Man Through the Ages

# The Russian Orthodox Church

## 10th to 20th Centuries

Chief Editor
Alexander Preobrazhensky,
D. Sc. (Hist.)

Progress Publishers

Moscow

Translated from the Russian by *Sergei Syrovatkin*
Designed by *Vadim Novikov*

РУССКАЯ
ПРАВОСЛАВНАЯ ЦЕРКОВЬ
X—XX вв.

*На английском языке*

© Progress Publishers 1988

*Printed in the Union of Soviet Socialist Republics*

$$P \frac{0400000000-611}{014(01)-88} 31-88$$

ISBN 5-01-000525-5

Institute of St. Sergiy of Radonezh in Paris, founded by Russian emigres, is also within the jurisdiction of the Constantinople Patriarchate.

The Church of Constantinople is a member of the World Council of Churches, at which it has a permanent representative.

Since 1972, the Church of Constantinople has been headed by Patriarch Dimitrios I, who bears the title of Archbishop of Constantinople—the New Rome and Ecumenical Patriarch. The Patriarch's residence is in Istanbul (ancient Constantinople).

*The Church of Alexandria.* It is just as ancient as the previous one, having received the status of a patriarchate simultaneously with the Church of Constantinople. However, numerically it is considerably inferior to the Church of Constantinople: there are only some 80,000 parishioners in it, who live in Egypt and in some other countries of the African continent.

The Church of Alexandria has 166 churches united in one archbishopric (of Alexandria) and 13 metropolitanates. Four of them are in Egypt, two in South Africa; Sudan, Libya, Zaïre, Cameroon, Zimbabwe, Ethiopia and Tanzania have one metropolitanate each.

It runs two monasteries, one of which, near Cairo, was built in the 4th century. The Church of Alexandria is regarded as the birthplace of monasticism: it is to this Church that St Anthony the Great (4th c.), the founder of Eastern monasticism, belonged.

The Church of Alexandria has within its jurisdiction the Eastern Research Institute.

Since 1968, the Church of Alexandria has been headed by Pope and Patriarch Nicolas VI of Alexandria and All Africa. His residence is in Alexandria.

The Church of Alexandria takes an active part in the ecumenical movement and is a member of the World Council of Churches. Its contacts with the Russian Orthodox Church are of long standing. The Moscow Patriarchate has a *podvorye*[1] in Alexandria, and the Alexandria Patriarchate a *podvorye* in Odessa.

---

[1] *Podvorye* (pl. *podvorya*)—originally a piece of city property owned by an outside owner (say, a monastery). Now often applied to a church given over to the use of a foreign Church as though it were her property and served by a representative of that Church.—*Tr.*

*The Antioch Church.* This Church appeared in the times of the Byzantine Empire, in which it was an important religious centre. At present, the city that gave this Church its name is on Turkish territory (Antakya), while the residence of the head of the Antioch Church is in Damascus (Syria).

The followers of the Antioch Church are Orthodox Syrians and Lebanese living not only in their native countries but also abroad. According to some sources, the Antioch Church has about a million followers, according to others, 1,370,000. Its 18 dioceses are scattered throughout the world and include parishes in Syria, the Lebanon, Iraq, Kuwait, Turkey, Iran, the Arabian Peninsula, in North and South America, Australia and New Zealand. There are three Exarchates in the Church: Australian, Mexican and Chilean.

Of the few cloisters of the Antioch Church, the most renowned in the Orthodox world are the Belmont Monastery near Tripoli (the Lebanon) and the Seidanai Convent near Damascus.

Theologians and clergymen are trained at the Belmont Theological Academy of St. John of Damascus and at a seminary, as well as at various schools of the Russian Orthodox Church.

The Antioch Church is a member of the World Council of Churches. It is headed by Patriarch Ignatius IV of Antioch and All the Orient, who has been occupying that post since 1979.

Permanent contacts with the Russian Orthodox Church are maintained through a *podvorye* of the Moscow Patriarchate in Beirut and a mission in Damascus. The Antioch Patriarchate has a *podvorye* in Moscow.

*The Orthodox Church of Jerusalem.* It is often described as the "cradle of Christianity" and the "mother of Christian Churches", and is one of the most ancient Orthodox Churches, whose heads were given the title of patriarch as early as the 5th century. According to various ecclesiastical sources, its followers number between 50 and 70 thousand; most of them are Arabs.

The Church has only 65 parishes with 60 priests. The parishes are united in two metropolitanates and one archbishopric.

The Brotherhood of the Holy Sepulchre has existed in the Church of Jerusalem since the 4th century. In the early 1980s, the Brotherhood numbered slightly more than 100 members.

The following monasteries of the Church of Jerusalem are the best known: the Holy Sepulchre Monastery in Jerusalem, the Bethlehem Monastery, the John the Baptist Monastery near Jordan, and the St. Savas Laura.

The Church has no theological schools of its own.

The Church of Jerusalem is headed by the Patriarch of the Holy City of Jerusalem and All Palestine, with a residence in Jerusalem. Since 1981, this position has been held by Diodoros I.

The Church of Jerusalem is a member of the World Council of Churches. It maintains contacts with the Moscow Patriarchate through the Russian Orthodox Mission in Jerusalem established in 1847.

*The Russian Church.* The origin of the Russian Church dates back to the "baptism of Russia" in 988—the official adoption by the Kievans of the Byzantine variety of Christianity on orders from the Kievan Grand Duke Vladimir Svyatoslavich and under pressure from the Duke's *druzhina* (bodyguard, armed force). The population of Kievan Rus was converted to the new faith by hierarchs and clergymen of the Constantinople Patriarchate.

At first, the Russian Church was a metropolitanate of the Church of Constantinople headed by Byzantine metropolitans appointed by the Ecumenical patriarch. Objective prerequisites for its independence only appeared with the rise of Moscow as an All-Russian centre to which the metropolitan's see was translated in the first half of the 14th century from Vladimir where it had been since the devastation of Kiev by the Tatar-Mongol invaders.

In 1448, the autocephaly of the Russian Church was proclaimed. It became to be headed by metropolitans elected by a council of Russian hierarchs, who did not have to be approved by the Patriarch of Constantinople. In 1589, Metropolitan Iov received the title of Patriarch of Moscow and All Russia, still retained by heads of the Russian Church. The patriarchal enthronement of Iov was attended by the heads of the Churches of Constantinople and Antioch. The Russian Church was listed as fifth in the diptych (the traditional list) of the Local Orthodox Churches—directly after the first four Eastern patriarchates.

Failing to secure the patriarch's support for his reforms, Peter I abolished the patriarchate in 1721, replacing it by a corporate form of administration. The Holy Governing Synod was made the administrative body of the Russian Church; it was not run by hierarchs but by state officials appointed by the czar. In 1723 the Synod was recognised by the Eastern patriarchs who called it their "equally honoured brother in Christ", possessing the right to perform and institute the same things as the four apostolic holy patriarchal thrones. This recognition indicated, among other things, that the Eastern patriarchs did not see Peter I's reforms as a departure from the Byzantine tradition of subordinating the Church directly to imperial power.

The synodal form of administration existed in the Russian Church for nearly two centuries and was only abolished in 1917, when the Local Council of 1917-1918 restored the Patriarchate.

According to the synodal report for 1913, the last prewar year, the Russian Church had, on the eve of the First World War, 67 dioceses within the country and one diocese in North America. It had 53,902 churches, 23,204 chapels and prayer-houses. Fifty-five churches were outside the Russian Empire. The number of followers of Orthodox Christianity was believed to be in the neighbourhood of 120 million.

On the eve of the October Revolution, more than 1,200 monasteries and convents existed—lauras, stauropegian monasteries, hermitages, *skete*s[1] and communities. There were four lauras: Kiev-Pechery, Pochayev-Dormition, Trinity-St. Sergiy, and St. Alexander-Nevskiy. The monasteries and convents possessed

---

[1] *Skete* (fr. Coptic *Schiet,* an extensive plain a day's journey from the Nitrian Mts.)—a semi-hermitic community consisting of a small brotherhood living in separate cells under the direction of an elder or *starets.—Tr.*

1,083,271 *dessiatinas* of land[1], wineries, tanneries, saw-mills, shops, printing-works, church-plate factories, etc.

The clergy included 168 hierarchs (three metropolitans, 26 archbishops, and 139 bishops) and 65,314 other members of the clergy (3,043 archpriests, 47,403 priests and 14,868 deacons). The Russian Church had three foreign missions—in Japan, China, and Urmia (Iran). Clergymen and theologians were trained at 57 theological seminaries and four theological academies.

The Orthodox parishes of Georgia, Armenia and Azerbaijan were united to form the Georgian Exarchate.

*The Georgian Church.* Christian communities headed by bishops existed in Georgia as early as the 4th century. They were subordinated to the Church of Antioch but separated from it in the middle of the 5th century. The Sixth Ecumenical Council of 681 confirmed the autocephaly of the Georgian Church, giving its head the same rights as the Eastern patriarchs.

In 1811, the Georgian Church became an Exarchate of the Russian Church. After the February Revolution, it regained autocephaly recognised by the Synod of the Russian Church in 1943.

The Georgian Church has 15 dioceses (some of which include Russian Orthodox parishes) and some 50 churches. There is an ancient monastery at Mtskheta (near Tbilisi), with a theological seminary attached to it. Besides, clerics of the Georgian Church receive secondary and higher theological education at the theological schools of the Moscow Patriarchate.

The Georgian Church is headed by Catholicos-Patriarch Iliya II of All Georgia, Archbishop of Mtskheta and Tbilisi, who has occupied that post since 1977. His residence is in Tbilisi. The Georgian Church is a member of the World Council of Churches.

*The Serbian Church.* Christianity of the Byzantine kind was introduced among the Serbs as early as the 9th century, but the history of the Serbian Church properly begins in the 13th century, when it gained

---

[1] *Dessiatina* equals 2.7 acres.— *Tr.*

autocephaly. In 1346, a patriarchate was established there.

The Serbian Church unites eight million believers both in Yugoslavia and abroad. It has 28 dioceses: 21 in Yugoslavia, three in Central and Western Europe (the centres of the dioceses are in Budapest, Timişoara and London), three in the USA and Canada, one in Australia and New Zealand, and runs several monasteries, one of which, the Chiliándary Monastery is on Mt Athos.

The Serbian Church has four theological seminaries—in Belgrade, Prizren, Sremski Karlovci and Krk. There is a theological department at the university of Belgrade. Serbian clergymen are also trained at theological schools of the Moscow Patriarchate.

The Serbian Church is headed (since 1958) by Gherman, Patriarch of Serbia, Archbishop of Peč, Metropolitan of Belgrade and Karlowitz. His residence is in Belgrade. Also in Belgrade there is a Russian patriarchal *podvorye* with a church. The Serbian Church is a member of the World Council of Churches.

*The Romanian Orthodox Church.* The basis of the Romanian Church were two metropolitanates which existed in the 14th century in Walachia and Moldova. It gained autocephaly only in 1885, and in 1925 received its present status of a patriarchate.

There are 16 million parishioners in the Romanian Church. They are united in five metropolitanates uniting 12 dioceses. There is one diocese in America and church districts in Jerusalem, Sofia, Vienna, London, and Baden-Baden.

The Romanian Church has about 100 cloisters. Clergymen and theologians are trained at four theological seminaries (at Bucharest, Cluj, Craiova, Buzău) and two university theological institutes (in Bucharest and Sibiu). There are also six schools training church choristers. Orthodox Romanians are also trained at theological educational establishments of the Russian Church.

Since 1977, the Romanian Church has been headed by His Beatitude Patriarch Justinian of All Romania, Locum Tenens of Caesarea in Cappadocia, Metropolitan of Ungro-Walachia, Archbishop of Bucharest. The

Romanian Church is a member of the World Council of Churches.

*The Bulgarian Church.* The mass baptism of the Bulgarians took place in 864, and in 870 the Church of Bulgaria received autonomy. In 919 it gained autocephaly, and in 927 became a patriarchate. When the country was conquered by the Greeks and the Turks, the Church of Bulgaria was subordinated to the Patriarch of Constantinople, who proclaimed it his Exarchate. In 1872, the Bulgarian Church refused to be subordinated to the Church of Constantinople, and in 1945 the latter consented to this. The Bulgarian Church again became autocephalous; since 1953 it is headed by a patriarch.

The Bulgarian Church is divided into 11 internal dioceses and three foreign ones (in New York, Detroit, and Ancona), with 12 metropolitans, 10 bishops and 2,000 priests (serving in 3,500 churches and chapels). There are 120 cloisters, of which the most important are the Rila, Bachkovo and the Trayan monasteries, and also the Zograf Monastery (on Mt. Athos).

The Bulgarian Church has two theological educational establishments: the Sofia Theological Academy named after St. Kliment of Ohrid, and the theological seminary at the Cherepish Monastery. Since 1971, the Bulgarian Church has been headed by Patriarch Maksim; his residence is in Sofia.

Since 1948, the Russian Church has had a *podvorye* in Sofia, and the Bulgarian Church, a *podvorye* in Moscow. The Bulgarian Church is a member of the World Council of Churches.

*The Orthodox Church of Cyprus.* It is one of the oldest Orthodox Churches. Suffice it to mention that the Third Ecumenical Council (431) placed it fifth (after the Patriarchates of Constantinople, Alexandria, Antioch and Jerusalem).

At present, the Church has 420,000 followers in six dioceses. Of the relatively few monasteries the best known are the Stavrovouni Monastery, the Kykko Monastery, the Machaira Monastery, the Apostle Barnabas Monastery, and others. The Church of Cyprus has a theological seminary which is also named after Apostle Barnabas.

The head of the Church of Cyprus bears the title of Archbishop of Nova Justiniana and All Cyprus. Between 1950 and 1977, this post was held by Archbishop Makarios III; he headed the Cypriots in the fight against the British colonialists who occupied the island in 1878. In 1960, Cyprus became an independent state, and Archbishop Makarios III was elected President of the republic. After the death of Makarios III in 1977, Archbishop Chrisostomos became the head of the Church of Cyprus. His residence is in Nicosia. The Church of Cyprus is a member of the World Council of Churches.

*The Church of Hellas.* Although Orthodoxy has existed in Greece for a very long time, the Church of Hellas became autocephalous only in 1850 (before that, it was under the Constantinople Patriarchate).

The Church of Hellas has some eight million parishioners in 77 dioceses, including several foreign ones. There are many monasteries and convents. At one of them (the Monastery of Pendeli near Athens), an Orthodox centre has been set up to promote links between the Church of Hellas and other Local Orthodox Churches.

Clergymen and theologians are trained at two theological departments and several theological seminaries. Graduates of the theological schools of the Moscow Patriarchate take an advance course at the theological department of the University of Athens. The Church is headed by Archbishop Seraphim of Athens and All Hellas, who has held this post since 1974. His residence is in Athens. The Church of Hellas is a member of the World Council of Churches.

*The Church of Albania.* It gained autocephaly in 1922. In the mid-1950s, it had four dioceses, and its followers numbered about 300,000. The Church was headed by Metropolitan Damian of Tirana and Durrës, Archbishop of All Albania, whose residence was in Tirana.

In 1967, the Albanian leadership announced the country's total atheisation. All churches were closed, and the clergy faced the necessity of changing their occupation.

However, the Church of Albania was still regarded as

existing even after 1967, at least nominally. Thus Archbishop Damian was invariably mentioned until January 1974 among the heads of autocephalous Orthodox Churches to whom the Moscow Patriarchate sent Christmas and Easter greetings. After 1974, the head of the Church of Albania was not mentioned in that list, neither was he listed in the *Orthodox Church Calendar for 1980,* where brief data on all the Local Orthodox Churches are published by the Moscow Patriarchate. It was not mentioned in its subsequent publications either.

*The Polish Church.* Orthodox dioceses existed in Poland since the 13th century, but the Polish Church finally gained autocephaly only in 1948. At present, it has some 500,000 parishioners in four dioceses and 20 districts. It runs 300 churches, where slightly more than 200 clergymen serve.

The Polish Church has a monastery (of St. Onufri in Liublin voivodship) and a convent (of Sts Martha and Maria in Bielostock voivodship). There are two educational establishments: a theological seminary and a section of Orthodox theology at the Christian Theological Academy in Warsaw. Besides, students from Poland are trained at theological schools of the Moscow Patriarchate. Since 1970, the Church has been headed by Metropolitan Basilios (Doroszkiewicz) of Warsaw and All Poland. His residence is in Warsaw. The Polish Church is a member of the World Council of Churches.

*The Orthodox Church of Czechoslovakia.* Byzantine Christianity began to be spread in Czechoslovakia as early as the 9th century, but the Orthodox Church of Czechoslovakia came into being as an organisational unit only in the middle of the 20th century, becoming autocephalous in 1951. It has four dioceses with some 150 parishes and 250,000 parishioners.

Clergymen are trained at the Orthodox Faculty of Theology in Prešov. Members of the Church of Czechoslovakia are also trained at the theological educational establishments of the Moscow Patriarchate.

The head of the Church bears the title of Metropolitan of Prague and All Czechoslovakia. Since 1964, this post has been held by Metropolitan Dorofej. His residence is in Prague. The Czechoslovak Church is a member of the World Council of Churches.

*The Orthodox Church in America.* This is the youngest Local Orthodox Church, not recognised so far by some of the other Churches. It emerged on the basis of church parishes established by Russian missionaries on the North American continent. At first, these parishes formed the North American Diocese of the Russian Church, which was reorganised, after the October Revolution of 1917, becoming an independent North American Metropolitan District. In the years that followed, the latter now maintained contacts with the Moscow Patriarchate, now broke off relations with it.

In 1969, the leadership of the North American metropolitanate finally realised the need to normalise relations with the Moscow Patriarchate. After a series of preliminary consultations and official meetings in Geneva, Tokyo and New York, the plenipotentiaries of the North American metropolitanate and of the Moscow Patriarchate signed on March 31, 1970 an agreement on the establishment of normal relations between the two Churches. On April 10, 1970, the Patriarch and the Synod of the Russian Church signed a document granting the Russian Orthodox Church in North America the status of the Autocephalous American Church.

At present, the American Church has 16 dioceses in Canada, the USA, and Latin America, numbering about a million followers united in 400 parishes. It has incorporated the Romanian and Albanian dioceses in the USA as well as the Old Catholics of Mexico, who have formed the Mexican Exarchate of the Orthodox Church in America.

The Orthodox Church in America has four monasteries and two convents, two theological seminaries (one of them in Alaska) and St Vladimir's Theological Seminary in Crestwood, N.Y. The Church also sends students to the theological schools of the Moscow Patriarchate.

Since 1977, the Orthodox Church in America has been headed by Theodosius, Archbishop of New York, Metropolitan of all America and Canada, whose residence is in New York. The Orthodox Church in America is a member of the World Council of Churches.

## AUTONOMOUS ORTHODOX CHURCHES

Just as autocephalous Orthodox Churches, autonomous ones are self-governing and independent in the handling of their internal problems. However, the election of the head of an autonomous Church is sanctioned by the head of the autocephalous Church which granted it autonomy; the fundamental documents and most important acts of an autonomous Church (such as the canonisation of saints, introduction of various canonical innovations, etc.) must also be sanctioned.

At present, there are three autonomous Orthodox Churches with a relatively small number of followers.

*The Orthodox Church of Finland.* Originally, the Orthodox parishes established in Finland were part of the Novgorod diocese of the Russian Church; since 1775, they were included in the St. Petersburg Metropolitanate. At the end of the 19th century, the Finland and Vyborg diocese of the Russian Church was established. In 1921, the Moscow Patriarchate granted the Church of Finland autonomy, and the latter came under the jurisdiction of the Patriarchate of Constantinople, retaining that status to the present.

There are some 75,000 parishioners in the Church of Finland. It consists of two metropolitanates—that of Karelia (with the see at Kuopio) headed by Archbishop Pavel, and that of Helsinki (or Helsingfors) headed by Metropolitan Ioann. The first metropolitanate has 16 churches and 39 chapels, the second, 16 churches and 15 chapels.

The Church has two monasteries and a convent. The overall number of monastics is less than 20.

Situated in Kuopio is an Orthodox Church Centre with the residence of Archbishop Pavel of Karelia and All Finland (in office since 1960), a church, a library, a church museum and a theological seminary. Apart from the seminary, clergymen are trained at the

Institute of Orthodoxy attached to the Theological Faculty of Helsinki University.

Under the aegis of the Orthodox Church of Finland are the Brotherhood of Sts Sergiy and Gherman of Valaam, the Association of Orthodox Priests, the Orthodox Youth Association, the Association of Orthodox Christian Students and other Orthodox Church societies. The Orthodox Church of Finland is a member of the World Council of Churches.

*The Sinai Church.* This is the oldest of the autonomous Orthodox Christian Churches: from the 7th century on, its head bore the title of bishop, and since the 9th century, the title of archbishop. At the same time it is one of the smallest of these Churches, consisting only of the St. Catherine the Great Martyr, Monastery on Mt. Sinai (Egypt) and 14 *podvorya* (three in Egypt and 11 in Greece, on Cyprus, in the Lebanon and Turkey).

The Sinai Monastery, with merely 20 monks, is a major depository of ancient manuscripts (284 Latin and 2,319 Greek) and some 2,000 icons.

The head of the Sinai Church and the Holy Hegumen of the monastery is Archbishop Damianos of Sinai, Pharan and Raifa (since 1973). In accordance with an ancient tradition, the head of the Sinai Church is consecrated by the patriarch of the Orthodox Church of Jerusalem, within those jurisdiction the Sinai Church lies.

*The Japanese Church.* The beginnings of Orthodoxy in Japan go back to the activities of the Russian missionaries in the second half of the 19th century. The head of the Russian Orthodox mission in Japan was Archbishop Nikolai (Kasatkin) who died in 1912. In 1970 he was canonised by the Moscow Patriarchate as the "apostle of Japan". He is a saint not only in the Russian Church but also in the Japanese one.

After the Second World War, the Orthodox Christian parishes in Japan, founded by Archbishop Nikolai and his followers were subordinated to the North American metropolitanate, despite the lack of any canonical basis for this. Simultaneously with the regulation of relations between the Moscow Patriarchate and the North American metropolitanate, former links between the Japanese and Russian Orthodox Churches were restored. The Russian Church included the Japanese one under its jurisdiction and granted it autonomy.

There are three dioceses in the Japanese Orthodox Church with some 36,000 believers, mostly Japanese. There are an Orthodox theological academy in Tokyo and some Sunday schools.

The Church is headed by Theodosius, Archbishop of Tokyo and Metropolitan of All Japan, consecrated in 1972 by the Patriarch of Moscow and All Russia. His residence is in Tokyo.

*Chapter I*

# CHRISTIANITY IN THE 10TH AND 11TH CENTURIES

The adoption of Christianity by Rus as a state religion was determined by a number of factors. In the 8th and 9th centuries, the early feudal system, a class system, emerged as a result of several interconnected processes: the development of the tribal nobility of the late stages of the primitive communal system into local princes; the development of confederations of tribes into state organisations, and of social inequality within traditional communities of various origins (in terms of functions and property) into class inequality. These processes involved the appearance, among servants, of slaves from the same tribe, along with foreign captives.

The formation of local principalities and the establishment, on their basis, in the 9th century of the ancient Russian state with its centre in Kiev, a state based on early feudal exploitation in the form of centralised rent (tribute, levies), required changes in the ideological sphere, in religion. Could the fairly primitive system of Slavic cults be brought in line with the new demands posed by the emergence of class society and the state? Attempts to set up a reformed pagan cult as an alternative to Christianity failed. These demands could best be met by a world religion established in late antiquity, adapted to the conditions of feudal society, and corresponding to the stage of development reached by Rus. As the dominant religion, Christianity deified class inequality, domination and subordination, the feudal structure of society, and state power, which fully accorded with the conditions in Rus.

Along with Eastern Slavs who worshipped the common old Slavic deities, the ancient Russian state incorporated non-Slavic tribes of the Baltic coast, the Volga region, and of the southern steppe, who had gods of their own. Replacement of all of them by a unified well-developed Christian religious system contributed to the consolidation of the ruling class and of the state.

In the Middle Ages, despite the considerable isolation of population groups and separate feudal worlds as political organisms, communication between peoples played an important role in the form of trade between remote countries, political and matrimonial alliances, the use of foreign mercenaries, and exchange of cultural achievements. In this situation, rulers of European states were interested in the adoption of a single religion, the Christian one, as part of the heritage of antiquity. This made them members of a unified cultural world formally equal to one another and opposed to pagan barbarians, although the real political conditions and other factors inevitably led to strife within that world and to the domination of some countries by others.

In the 9th and 10th centuries, Rus was traditionally linked both with Constantinople (Tsargrad or "the tsar's city", in Russian) and with the Slavs in Central Europe and in the Balkan Peninsula who were in close contact with Byzantium. These ties largely determined the ecclesiastical orientation of Rus towards the Eastern Christian world with its equality of the languages of all the Christian peoples who had writing systems of their own, orientation towards the Constantinople see in the glamorous capital of the ancient empire; conversion to Christianity offered a good basis for attaining the same status as that empire.

Christianity was known in Rus even before the official adoption of that faith. As early as the 840s, Ibn-Khordadbek mentioned Christian Slavs who traded with the Orient. According to Byzantine sources (Patriarch Photius and others), Rus was baptised soon after the 860 campaign against Constantinople. Byzantium, too, had a great interest in converting its northern neighbours to Christianity; it would not only weaken their pressure against the empire but also create the premises for incorporating Rus within the sphere of Byzantine political influence. At that time, though, Christianity did not penetrate deep, being probably restricted to the higher aristocracy and unrecognised even by some Kievan princes. It is possible that a missionary archbishop, sent at that time to Rus, was remembered in the 11th century as one of the first metropolitans, Mikhail or Leon. The 944 treaty with Byzantium mentions Christians in Rus ("those who were baptised"), and also the church of St Elijah, probably in Kiev. Grand Duke Igor's wife Olga was a Christian; after 945 she became head of the ancient Russian state. Her son Svyatoslav, though, refused to give up the traditional pagan religion.

Christianity as a state religion was adopted by Svyatoslav's son Vladimir, Grand Duke of Kiev (980-1015), who realised the need for a reform of the religious cult but attempted at first to avert the victory of Christianity by establishing an international pagan pantheon headed by Perun, which personified the new social relations of early feudal society. However, the reform, accompanied by persecution of Christians, proved a failure; it was followed by the destruction of the newly established pantheon and by official Christianisation.

That event was precipitated by the course of the political relations between Rus and Byzantium in the late 980s. When he was fighting against Byzantine rebel Bardas Phocas, a general who aspired to ascend to the imperial throne and had considerable forces at his disposal, Basil II appealed to Prince Vladimir, scattering generous promises in exchange for his aid. According to Jahja of Antioch, an Arab Christian historian of the 11th century, the treaty by which 6,000 Russian troops were sent to the emperor's aid stipulated that the "Czar of Russians" Vladimir would marry Anna, sister of Emperor Basil, and that his country would embrace Christianity. That agreement could be concluded in the winter of 987-988. After his victory over the rebel and consolidation of his power, the emperor had to fulfil his obligations under the treaty and give away his sister Anna in marriage to the Kiev Prince. That was a rare exception in the empire's political practices; shortly before that, the suit of the son of the German emperor, the future Otto II, for the hand of the porphyrogene princess was rejected.[1] To fulfil the terms of the treaty Prince Vladimir had to besiege and take by storm in 989 an important Byzantine possession in the Crimea—the city of Korsun (Chersonesus)[2] which had an episcopal see. That Byzantine possession was returned to the emperor as a *ven* or bride-money.

For the treaty to become effective at the earliest possible date, the baptism of Vladimir, who received the Christian name of Vasiliy in honour of Emperor Basil II's patron, St. Basil the Great, may have taken place already at the time of the stay of that emperor's embassy in Kiev, that is to say, early in 988,[3] although the Korsun legend of *The Tale of Bygone Years,* and *The Life of Vladimir* dependent on it, links this up only with the Korsun campaign. As for the baptism of the Kievans, the sources offer contradicting evidence on

---

[1] G. Ostrogorsky. *Geschichte des byzantinischen Staates,* München, 1963, p. 100.

[2] According to *The Tale of Bygone Years,* Vladimir decided to be baptised if he succeeded in taking Korsun, and demanded the bride to be handed over to him after that success, saying that he would threaten Constantinople if his demand were not met (PSRL, Moscow, 1962, Vol. 2, columns 95-96). This is contradicted by the evidence of Iakov Mnich's *Memory and Praise* (see next footnote). Recently the suggestion has been put forward that Korsun was taken by Vladimir by agreement with Emperor Basil, for the city had gone over to the usurper Bardas Phocas's side. See A. Poppe. *The Political Background to the Baptism of Rus. Byzantine-Russian Relations Between 986-989.* Dumbarton Oaks Papers, 30, 1976; also A. V. Poppe. "O prichine pokhoda Vladimira Svyatoslavicha na Korsun 988-989" (On the Causes of Vladimir Svyatoslavich's Campaign Against Korsun in 988-989). In: *Vestnik MGU. Istoriya,* 1978, No. 2, pp. 49-50.

[3] According to *Memory and Praise* by Iakov Mnich, an 11th-century author, Vladimir was baptised "in the tenth year after the murder of his brother Yaropolk", which happened in 978, and lived for 28 years after the baptism. This points to the 6495th March year, or 987-988, which is confirmed by a reference to his taking Korsun in the third year after the baptism (the 6497th March year, or 989-990) [See A. A. Zimin. "Pamyat i pokhvala Iakova Mnikha i zhitiye knyazya Vladimira po drevneishemu spisku" (Iakov Mnich's Memory and Praise and the Oldest Copy of the Life of Prince Vladimir). In: *Kratkiye soobshcheniya Instituta Slavyanovedeniya AN SSSR* (Brief Reports of the Institute of Slavic Studies of the USSR Academy of Sciences), Moscow, 1963, Vol. 37, p. 72]. A March vear began on March 1 and ended on February 28.

the date. Along with the traditional date, 988, researchers put forward evidence both for earlier and later dates—for instance 990.[1] According to *The Tale of Bygone Years,* Kievans were baptised in the Dnieper, according to the *Life of Vladimir,* in the Pochaina, a tributary of the Dnieper. After Vladimir's return from Korsun and the arrival of priests from Constantinople and Korsun, the conversion to Christianity must have indeed assumed a greater scope.

The replacement of one religious cult by another was accompanied by the destruction of formerly worshipped effigies of gods now publicly desecrated by the prince's servants, and by the erection of churches on the former sites of pagan idols and temples. Thus the St. Basil's Church, dedicated to the above-mentioned St Basil the Great, was erected on the hill in Kiev where the Perun idol had stood; the Nativity Church was built in Peryn near Novgorod, where a pagan temple had been situated. According to *The Tale of Bygone Years,* Vladimir "began to build churches in cities and to appoint priests, and people in all the cities and villages were baptised".

Conversion to Christianity was forcibly carried out by the prince and the evolving church organisation in the teeth of resistance not only on the part of pagan priests but also of various strata of the population. Metropolitan Ilarion of Kiev admitted that the baptism in Kiev was forcible: "No one resisted the prince's order pleasing unto God, and everyone was baptised—if not of their own free will then out of fear of the giver of orders, for his religion was connected with power." The resistance to the replacement of the traditional cult was all the stronger in the other cities. In Novgorod, the legend has been preserved of the introduction of Christianity there by Bishop Ioakim of Korsun and the prince's generals Dobrynya and Putyata, "Putyata baptising with the sword and Dobrynya, with fire".[2]

---

[1] O. M. Rapov. "O date prinyatiya khristianstva knyazem Vladimirom i kievlyanami" (On the Date of Adoption of Christianity by Prince Vladimir and the Kievans). In: *Voprosy istorii,* 1984, No. 6, pp. 44-45.

[2] V. N. Tatishchev. *Istoriya Rossiiskaya* (A History of Russia), Moscow-Leningrad, 1962, Vol. I, p. 113.

\* \* \*

Soon after the official introduction of Christianity, the first church organisation was set up in Russia as part of the diocese of the Archbishop (Patriarch) of Constantinople. It was headed by a metropolitan sent from Constantinople, who had his see at St. Sofia's Cathedral in Kiev. Ye. Golubinsky's view that the original residence of the metropolitan was in Pereyaslavl is not borne out by contemporary research.

The date of the establishment of the Kievan metropolitanate is determined from indirect data, as there is nothing in the Russian sources on this point. The founding of the cathedral was preceded by the building (in 990-995/6) of the stone Tithe Church of the Mother of God, to which one-tenth of the prince's income was handed over.[1] Judging by the position of the Russian metropolitanate among other metropolitanates in the list of the sees of the Patriarchate of Constantinople in the 1080s, it already existed in 997, which means that it was founded in 996-997.[2] The wooden St. Sofia's Cathedral must have been burnt down several times before the stone building that still stands was erected in 1037—early 1040s.

The church administration in important political and administrative centres was in the hands of bishops subordinated to the metropolitan. In the times of Vladimir and in the first decades of the reign of Yaroslav, bishop's sees (bishoprics) were apparently established in Byelgorod, Novgorod, Polotsk, Chernigov, Pereyaslavl and some other cities. That was a time of Christianisation of the bulk of the population and the spreading of ecclesiastical power through most of the state's territory. All the bishoprics were set up in the most important centres of the state then in the process of feudalisation.

In the middle and the second half of the 11th

---

[1] Evidence of construction to be found in *The Tale of Bygone Years,* Iakov Mnich's *Memory and Praise,* and Prince Vladimir's statute on tithes.

[2] G. Lowmieński. "Review of A. Poppe. *Państwo i kościół na Rusi w XI wieku,* 1968"—*Kwartalnik historyczny,* 1970, Nos. 3-4, pp. 792-793.

century that process was complemented by another, just as important for the development and consolidation of the state. In that period, bishoprics were founded on territories developed by the Kievan princes—in the nomadic steppe, south of Kiev—and in the colonised areas of the north-east. In the 1030s and 1040s, soon after the founding of a new line of fortifications along the Ros River and some successes in the subjugation of the Pechenegs, a see was set up in Yuryev-City, named after the patron of its founder, Yaroslav (Yuriy). That bishopric was apparently intended to promote Christianisation and subjugation of the nomads closest to Kiev. The setting up of a see in Rostov can be placed in the 1070s or 1080s. In the land of Rostov, Christianity was not widespread in the 11th century, as both the Russians and the Merya hardly obeyed state power and the Church, as indicated both by the predominant burial rites and by the uprising recorded in the Chronicle under 1071. Thus the see established under these political conditions was to further closer links between this region and Kiev. The ancient archbishop's cathedra in Tmutarakan, the centre of a politically and economically important old Russian principality on the shores of the Black and Azov seas, was also connected with the Russian church organisation in the 11th century.

The beginning of feudal division in Russia and the establishment, after the death of Yaroslav, of the triumvirate of princes (Izyaslav in Kiev, Svyatoslav in Chernigov and Vsevolod in Pereyaslavl) may have been a factor in the emergence of new metropolitanates—those of Chernigov and Pereyaslavl, evidence of which is to be found in some sources. We have data on Metropolitan Neofit of Chernigov, mentioned in 1072, and two metropolitans of Pereyaslavl—Leontiy, the author of the epistle on *opresnoki* (unleavened communion bread), and Ephraem, who consecrated the Cathedral of St. Michael the Archangel. One of these dioceses, headed by a metropolitan, covered the vast principality of Chernigov stretching from Chernigov in the west to Ryazan and Murom in the east, i.e., to the land of the Vyatichi; the other diocese served the interests of the princes of Pereyaslavl, who were also lords in the lands of Suzdal and Belozersk; that diocese also had control of Smolensk.

The existence in Russia of three metropolitanates (the two new ones must have been titular, i.e., subordinated directly to the patriarch, having no bishops under them) was a considerable political achievement for Yaroslav's sons, whose demands were met by Constantinople. When power was again concentrated in the hands of the prince of Kiev (after 1076), he was also able to concentrate the Russian church administration in the hands of a metropolitan subject to him.

In the reign of Yaroslav the Wise, the first Russian, instead of a Greek, Metropolitan was inducted in Kiev. He was priest Ilarion of the prince's court church in the village of Berestovo, a highly educated person with a brilliant literary gift. In violation of the tradition established in Constantinople, he was nominated by the prince and confirmed by a council of bishops in Kiev, but there is no evidence that he was consecrated by the patriarch, although his name was not later excluded from the list of the metropolitans of Kiev. At the same time the unexpected new consecration of St. Sofia's Cathedral by the Greek metropolitan Ephraem, who succeeded Ilarion, is apparently an indication of the fact that the patriarch did not regard his service in that church as canonical. In his religious-political treatise *Discourse on Law and Grace,* Ilarion put forward arguments in favour of Rus's equality with other Christian powers and of canonisation of Prince Vladimir, which did not take place until the 13th century. The Statute on Church Courts, compiled by Prince Yaroslav with Metropolitan Ilarion's participation, set down the standards of Russian law adapted to the needs of the Christian Church; they differed considerably both from the standards of the canonical ecclesiastical law and the Byzantine criminal law.

\* \* \*

The character of the dominant form of expropriation of surplus products from the direct producer left an imprint on the forms of support of the church organisation. From its emergence in the late 10th to the end of the 11th century, i.e., during the first century of its history, the characteristic form of support was a centralised tithe paid by the state, or the prince, to the Church from the tributes and other forms of the prince's court's income, including court fines. Up to the last quarter of the 11th century there were no indications in the sources that episcopal sees, the individual churches or the first cloisters owned any land property that would make them feudals enjoying certain immunities and economically independent of the prince's power. Sources of the 11th and 12th centuries unanimously indicate that the Church received one-tenth of the prince's tributes and an income from the prince's court of justice. That was true not only of the Tithe Church and episcopal cathedrals but also of the churches of cities and monasteries, such as the Church of Sts Boris and Gleb in Vyshgorod and the Church of the Mother of God at the Pechery Monastery.[1]

Along with this basic form of support, those elements of the church organisation which possessed jurisdiction (i.e., episcopal sees and their local officials, the *tiuns*) received income as officers of church courts. In the 11th century their jurisdiction was extended to family and marriage matters. With the expansion of the church organisation itself the number of conflicts within the Church also grew. All this was given legal form in the original statute of Prince Yaroslav and Metropolitan Ilarion on church courts passed in the middle of the 11th century. The right to administer justice gave the Church additional sources of livelihood.

Studies in the history of the formation of the old Russian church organisation have shown that in the initial period of its existence in the late 10th and in the 11th century, the Church had little chance of following foreign models—it adapted itself as best it could to those determinant local conditions which could make easier the existence of this organisation brought from the outside, and facilitate its gradual incorpora-

---

[1] PSRL, Vol. 2, columns 492-493.

tion in society. The local or "national" character of the original Russian Church is clear from various facts, such as the tithe support for the new cult on the old, pagan principle, the incorporation in early church legislation in Rus of the norms and principles of the ancient Russian barbarian and early feudal (early class) secular law. Of this nature is also, among many other similar facts, the territorial-administrative structure of the church organisation with one metropolitan and a small number of bishoprics (up to 10 in the 11th century, up to 16 in the first half of the 13th century)—a replica of the system of subordination of the old Russian principalities to Kiev, so different from the church system on Byzantine territory (more than 300 bishoprics in the 9th century,[1] 80 metropolitanates and 32 archbishoprics according to the List of the 11th century[2]). Golubinsky believed this specificity of the church system to be a "distinguishing characteristic feature" of the Russian Church, which introduced a new spirit in its administration.[3] The Kievan metropolitanate united, except for a short period in the second half of the 11th century, the entire territory of the ancient Russian state; in other words, it was the centre of a national Church.

The relationship between secular and ecclesiastical power in 11th-century Rus can therefore be seen not as an imitation, voluntary or involuntary, of the subordinate position of the church organisation in relation to imperial power in Byzantium but as a local phenomenon determined by the conditions of its emergence and economic position in the first period. Financial dependence of sees, monasteries and churches on princely power at the end of the 10th and in the 11th century, along with the active role played by that power in the replacement of the state pagan cult by the Christian one, is the factor which determined from the outset the

---

[1] Ye. Ye. Golubinsky. *Istoriya russkoy tserkvi* (A History of the Russian Church), Moscow, 1901, Vol. I, Part I, pp. 368-369.

[2] A. Poppe. "Russkiye metropolii Konstantinopolskoi patriarkhii v XI v." (Russian Metropolitanates of the Constantinople Patriarchate in the 11th Century). In: *Vizantiyskiy vremennik,* Moscow, 1968, Vol. 28, pp. 99-100.

[3] Ye. Ye. Golubinskiy. Op. cit., Vol. I, Part I, p. 341.

character of the relations between the two powers in Rus in the political and other spheres. This is all the more important as there is indubitable similarity in the relationship between state and Church in ancient Rus and in Western Europe before Pope Gregory VII's reforms in the middle of the 11th century.

The collaboration between the grand-ducal and church organisations was expressed in the formation in the first half of the 11th century of an extensive ecclesiastical jurisdiction covering marriage and divorce, relations within the family, conflicts involved in the defence of honour, some cases of inheritance, and conflicts within the Church. Cases were considered by episcopal officials who thus handled a vast variety of problems of everyday family life as well as issues arising from the replacement of the traditional communal marital norms and customs by the new, Christian norms of class society.

\* \* \*

The need to protect the feudals—the princes and their *druzhinas,* to suppress the actions against the new system, caused the emergence of the corresponding branches of law and the norms which later formed the Russkaya Pravda or remained as customs (replacement of blood feuds in cases of murder by state punishment, responsibility for violation of property rights, etc.). That was the first stage in the formation of public law of the state, undergoing the process of feudalisation, a stage restricted by the needs and possibilities of the prince's power, still relatively weak economically and politically. Other conflicts, practically just as frequent but less dangerous to the new system, conflicts within the classes rather than between them, remained traditionally within the jurisdiction of the pre-state bodies— communes and large families. Fairly soon, even before the middle of the 11th century, the Church in Rus identified the spheres of administration that had not been appropriated by the state. Borrowing the norms and standards of ancient Russian right and giving them Christian form, the Church took over a large number of new social institutions without any resistance from the state and without encroaching on the prince's jurisdiction, either. It thus helped the feudal power to consolidate the new system and the corresponding forms of social links—the Christian family, marriage, and to regulate relations between relatives.

Introduced by the princes at the time of the formation and initial development of feudal relations, Christianity was called upon to further that process; however, during the first century it was not widespread, being restricted to the upper stratum of society—the princes' families, *druzhinas*, the rich city-dwellers, and probably the upper stratum of the local communes, judging by their position during the 1071 uprising in Suzdal. Metropolitan Ioann II noted in the 1080s that Christian marriage rites were only observed by princes and boyars, while the common people continued to follow the pagan rites.[1] Prince Vladimir's Statute On Tithes stipulated that it was effective in "cities and *pogosts* where Christians live".[2] The Christianisation of outlying areas encountered serious difficulties. There is a record of the bishop Leontiy of Rostov being killed by local pagans.[3] Magicians played an important role in the peasant and city unrest of the 11th century, setting themselves and their faith in opposition to the princely power and the Church; the people's masses followed them. During the 1071 uprising in Novgorod, only Prince Gleb and his *druzhina* took the side of the bishop at the critical moment in the rebellion, while the people all followed the magician, and only the killing of the latter by the prince restored the authority of the Church.

The Christianisation of society led to the ousting and destruction not only of the pagan cult but also of the folk arts connected with it—decorative, music and choreographic. The traditional dances and picturesque rites were declared to be the "Devil's games", and folk musical instruments—psalteries, pipes, horns, etc.—were often destroyed. However, considerable elements

---

[1] RIB, St. Petersburg, 1908, Vol. VI, column 18.

[2] DKU, Moscow, 1976, p. 15.

[3] *Paterik Kievskogo Pecherskogo monastyrya* (Lives of the Fathers of the Kiev-Pechery Monastery), St. Petersburg, 1911, p. 76.

of traditional beliefs and rites survived in the Christian times, which resulted in the so-called double faith—the merging of pagan and Christian elements in some cultural spheres. The influence of the pagan worldview enriched the culture of feudal society, its literature (cf. *The Lay of Igor's Host*) and art.

It must be taken into account that basically, as an erroneous idealist belief that the world is governed by supernatural forces independent of man, Christianity was no different from paganism, and replacement of one set of cults by another did not free man from worshipping such forces.

However, the introduction of Christianity in Rus, just as in the other countries of Europe, had a positive effect. It promoted the consolidation of the progressive feudal class system and helped to overcome elements of tribal relations, to establish monogamy as the only form of marriage, permanent family as a divine institution ("what God united, man cannot dissolve"), and a ban on intercourse and marriage between close relatives conducive to degeneracy.

Christianity recognised the existence of slavery and other forms of social dependence as lawful and inevitable, protesting merely against abuse of power by the master in relation to his servant; it called for the manumission of infirm old men and concubines but not for abolition of this form of exploitation. The freeing of a serf was ordered for the master's serious crime—say, as a heretical deviation.[1] The clergy owned serfs; thus Bishop Stefan of Novgorod "was strangled by his serfs" (1068).[2] The cloisters, though, did not use serf labour.

Christianity brought with it the concepts, evolved in ancient Rome and in Byzantium, of the need for domination by and subordination to state power. Outstanding works of architecture, painting, jewellery, printing, literature, hymnography were produced for the new cult; their significance, however, was not

---

[1] S. I. Smirnov. *Materialy dlya istorii drevnerusskoi pokayannoi distsipliny* (Materials for a History of the Ancient Russian Discipline of Penance), Moscow, 1912, p. 180.

[2] NPL, Moscow-Leningrad, 1950, p. 473.

limited to their applied ecclesiastical use, although their origin was determined primarily by that use. The ancient Russian system of writing, which came into being before the end of the 10th century, was officially recognised by the Church under the new conditions and became widespread, going far beyond the needs of the cult; as birch-bark records show, it was widely used by city-dwellers for their needs. Through translations of Byzantine and some West European books, Rus became familiar with the achievements of classical and medieval literature, historiography, philosophy and natural science.

*Chapter II*

# CHRISTIANITY AND THE CHURCH IN THE 12TH-14TH CENTURIES

The development of feudal relations, the spreading of the patrimonial estate system of exploitation side by side with the early state system, considerably strengthened church organisations and changed their economic basis, which considerably enhanced their influence on the country's life.

In the late 11th and the early 12th century, a new source of material support for the Church—land property—appeared. Increasing in the 12th and 13th centuries, it turned the Christian cult organisation into a feudal system. The Church's landed estates evolved both out of princely possessions where personally free peasants lived in communities and out of villages and unpopulated but cultivated territories, handed over to the Church as gifts or by testament. The Church also appropriated villages and territories that did not form part of landed estates but were merely under the prince's supreme jurisdiction.

The first records of lands handed over to the Church of the Mother of God of the Pechery Monastery in the 1060s and early 1070s, mention them as a form of early feudal living—the allotment of tributes from certain districts in various parts of the state,[1] but in the late 11th and in the first half of the 12th century, the cloisters and the see of Smolensk were already given definite villages and arable lands. Metropolitan Yefrem of Pereyaslavl (c. 1089-1091) gave the Pechery Monas-

---

[1] PSRL, Vol. 2, columns 492-493.

tery a farmstead at Suzdal "with villages"; a grant to the St. Panteleimon Monastery of Novgorod dating from the 1130s records a transfer of villages and other lands. Villages, along with tithes, were granted to the Cathedral of the Smolensk Icon of the Mother of God on the occasion of an episcopal cathedra being instituted there in 1136. The Church of the Mother of God in Vladimir, which was intended by Andrei Bogolyubsky as the cathedra of the new metropolitan, was also granted "great possessions, immunities, tributes, the best villages, a tithe of his herds, and a one-tenth tax on trade..."[1] Beginning with the 12th century, ownership of land by church bodies (monasteries and sees) emerged simultaneously with their foundation, and that was typical of later times, too. There are records from the 12th and 13th centuries of the ownership by the Church of the Mother of God in Vladimir and by the Tithe Church in Kiev (which must have retained its traditional functions of collection and distribution of church income) of cities, including Polonnoye, Gorokhovets and others not listed by name.[2]

The traditional tithe also changed its character. The tithe from administration of justice was abolished or replaced by fixed sums (the middle of the 12th century). The tithe ceased to be a share of the centralised state rent, becoming a special tax collected by special officials—tithe collectors (the second half of the 12th century).

In the first quarter of the 13th century the possessions of church sees were already so great that Bishop Simon of Vladimir and Rostov proudly mentioned that fact in his epistle to Polikarp: "They have so many cities and villages, and collect tithes all over that land"[3]

---

[1] PRSL, Moscow, 1962, Vol. 1, column 348.

[2] Ya. N. Shchapov, "Tserkov v sisteme gosudarstvennoi vlasti Drevnei Rusi". In: *Drevnerusskoye gosudarstvo i yego mezhdunarodnoye znacheniye* ("Church in the System of State Power in Ancient Rus". In: *The Ancient Russian State and Its International Position*), Moscow, 1965, pp. 333-336.

[3] *Kievo-Pecherskiy paterik* (Lives of the Kiev-Pechery Fathers), Kiev, 1930, p. 130.

The transformation of the Church into a landowner considerably expanded and consolidated the determinant socio-economic structure of ancient Russian society in the 12th-14th centuries. Church organisations possessed lands, along with peasants living on them, as their property, and had an interest in increasing their number. The practice of handing over lands to cloisters by feudals by testament or spiritual will, to ensure prayers for the remission of the testator's sins after his death, led to a constant and at that time unlimited increase of church property. The handing over of lands to ecclesiastical establishments was accompanied by a ban on the transfer, including sale, of these lands to other owners, and under favourable conditions that ban was legally valid over several generations, which expanded church ownership of land almost infinitely. That made such ownership privileged from the very outset, and the extent of the privileges increased in the second half of the 13th century after the Church was relieved of the duty to the Horde.

The system of ecclesiastical feudal ownership was built on an organisational basis different from that of secular ownership. The feudal land structure involved hierarchical subordination of small feudal owners to bigger ones, including the grand duke of the land who, being the suzerain of the appanage princes and boyars, possessed some feudal rights to the lands of these his vassals. The ancient Russian church organisation, uniform in its structure, was not the supreme owner, in the person of the metropolitan, of all the lands belonging to individual sees, cloisters or churches; neither did a bishopric have such rights to the church lands in its diocese. Each of the church units, each cathedral or monastery church (say, the churches of St. Sofia, of the Mother of God, of Our Saviour, of St. George, etc.) was the nominal owner of real estate and movable property handed over directly to them or even to a definite throne. The feudal structure of the church organisation was thus determined, on the one hand, by the administrative structure involving subordination of the church units to an episcopal, and later the metropolitan centre, and on the other hand, by maintaining the ownership of land by concrete cloisters and churches, a system in which the metropolitan and episcopal cathedrals were no different, as owners of lands handed over to them, from the individual churches without administrative rights or the monasteries.

\* \* \*

During the 12th and the first half of the 13th century the structure of the church organisation continued to develop: bishoprics appeared in Smolensk, Galich, and, at the end of the 12th century, in Ryazan; early in the 13th century, with the political strengthening of the principality of Vladimir and Suzdal, it was also granted a diocese of its own, which became separate from that of Rostov (1214). Bishoprics were also instituted in south-western Russia, in Peremyshl (Przemyśl in Poland) and Ugrovsk. Some cathedras were moved to new localities, and others closed down.

An attempt to institute in Russia a metropolitanate opposed to the Kievan one was undertaken by Prince Andrei Bogolyubsky in the 1160s, but it failed. The policy of the prince of Vladimir, who strove for a unification of Rus and acted in concert with a local churchman, a candidate for the metropolitanate, was directed against Constantinople's creature in Kiev and could not be approved of or recognised by the emperor and the patriarch.[1]

Of the Russian episcopal sees of that time, only the Novgorod see received the status of an archbishopric. The appearance of that institution may probably be linked with the work of His Grace Ivan Popyan (1110-1130) referred to as an archbishop in the chronicles.[2] In the years of his office the conditions matured that soon resulted in the establishment of the republican system in Novgorod. But the irreversible development of Novgorod along republican lines not

---

[1] N. N. Voronin. "Andrei Bogolyubski i Luka Khrizoverg (Iz istorii russko-vizantiyskikh otnosheniy XII v.)" [Andrei Bogolyubsky and Luka Chryzoverg (From the History of Russian-Byzantine Relations in the 12th c.)]. In: *Vizantiyskiy vremennik*, Moscow, 1962, Vol. 21, pp. 36-42.

[2] NPL, pp. 19, 22.

only preserved the new title of the local hierarchs but also changed the procedure of their induction. Beginning with Nifont's successor, Arkadiy (1156), the hierarchs of Novgorod were elected locally, not appointed by Kiev, but the metropolitan retained the right of consecration. It is not clear why the archbishops of Novgorod sometimes received that title only after a period of service and not at their induction. In any case that title had a different significance in Rus, as compared to the Church of Constantinople, where the title of autocephalic archbishop was conferred on a see directly subordinated to the patriarch rather than to a local metropolitan.[1] Thus the procedure of conferring the archbishop's power and his title in Novgorod, which developed in the 12th century along republican lines, fully accorded with the special and very significant position of the bishopric in the republican administration of Novgorod in the 14th and 15th centuries.

The institution of new sees led to the division of the territories of the dioceses, which furthered the spreading of the church organisation, of Christianity and its ideology in society. This division could not keep up with the splintering of princely power in the process of intensifying feudal fragmentation but it followed in the wake of that process, and where the balance of political forces in Rus was favourable to a prince, the capital, and sometimes the territory of the principality, coincided with the new diocese.

Along with the emergence of new sees, other bodies of administration came into being, anticipating and complementing the former process. Archbishop's vicars and representatives of the episcopal courts and administration appeared in the outlying districts of dioceses, in the centres of principalities which had not yet gained church autonomy, and in major cities. This institution probably appeared in the diocese in towns as well as at the various sees in the 12th century. They may have been installed especially for the administration of justice at the time of significant growth of the

---

[1] H. G. Beck. *Kirche und theologische Literatur im Byzantinischen Reich*, München, 1959, pp. 67-68.

Church's jurisdiction in the 12th century. It was a local institution which did not emerge from the very beginning of the church organisation but only at a time when it was adapted to the conditions of the ancient Russian social and state structure.

Church feudals had not only ecclesiastical but also civil and criminal jurisdiction over the population that belonged to them by the right of feudal ownership. This can be deduced from indirect data by extrapolating the basic monastery regulations on the church holdings and in view of the gradual reduction of the judicial immunity of the Moscow metropolitan see in the 15th century.[1]

Compared to the 11th century, the sees retained or even expanded their earlier spheres of jurisdiction—over the whole of Rus Christian population in matters that were not subject to princes' courts ("episcopal litigation" or "church courts", according to the terminology of the sources), and over certain groups of that population regardless of the territory where they lived, in cases of all types ("church people", in the same terminology).

An important instrument of forming the class of persons dependent on the Church was the extension of its jurisdiction to those groups of the population which found themselves outside the traditional groups of the early class social structure subject to princely jurisdiction. In the 11th century, "church people" included only monks, clergymen and members of their families, whereas in the 12th and 13th centuries that list grew considerably. Church people now included peasants, direct producers who fell under the feudal domination of the Church, people whose subordination was in the interest of the Church (e.g. pilgrims), and, finally, those who had no means of livelihood because of infirmity (blind men, lame men, etc.), who lived on the charity of the Church and promoted the propaganda of its ideology.

A significant source of the Church's material support

---

[1] S. B. Veselovsky. *Feodalnoye zemlevladeniye v Severo-Vostochnoy Rusi* (Feudal Landownership in North-Eastern Rus), Moscow-Leningrad, 1947, Vol. 1, pp. 401-412.

was at that time yet another sphere of its jurisdiction throughout the country—family and marriage cases. In the 12th and 13th centuries, the Church extended its jurisdiction to include litigation between spouses about property, cases involving religious cults of other Churches (Moslem, Judaic) and pagan cults, the use of folk medicine mixed with pagan magic and cases of death involving the use of these means. The range of cases formerly also within episcopal courts jurisdiction was likewise extended to cover marriages and contacts with persons of non-Christian faiths, relations within the family, etc.

The 12th and 13th centuries saw a continued expansion of the church jurisdiction. Spreading its judicial power throughout the country in the wake of princely power, the old Russian Church took a large new group of institutions in its hands, usually without encountering opposition from the state and objectively helping state authorities in consolidating the class system. At the same time the expansion of the church jurisdiction sometimes came in conflict with that of the princes—in cases of property inheritance, theft of agricultural and home-industry products.

Towards the end of the 12th century, the Church extended its rights to cover such an institution of city life as the weights and measures service. According to the statutes of Vladimir and Vsevolod, and the treaties between Russian principalities and Riga and Lübeck, episcopal sees began to supervise and, consequently, to administer justice in this sphere. We have no data on whether that service emerged in Rus only at that time, and whether it was in the hands of the Church from the outset or was transferred from some secular, urban or princes' bodies to local bishops and the clergy of cathedrals.[1]

The weakening of direct economic dependence of the Church on the princes' power due to the growth of its land property transformed episcopal sees into

---

[1] Ya. N. Shchapov. "Iz istorii gorodskogo upravleniya v Drevney Rusi (Sluzhba mer i vesov)". In: *Goroda feodalnoy Rossii* [From the History of City Administration in Ancient Rus (The Service of Weights and Measures). In: *The Cities of Feudal Russia*], Moscow, 1966.

independent economic organisms potentially autonomous in other spheres of activity as well. As a result, the interests of ecclesiastical bodies could not come in conflict with those of the princes' power in nonconfessional and non-ideological spheres. Records of this appear in the second half of the 12th century, when political activity of sees and bishops sometimes led to conflicts with princes. Such instances also occurred in north-eastern Rus, where the bishops Leon and Feodor gained notoriety for their money-grubbing and abuses of power in Suzdal and Vladimir, and in other centres. Evidence of this is also provided by the differences in the attitude of the heads of Russian dioceses to the induction of the metropolitan of Kiev by Prince Izyaslav, in violation of the established tradition of the metropolitan being sent from Constantinople. At the council, two of the eight bishops, Nifont of Novgorod and Manuil of Smolensk opposed the grand duke's desire to induct a local metropolitan, and one bishop, that of Polotsk, did not come to the council at all; the consecration of Kliment was confirmed by five bishops. The very comparison of the case of Metropolitan Ilarion in 1051 and Metropolitan Kliment in 1147 shows the considerable change in the position of the hierarchs of the Russian Church that occurred in the intervening one hundred years, although it is more than probable that there were more Greeks among the members of the council that elected Ilarion than in the middle of the 12th century. This new position of bishops as political figures might be a factor in determining their attitude to the consecration of the metropolitan in Kiev without the patriarch's blessing and to the grand duke's candidate.

As a rule, bishops did not participate in the conferences of princes that gathered to handle matters of state. At the same time there are records of the participation of hierarchs in princes' councils[1] when the latter discussed such questions as the accession of some

---

[1] V. T. Pashuto. "Cherty politicheskogo stroya Drevney Rusi". In: *Drevnerusskoye gosudarstvo i yego mezhdunarodnoye znacheniye* (Some Features of the Political System in Ancient Rus. In: *The Ancient Russian State and Its International Significance*), Moscow, 1965, pp. 13-24.

prince to the throne, mostly in circumvention of the established tradition. Participation of the higher dignitaries of the Church in these councils was supposed to make the decisions of these councils, expressing the princes' will, more authoritative, confirmed by heavenly power, as it were.

But that did not have much effect, as a rule. In 1164, the bishop of Chernigov swore falsely, kissing the cross, and thus misled the princess and the city authorities, helping to hand the city over to Svyatoslav Vsevolodovich.[1] In Galich, the participation of higher church dignitaries in the council called by Yaroslav Osmomysl in 1187 did not prevent the handing over of the throne of Galich after the prince's death to Vladimir, not Oleg.[2] The advice of Bishop Ioann of Suzdal in 1211 to deprive the oldest son, Konstantin, of the throne of Vladimir for his disobedience[3] played an important role, determining for a certain period the hierarchy among the Vsevolodovichi after the death of their father.

However, secular power, the power of grand dukes and boyars, continued to determine the political development in Rus in the 12th and 13th centuries both in the centre and locally. A graphic expression of this was the trial at a purely secular council of princes in Suzdal in 1229 of the former local bishop Kirill I, renowned for his wealth, apparently in connection with his greed and extortionist practices, which ended in his being dispossessed.[4]

Through its hierarchs, the Russian Church influenced the country's political life.[5] The dignitaries of the Church acted not so much as bodies of power as an

---

[1] PSRL, Vol. 2, columns 522-523; B. A. Rybakov. "Drevnosti Chernigova" (The Antiquities of Chernigov), MIA, No. 11, Moscow-Leningrad, 1949, p. 94.

[2] PSRL, Vol. 2, column 657.

[3] PSRL, Vol. 10, columns 63-64; Vol. 25, p. 103; S. M. Solovyov. *Istoriya Rossii s drevneishikh vremyon* (A History of Russia from the Times Ancient), Book I, Moscow, 1959, Vol. 2, pp. 604-607.

[4] PSRL, Vol. 1, column 452; Ye. Ye. Golubinsky. Op. cit., Vol. 1, Part I, pp. 553-554.

[5] S. M. Solovyov. Op. cit., Book 2, Vol. 3, Moscow, 1960, Vol. 3, pp. 62-63.

ideological and political factor on which the success of a given side in the struggle of groups of princes and citizens largely depended. A study of the role of the Church's head in the political life of Novgorod in the first third of the 13th century indicates that here, too, the archbishops were creatures of princes and boyar parties, and they occupied the see only as long as the princes with whom they were connected managed to stay in power.[1]

But the participation of church bodies in the administration of justice and in other public services was not restricted to the bishops. Towards the end of the 12th century and the beginning of the 13th, the office of the archimandrite of Novgorod became a special institution that rivalled the episcopal see. That was a new institution of city administration (a magistracy) that officially represented the interests of the numerous black clergy and monastics in the person of the archimandrite of Novgorod. The city *veche* or people's assembly elected one of the fathers superior of a Novgorod monastery head of that magistracy; during his term in that new capacity he must have retained the right to his crozier, the reason for that being that it was limited, restricted in time.[2] Thus in this field, too, the political activity of the ecclesiastical (monastic) organisation involved a strengthening of its economic basis and social role, in the first place in Novgorod, although there are indications of the existence in the late 12th century of a monastic organisation in Kiev, too.[3]

\* \* \*

The canonisation of saints in Rus was a means of spreading the Christian cult resting on local, ancient Russian foundations, one that made a considerable ideological impact on the masses. At the same time it had political significance, as it made real political and

---

[1] A. S. Khoroshev. *Tserkov v sotsialno-politicheskoy sisteme Novgorodskoy feodalnoy respubliki* (The Church in the Socio-political System of the Novgorod Feudal Republic), Moscow, 1980, pp. 41-48.

[2] V. L. Yanin. *Ocherki kompleksnogo istochnikovedeniya* (Essays in Comprehensive Source Studies), Moscow, 1978, pp. 136-149.

[3] PSRL, Vol. 2, column 682.

church figures connected with princely dynasties and monasteries objects of worship. Thus the first canonisation of the princes Boris and Gleb, the brothers of Yaroslav the Wise, sanctified, as it were, the authority of the entire princely clan of Yaroslav's descendants, the more so since it proved impossible, until the 13th century, to make the Greek metropolitans canonise Vladimir, Russia's official baptist who had a well-known pagan past. However, the cult of Sts Boris and Gleb, to which such great importance was attached also had in the second half of the 11th century the concrete political meaning of strengthening "legal" princely power and of condemning murder as a means of settling problems of succession to the throne. That was why the cult of the princes was widespread even outside Rus. Internationally, there was also another aspect to this cult: ancient Russian princes now had their own "intercessors" from among the members of their family—something that no other head of any neighbouring state could boast of. According to *The Tale of Bygone Years*, the Kievan metropolitan Georgios, of Greek origin, who participated in the translation of the relics of the two brothers in 1072, did not support their cult up to the moment of the miracle that occurred during the proceedings. The canonisation of Alexander Nevskiy had the same significance for the principality of Vladimir and Suzdal. As early as the 1280s, his cult was locally worshipped under his son Dmitriy Aleksandrovich, confirming the latter's right to the grand-ducal throne, as was clearly said in the life of that saint written at the prince's Monastery of the Nativity at Vladimir.[1] Alexander Nevskiy was officially canonised in 1281.

In the 12th century, two churchmen were canonised—Feodosiy of Pechery, Father Superior of the Kiev-Pechery Monastery and an ideologue of Orthodoxy and monasticism (1108), and Bishop Leontiy of Rostov, the missionary who converted the principality of Rostov to Christianity (1191-1194).

---

[1] Yu. K. Begunov. *Pamyatnik russkoy literatury XIII veka "Slovo o pogibeli Russkoy zemli"* (*The Tale of the Ruin of the Russian Land:* A Monument of 13th-Century Russian Literature), Moscow-Leningrad, 1965, pp. 61, 71.

\* \* \*

The ideologues of all Churches, including the Orthodox one, preached the exclusiveness of their doctrine, considering all the other Churches as erring. At a time when the community of the religious cult as an element of feudal culture was one of the constituent features of nationality, this furthered the nationality's consolidation and the strengthening of the state, and, under the conditions of foreign enslavement, helped to preserve the ethnos. Connected with this were the bans on contacts with members of other faiths, on eating forbidden food, and on marriages with members of other confessions. After the division of the Western and Eastern Christian Churches in the middle of the 11th century, Greek hierarchs in Rus just as Russian churchmen, such as Feodosiy of Pechery (of the Caves) engaged in anti-Latin propaganda, but it met with no response either among the ruling feudal class or among urban craftsmen or any other strata. Military actions of Catholic countries against Rus naturally evoked outbreaks of anti-Catholic feeling. Of this nature was the antipathy to Poland in the Kiev-Pechery paterik, undoubtedly connected with the Polish campaigns against Kiev in the 11th century.

Closely connected with princes' thrones, the Russian Church did not give up its contacts with Western countries, either, and adopted an independent line in selecting cultic elements. Thus, the 1056-1057 calendar in the Ostromir Gospel included remembrance of the Italian saints Appolinaris, Bishop of Ravenna, and Vitus; at the end of the 11th century, the cult of St. Nicolas, Bishop of Myra in Lycia, was instituted in Rus on the occasion of the translation of his relics to the city of Bari, Italy, although it was not recognised by the Byzantine Church.

A noticeable change in the attitude to the Western Church was linked with the feudal aggression in the 13th century, under the Catholic slogans of a crusade against the unchristianised peoples of the Eastern Baltic region subject to Rus. The aggression was organised by the Livonian Order; Swedish and Danish knights also took part in this crusade, supported ideologically and politically by the Pope. The onslaught on the Russian lands was beaten back by the people's volunteer corps of Novgorod and Pskov, and it undoubtedly evoked considerable antipathy towards the Western Church and everything connected with it. Prince Alexander of Vladimir and Suzdal, named Nevskiy after his victory on the Neva, was, as we have already mentioned, canonised by the Church as early as the 1280s.

\* \* \*

The Tatar-Mongol invasion inflicted terrible devastation on Rus. It was a terrible setback for the country; vast numbers of people perished or were driven into captivity; great material values were destroyed, and whole cities (Kiev, Ryazan, Lutsk, Vladimir, Suzdal, Rostov, and others), as well as a number of handicrafts and industries, ceased to exist. Churches and the landed estates of churches and monasteries suffered greatly.

The establishment of the Horde's domination over Russian principalities somewhat altered the position of the Church. It now dealt not only with the power of the princes but also with a foreign political force, establishing relations with it on the recognition of its legality and divine origin. In exchange for that, the khans recognised the special position of the Church in the Russian principalities, confirmed the immunity of the church possessions, and exempted the Church from the heavy taxes collected by the conquerors, from the obligation to send troops from church lands during Tatar campaigns. The metropolitan in Rus had to go to the Horde and get the *yarlyk* or decree there, confirming the rights of the Church, in the same way as the princes received from the khan their *yarlyk* confirming their right to the grand-ducal throne. Thus the Russian Church, just as the princes, became a vassal of the khans, and the hierarchs who headed it were now able to protect their interests politically as well as economically, which made them active participants in the political struggle in Rus in the 14th and 15th centuries. The first *yarlyk* or metropolitan's charter of immunity was received by Metropolitan Kirill from Khan Mengu-Timur in 1267.[1]

According to that document the clergy were obliged "to pray God with a pure heart for the khan and his family, and to bless him", which it did, appreciating the "benevolence towards the Holy Church on the part of the infidels and the pagans". It was highly important for the conquerors to have a political, economic and, primarily, ideological force in Rus which might influence Russian society to obey "those sent by God". The Horde's long oppression of Rus, the defeats of anti-Horde uprisings, and a constraint in the conduct of the princes, who avoided open action against the invaders, can to some extent be explained by that position of the official Church. Only the action of Dmitriy Donskoy supported by St. Sergiy of Radonezh, father superior of a monastery, who broke with that antinational tradition, led to the victory in the battle on the Kulikovo Field. At the same time the Church played an important role in 14th-century Rus in ensuring the unity of the Russian people and in the desire to get rid of the yoke imposed by the heterodox conquerors.

The 13th century was a decisive stage in the spreading of Christianity among the masses of the population. The last references to magicians among the properly Russian population disappear (the last record of the burning at stake of four magicians in Novgorod, dates from 1227).[2] Burials in burial mounds were no longer practised; the burial rites became Christian in rural areas as well as in the cities. Pagan symbols, formerly widely used in jewellery, gradually disappeared, while the number of liturgical books and icons that survived from the 13th and 14th centuries increased considerably. Thus four times as many gospels have survived from the 14th century as from the 11th-13th centuries taken together. This is connected with the vigorous activity of the Church which became, by the 13th century, a significant factor in the development of Rus and was now able to interfere in

---

[1] PSRL, Moscow, 1965, Vol. 15, issue I, column 32.
[2] NPL, p. 65.

society's life and to impose a strict religious censorship. The terrible decades of the foreign conquest and yoke may have contributed to the rise in Christian religiousity.

\* \* \*

Changes in the position of Russian principalities in the 13th and 14th centuries, linked with the incorporation of most of them in the Horde (the middle of the 13th century) and the Grand Dukedom of Lithuania (the middle of the 14th century) led to a partial restructuring of the administration of the Church. In 1299, Metropolitan Maksim of Kiev, a Greek by origin, "unable to stand the Tatar violence, left his metropolitanate in Kiev" and moved to Vladimir of Suzdal, where the future cathedral had been built already in the times of Andrey Bogolyubsky. In the course of time, that move played a very important role in the development of north-eastern Rus, for the metropolis took an active part as a political force, in the struggle (in the 14th and 15th centuries) for the reunification of Russian lands round Moscow.

In the 13th century, the oldest episcopal sees were closed down in Belgorod, Yuryev and Pereyaslavl, the devastated southern regions of Rus. At the same time, new sees were instituted in Tver (in the last quarter of the 13th century) and in Suzdal (in the 14th century). In the middle of the 14th century, a nominal episcopate was established in Kolomna, whose head was the metropolitan's vicar. In the course of political struggles, some bishops (those of Suzdal and Rostov) received, close to the end of the century, the title of archbishop, which they subsequently lost.

In the struggle among the major feudal centres and the princes who headed them, metropolitans and bishops were used (and themselves acted) as a real political force capable of shifting the balance of power in favour of a given candidate to a *yarlyk* and the right to a grand dukedom or metropolitan's see. In the course of that struggle between Moscow and Tver, the conditions were created for moving the metropolitan's cathedra from Vladimir to Moscow (before 1326), which was an act of strong support for the future capital of the centralised Russian state on the part of the Church. At the same time Dmitriy Donskoy's attempt to secure the cathedra for his priest Mityai met with considerable opposition on the part of the higher clergy and ended, after 13 years of struggle, with the recognition by the grand duke of Metropolitan Cyprian, a creature of Constantinople, who had occupied the metropolitan's cathedra in the Lithuanian Grand Dukedom.

\* \* \*

The Church's missionary activities were one of the means of incorporating the neighbouring peoples in the Russian principalities. The neighbouring tribes became the object of archaic forms of exploitation traditional for the outlying areas of Rus with a view to spreading the religion and culture of class society, and in the Eastern Baltic region, in competition with the crusades under Catholic slogans, also with a view to preserving the local forms of the early feudal organisation of society. In the northern part of Latgale, subordinated to Pskov, Christianity was introduced in 1207, which was intended as a barrier to stop the advance of the Order; in 1210, under their peace treaty with the Ests, the Novgorod authorities also baptised some of the Ests' leaders.[1] In 1227, on orders from Prince Yaroslav Vsevolodovich of Novgorod, almost the whole of Karelia[2] was baptised. Adoption of Christianity offered the "elders" of the neighbouring tribes the chance of entering the feudal service of some Russian prince, which strengthened their authority over their tribesmen, as we can see from the fate of Pelgusiy-Filipp an Izhoran, who took part in the victorious battle of Novgorod against the Swedish fleet on the Neva in

---

[1] V. T. Pashuto. "Osobennosti struktury Drevnerusskogo gosudarstva". In: *Obrazovaniye Drevnerusskogo gosudarstva i yego mezhdunarodnoye znacheniye* (Some Features of the Structure of the Ancient Russian State. In: The Formation of the Ancient Russian State and Its International Significance), p. 115.

[2] PSRL, Vol. I, column 449.

1240.[1] In 12th-century Novgorod, norms of penance were recorded which were imposed on "a Bulgarian, a Polovtsian, a Chud" on baptism, which shows that this was a normal occurrence[2].

Great attention was also paid to the Christianisation of the Volga and Kama regions. After the conquest of Rus by the Horde, an episcopal seat was established at Sarai, the Horde's capital, in 1261. Although the khans themselves could have been interested in its institution enabling them to have a plenipotentiary representative of the Russian metropolitan, who could serve as a contact with Byzantium, this was also an official channel for working among the Russian population in the Horde and for converting to Christianity the Mongols themselves and the other heterodox peoples of the Khanate. Bishop Theognostus of Sarai studied the question of how adult "Tatars" should be baptised in accordance with Orthodox rules.[3] Even members of the khan's family embraced Christianity—such as Peter, a nephew of Khan Batu, the "Czarevich of the Horde", and others. Besides, the Russian metropolitan's representative at Sarai was important as an instrument of opposing the influence of the Pope's throne, which kept sending missions to these remote lands to try to convert the khans to Catholicism. The Sarai diocese also included the southern Russian lands of the former Pereyaslavl bishopric.

The Komi-Zirani, tribes that paid tribute to the Grand Dukedom of Moscow, were also Christianised. The conversion of these tribes was begun by an educated missionary, a monk from Ustyug called Stefan and nicknamed Khrap. Not only did he learn the Zirani language, but also created a special ("Permian") alphabet for it and translated liturgical

---

[1] NPL, pp. 392, 393. See Yu. K. Begunov. "Drevnerusskiye istochniki ob izhortze Pelgusii-Filippe, uchastnike Nevskoy bitvy 1240 g.". In: *Drevneyshiye gosudarstva na territorii SSSR, Yezhegodnik 1982* (Ancient Russian Sources on Izhorian Pelgusiy Filipp, Fighter in the 1240 Battle of the Neva. In: The Earliest States on the Territory of the USSR, Yearbook 1982), Moscow, 1983, pp. 76-85.

[2] RIB, Vol. VI, column 33.

[3] Ibid., column 129; see M. D. Poluboyarinova. *Russkiye Lyudi v Zolotoy Orde* (Russian People in the Golden Horde), Moscow, 1978.

books into Komi. After burning down pagan prayer-houses and idols, he succeeded in Christianising part of the land. In 1383 he was made bishop of the new Perm diocese at Ust-Vym, which was instrumental in converting the whole of the land of Perm to Christianity. The new bishop became the grand duke's vicegerent in this area, concentrating in his hands both secular and ecclesiastical power.

The second half of the 14th century marked the beginning of a new stage in the development of monasteries, which made these ecclesiastical bodies major landowners in north-eastern Rus. That process was begun as early as 1357 by Sergiy of Radonezh, who founded the Trinity Monastery, and was later continued with Metropolitan Aleksey's support. Some 40 monasteries were founded, so that the territory from Zvenigorod near Moscow to the White Sea was covered by a network of church estates. They were founded in areas where feudal relations were but poorly developed, and where there were untouched land resources. The peasants often rebelled against the new landowners. But it was the cloisters, helped by state authority, that emerged victorious as a rule. Only in their conflicts with local feudals did they have to back down or seek compromises.[1] The success of the cloisters was also connected with the expansion of ploughing and truck gardening by them in the north with its cheap manpower, where previously only grazing was practised, and with the closely interrelated economic and ideological activity of these ecclesiastical organisations.

\* \* \*

The domination of religious ideology in medieval society resulted in rebellions against the feudal system and the Church which took the form of intra-religious strife. We have vague, much later reports of heretical ideas and actions in Rus going back to the 11th-13th centuries. For the 14th century we have documentary

---

[1] I. U. Budovnits. *Monastyri na Rusi i borba s nimi krestyan v XIV—XVI vv.* (Monasteries in Rus and the Peasants' Struggle Against Them in the 14th-16th Centuries), Moscow, 1966, pp. 135, 362.

evidence of heresies. The most important of these actions was the *Strigolniki* movement which began in the middle of the century among the democratic strata of city-dwellers in Novgorod and became further developed in Pskov. That was a rationalistic doctrine directed against the state Church as a cultic organisation. The *Strigolniki* rejected the church hierarchy and the accepted system of the induction of clergymen, the priests' mediating role between man and God. They opposed church sacraments. Rejecting the dominant feudal Church, they advocated instead a democratic community of Christians possessing no property and headed by teachers whose authority was based on the example they set and not on their position.[1] That was an attempt to replace the feudal Church by an ideal, though remote from reality, early Christian organisation, which was dangerous both to the Church itself and to the state connected with it. In 1375, the heretics were publicly executed in Novgorod, but that did not put an end to the heresy's existence, and the metropolitan of Moscow and the patriarch of Constantinople joined in the fight against it.

In the 13th and 14th centuries, having penetrated much deeper in the consciousness of the people than previously, Christianity acquired greater opportunities for development in Rus. In the times of the Tatar-Mongol yoke, when traditional relations with other European countries, with which Rus had previously been closely connected, were made more difficult, Christianity in the form of Orthodoxy remained an important channel of communication with the European world. The Slavic countries in the Balkan Peninsula, Walachia, Byzantium and Georgia belonged to the same cultural circle, based on the same principle which was natural for the Middle Ages, as the Russian lands divided among several states. Under these conditions, Christian literature, art and philosophy, concentrated in the hands of and spread primarily by the Church, were an important component of the

---

[1] N. A. Kazakova and Ya. S. Lurye. *Antifeodalniye yereticheskiye dvizheniya na Rusi XIV—nachala XVI vekov* (Anti-feudal Heretical Movements in Rus in the 14th—Early 16th Centuries), Moscow-Leningrad, 1955, pp. 52-55.

ideological life of Rus which linked it to states of the same type and offered it a chance of cultural exchange with them. Another source of cultural impulses was in that epoch the heritage of ancient Rus with its high culture and many-sided links. Such Russian cities as Pskov and Novgorod retained their links with Western countries, and western Russian lands developed in close contact with Lithuania, Poland, Bohemia, and Hungary.

Soon after the defeat of the Horde, the Russian Church felt the need for close ties with the Christian world to help it restore the Russian written tradition in the field of law. Many sees in Russia were left without codes of law which they needed in their administrative and judicial activity, which hampered the performance of the Church's traditional functions. In 1261, Metropolitan Kirill ordered from Bulgaria a new book of guidance which included commentaries by Byzantine jurists; in the 13th-15th centuries, it became widely known throughout Rus. It was revised several times, with interpolations from ancient Rus own heritage (the Russkaya Pravda, the statutes of princes Vladimir and Yaroslav, etc.).

The community of the Eastern Christian world in the 14th century was manifested in many areas of culture, in particular in the spreading in Rus of the religious-philosophical doctrine of hesychasm, which came from Byzantium. Evolved by Gregory Palamas, a hermit of Mt. Athos, in his controversy against the then prevalent ideas of theological rationalism defended by Varlaam, that mystic doctrine was based on the idea of "divine energy" supporting the whole of the terrestrial world (1341).

In Rus, these views were reflected in the philosophical argument between Archbishop Vasiliy Kalika of Novgorod, and Bishop Feodor of Tver (1347). The argument centred on the "concrete" question whether paradise existed on the earth, if only in remote overseas lands inaccessible to man, as Vasiliy believed, or whether it was mental only, existing in man himself when he was illuminated by "divine light". That was the view supported by some clergymen in Tver, who shared the doctrine of Palamas, thus showing their acquaintance with the latest philosophical ideas of Eastern Christianity.

In another sphere of church life, the doctrine of hesychasts was reflected in the wide spreading of cenobitic Rules in Russian monasteries instead of the Rules advocated in vain by Feodosiy of Pechery as early as the 11th century. Quite possibly it was a factor in the formation in the 14th and 15th centuries of a great many new monasteries in north-eastern Rus as monastic collectives rather than as hermitages of individual zealots,[1] although the latter's role in the emergence of new monasteries is beyond doubt. In the 14th and 15th centuries the monks at Russian monasteries, both old and new, read and copied, with great understanding numerous ascetic and contemplative works of the 6th-14th centuries from Byzantium (by John Climacus, Dorotheus, Isaac Cyrus, Simeon the New Theologian, Gregory of Sinai, and others) which laid down the foundations of that religious-philosophical doctrine.

---

[1] G. M. Prokhorov. "Isihazm i obshchestvennaya mysl v Vostochnoy Yevrope v XIV v.". In: *Trudy otdela drevnerusskoy literatury* (Hesychasm and Social Thought in Eastern Europe in the 14th Century. In: TODRL, Leningrad, 1968, Vol. 23, p. 106.

*Chapter III*

# THE ORTHODOX CHURCH IN THE 15TH AND 16TH CENTURIES

The Orthodox Church in medieval Rus was a major landowner; it enjoyed the same feudal privileges as the princes. Metropolitans, bishops, monasteries and cathedrals owned arable lands with peasants living on them, fisheries and hunting grounds. The most valuable estates were granted to the metropolitans in the 14th century by the grand dukes. Novgorod's Sofia House with the archbishop at the head had extensive land possessions. The monasteries gained most of their possessions in the 15th century through seizure of deserted lands of peasants, and in the 16th century, through absorption of the possessions of the boyars who fell into disfavour. In that period, the number of monasteries grew rapidly, and their colonising and economic activities increased both in the centre and in the outlying districts. According to V. O. Klyuchevsky, 84 monasteries appeared in the 15th century, including 27 in the cities, and in the 16th century, 86 (35 of these in the cities). In all, 254 monasteries were founded in Rus in the 14th-16th centuries, 104 of them in the cities and their environs.[1]

Towards the middle of the 15th century, the development of feudal relations brought about the introduction of wide-ranging judicial and fiscal immunities of the church possessions. The statutory contractual charter signed by Grand Duke Vasiliy I

---

[1] V. O. Klyuchevsky. *Sochineniya* (Works), Moscow, 1957, Part 2, p. 247.

Dmitrievich and Metropolitan Cyprian on June 28, 1404, "On Church People and Land Possessions" defined the relationship between grand dukes and metropolitans at the time of the formation of the centralised Russian state. The charter has survived as a document (without the names of the prince and the metropolitan) defining the seignorial rights of the grand duke and the privileges of Moscow metropolitans during the whole of the 15th century. The text is close to the contractual charters of princes and metropolitans. The metropolitan was granted complete judicial and partial tax immunity within his possessions; the exceptions were the duties paid by the metropolitan's traders as part of the tribute to the Golden Horde.[1] Bishops and monasteries also received princes' charters granting various privileges.[2] The peasants who toiled on the lands of the clergy were tied to the latter by feudal dependence and were obliged to carry out various tasks, including the building of churches, the erection of monastery walls and fortifications, the construction of palaces, the cleaning of ponds, etc. During Christian feasts, they were obliged to bring gifts to their Father Superior, "whatever they had in their hands".[3]

As the sources show, the clergy attempted to restrict the freedom of the peasants' movement from one master to another. In the mid 1460s Ivan III Vasilyevich's charter addressed to Prince I. V. Obolensky, Vicegerent of Yaroslavl, stipulated that the peasants of the Trinity-St. Sergiy Monastery could only leave their masters in autumn, on St. George's Day. The charter was the result of the monks' complaint that the peasants were leaving the monastery possessions to settle on the grand duke's lands.[4] In the late 15th and the early 16th centuries, there was a sharp rise in the

---

[1] PRP, Moscow, 1955, Issue 3, pp. 421-423, 432-436.

[2] See the charter, signed by Prince Vasiliy I Dmitrievich on February 20, 1423, granting privileges and immunities to the Archimandrite of the Monastery of Our Saviour and the Annunciation entitling him to the wastelands of Lyskovo and Kurmysh in the district of Nizhniy Novgorod (PRP, Issue 3, pp. 98-99).

[3] PRP, Issue 3, p. 424.

[4] PRP, Issue 3, pp. 93-94.

struggle of the peasants for land; 84 per cent of all the conflicts over land involved, according to A. D. Gorsky's observations, litigation between church feudals and the "black" and palace peasants.[1]

Apart from feudal rent, traditional tithes also went to the Church's treasury. The wealth of the clergy, and especially of the cloisters, accumulated through usury and commerce, as well as the performance of various rites and "voluntary" collections among the population. We have an interesting record (dating, it is true, from the middle of the 17th century) as to the size of the money (apart from rent) paid to the treasury of the patriarch (formerly metropolitan) from one cathedral church only—that of Yuryevets Povolzhskiy in the patriarch's *volost*. The receipt-book of the Patriarch's Fiscal Department for the year 1653 records that Archpriest Avvakum collected, between April 1 and August 26, 1652, "10 roubles 13 altyns [three-kopeck pieces.— *Tr.*] 2 dengas [half-kopeck pieces] from 34 minors, 37 bigamists, 4 trigamists, from 16 funeral and 4 bastardy duties; also 17 roubles and 17 altyns feudal money; also 5 roubles and 10 altyns from court cases and retrials..."[2] The sum of the income "apart from the rent" was large for those times, but the bulk of the Church's vast material wealth, or rather the wealth of its hierarchs, came from the feudal rent exacted from the peasant population living in bondage on church lands.

Up to the middle of the 15th century the Russian metropolitanate formed part of the Constantinople Patriarchate, and the metropolitans were appointed to the see of Kiev and All Russia by the patriarch of Constantinople. This fact of foreign policy, along with other, internal circumstances (certain feudal privileges), material wealth, and increased ideological and political role of the Church during the yoke of the Horde, promoted the relative independence of the metropolitan see in the state. In the hard times of Mongolian

---

[1] A. D. Gorsky. *Borba krestyan za zemlyu na Rusi v XV-nachale XVI veka* (The Struggle of the Peasants for Land in Rus in the 15th and early 16th Centuries), Moscow, 1974, p. 107.

[2] TsGADA, reg. 235, case 2, book 33, sheet 602 (reverse).

oppression, the grand duke, pursuing the policy of gathering the lands round Moscow, had an interest in the alliance with the metropolitans. Russian candidates were sent to Constantinople, but not all of them succeded in ascending to the metropolitan throne. Thus in 1434-1435, after the death of Metropolitan Photius, a Greek by birth, Bishop Iona of Ryazan was sent to Constantinople "to be inducted". But the patriarch of Constantinople rejected him as a candidate, raising in 1436 the Greek Isidore to the metropolitan throne of Moscow.[1]

In view of the Turkish threat, and hoping to get military aid from Rome, the Greek clergy, headed by the patriarch and the emperor, concluded in 1439 a union with the Catholic Church at the Ferrara-Florence Council, recognising the Roman Pope's supreme authority. Metropolitan Isidore of Moscow, who was present at the council, showed himself a confirmed supporter of the union.[2] For the Russian state, still weak at the time, recognition of the union would also mean political dependence on the Pope. Grand Duke Vasiliy II Vasilyevich did not recognise the union (later the Greeks themselves renounced it), and Isidore was taken, after a service at the Cathedral of the Dormition, to the Chudov Monastery (The Monastery of St. Michael's Miracle); later he was given a chance to leave Rus. On December 15, 1448, a council of Russian bishops elevated Bishop Iona of Ryazan to the metropolitan throne.

After the conquest of Constantinople by Othman Turks in 1453, Moscow metropolitans, elected by the Local Councils, no longer went to Constantinople. In this way the Orthodox Church in Rus became independent and in fact autocephalous, although it remained, according to church law, within the patriarchate of Constantinople. The year 1458 saw the separation of the Moscow and Kiev metropolitanates; the latter

---

[1] Ye. Ye. Golubinsky. *Istoriya russkoy tserkvi* (A History of the Russian Church), Moscow, 1900, Vol. 2, Part I, p. 419.

[2] In Golubinsky's view, as they went to the council, the Greeks, who regarded Isidore as a "great philosopher", hoped to avoid with his aid any concessions to the Roman curia on questions of dogma (Ye. Ye. Golubinsky. Op. cit., Vol. 2, Part I, pp. 423-424).

included some Russian lands which were part of the Grand Dukedom of Lithuania. The elevation to the Kievan metropolitanate of another metropolitan indicated an attempt by the patriarch of Constantinople to challenge the autocephaly of the Moscow (Russian) Church, which had just asserted itself *de facto*.[1] The balance of power between the secular and church authority in the Russian state changed in favour of the former, although the relationship between the grand dukes and the higher hierarchs were often aggravated by the vicissitudes of the struggle for state centralisation.

Thanks to tradition, vast wealth and extensive privileges, the Church was a sort of a state within the state, as it were. In his possessions, the metropolitan wielded unlimited power over the church people—it was not for nothing that he bore the title of *vladyka,* or lord.[2] Boyars, *stolniks* [Russian courtiers inferior in rank to boyars.— *Tr.*], children of boyars of various ranks, and other courtiers served at the metropolitan's court in the Kremlin. The metropolitan had a steward, a treasurer, scriveners and clerks. The positions in which noble and middle-ranking families served were hereditary. Some of the higher-ranking metropolitan's courtiers later served the patriarchs as well.[3] In the 15th and 16th centuries, there were 18 dioceses on Russian territory, with metropolitanates in Moscow and Kiev.[4] The hierarchs of Novgorod and Rostov had the rank of archbishop. As a rule, the metropolitans nominated bishops from among monks of noble origin, archimandrites and fathers superior of major privileged monasteries. According to a tradition inher-

---

[1] See Ya. N. Shchapov, *Vostochnoslavyanskiye i yuzhnoslavyanskiye rukopisnye knigi v sobraniyakh Polskoy narodnoy respubliki* (Eastern Slavic and Southern Slavic MS Books in the Collections of the Polish People's Republic), Moscow, 1976, Vol. 2, Appendix, No. 52, pp. 145-147; Ye. V. Belyakova. "K istorii uchrezhdeniya avtokefalii russkoy tserkvi". In: *Rossiya na putyakh tsentralizatsii* (On the History of Instituting the Autocephaly of the Russian Church. In: Russia's Path Towards Centralisation), Moscow, 1982, pp. 152-156.

[2] DDG, Moscow, 1950, Vol. 3, p. 14.

[3] S. B. Veselovsky. Op. cit., pp. 423-427.

[4] Ye. Ye. Golubinsky. Op. cit., Moscow, 1911, Vol. 2. Part II, pp. 26-32.

ited from Byzantium, the candidate paid the metropolitan a tax at induction.

The higher hierarchs gathered at councils which handled the most important problems of church administration and the life of the Church. According to canonical rules, the councils were regarded as the highest legislative bodies in church matters, but they were not convened regularly. The hierarch who found it impossible to attend a council sent in a message. Only the signatures of the higher hierarchs were regarded as necessary to make the Council's decisions valid. We know from the Nikon Chronicle that the 1401 Council was attended by seven bishops. At that council, Metropolitan Cyprian censured Archbishop Ioann of Novgorod and Bishop Savva of Lutsk. The reason for punishing the archbishop of Novgorod, who was compelled to give up his see and sent to the Chudov Monastery, was his striving for independence, in particular the refusal to recognise the metropolitan's right to hold the highest Court of Appeal for the citizenry of Novgorod, and, consequently, to the court tax ("monthly court"). After three years and four months Ioann was forgiven and returned to the archbishop's throne in Novgorod.[1]

The Church Councils of 1503, 1504, 1551, 1553, 1580-1584 discussed the secularisation of church lands, and passed decisions on the stamping out of heretical freethinking. The Councils were invariably attended by representatives of secular power: the grand duke or the heir apparent, members of the Boyar Duma (Council) and state officials. Intruding into the sphere of church administration and land ownership, as well as the ideological struggle within the Church, secular authority sought to subordinate the Church.

Orthodox ecclesiastics were traditionally divided into the black clergy and the white. The former included the upper echelons of the church hierarchy and the numerous monasteries. In the 15th and 16th centuries most of the monasteries were cenobitic, although as late as the beginning of the 16th centuries there existed

---

[1] Ye. Ye. Golubinsky. Op. cit., Vol. 2, Part I, p. 319, footnote 2.

monasteries following the cellular Rules.¹ Council elders *(startsi)* headed by the hegumen (father superior) administered the monastic commune. The major privileged monasteries were headed by archimandrites appointed by the grand duke or the metropolitan. Monastic estate managers (cellarers), treasurers and clerks were elected from among the council *startsi*. The founders and hegumens of monasteries drafted cenobitic Rules prescribing an ascetic mode of life "in accordance with the rules of the holy fathers"—the wearing of definite types of dress, observance of celibacy, and rejection of earthly pleasures. Actually, these rules were not observed. Metropolitans and other higher hierarchs denounced monastics and their licentious conduct. In his speech at the 1551 Church Council, or Stoglav (One Hundred Heads), Czar Ivan IV said that people took monastic vows, among other reasons, "for the sake of the body's quiet, to indulge in constant drinking". Along with other problems, the councils' resolutions dealt with the question of improving monastic discipline.²

Up to the beginning of the 16th century, some monasteries had women living in. The ideologues of monasticism protested against this. The 1503 Church Council declared that "monks and nuns will not live in the same cloister". At monasteries, the service was to be conducted by hegumens and at convents, by parish priests. The Council's decision forbade widowed priests and deacons to conduct services [3] (that decision was confirmed at the Stoglav Council of 1551), and bishops were forbidden to exact payments for the induction of priests (the rule was in force only until 1505).

In the 15th and 16th centuries monasteries became major estates. Thus, in 1601 the Byeloye Ozero Monastery of St. Kirill owned 11 large and 5 smaller villages, 607 hamlets and 320 wastelands.⁴ The wealth

---

[1] I. U. Budovnits. Op. cit., pp. 75-76; for details of the Rules determining the order of monastic life and of church service see P. Kazansky. *Istoriya pravoslavnogo russkogo monashestva* (The History of the Russian Orthodox Monasticism), Moscow, 1855, pp. 28-40.

[2] *Stoglav*, St. Petersburg, 1863, pp. 44, 204-205 ff.

[3] PSRL, St. Petersburg, 1901, Vol. 12, p. 257.

[4] A. I. Kopanev. *Istoriya zemlevladeniya Byelozerskogo kraya v*

of the Trinity-St. Sergiy, Solovki and the St. Simon monasteries of Moscow and others rivalled that of the Byeloye Ozero Monastery of St. Kirill. Members of the dominant feudal class who took monastic vows formed a privileged group among the monks; it played a prominent role in the political and ideological struggle. One of such privileged monks was Iosif, hegumen of the Volokolamsk Monastery, an offspring of the family of the Sanins, noblemen from the environs of Moscow. He was a zealous ideologue of monasticism, champion of monastic asceticism, and an outstanding publicist of those times; he advocated monastic landownership but censured the monks' avarice, and also insisted on harsher reprisals against heretics.[1] The opponent of the "Iosifites", Vassian Kosoy (the Squint-eyed—*Ed.*), a monk of the Monastery of St. Kirill from the ancient boyar family of the Patrikeyevs who fell into disfavour at the end of the 15th century, under Ivan III, protested in his publicistic writings against "avarice" and against executing heretics.[2] Ordinary monks worked on the monastery estates side by side with peasants and serfs.

The role must be stressed of monasteries and bishoprics in the development of medieval culture. Major monasteries had libraries and schools for the instruction of adolescents in "book wisdom"; chronicles were written here, and groups of icon-painters and architects were formed. Liturgical books and textbooks were translated from Greek, Latin, and other languages.

The white or parish clergy were extremely numerous in Rus. Priests and deacons were mostly ordained on the hereditary principle. The practice was fairly frequent of townspeople and village communities electing priests from their midst. The white clergy had to work

---

*XV-XVI vv.* (The History of Landownership in Byelozersk Land in the 15th and 16th Centuries), Moscow-Leningrad, 1951, p. 140.

[1] *Poslaniya Iosifa Volotskogo* (The Epistles of Iosif of Volotsk), Moscow-Leningrad, 1959, pp. 366-367.

[2] N. A. Kazakova. *Ocherki po istorii russkoy obshchestvennoy mysli: Pervaya tret XVI veka* (Essays on the History of Russian Social Thought: The First Third of the 16th Century), Moscow, 1970, pp. 87-154.

for their living—to plough land and practise various trades. On the one hand, the parish clergy spread among the masses the political and religious ideas of the ruling class, and, on the other, they had close ties with the broad circles of the population, and were themselves influenced by them.[1] Apart from priests and deacons, the clergy of a parish included junior deacons, sextons, choristers, bell-ringers, prosphora-bakers; the church people also included beggars, cripples, God's fools, widows, and some categories of bondsmen. Intensified social and property stratification amidst the white clergy led, about the middle of the 16th century, to the emergence of a privileged stratum—archpriests and churchwardens.

According to canonical law, the clergy, both black and white, were subject to the government and jurisdiction of the bodies of church authority. In this connection, Metropolitan Cyprian wrote to the people of Pskov: "It is unseemly for laymen either to try the priest, or to punish him, or to condemn him, or to say a word against him; the hierarch who ordains them, he alone judges them, and punishes them, and teaches them."[2]

In the Middle Ages, the Church played a great role in all the spheres of life of the state and society. In issuing their decrees, the grand dukes turned to the metropolitans for advice and blessing. The higher hierarchs were present at the sittings of the Boyar Duma and the Councils of the Land. The clergy had the right to plead for those in disgrace. Although the Church was an ally of the grand dukes, the relations between the allies during the formation of the centralised state were rather complicated. Tension often arose

---

[1] M. N. Tikhomirov. *Drevnerusskiye goroda* (Ancient Russian Cities), Moscow, 1956, pp. 166-180; N. V. Ustyugov and N. S. Chayev. "Russkaya tserkov v XVII v." In: *Russkoye gosudarstvo v XVII veke: Noviye yavleniya v sotsialno-ekonomicheskoy, politicheskoy i kulturnoy zhizni* (The Russian Church in the 17th Century. In: The Russian State in the 17th Century: New Phenomena in the Socio-Economic, Political and Cultural Life. A Collection of Articles), Moscow, 1961, p. 296.

[2] Makariy. *Istoriya russkoy tserkvi* (A History of the Russian Church), St. Petersburg, 1886, Vol. 5, p. 11.

under the metropolitans Cyprian the Bulgarian and Photius the Greek, as they strove to maintain the Church's independence by various means, including personal contacts with the patriarchate of Constantinople.

In 1445, after the defeat of the Russian army by Khan Ulug Mohammed, a conspiracy was formed against Grand Duke Vasiliy II Vasilyevich, headed by the appanage princes of Galich. Boyars, merchants and members of the black clergy took part in the conspiracy. Even monks from the Trinity-St. Sergiy Monastery patronised by the princes of Moscow, participated in the conspiracy. Vasiliy II was seized at the monastery and, after being blinded, was sent under guard to Uglich. When Moscow was seized by appanage Prince Dmitriy Shemyaka, he was supported by "bishops and archimandrites of the whole land, and honest hegumens and presbyters..."[1] Bishop Iona of Ryazan was also on the side of the appanage princes. After the expulsion of Shemyaka from Moscow, the higher clergy accused him of disobedience to the grand duke and of disturbing the peace. Needing the support of the Church, Vasiliy II made a compromise with the Lords Spiritual, giving his consent to the elevation of Iona to the metropolitan throne by a council of Russian bishops. The alliance of secular and ecclesiastical authority, which seemed shaky for a while, was now restored, and some of the higher clergy began to call Vasiliy II "God-crowned Czar of all Russia", a title only Byzantine emperors were honoured with.[2] In the middle of the 16th century, under Metropolitan Makariy, Iona was canonised and included in the state pantheon of saints as a "great miracle worker".[3]

When the centralised state became stronger, and the Russian people threw off the Horde's yoke, relations between the clergy and the grand dukes became

---

[1] PSRL, St. Petersburg, 1910, Vol. 23, p. 153.

[2] M. A. Dyakonov. *Ocherki obshchestvennogo i gosudarstvennogo stroya Drevney Rusi* (Essays on the Social and State System of Ancient Rus), St. Petersburg, 1910, p. 415.

[3] A. S. Khoroshev. *Politicheskaya istoriya russkoy kanonizatsii XI-XVI vv.* (A Political History of Russian Canonisation in the 11th-16th Centuries), Moscow, 1986, pp. 106, 107, 172 ff.

strained. Needing land resources to reward members of his service class, Ivan III Vasilyevich made attempts to secularise church lands.[1] The government supported the programme of the "non-hoarders", whose ideologue was Nil of the Sora. According to Nil's hermitage rules, the life of monks must be based on earning everything that was necessary "by the labour of their hands". Hoarding "of the fruit of the labour of others gathered by force" was strictly forbidden.[2]

The orthodox clergy, headed by Iosif of Volotsk [Volokolamsk— *Tr.*] and Archbishop Gennadiy of Novgorod, took up a position hostile to the grand duke. Nil of the Sora, called to Moscow, supported the government's programme at the church council.

The "Iosifite" majority at the Council, headed by Metropolitan Simon, rejected Ivan III's secularisation plans referring to the ancient tradition dating from the times of the Kievan princes. The canonical justification in the Council's decision of the "legality" of monastic landownership contained references to the spurious charter of Czar Constantine ("Constantine's gift"), the ruling of the Council of Carthago, and the lives of saints. After the Church Council, Ivan III, unwilling to face an open conflict with the higher hierarchs, gave up his secularisation plans and established closer contacts with Iosif, the Hegumen of Volotsk, promising him to visit harsher reprisals on heretics.

The desire of secular powers to secularise at least part of the ecclesiastic hierarchs' possessions marked the domestic policy of Grand Duke Vasiliy III Ivanovich: maintaining an alliance with the "Iosifites" that controlled the Church, he also expressed himself

---

[1] Secularisation actually meant practical measures by the state to redistribute feudal holdings. In this particular case we do not associate the term with the intellectual movement meaning the change "in the general notions of the cosmic and metaphysical order of things.". [See V. Bosuma. "Sekulyarizatsiya obshchestva v XVII v." *XIII Mezhdunarodnyi kongress istoricheskikh nauk. Moskva. 16-23 avgusta 1970.* ("Secularisation of Society in the 17th Century". In: *Thirteenth International Historical Congress. Moscow. August 16-23, 1970*), Moscow, 1970.] Secularisation in a broader sense was launched in Russia in the 17th-18th centuries.

[2] M. S. Borovkova-Maikova. *Nila Sorskogo Predaniye i ustav* (The Legend and Statute of Nil of the Sora), St. Petersburg, 1912, pp. 5-7.

in favour of the "non-hoarders", bringing closer to his court Vassian Kosoy. A follower of Nil of the Sora, Vassian condemned church landownership, recognising the right of only cathedral churches to own lands the income from which was to meet the needs of the impoverished and cripples. He criticised the mode of life at monasteries, pointing to the hard life of peasants at villages belonging to the monasteries, disapproved of the policy of harsh reprisals against heretics, and had his own views on questions of dogma. The positions of "non-hoarders" at the court were strengthened with the arrival from Mt. Athos in Moscow of a talented and educated monk Maksim the Greek, commissioned by the grand duke to translate and correct liturgical books.

Maksim the Greek became close to some princes and boyars as well as learned men. His writings criticised licentiousness of the monks and the excesses of "hoarding" on the part of the monasteries. In defence of the peasants, he wrote of the heavy burden they carried, working for the monasteries; he particularly denounced the monasteries' usury, calling it "an impious business", and the monks, "cruel extortioners". Maksim the Greek's publicistic activities aroused the anger of the "Iosifites". Metropolitan Daniil, a zealous follower of the Hegumen of Volotsk, supported Vasiliy III when he divorced Solomonia Saburova, and got the Church Council condemn Maksim, using trumped-up charges. In 1525, Maksim the Greek was incarcerated in the dungeon of the Volokolamsk Monastery, and six years later, after a retrial, moved to a monastery at Tver.[1] At that time, Vassian Patrikeyev was also condemned and secluded at the Volokolamsk Monastery of St. Iosif where he soon died. Metropolitan Daniil celebrated a complete victory over his ideological enemies. Thus did the hierarchs make short work of anyone who dared to oppose the Church's feudal privileges.

The monasteries' lands continued to increase under Ivan IV Vasilyevich the Terrible. In the middle of the 16th century, according to the Englishman Clement

---

[1] Maksim the Greek was only freed under Ivan the Terrible; he spent his last years at the Trinity-St. Sergiy Monastery.

Adam's report, the monasteries possessed a third of the arable lands.[1] At the Stoglav Council of 1551, Czar Ivan IV raised the question whether it was proper for the monasteries to own such vast lands. In its "Reply", the Council, headed by Metropolitan Makariy, defended church and monastic landownership. Those who encroached on that right ran the risk of excommunication. A compromise was achieved between ecclesiastical and secular authorities: cloisters could now buy new lands only by the permission of the czar. The lands granted to the clergy during the Boyar reign (late 1530s-early 1540s) were handed back to the czar. That was the first legislative restriction of monastic landownership in the history of Russia.

Ivan the Terrible persistently implemented a policy of splitting the unity of the clergy and the subordination of the Church to state authority. The czar used the authority of the *vladykas* to further his aims, but he brooked no signs of independence on their part. Thus on his orders the dethroned Metropolitan Filipp, Archbishop Gherman of Kazan, Hegumen Korniliy of the Pskov-Pechery Monastery, were all executed; Archbishop Pimen of Novgorod was sent to gaol, and so on. At the 1580 Church Council, relying on servicemen and supported by the white clergy, Ivan the Terrible, with the acquiescence of the higher hierarchs, pressed a resolution depriving cloisters and churches of the right to buy privately owned land.[2] The 1584 Church Council, already in the reign of Fyodor Ivanovich, confirmed the decision of the 1580 Council and cancelled certain fiscal immunities of the black clergy.

The spiritual life in Russia in the 15th and 16th centuries was dominated by the Church. The feudalised Christian doctrine existed in its most orthodox dogmatic form in combination with a conservative system of views of the world, society and man. Relying on its great wealth, the Church endeavoured to establish a total spiritual monopoly, fighting against

---

[1] *Zhurnal Ministerstva narodnogo prosveshcheniya* (The Journal of the Ministry of Public Education), St. Petersburg, 1838, Part 20, No. 10, p. 62.

[2] SGGD, Moscow, 1813, Vol. 1, p. 200.

pagan survivals, popular amusements, and the spreading of other religions, particularly Catholicism and Lutheranism. Intolerance to other religions was graphically expressed in a formula inherited by printed denunciatory literature from handwritten books: "Since, according to the Apostle, there is one God and one faith, all the other faiths are not faiths but heresies and schisms."[1] The clergy of other Christian Churches displayed the same bigoted attitude to members of other faiths. The Church fought especially fiercely against the heretic movement aimed, just as all reformation movements in Europe, against "the spiritual dictatorship of the Church".[2] While adhering to a religious-idealistic worldview (in its Christian form), heretics criticised the dogmas, rites, and the church hierarchy, and some even went as far as criticising the feudal system and the oppression of the people under this system. The heretic movement was triggered off by a rise in the antifeudal struggles of tradepeople and peasants, and by the development of social and philosophical thought.

In the first quarter of the 15th century, there was a revival of the *Strigolniki* movement in Pskov; in its content, their doctrine was close to the official heresy of the Middle Ages. Pskov maintained close contacts with the Lithuanian Grand Dukedom and Livonian cities, and it had well-developed trading quarters. The interest of the townspeople for religious questions was also stimulated by the political struggle of the Pskov republic for the independence of its Church from the archbishop of Novgorod. The Snetogorsk Monastery of Pskov where the *startsi* and privileged monks formed a group separated from the rest of the brotherhood, became one of the hotbeds of opposition.

The *Strigolniki* of Pskov, just as their predecessors in Novgorod, opposed monasticism, rejected the hierarchy and the sacraments, and recognised the right of common laymen to interpret doctrines of the faith. The most radical of the heretics, who had unorthodox views

---

[1] *Kniga o vere* (The Book of Faith), Moscow, 1648, Preface.

[2] F. Engels. "Introduction to *Dialectics of Nature*", K. Marx and F. Engels, *Selected Works* in three volumes, Vol. Three, Progress Publishers, Moscow, 1976, p. 42.

of the crucial dogma of Triune God, doubted the divine origin of the Christ of the Gospel, and did not believe in the resurrection of the dead. The Church fought against the heresy together with the secular authorities of Pskov. Metropolitan Photius' denunciatory epistle to Pskov of September 23, 1427 (one of his four known epistles against heretics), announced that the *Strigolniki* had been caught and their leaders apparently executed; thus the *Strigolniki* heresy was suppressed, but their rationalist ideas lived on.

At the end of the 15th century, aggravation of social and class contradictions, the struggle between "non-hoarders" and "Iosifites", involving worldview problems, and the increased scope of the peasant movement against ecclesiastical feudals, created a situation in the country that was favourable to the rise of heresies. Religious questions were widely discussed, which was noted by Iosif of Volotsk with disapproval. Novgorod with its wide international trade and political links, highly developed handicrafts, and high standard of urban life and heretical traditions became the centre of the inception and spreading of heresies.

The heresy in Novgorod grew stronger at the time of Novgorod's joining to Moscow, when the secularisation of church land possessions became a vital issue. Iosif of Volotsk and Archbishop Gennadiy of Novgorod insisted that the heresy was fathered by the "Jewish heretic" called Skhariya who came to Novgorod in 1471 with the retinue of Prince Mikhail Olelkovich (Aleksandrovich) from the Grand Dukedom of Lithuania. 19th-century church historians stressed in this connection the dependence of heretical views on Judaism, calling the members of the movement Judaisers.[1] The question of the origin of the heresy still remains debatable. The Soviet researcher Ya. S. Lurye rejects the view that Skhariya was a real personality.[2] I. N. Golenishchev-Kutuzov expressed the opinion that

---

[1] Ye. Ye. Golubinsky. Op. cit., Vol. 2, Part I, pp. 560-563.

[2] N. A. Kazakova and Ya. S. Lurye. *Antifeodalniye yereticheskiye dvizheniya na Rusi XIV—nachala XVI vekov* (Anti-feudal Heretical Movements in Rus in the 14th—Early 16th Centuries), Moscow-Leningrad, 1955, pp. 113-114.

the Taborites influenced the views of heretics both in the Grand Dukedom of Lithuania and in Novgorod.[1] The rationalist conceptions of Novgorod heretics clearly show certain affinities with those of the radical wing of the *Strigolniki* of Pskov. That fact was also noted by the churchmen who fought against the heresy. Thus in his message to the 1490 Church Council, Archbishop Gennadiy, exposing a Novgorod monk Zakhar (who denounced the hierarchs) as a heretic, called him a *Strigolnik*.[2]

Rejecting the spiritual hierarchy and the church sacraments, the heretics of Novgorod refused to worship the relics of saints and icons—"things created by the hand of man". The main point of their doctrine was an unorthodox interpretation of the dogma of a Triune God. The Trinity conception was defended by Iosif of Volotsk and Archbishop Gennadiy of Novgorod. In their words, the heretic dogmas "abused Christ the Son of God and His Most Pure Mother, and desecrated holy icons..."[3] The heretics took interest in practical astronomy and mathematics. The heretics of Novgorod knew the works of Menander, the famous playwright of antiquity; of the 12th-century Jewish philosopher Moses Maimonides and of El Ghazzali, an Arab scholar of the late 11th-early 12th centuries.[4] The heretics of Novgorod were headed by members of the white clergy—Archpriest Gavriil of the St. Sofia Cathedral and the priests Aleksey and Denis. The heresy became widespread among trade people, its preachers "enticing many common people".

In the mid 1480s, a circle of free-thinkers was formed in Moscow, headed by Fyodor Kuritsyn, a clerk

---

[1] I. N. Golenishchev-Kutuzov. "Gumanism u vostochnykh slavyan (Ukraina i Belorussiya)". In: *Mezhdunarodnyi syezd slavistov (Sofiya, sentyabr 1963): Doklady sovetskoy delegatsii* [Humanism among Eastern Slavs (The Ukraine, Byelorussia). In: The Fifth International Congress of Slavists (Sofia, September 1963): Reports by the Soviet Delegation], Moscow, 1963, p. 9.

[2] N. A. Kazakova, Ya. S. Lurye. Op. cit., *Appendix*, pp. 378-379.

[3] Ibid.

[4] A. I. Klibanov. *Reformatsionniye dvizheniya v Rossii v XIV—pervoy polovine XVI v.* (Reformation Movements in Russia in the 14th-first half of the 16th Centuries), Moscow, 1960, pp. 292, 387.

in the Boyar Duma, on his return from Hungary, where he was sent in 1481 by Grand Duke Ivan III on an important diplomatic mission.[1] The priests Aleksey and Denis were transferred from Novgorod to Kremlin cathedrals. The circle was patronised by Yelena Voloshanka, the grand duke's daughter-in-law and daughter of Stefan of Moldavia. Moscow heretics were critical of the institution of monasticism and of ecclesiastical hierarchy. They took a distinctly rationalist attitude to some texts of the Holy Scripture. In the struggle between "non-hoarders" and "Iosifites", the views of the Moscow free-thinkers expressed the spiritual interests of the progressive part of society.

Members of this circle in the capital displayed an interest in philosophical and scientific knowledge. Thus Fyodor Kuritsyn gave an unorthodox interpretation of the freedom of will which he defined in terms of human knowledge and education rather than of divine Providence. Fyodor Kuritsyn's heritage includes his *Laodicean Message,* a monument of philosophical thought, and a literary work—*The Tale of General Dracula.*[2] Another member of the circle of heretics, Ivan Chorniy (the Black), copies *The Hellenic Chronicler* describing the events of world history, and a collection of Biblical books, with numerous heretical marginal notes.

The orthodox clergy demanded that the heretics be executed. Archbishop Gennadiy of Novgorod insisted that "they must be executed, burnt and hanged", citing the actions of the Catholic inquisition in Spain and Italy in support of his demand. For political considerations,

---

[1] K. V. Bazilevich. *Vneshnyaya politika Russkogo tsentralizovannogo gosudarstva: Vtoraya polovina XV veka* (The Russian Centralised State's Foreign Policy: The Second Half of the 15th Century), Moscow, 1952, p. 415; Ya. S. Lurye. *Ideologicheskaya borba v russkoy publitsistike kontsa XV—nachala XVI veka* (Ideological Struggle Among Russian Publicistic Writers of the Late 15th-Early 16th Centuries), Moscow-Leningrad, 1960, p. 141.

[2] F. I. Lilienfeld. "Ioann Tritemiy i Fyodor Kuritsyn. O nekotorykh chertakh rannego Rennessansa na Rusi i v Germanii" (Johannes Trithemius and Fyodor Kuritsyn. Some Features of the Early Renaissance in Rus and Germany). In: *Kulturnoye naslediye drevney Rusi: istoki, stanovleniye, traditsii* (The Cultural Heritage of Ancient Rus: Origins, Development and Traditions), Moscow, 1976, pp. 116-123.

Grand Duke Ivan III Vasilyevich was slow in resorting to reprisals, seeking to make the clergy accept his secularisation plans, if only partially. At the Church Council of 1490, convened to try the heretics of Novgorod, the latter were defended by Metropolitan Zosima, later also accused of heresy by Iosif of Volotsk. Ivan III did not consent to condemn the heretics to death; they were excommunicated, some were secluded in remote monasteries, others sent to Novgorod.

Archbishop Gennadiy subjected the condemned men to public desecration: they were dressed in fools' clothes, and made to ride with their faces to the horses' tails, hands tied behind their backs; on their heads were pointed birchbark helmets with the words "This is the Satan's host!" inscribed on them. The procession moved through the city streets, and the citizens were expected to mock at them. Then the birchbark caps were burnt on their heads, and the heretics themselves were subjected to corporal punishment. It may well be that in following this inquisitorial procedure, the archbishop of Novgorod imitated the king of Spain. The final trial of the heretics, mostly participants of the Moscow circle, took place at the 1504 Church Council. The accused were condemned to death. Fyodor Kuritsyn's brother Ivan Volk (the Wolf), Dmitriy Konoplyov and Ivan Maksimov were burnt in a log cabin on the ice of the Moskva. Some heretics were also executed in Novgorod.

Despite the persecution and executions, the Church was unable to eradicate free thought. Around 1553, Matvey Bashkin organised a circle of the gentry in Moscow. Bashkin came from a family of petty boyars who sent their children to the court of Ivan IV. The circle continued and further developed the heretical traditions of the Moscow free-thinkers of the late 15th-early 16th centuries. Rejecting the official Church with its feudal hierarchical system, Matvey Bashkin opposed to it "a council of the faithful"; he refused to worship icons and rejected the most important church sacraments. Bashkin's social projects went further than his predecessors'. His circle rejected the institution of serfdom and all forms of bondage. After trial by a Church council, Matvey Bashkin was incarcerated at the Volokolamsk Monastery of St. Iosif and after a retrial in 1554, burnt at the stake.[1]

In the 1550s, the "new teaching" of Feodosiy Kosoy, a runaway Moscow serf, became widespread among the lower strata of townspeople and part of suburban peasants. Its opponents among the reactionary clergy called it a "slaves' teaching". Feodosiy Kosoy's views took shape in the midst of acute social contradictions and class actions of the townspeople in Moscow. These views represented the most radical trend in the heretical movement of the 15th and 16th centuries.[2] Feodosiy Kosoy protested not only against the feudal organisation of the Church but also against the entire social system based on exploitation of man by man. He substantiated his views through a rationalist reinterpretation of some texts of the Holy Scripture (the Gospel, Books of the Apostles, and others).

Following his predecessors, Feodosiy rejected the dogma of the triune nature of divinity, declaring that God, the creator of Heaven and Earth, is one. He visualised Christ as a "preceptor" of the common people. Church rites and sacraments, prayers, worshipping the cross and icons, observance of fasts were all "human legends", according to Feodosiy. The social aspects of his views found expression in his rejection of the church hierarchy, the institution of monasticism, church landownership and obedience to the authorities. Feodosiy preached equality of all men and religions before God, opposing the powers that be and protesting against wars whose burden fell on the toiling people. In Feodosiy's homilies, the evangelical formula "Love thy neighbour" was not an abstract precept but one filled with living human content. Around 1554-1555, Feodosiy Kosoy was caught and taken to Moscow, to be tried by a Church Council. Together with his associates he managed to escape from a monastery gaol

---

[1] We have a record of the investigation into Matvey Bashkin's case [A. A. Zimin. *I. S. Peresvetov i yego sovremenniki* (I. S. Peresvetov and His Contemporaries), Moscow, 1958, pp. 168-181].

[2] We have no data on the works of Feodosiy Kosoy. His teaching was denounced by monk Zinoviy, a church writer of the 16th century [Zinoviy Otensky, *Poslaniye mnogoslovnoye* (A Message of Many Words), St. Petersburg, 1880].

to the Grand Dukedom of Lithuania, where he continued to preach. Feodosiy Kosoy's followers were active among townspeople and peasants in the 1560s.

In the 16th century, the major monasteries and bishoprics retained their significance as centres of medieval culture and Christian scholarship. Although the conservative role of the Church began to tell on the development of social thought, education and art, the non-orthodox and humanist ideas of the heretics in 15th- and 16th-century Russia did not evolve into a programme of reform of the dominant Church, and the heretical movement did not develop into a people's Reformation, as was the case in advanced European countries.

After the defeat of the heretics and the failure of the far-reaching plans for the secularisation of church lands, the alliance of secular power and the clergy grew stronger. Expressing the interests of church hierarchs who supported the government on condition that the positions of the Church in the state were to be preserved and consolidated, Iosif of Volotsk made an attempt to substantiate the divine origin of grand-ducal authority. Church writers gave literary form to the pretentious idea that Moscow was the "third Rome", and the Russian Church the only guardian of "true" Christianity after the Union Decree of Florence and the conquest of Byzantium by Othmans. In the same period, legends became current among the feudals about the descent of Moscovite grand dukes from Byzantine and Roman emperors.

Endeavouring to consolidate the influence of the upper echelons of the church hierarchy, Metropolitan Makariy of "Iosifite" convictions, came up with the initiative of Ivan IV's coronation as czar. The magnificent ceremony conducted on January 16, 1547, by the metropolitan and bishops at the Dormition Cathedral, and the high title of czar (never conferred on appanage princes), bestowed on the young grand duke by the metropolitan—all this demonstrated not only the enhanced authority of Russia in international relations but also the Church's political role in the state.

Metropolitan Makariy did a great deal to make Church ideology the ideology of the whole state. In the middle of the 16th century measures were taken to centralise canonisation acts: the Church Councils of 1547 and 1549 canonised local saints on a mass scale. The decisions of the 1551 Stoglav Council were also intended to consolidate and centralise the church organisation.

An important event of Russia's political and church history of the late 16th century was the establishment of a patriarchate. Indeed, the Russian Church, which represented the official ideology of a powerful independent state, which sanctified the authority of the czars who saw themselves as heirs of Byzantine emperors, formally continued to be part of the Constantinople Patriarchate. In the mid 15th century, the Moscow metropolitanate became factually independent, but the Eastern patriarchs, who were at the time under the Turkish yoke and turned to Russia for material and, sometimes political, aid, refused to recognise the autocephaly of the Russian Church on the legal canonical plane. Towards the end of the 16th century, the entire course of political development made inevitable the ending of the Moscow metropolitanate's formal dependence on the patriarch of Constantinople and the bringing of its legal status to conformity with its actual independent position. In the system of the Eastern Churches, which arose, just as the Roman curia, in late antiquity, the patriarch of Constantinople, who bore the title of "Ecumenical Patriarch", came first; next in rank was the patriarch of Alexandria with the title of "Pope and Judge of the World", followed by the Antiochene and Jerusalem patriarchs. The institution of the patriarchate was also made necessary by the growing threat of Catholicism in the southwestern lands of Russia, whose Orthodox population needed an authoritative protector.

In 1586, Patriarch Ioakim of Antioch arrived in Moscow to beg for aid to the Eastern Orthodox Church. The negotiations concerning the establishment of the patriarchate were secretly conducted by Boris Godunov, a boyar. Without the consent of the Ecumenical Council, Ioakim did not dare to perform that "great" deed. He was asked to promote that cause in his contacts with the Eastern patriarchs. In 1588,

Patriarch Jeremiah II of Constantinople came to Moscow himself. That was an opportune moment, and it was decided to press him to agree to the induction of a patriarch. At first, he himself was suggested to stay in Russia as a patriarch, but when he consented to that, it was proposed that his seat should be in Vladimir—a condition which made the Ecumenical Patriarch refuse to stay in Russia.

After that, the events took an official turn. In January 1589, a Church Council was convened in the czar's chambers, and in the presence of the czar and of the Boyar Duma, Jeremiah II considered three patriarchal candidates (according to a procedure that had been in effect under Byzantine emperors), selecting Metropolitan Iov, a protégé of Boris Godunov. The ceremony of Patriarch Iov's consecration at the Dormition Cathedral was extremely solemn and magnificent. After the ceremony, the Charter on the election of the patriarch was drafted and signed by the patriarchs of Constantinople and Moscow and by other hierarchs. According to that Charter, patriarchs of Moscow and All Russia were to be elected by Local Councils and confirmed by the czar; they had to notify Eastern patriarchs of their election. Simultaneously, four metropolitanates were established—those of Novgorod and Rostov and two new ones, of Kazan and Krutitsy; six archbishoprics: in Tver, Vologda, Suzdal, Ryazan, Smolensk, and Nizhniy Novgorod; eight bishoprics: in Kolomna, Pskov, Ustyug, Rzhev, Bryansk, Chernigov, Byeloe Ozero and Dmitrov.[1] Patriarch Jeremiah II and his retinue were showered with precious gifts; they also received the financial aid they were asking for and left in May 1589 for Constantinople.

The institution of a patriarchate in Russia was confirmed by canonical acts of Constantinople Councils of Eastern hierarchs in May 1590 and February 1593. The Council charters signed by the hierarchs (with authentic and counterfeit signatures on the 1590

---

[1] P. Lapin. *Sobor kak vysshiy organ tserkovnoy vlasti: Istoriko-kanonicheskiy ocherk* (The Church Council as the Supreme Body of Church Authority: A Historico-Canonical Essay), Kazan, 1909, pp. 181-215.

Charter and authentic ones on the 1593 Charter)[1] were brought to Moscow and are now kept in Soviet archives. The Moscow Patriarch was placed not third, as the czar's government hoped for (next in rank after the patriarchs of Constantinople and Alexandria) but fifth, after the Patriarch of Jerusalem, and sixth in the overall system of the Western and Eastern Churches.

A great role in the establishment of the patriarchate and the election of Iov to the patriarchal throne was played by Boris Godunov, the actual ruler of the Russian state. That was a major diplomatic and political triumph for him. The event itself marked a step in the subordination of the Church to the state. At the same time, the prestige of the Russian Church in international affairs and, in the first place, in the system of the Eastern autocephalous Churches, grew considerably.

\* \* \*

Church history of the 16th century ends with the events of the Time of Troubles. A terrible natural calamity befell Russia in the early 17th century—crop failures in three successive years (1601-1603). An eyewitness, the Dutchman Isaac Massa, reports that "a third of the Muscovite czardom died of starvation".[2] In those years of the people's suffering the hierarchs used their great wealth to strengthen their influence in society, to increase their riches and to put the peasants in feudal bondage, rather than to relieve the sufferings of the famine-stricken. Conducting *molebens,* litanies of the departed, and calling for patience, the clergy sought to reconcile the hungry and the replete, the poor and the rich. Unrestrained profiteering in grain

---

[1] B. L. Fonkich. "Grecheskiye gramoty sovetskikh khranilishch: Iz istorii uchrezhdeniya patriarshestva v Rossii: Sobornye gramoty 1590 i 1593 gg." In: *Problemy paleografii i kodikologii v SSSR* (Greek Charters in Soviet Archives: From the History of the Institution of the Patriarchate in Russia: Church Council Charters of 1590 and 1593. In: Problems of Palaeography and Codicology in the USSR), Moscow, 1974, pp. 251-260.

[2] I. Massa. *Kratkoye izvestiye o Moskovii v nachale XVII v.* (A Short Report on Muscovy in the Early 17th Century), Moscow, 1937, p. 61.

flourished in the country; not only secular feudals, merchants and rich peasants but also monasteries and the clergy engaged in it.

During the Peasant War of 1606-1607, in which the peasants were led by Ivan Bolotnikov, the clergy of Moscow headed by Patriarch Ghermoghen sent pastoral messages throughout the country calling the rebels "evil-doers", "brigands", "thieves", and "apostates" who renounced God and the Christian faith. Forgetting all about religious camouflage, the authors of the messages described the goals of the people's struggle as extremely dangerous for the feudal system: "forgetting the fear of God, the weeds have risen, wanting to swallow the ears of wheat". During the foreign intervention, some of the Muscovite clergy went over to the Polish invaders' side. According to the author of *A New Tale of the Glorious Russian Czardom and the Great State of Muscovy*, some of the Muscovite priests and monks "went over to the enemy and did their bidding". When a broad national liberation movement of the people, in which the parish clergy took an active part, got under way, some hierarchs supported the movement. Late in 1610, Patriarch Ghermoghen began to send out messages calling on the people to rise in arms against the invaders. Seizing the Kremlin, the Poles incarcerated him in a dungeon under the Chudov Monastery, where he was starved to death.[1]

---

[1] N. F. Droblenkova. *Novaya povest o preslavnom Rossiyskom tsarstve i sovremennaya yei agitatsionnaya patrioticheskaya pismennost* (A New Tale of the Glorious Russian State and Contemporary Patriotic Writings), Moscow-Leningrad, 1960.

*Chapter IV*

# THE RUSSIAN CHURCH AND STATE IN THE 17TH CENTURY

In the history of the Russian Orthodox Church, the 17th century is traditionally called the patriarchal period, its head in this period being a patriarch whose title was "the Great Most Holy Lord Patriarch of Moscow and All Russia and of All the Northern Countries".[1] During the century, eight patriarchs succeeded one another on the patriarchal throne: Filaret (1619-1633), Ioasaf I (1634-1638), Iosif (1642-1652), Nikon (1652-1658), Ioasaf II (1667-1672), Pitirim (1672-1673), Ioakim (1674-1690), and Adrian (1690-1700). In the inter-patriarchal period (between 1658, the year when Nikon left the throne, and the election of Ioasaf II), the highest body of church authority, was the Church Council. Metropolitan of Krutitsy was usually appointed the Patriarchal Locum Tenens.

The patriarch ruled the Church together with the council of the higher hierarchs—metropolitans, archbishops, bishops and archimandrites of the major privileged monasteries. During the patriarchal period, Church Councils were convened frequently if irregularly. The Councils settled legislative problems involving the entire local church system and administration, discussed questions of dogma, church discipline and reforms, took measures against popular anti-church movements, elected patriarchs and other high hierarchs, and established new dioceses. The presence of the hierarchs (metropolitans, and bishops) at the

---

[1] AI, St. Petersburg, 1842, Vol. 5, No. 186, p. 322.

Councils was obligatory. Fathers superior of monasteries and members of the white clergy—archpriests, priests and deacons—were sometimes invited to Councils, but only the higher clergy had the deciding vote, and only the hierarchs had the right to sign the Councils' decisions.[1]

The question of Church Councils, of the number of their participants and composition, requires special research. A study of pre-revolutionary literature has shown that Church Councils were convened fairly frequently during the whole of the 17th century.[2] Some of the Councils were "incomplete", i.e., they were not attended by all the higher hierarchs and dealt mainly with the current administrative and judicial affairs. The greater Church Councils, e.g., those of 1656, 1660, 1666-1667, were attended by the Eastern higher hierarchs, learned theologians and representatives of the clergy of the South-Western Russian Church. Apart from the ecclesiastics, the Councils were always attended by the czar and members of the Boyar Duma. Representatives of the secular authority, except for the czar, never expressed their views at the Councils, and none of them, not even the czar, signed the Council resolutions. To convene a church Councils, a charter was issued in the name of the czar, the patriarch and the Sanctified Council.[3] Some time in the middle of the 17th century, particularly in the inter-patriarchal period, the role of the czar in the Councils' activities and in the handling of all church matters began to grow. The higher clergy also took part in the work of the Councils of the Land convened several times in the first half of the century. Church Councils and Councils of the Land often worked at the same time.

There were 24 dioceses in Russia at the end of the

---

[1] Makariy. Op. cit., Vol. 12, p. 11.

[2] N. F. Kapterev. *Tsar i tserkovnye sobory XVI i XVII stoletiy,* (The Czar and the Church Councils of the 16th and 17th Centuries), Sergiyev Posad, 1906; P. Lapin, *Sobor kak vysshiy organ tserkovnoy vlasti: Istoriko-kanonicheskiy ocherk* (The Church Council as the Highest Organ of Church Authority: A Historico-Canonical Essay), Kazan, 1909, pp. 289-318.

[3] The Sanctified Council was an "incomplete" council consisting of bishops and archimandrites who came to the capital to attend to various church matters.

17th century (from 1700 records).¹ The largest of these was the patriarchate, followed by metropolitanates, archbishoprics and bishoprics. When new dioceses were formed, the bishops received from the government landed estates with serfs living on them. At different periods in the 17th century the number of monasteries varied. There were 494 independent monasteries and convents in European Russia in 1653, and in 1700, 426 independent monasteries and 174 monasteries attached to the former, all of which had estates.² The 17th century saw the emergence and development of patriarchal monasteries into major allodial landowners: the Novyi Ierusalim (New Jerusalem) Monastery near Moscow; the Lake Valdai Monastery of the Iverskaya Icon of the Mother of God; the Cross Monastery on Kiy Island in the district of Kargopol. Monasteries without landed estates also appeared—such as the Annunciation Monastery in Vyazniki of the district of Vladimir, the Zolotnikovskaya Wilderness in the district of Gorokhovets, and others. Schismatics' sketes cannot be counted for lack of any data on them. At the same time a number of monasteries became parish churches, since the 1681 Church Council forbade the building of new monasteries. Some were closed down, others attached to diocesan houses. In the last quarter of the 17th century, some 13,000 churches functioned in Russia; there were not more than 140,000 monks and nuns (or the black clergy) and churchmen with their families at that time.³

---

[1] Ya. Ye. Vodarsky. *Naseleniye Rossii v kontse XVII—nachale XVIII veka: Chislennost, soslovno-klassovyi sostav, razmeshcheniye* (Russia's Population in the late 17th-early 18th Centuries: The Size, Estates and Classes, Distribution), Moscow, 1977, pp. 82-83.

[2] For a map of Russia indicating the location of monasteries see: Ya. Ye. Vodarsky. "Tserkovnye organizatsii i ikh krepostnye krestyane vo vtoroy polovine XVII—nachale XVIII v.". In: *Istoricheskaya geografiya Rossii; XII—nachalo XX v. Sb. statey k 70-letiyu L. G. Beskrovnogo* (Church Organisations and Their Serfs in the Second Half of the 17th and Early 18th Centuries. In: A Historical Geography of Russia: 12th-Early 20th Centuries. A Collection of Articles on L. G. Beskrovny's 70th Anniversary), Moscow, 1975, pp. 70-96.

[3] Ya. Ye. Vodarsky. *Naseleniye Rossii v kontse XVII—nachale XVIII veka*, p. 87; only those churches were taken into account which paid taxes.

Just as in the 16th century, the Church remained the most powerful feudal economic organisation in the country. Patriarchs, bishops, monasteries and cathedral churches owned in the beginning of the 17th century about a third of all the feudal possessions,[1] which continued to grow during the whole of the century. Thus, the patriarchal possessions grew through acquisition of lands and the czar's grants under Filaret (the father of Czar Mikhail Fyodorovich, the actual ruler in the state), Iosif, and Patriarch Nikon. Under Ioakim and Adrian, several monasteries were attached to the Patriarchal house.[2]

Censuses of tax-liable homesteads on the lands owned by the clergy indicate a growth of church landownership. According to the census books of 1646 and the 1654-1666 receipt-books of the Monastery Department, there were 6,432 peasant homesteads in the patriarch's landed estates and 87,908 homesteads on the lands of the monasteries.[3] The number of peasant homesteads owned by the patriarch, the bishops and the monasteries grew considerably at the end of the century (compared to the 1650s). Relying on an analysis of a summary of the 1678 census, I. Bulygin established that the patriarch owned 9,084 peasant homesteads (6.1 per cent of all homesteads owned by the clergy), and 395 monasteries and convents owned 116,137 homesteads (77.9 per cent of the total number). In all, there were 148,997 peasant homesteads on church lands owned by the patriarch, the hierarchs, the cloisters and the churches.[4] By 1700, the possessions of the clergy, and especially of the patriarch, had grown again.

---

[1] A. G. Mankov. *Ulozheniye 1649 goda—kodeks feodalnogo prava Rossii* (The 1649 Code—a Code of Feudal Law in Russia), Leningrad, 1980, p. 195.

[2] M. I. Gorchakov. *O zemelnykh vladeniyakh vserossiyskikh mitropolitov, patriarkhov i sv. Sinoda (988-1738)* [On the Land Possessions of Metropolitan and Patriarchs of All Russia and the Holy Synod (988-1738)], St. Petersburg, 1871, p. 330.

[3] Ibid., p. 343. *Appendix*, pp. 88, 92-93.

[4] I. A. Bulygin. *Monastyrskiye krestyane Rossii v pervoy chetverti XVIII veka* (The Monastery Peasants of Russia in the First Quarter of the 18th Century), Moscow, 1977, pp. 41-45.

The Church's vast lands and finances enabled the higher hierarchs to retain their feudal privileges. Just as in the 16th century, the patriarch, the metropolitans and the bishops had the right to employ their own men. The patriarch's estates were controlled judicially, financially and administratively through the departments at the Patriarch's Court in the Kremlin, staffed with members of the gentry and boyars' children. Depending on their position in the official hierarchy, the patriarch's employees received a remuneration (in land and money) which varied in size, falling into several categories. In the middle of the century, there were five categories of remuneration. Towards the end of the century, the number of categories grew from five to ten.[1] Under Patriarch Ioakim, the number of employed rose to 209 (1690); under Patriarch Adrian that number again increased somewhat.[2] The Patriarch's court was the highest judicial instance in the whole state of Russia as far as crimes against religion and the Church were concerned. According to the 1649 Code (Statute), the highest court of appeal in relation to the patriarch's court was the Court of the czar and of the Boyar Duma.

The relations between the secular and ecclesiastical authorities in the 17th century were extremely complicated. On the one hand, the state endeavoured to weaken the Church's economic might, to subordinate it to the state system of administration, and to deprive the hierarchs of their feudal privileges; on the other hand, the state acted as a legal and punitive force guarding the Church. The contradictions of the government's policy were reflected in the new code of law. Church estates were a drain on the state's land resources, and that caused discontent among the gentry, who saw church lands as a real reserve that might be used by the government as a means of rewarding them for service by grants of land. That was why the secularisation of church possessions was such a burning issue at the 1648-1649 Council of the Land. In

---

[1] N. V. Ustyugov and N. S. Chayev. *Russkaya tserkov v 17 v.* (The Russian Church in the 17th Century), p. 301.

[2] M. I. Gorchakov. Op. cit., p. 403.

November 1648 "all the elected people of the whole Land" handed in a petition to the czar insisting that lands acquired since 1580 be taken away from the patriarch, the bishops and the monasteries. They proposed to distribute those lands "selectively among servicemen who had little or no land, or owned land without peasants, among the gentry and boyars' children".[1]

Under their pressure decrees were adopted which were aimed at limiting church possessions, effecting their partial secularisation, and depriving the hierarchs of their feudal privileges. An article was included in the Code which forbade Lords Spiritual and monasteries to buy and to accept as security or payment for prayers for the dead lands that were bought or received as emolument for service. Landowners taking monastic vows had to hand over their lands to kinsmen, who were obliged to pay for the former owner's upkeep.[2] An important legislative act was the confiscation of feudals' possessions in the cities (the so-called white boroughs). In 1649-1652, most of the hierarchs' and monasteries' holdings and city houses (more than 60 per cent of them) were confiscated and handed over to boroughs.[3] But the clergy continued, in circumvention of the law, to acquire houses in cities and commercial and industrial villages.

The 1648-1649 Council of the Land set up the Monastery Department whose jurisdiction covered civil (including criminal), fiscal (state duties and taxes) and estate cases involving the clergy and people dependent on the Church. The Code thus proclaimed for the first time equal cognizance in non-spiritual cases of the laity and all the churchmen, from the metropolitan to the monastery peasant. The Monastery Department was run by an *okolnichiy* (member of a social group with a

---

[1] L. V. Cherepnin. *Zemskiye sobory Russkogo gosudarstva v XVI-XVII vv.* (Councils of the Land of the Russian State in the 16th and 17th Centuries), Moscow, 1978, pp. 298-299.

[2] PRP, Moscow, 1957, Issue 6, Chapter XVII, pp. 256-258.

[3] P. P. Smirnov. *Posadskiye lyudi i ikh klassovaya borba do serediny XVII v.* (Townspeople and Their Class Struggle Until the Middle of the 17th Century), Moscow-Leningrad, 1948, Vol. 2, pp. 593-605; A. G. Mankov. Op. cit., p. 196.

status second to that of boyars.— *Tr*.) and his secretaries. The higher hierarchs were disgruntled at the establishment of the Monastery Department. At the greater Church Council of 1666-1667, which, in fulfillment of the czar's desire, condemned Nikon, the government made certain concessions to the Church, restoring the patriarch's jurisdiction over the clergy in civil matters. After the Council, the Monastery Department was abolished.

In the 17th century, church ideology continued to prevail, although new tendencies were becoming apparent almost in all the spheres of spiritual life, penetrating even into religious art (cf. some features of realism in cultic structures and icon painting). However, only at the end of the century did the government of Czar Peter I Alekseyevich embarked on the path of irreversible secularisation of culture and of its emancipation from the control of the Church. And yet, even in that difficult period when the Church tradition formed still "a great conservative force",[1] there was an apparent growth of rationalism and free-thinking, and a search for new religious forms of thinking; secular literature, art and education began to develop. In the absence of a system of ideological means and corresponding institutions for the substantiation and maintenance of its domination, the landowners' state needed not only the traditional ecclesiastical ideology but also the Church's ramified feudal organisation for implementing a serfdom-based domestic policy throughout that state.

Amidst aggravated class contradictions, and the people's growing anticlerical movement, the state took the Church, its entire organisation, hierarchy and dogmas, under the protection of the law. The 1649 Code was the first secular legislative document codifying the *corpus delicti* of the so-called "criminal acts" against the Church, putting them before all the other crimes. Before this Code, such "crimes" had been mostly considered in the nomocanon books—

---

[1] F. Engels. "Ludwig Feuerbach and the End of Classical German Philosophy", K. Marx and F. Engels, *Selected Works* in three volumes, Vol. 3, p. 374.

monuments of ecclesiastical law.¹ The first chapter of the Code is called "On Blasphemers and Church Rebels", while the chapter "On the Czar's Honour, and How the Czar's Health Is to Be Protected" comes second. "Blasphemy" was taken to mean any act directed against dogma, including disruption of church service. Blasphemy was punishable by death. We can judge of the pressure of real life on the legislators and of the most characteristic manifestations of church disobedience from the fact that the law protected the office of the service in the church and the clergy's honour.

The social conflicts within the clergy grew more pronounced; the gap between the upper echelons of the church hierarchy and the lower parish clergy increased. The position of the latter noticeably deteriorated; the red tape involved in ordination entailed bribe-taking on the part of hierarchs' clerks, and ordination duties grew. Hierarchs punished and jailed priests who fell in arrears with payments of duties. All this bred discontent with the hierarchs among the lower clergy closely linked with the townspeople and the peasant community. The people were indignant about the life of luxury which the princes of the Church led, and this indignation rose especially in Nikon's patriarchate. Anticlerical sentiments were reflected in the fall of the clergy's authority and the revival of pagan rituals and amusements.

It was the government's policy to support the Church's authority. This aim was pursued by a circle of "theophiles" consisting of laymen and ecclesiastics and functioning at the czar's Court in 1646-1653; it was formed after the accession to the throne of Czar Aleksey Mikhailovich (1645) and headed by Stefan Vnifantyev,² the czar's tutor and Archpriest of the Annunciation Cathedral in the Kremlin, distinguished for his erudi-

---

[1] Ya. N. Shchapov. *Vizantiyskoye i yuzhnoslavyanskoye pravovoye naslediye na Rusi v XI-XIII vv.* (Byzantine and Southern-Slavic Legal Heritage in Rus in the 11th-13th Centuries), Moscow, 1978.

[2] Stefan's surname is spelled Vonifatvev in the literature; we accept the more precise spelling found in his MSS and in the archive documents of the 17th century.

tion, broad political views and spiritual interests. Some of the men close to the czar and Vnifantyev were F. M. Rtishchev, *okolnichiy* since 1655, renowned for his contribution to the development of education; Simeon (in schema Spiridon) Potyomkin, a European-educated nobleman from Smolensk who often visited Moscow; and Prince A. M. Lvov, head of the Printing House. The all-powerful boyar B. I. Morozov patronised the circle. Connected with it were also the leading editors of the Printing House, icon-painters of the Armoury and court musicians (composers and choristers).[1]

This circle also included ecclesiastics: Nikon, the talented and vigorous archimandrite of the Monastery of Our Saviour (metropolitan of Novgorod since 1649 and patriarch since 1652), who enjoyed the good graces of the czar and his confessor, and Ivan Neronov, the popular dean of the Cathedral of the Kazan Icon of the Mother of God in Red Square, invited from Nizhniy Novgorod. Close to the "spiritual brotherhood of the capital" were Archpriests Daniil of Kostroma, Login of Murom, Avvakum of Yuryevets-Povolskiy, and Daniil of Temnikov. These members of the white clergy, closely linked with the commercial and industrial circles, spread the ideas of the Moscow circle in the provinces.

The "theophiles" were the exponents of the religious and enlightenment orientation of the government, part of the ruling class and of the privileged upper stratum of the townspeople at a time of aggravation of class contradictions and a fall in the authority of the higher clergy. Widely differing in their estate background, level of education, and socio-political views, the mem-

---

[1] A. I. Rogov. *Muzykalnaya estetika Rossii XI-XVIII vv.* (Musical Aesthetics in Russia in the 11th-18th Centuries), Moscow, 1973, pp. 16-17 (on the role of the court circle in the development of the singing and rhetorical liturgical art); Ye. S. Ovchinnikova, *Tserkov Troitsy v Nikitnikakh: Pamyatnik zhivopisi i zodchestva XVII v.* (The Trinity Church in Nikitniki: A Monument of 17th-Century Painting and Architecture), Moscow, 1970 (the views of the icon-painters who did the murals in the church were close to those of the "theophiles"); V. S. Rumyantseva. *Narodnoye antitserkovnoye dvizheniye v Rossii v XVII v.* (The Popular Anticlerical Movement in Russia in the 17th Century), Moscow, 1986, pp. 31-65.

bers of the circle were united for a while by the outstanding personality of Stefan Vnifantyev and his programme for a spiritual and moral revival of society.

The leaders of the governmental circle set themselves the aim of enhancing the authority of the official Church through promoting cultural and educational activities: establishment of schools of the European type for teaching young men foreign languages, the sciences and theology; the spreading of literacy and printed liturgical books as well as textbooks; and through regulation of church practices: replacement of the many-voiced singing in churches by one-voice singing and reading,[1] and introduction of sermons and exhortations in the churches. Rtishchev, Vnifantyev and Nikon maintained cultural contacts with South-Western scholars, the Kiev-Pechery Lavra, the Kiev (Educational) Monastery, and centres of fraternal movements in the Ukraine, Byelorussia and Lithuania. In their domestic churches and chapels, they began to introduce part-singing on the Ukrainian model. Books by Ukrainian, Byelorussian and Polish Orthodox polemicists were brought out at the Printing House. In 1649, the Smaller Catechism by Pyotr Mogila, Rector of the Kiev Academy, was published in Moscow. That was the first popular exposition of the foundations of Christian dogma in the form of questions and answers. The Moscow Printing House issued a great number of textbooks for traditional primary education, ABC books, Psalters and Books of Hours;[2] in 1648, a new textbook was published that was especially necessary for secondary and higher schools—a *Grammar* by the Byelorussian scholar Meletiy Smotritsky.

---

[1] To reduce the time of church service, the clergy of the 17th century accepted the many-voiced mode, the priest, the deacon and the choir all singing their parts simultaneously. The "theophiles" called this sort of divine service "heretical noise".

[2] A. S. Zernova. *Knigi kirillovskoy pechati, izdannye v Moskve v XVI-XVII vekakh: Svodnyi katalog* (Books in Cyrillic Alphabet Published in Moscow in the 16th and 17th Centuries: A Complete Catalogue), Moscow, 1958, pp. 65-76; I. V. Pozdeyeva. *Noviye materialy dlya opisaniya izdaniy moskovskogo Pechatnogo dvora: pervaya polovina XVII v.* (New Materials for Describing the Editions of Moscow's Printing House: Early Half of the 17th Century), Moscow, 1986, pp. 17-29.

After the death of the inactive Patriarch Iosif on June 25, 1652, the Church Council elevated, in compliance with the wishes of the czar, Metropolitan Nikon of Novgorod to their patriarchal throne. An active member of the Court circle, he became, through his exceptional intellect and other natural gifts (especially in architecture), one of the closest persons to Czar Aleksey Mikhailovich. Son of a Mordvinian peasant from Nizhniy Novgorod, he traversed the thorny path from rural priest to patriarch. As he ascended to the highest rung of the social and church hierarchy, he retained all his natural vigour and at the same time acquired some traits of an imperious feudal lord; numerous contemporaries' accounts speak of his arrogance, stern temper, and love for luxury and splendour.

Nikon's principal objectives became obvious in the very first days of his patriarchate: the strengthening of the patriarch's power; enhancing its authority not only in society's spiritual life but also in state affairs; and reforms in the Church. Domestic factors and goals of foreign policy prompted the concrete path of reorganising church (mostly liturgical) practices: the unification of rites, offices and liturgical books on the Greek model. The orientation towards the Greek liturgical practice of the 17th century and, accordingly, the South-Russian book learning became clear already under the "theophiles", who ran the affairs of the Church under Patriarch Iosif. However, they could not control the anticlerical ferment in the country; the divine service, long as it was, became even longer with the introduction of the one-voiced mode and of sermons, which caused an almost universal discontent. The leading editors of the Printing House, connected with the "theophiles" and aware of the need for revising the books, were not trained well enough to unify the liturgical books on the printed Greek model with due consideration for the grammatical and stylistic requirements of the times.

Nikon realised the importance of the printed word better than any of his predecessors on the patriarchal throne. As aptly noted by I. D. Mansvetov, in the second half of the 17th century, the patriarchs began to exercise a tighter control of the work of the Printing

House and the editors. In his view, no one else but Patriarch Nikon was the initiator of censorship in the modern times.[1] It was no accident that Nikon paid great attention to the Printing House already in his office of the metropolitan of Novgorod. Thus he pulled strings to have Archimandrite Silvestr of the St. Andronik's Monastery of Our Saviour appointed editor instead of Mikhail Rogov condemned for *Cyril's Book*. Early in 1652, he recommended senior chorister Evfimiy of the Chudov Monastery, pupil of Yepifaniy Slavinetskiy, for the post vacated by the death of editor Shestak Martemyanov. In November 1652, the editors *starets* Iosif (Ivan Nasedka in the world) and *starets* Savvatiy were dismissed and sent into exile. The youngest editor, layman Sila Grigoryev, was discharged, and Matvey, a chorister of the Monastery of Our Saviour, was appointed in his place.

The Printing House, previously controlled by the Grand Palace Department, was handed over to Nikon by the czar late in 1653. Nikon entrusted supervision of its work to above-mentioned Silvestr, promoted to Metropolitan of Krutitsy. In January 1654, Ivan Ozerov, graduate of the Kiev Academy who began his education at Vnifantyev's Graeco-Latin school, was included among the editors. *Starets* Arseniy the Greek, who knew many languages, was recalled by Nikon from the Solovki Monastery. In March 1654, Arseniy became first editor.[2] Yepifaniy Slavinetsky, a close associate of the patriarch, exerted a considerable influence on the

---

[1] I. D. Mansvetov. "Kak u nas pravilis tserkovnye knigi: Materialy dlya istorii knizhnoy spravy v XVII stoletii po bumagam arkhiva Tipografskoy biblioteki v Moskve". In: *Tvoreniya svyatykh otsov v russkom perevode, izdavayemye pri Moskovskoy dukhovnoy akademii* (How Church Books Were Edited in Russia: Materials for the History of Book Publishing in the 17th Century from the Papers of the Archives of the Printer's Library in Moscow. In: Works of the Holy Fathers in Russian Translation Published by the Moscow Theological Academy), Moscow, 1883, Book 4, pp. 543 ff.

[2] A. Golubtsov. *Preniya o vere, vyzvannye delom korolevicha Valdemara i tsarevny Iriny Mikhailovny* (Debate on Faith Caused by the Case of Prince Waldemar and Czarevna Irina Mikhailovna), Moscow, 1891, pp. 125 ff.; P. F. Nikolayevsky. "Moskovskiy pechatnyi dvor pri patriarkhe Nikone" (The Moscow Printing House under Patriarch Nikon). In: *Khristianskoye chteniye*, 1891, No. 7/12.

work of the Printing House as philologist, translator and author of prefaces to printed books. In Nikolayevsky's view, Nikon endeavoured to make the Printing House the "principal instrument" of his activity. N. M. Nikolsky writes that Nikon undertook the solution of the problem of a church reform that was long overdure only "in connection with the triumph of technology in book printing".[1]

The reforms were also made necessary by certain factors of foreign policy. They were implemented at a time when the prestige of the Russian state on the international scene increased, and when the Ukraine and Byelorussia were reunited with Russia, bound as they were by the ties of a common historical fate. Greek, Ukrainian and Byelorussian scholars were invited to participate in the work of identifying church rites, offices and books in order to attract to Moscow's side the higher clergy of Little Russia connected with the patriarch of Constantinople (in the 1650s-1680s, the dioceses of Smolensk, Polotsk, Pereyaslavl, and Chernigov, and the metropolitanate of Kiev were reunited with the Moscow Patriarchate).[2] Besides, the political allies of the Russian state among the Greek and South-Russian clergy were inclined to the idea of Russia as the centre of the Orthodox East.

The Psalter published on February 11, 1653, contains an article on bows, the three-finger sign of the cross, and the reduction of bows to the ground during prayer.

In February and March of the same year, a *Memorandum* was sent to the churches of Moscow by patriarchal decree; its content was described in Archpriest Avvakum's autobiographical *Life:* "According to the traditions of Holy Apostles and Holy Fathers, it is not seemly to throw yourselves on your knees in

---

[1] *Khristianskoye chteniye*, 1891, No. 7/12, p. 186; N. M. Nikolsky. *Istoriya russkoy tserkvi* (A History of the Russian Church), Moscow, 1983, 3rd ed., p. 130.

[2] I. M. Pokrovsky. *Russkiye yeparkhii v XVI-XIX vv.: Ikh otkrytiye, sostav i predely. Opyt tserkovno-istoricheskogo, statisticheskogo i geograficheskogo issledovaniya* (Russian Dioceses in the 16th-19th Centuries: Their Establishment, Structure and Boundaries. An Essay in Ecclesiastical-Historical, Statistical and Geographical Investigation), Kazan, 1897, Vol. I, pp. 464-487.

church, but you should bow from the waist, and you should also make the sign of the cross with three fingers."[1] According to canonical rules, the clergy were obliged to obey their "supreme pastor". The alarmed brotherhood now gravitated towards Ivan Neronov as their head, and Nikon not only ceased to consult them but would not even let his former friends into the Cross Chamber (the patriarch's official reception room). The latter saw the *Memorandum* as the beginning of disfavour. In 1653 and 1654, almost all "theophiles" were sent into exile or thrown into monastery dungeons, although the reforms were not yet in full swing, and neither did they have the sanction of the Church Council. Leaving the basis of the Orthodox dogma intact, Nikon's reforms made the divine service conform to certain rationalist requirements. As a result of the changes, the liturgy was shortened (so that the issue of one-voiced singing and reading no longer arose), as were the offices of baptism, penance, matins, anointing, and the texts of prayers; genuflection ("throwing oneself to the knees") was abolished, and so on.[2]

One of the aspects of the axiological consciousness of that epoch was a religious or practical-spiritual attitude to the world and society. In the Middle Ages, each individual lived his life not only in the system of production relations, expressed through property, commerce and politics, but also in ritual forms established by the Church as obligatory and strictly observed: baptism, wedding ceremony, confession, communion, liturgy, funeral rites according to the Orthodox mode, remembering the dead.

One of the reforms affecting the entire society was the replacement of the two-fingered sign of the cross by the three-fingered one, and of the "three-part" or eight-point cross depicting the crucifiction by the "two-part" or four-point one; the change over from following the sun to heading against the sun during processions at baptism, wedding, and other ceremonies;

---

[1] "Pamyatniki istorii staroobryadchestva XVII v." Monuments of the History of Old Belief in the 17th Century), In: RIB, Leningrad, 1927, Vol. 39, column 15.

[2] *Materialy,* Moscow, 1881, Vol. 6, pp. 21-45.

the reduction of the number of prosphoras from seven to five for proskomedia (at the beginning of the liturgy). Book corrections included a change in the spelling of the Russian word for Jesus (*Iisus* instead of the widespread *Isus*); and replacement of certain texts in *The Creed*, of which each member was regarded as inviolable: "life-giving God" for "true and life-giving God", and "his kingdom will be unending" for "his kingdom is unending". At the end of a psalm, the word "hallelujah" was to be repeated three times, not twice as before, etc. The stylistic editing of liturgical books followed the system of the three styles of literary speech.[1]

In the spring of 1654, Nikon convened a Church Council. Under pressure from the czar, the Council approved of the new rites and the changes in liturgical texts. Bishop Pavel of Kolomna, who protested against the reforms at the Council, was banned by Nikon from performing his ecclesiastical duties and banished to the district of Novgorod, where he soon tragically died.[2] The patriarch was authorised to continue implementing reforms. The wording of the Council decision was, however, fairly careful: only those rites and offices were to be revised which did not conform to the ancient Russian and Greek ones. At the same Council Nikon made a speech in which he declared that the books printed in Moscow deviated from the Greek and Old Slavonic ones, and that contemporary Russian rites were "new inventions".[3] In actual fact, Russian rites were no different from the ancient ones or the rites of Greek antiquity; studies by Golubinsky and Kapterev have shown that there were differences in the rites during the Middle Ages both in the Greek and in the Russian Churches; thus both the two-fingered and

---

[1] Makariy. *Istoriya russkogo raskola, izvestnogo pod imenem staroobryadstva* (The History of the Russian Schism Known as Old Belief), St. Petersburg, 1889, pp. 108 ff.; V. P. Vompersky, *Stilisticheskoye ucheniye M. V. Lomonosova i teoriya tryokh stiley* (M. V. Lomonosov's Stylistic Doctrine and the Theory of Three Styles), Moscow 1970, pp. 21-24.

[2] RIB, Vol. 39, column 15.

[3] N. I. Subbotin. *Deyaniya moskovskogo tserkovnogo sobora, byvshego v tsarskikh palatakh* (The Acts of the Moscow Church Council in the Czar's Chambers), Moscow, 1873, p. 17.

three-fingered signs of the cross were used. However, to achieve uniformity in the rites of the Russian church practice and that of the Eastern Slavic peoples it was necessary to introduce certain changes in the Russian rites and ceremonies following the Greek mode used in all the Orthodox countries.

Replacement of old rites and ceremonies by Greek ones destroyed in some cases long-established traditions and customs in the Russian liturgical practice. It was precisely against this sort of unnecessary break from the tradition, and especially against implementing it by drastic measures, that Patriarch Paisius of Constantinople warned Nikon, believing that certain differences in the rites of the Orthodox Churches were canonically justified, provided there was unity in the cult and the dogmas. In his patriarchal epistle brought to Moscow in May 1655, Paisius begged Nikon not to allow debate within the Church over rites and order of ceremonies.[1] Ultimately Nikon recognised the correctness of both old and new rites.[2] As investigation of documents shows, the government of Czar Aleksey Mikhailovich persecuted schismatics for refusal to obey the Church rather than for their adherence to the old rites.

Friendship with Czar Aleksey Mikhailovich gave Nikon access to state affairs. He took part in diplomatic negotiations, and during the czar's military campaigns became an autocratic ruler in the capital. Nikon's political line is usually described in the literature (prerevolutionary and foreign[3]) as historically doomed opposition to the government's policy of subordinating the Church to the state, a policy which gathered momentum after the 1649 Code (incidentally, it was N. F. Kapterev who started this particular ball rolling). The view expressed by Nikon after 1658, that "priest-

---

[1] N. F. Kapterev. *Patriarkh Nikon i tsar Aleksei Mikhailovich* (Patriarch Nikon and Czar Aleksey Mikhailovich). Sergiyev Posad. 1909, Vol. I, p. 260.

[2] Ivan (in schema Grigoriy) Neronov, who refused to accept the Church reform, was allowed by Nikon to conduct services according to the old rites and books (*Materialy*, Vol. I, p. 11).

[3] A. V. Kartashev. *Ocherki po istorii russkoy tserkvi* (Essays in the History of the Russian Church), Paris, 1959, Vol. 2, pp. 194-200.

hood is greater than czardom"[1] is interpreted one-sidedly: being a patriarch, he endeavoured to place church authority in the sate higher than the authority of the czar. This problem still awaits an investigation; we shall merely present here certain observations made in the perusal of the sources, which permit a different opinion of the patriarch's ideological position and of the nature of his views.

One of the leaders of the court circle of "theophiles"-enlighteners and a close associate of the czar's tutor Stefan Vnifantyev, Nikon began, on accession to the patriarchal throne, to criticise the 1649 Code sharply and openly.[2] This placed him in direct opposition to the ruling boyar group headed by Prince N. I. Odoyevsky. His denunciatory sallies against the *Statutory Book,* whose content remains unknown, were widespread not only at court and throughout the capital but also throughout the land (it may well be that Nikon's critique of the Code became known to the Don Cossacks),[3] causing the boyars' hatred and anger. In the final analysis, it was Nikon's opposition to the boyars, who were in control of the state, that became the cause of the coolness shown him later by the czar and the Court, and of his condemnation by the Church Council.

At the time of the impending rupture with the czar, who ceased to attend patriarchal services in the cathedral church and forbade Nikon to be called "Great Lord", the proud and touchy Nikon, after a liturgy at the Dormition Cathedral on July 10, 1658,

---

[1] *Zapiski Otdeleniya russkoy i slavyanskoy arkheologii* (Papers of the Department of Russian and Slavic Archaeology), St. Petersburg, 1861, Vol. 2, p. 436.

[2] "Rospis spornykh rechey protopopa Ivana Neronova s patriarkhom Nikonom" (Records of the Controversy Between Archpriest Ivan Neronov and Patriarch Nikon). In: *Materialy,* Vol. I, p. 48 (dated November 1653).

[3] This can be assumed on the basis of reports of the Archimandrite of the St. Ferapont Monastery where Nikon was held during his exile. In 1668 the informer wrote to the czar that Nikon had told him, personally: "Don Cossacks came to me in the Resurrection Monastery [The Novyi Ierusalim Monastery.—*Author*], saying, 'If you wish, we shall put you back on the patriarchal throne, we shall gather free men, the boyars' people'" (S. M. Solovyov. Op. cit., Moscow, 1961, Book 6, Vol. XI, p. 274).

took off his precious patriarchal vestments, put on a poor monk's attire and left his patriarchal seat for his house monastery at Novyi Ierusalim. We shall not assert, following Kapterev and others, that that was merely a demonstration, and that Nikon hoped to return to the patriarchal throne.[1] In any case, Nikon rejected the czar's request not to abandon the patriarchate conveyed through a boyar in attendance, Prince A. N. Trubetskoy; his reply to the czar said: "I will not go back on my word; and then I promised a long time ago that I would not be a patriarch."[2] Later the patriarch, abandoned by everyone, changed his mind.

According to canonical rules, a patriarch who did not divert himself of the office could only be replaced by a Church Council of local bishops, attended by the higher Eastern hierarchs. The arrival of Greek ecclesiastics in Moscow was delayed for quite a long time. In the inter-patriarchal period (1658-1666) Nikon lived at the Novyi Ierusalim Monastery near Moscow, seeking a reconciliation with the czar. The Church Council of 1666-1667, attended by Patriarch Paisius of Alexandria, Patriarch Macarius of Antioch and several Greek hierarchs, condemned Nikon, deposed him and sent him as an ordinary monk into exile to the St. Ferapont Monastery. His reforms were canonically confirmed by the Church Council. The schismatics were excommunicated, anathematised and outlawed in terms of secular laws.[3] Orthodox Ukrainians, Byelorussians and Poles, who did not accept the reforms, called this Council of

---

[1] N. F. Kapterev. Op. cit., pp. 163 ff.; N. Korenevsky. *Tserkovnye voprosy v Moskovskom gosudarstve v polovine XVII veka: Deyatelnost patriarkha Nikona* (Church Issues in the State of Muscovy in the Middle of the 17th Century: The Activities of Patriarch Nikon), Kiev, 1912.

[2] *Delo o patriarkhe Nikone: Izdaniye Arkheograficheskoy komissii po dokumentam Moskovskoy Sinodalnoy (byvshey Patriarshey) biblioteki* [The Case of Patriarch Nikon: Published by the Archaeographic Commission from the Documents of the Moscow Synodal (formerly Patriarchal) Library], St. Petersburg, 1897, p. 15; N. Gibbenet. *Istoricheskoye issledovaniye dela patriarkha Nikona* (A Historical Study of Patriarch Nikon's Case), St. Petersburg, 1882-1884, Parts 1-2.

[3] The 1971 Local Council of the Russian Church cancelled the decision of the 1666-1667 Council concerning the anathematising of the schematics.

Moscow, just as the Council of Ferrara and Florence of 1438-1439, the "eighth" council, counterposing it to the seven Ecumenical Councils.[1]

The Church Council charged Nikon with a crime against the state (the gravest of all his transgressions)— the fact that he dared to criticise the Code while holding the office of patriarch. In his "Reply" to Boyar Streshnev's questions Nikon touched but slightly on the activities of the "statutory" Council involving civil matters (which was understandable, Nikon being a patriarch in disgrace). His indignation at and dislike for the Monastery Department, which intruded into church-allodial matters, are those of a typical feudal hierarch. But the principal content of the "Reply", in our view, has to do with the problem of relationship between the authority of the Church and the czar—a vital issue of that epoch. Here Nikon appears in quite a different light—as a convinced opponent of the autocratic (tyrannical) ideology with well-developed absolutist tendencies, which equated the czar, a mere man, with God, and usurped the power of the highest spiritual authority in society.[2]

That Nikon's complex case has not been adequately studied is clear from the fact that his views as a statesman of his epoch are not taken into account, and that his close ideological contacts with the Court circle of enlighteners are ignored. His testimony at the Church Council confirms that his opposition was not limited to church issues only (as believed by most authors). The disgraced Nikon called the Council of the Land of 1648-1649, which sanctioned the serf-owners' Code, canonically and juridically illegal act of a small group of boyars: "That statutory lawless book is merely evidence of their [the boyars'.— *Author*] lawlessness." Nikon called Prince Odoyevsky, head of the Statutory Commission and of the ruling boyar clique, an "enemy of God and of all truth", and an "blasphemer".[3] Just as Archpriest Avvakum, condemned

---

[1] V. S. Rumyantseva. Op. cit., pp. 123 ff.

[2] *Zapiski Otdeleniya russkoy i slavyanskoy arkheologii* (Papers of the Department of Russian and Slavic Archaeology), Vol. 2, pp. 423-431.

[3] *Zapiski Otdeleniya russkoy i slavyanskoy arkheologii*. Vol. 2, p. 427.

by the same Church Council, Nikon appealed to the czar, reminding him of the times when young Aleksey Mikhailovich shared the views of the "theophiles".[1]

In a state based on feudal ownership, Nikon could not conceive of the role of the Church without landownership, without privileges, without a hierarchical system and a strong, centralised authority of the patriarch. At the same time he saw the Church as a social institution called upon to oppose the unlimited power of the boyars hating the people.

Nikon's ideological opponents among the "theophiles", including Ivan (Grigoriy) Neronov, Avvakum, Deacon Fyodor and others, championed the development of *sobornost* (from the Russian *sobor*, which means "assembly", "synod".— *Tr.*) in church administration; they sharply criticised Nikon's Councils, which did not express the interests of all the clergy and laity; and they saw the actions of the patriarch, who tolerated no objections to his initiatives, as a deviation from canonical rules. Besides, it can be assumed from their critique of church authorities that the "theophiles" also protested against the hierarchical structure of the Church organised, just as the ruling class, on a feudal basis.[2] Thus Neronov drew the attention of Czar Aleksey Mikhailovich to the gap between the hierarchs and the lower echelons of the ecclesiastics.[3]

Churchmen from south-western Russia and from Poland also took part in the struggle over the church reform within the Court, among the clergy of the capital and among the common townspeople. In the context of close contacts between the peoples of Eastern and Western Europe they opposed the supremacy of the Roman Pope, and pointed to the contrast between the ecclesiastical practices in Europe at the end

---

[1] See V. S. Rumyantseva. "Kruzhok Stefana Vnifantyeva". In: *Obshchestvo i gosudarstvo feodalnoy Rossii. Sb. statey, posvyashchonnyi 70-letiyu akademika L. V. Cherepnina* (Stefan Vnifantyev's Circle. In: Society and the State in Feudal Russia. A Collection of Articles on the Occasion of Academician L. V. Cherepnin's 70th Anniversary), Moscow, 1975, pp. 178-188. The whole question needs further study.

[2] See F. Engels, "Socialism: Utopian and Scientific", K. Marx and F. Engels, *Selected Works* in three volumes, Vol. Three, pp. 103-104.

[3] *Materialy*, Vol. 1, pp. 174-176.

of the 16th and in the first half of the 17th century, and the epoch of the seven Ecumenical Councils (before the division of the Christian Churches into Eastern and Western) and the late classical (Apostolic) times.[1] The views of the Ukrainian, Byelorussian, and Polish Orthodox polemicists, just as those of Patriarch Nikon, as regards the ecumenical Church, rested on an essentially identical ideological basis.[2]

The struggle against church reforms merged with a popular movement known since the end of the 1650s as the Schism.[3] Two trends were distinguishable in it. One of these was the *staroobryadchestvo* or Old Ritualists[4] movement, mostly represented by common townspeople, the commercial-industrial upper stratum, the white clergy, and departmental clerks. The ideologues of the Old Believers, Archpriest Avvakum, Deacon Fyodor, Dosifey, Ivan Dementyev and many others, sharply denounced the higher clergy and secular powers, even including the czar, but they never opposed the foundations of Christian dogma. Among the peasants and plebeians, the Old Belief was combined with Kapiton's faith[5]—the most radical trend in

---

[1] See the works of Spiridon Potyomkin: RO GBL, reg. 292 (The S. P. Stroyev collection), No. 47; V. S. Rumyantseva. Op. cit., pp. 119-126.

[2] In the heat of the debate, the polemicists who opposed Nikon's reforms attributed them to the "Latin" influence. 19th-century authors persistently ascribed to Nikon certain Papist tendencies (the placing of church authority above the czar's) uncharacteristic of the Orthodox tradition. See: *Kniga o vere* (The Book of Faith), Moscow, 1648; N. F. Kapterev. *Patriarch Nikon and Czar Aleksey Mikhailovich*, Vol. I.

[3] The name was given to the movement by the ecclesiastics. The term *raskol* ("schism", "dissent") was first used in 1652 (i.e., before Nikon's reforms) by Metropolitan Iona of Rostov to refer to the common people who rejected the authority of the spiritual fathers (AI, St. Petersburg, 1842, Vol. 4, No. 62, pp. 174-175).

[4] The term *staroobryadchestvo* ("old ritualism") does not occur in 17th-century sources. Its origin dates from the 18th century. The ideologues of the early "old ritualism" called themselves "the faithful", "true believers", and "lovers of old times"; at the end of the century they came to be called Old Believers (PDP, St. Petersburg, 1895, Vol. 108, p. 10).

[5] After the name of the peasant preacher *starets* Kapiton, who began an anti-church campaign long before Patriarch Nikon's reforms.

the popular movement spreadheaded against the social foundations of feudal society. Its adherents rejected the institution of priesthood, church sacraments, and many rites. Some of the schismatics of the Kapiton variety criticised the dogma of the Triune God. The early Schism (the 1640s-1680s) expressed, in religious form, a critique of the earthly affairs, and in the first place a protest against serfdom, as well as the people's Utopian hopes for a social transformation of society.

After Nikon's departure from the patriarchal throne and the Church Council of 1666-1667, which condemned the "theophiles", who were arguing with one another, the Church and the state began a fierce persecution of the Schism, relying on the *streltsy* corps as a military force (incidentally, there had been no mass persecutions of the Schism under Nikon). Investigations of the schismatics' cases were run by the most important central establishments: the Ambassadorial, Secret, Rating and Novgorod Departments. *Streltsy* detachments burnt down the schismatics' *sketes* "wildernesses" and monastic cells in the forests. Adherents of the Old and Kapiton's Belief were tortured, burnt at the stake or thrown into gloomy monastery dungeons. The stamping out of the popular movement "by fire and sword" caused a wave of self-immolations. Documents show that the peasants chose self-immolation when their cottages were surrounded by the *streltsy*, forcing them to obey the authorities and to attend the church. Women also took an active part in the movement.

Churchmen were intolerant of other confessions and of religious free-thinking. Throughout the history of the Schism, just as of all the other popular movements of the 17th century (peasant and townspeople's uprisings), the Church was the ideological headquarters of the czar's government and of the feudal class. True, this did not rule out isolated instances of participation of the lower- and middle-ranking clergy in the rebellions or of their running away to dissidents' *sketes.*

Spiritual culture controlled by the Church did not yet lose its positive potential in the 17th century. "Masters of literacy" mostly came from the lower clergy. It was through their enlightenment activities that the network of elementary schools to teach reading and writing in Old Church Slavonic and Russian was expanded. In the major cities, churches and cathedrals founded free schools for the children of poor townspeople and suburban peasants.

Scholars who worked on progressive ideas and new, secular forms of culture and education lived at monasteries. In the 1650s, learned Byelorussians and Ukrainians settled at the St. Andrew Educational Monastery founded by the *okolnichiy* F. M. Rtishchev; here they translated books and taught children and adolescents Polish, Greek and Latin, as well as the secular sciences. The Chudov Monastery in the Kremlin had a school named after Metropolitan Aleksey, run by Yepifaniy Slavinetsky, a learned philologist. On settling upon his arrival in Moscow at the Zaikonospasskiy Monastery, Simeon Polotsky opened a Latin school for the young clerks of the Secret Department. His disciple Silvestr Medvedev, who took the monastic vows in order to be able to study science, continued his teacher's cause. A European-type school functioned at the Epiphany Monastery in Kitay-gorod. In October 1687, the first higher educational establishment of Russia, the Slavonic-Greek-Latin Academy, was opened at the Zaikonospasskiy Monastery. Its first rectors were the Greek brothers Sophronius and Ioannikius Likhuds, graduates of Padua University in Italy.[1] Later, Peter I's cultural and educational reforms ousted the ecclesiastics out of their most important spheres.

---

[1] A. A. Prozorovsky. *Silvestr Medvedev: (Yego zhizn i deyatelnost): Opyt tserkovno-istoricheskogo issledovaniya* [Silvestr Medvedev: (His Life and Activities): An Essay in Research in the History of the Church], ChOIDR, 1896, Book 2. See part. IV; DRV, Moscow, 1791, Vol. 16, p. 208; M. Smentsovsky. *Bratya Likhudy* (The Likhud Brothers). St. Petersburg, 1899; A. I. Rogov. "Shkola i prosveshcheniye", *Ocherki russkoy kultury XVII veka* (Schools and Education. In: Essays in Russian Culture of the 17th Century), Moscow, 1979. Part 2, pp. 276-287; V. S. Rumyantseva, "Shkolnoye obrazovaniye na Rusi v XVI-XVII vv." (School Education in Russia in the 16th and 17th Centuries). In: *Sovetskaya pedagogika* (Soviet Pedagogics), Moscow, 1983, No. 1, pp. 105-113; A. P. Bogdanov. "Silvestr Medvedev". In: *Voprosy istorii,* Moscow, 1988, No. 2, pp. 84-98.

*Chapter V*

# THE RUSSIAN CHURCH IN THE 18TH CENTURY

The 18th century occupies a special place in the history of the Russian Church. Probably no other period brought as many changes in the Church as that age. These changes radically altered the position of the Church and determined its future development.

Relations of feudal serfdom continued to disintegrate in that century, and new, bourgeois, relations continued to develop. Important changes occurred in the political system: a monarchy based on representation of the estates was replaced by absolutism. Class struggle grew more and more acute, reaching its climax in the peasant war led by Yemelyan Pugachov. Significant developments took place in science, social thought and culture. Providentialism, a religious world outlook, gave way to rationalism which explained all phenomena in Nature and society from the positions of reason. The ideology of enlightenment came into being and began to develop further, and at the end of the century revolutionary-democratic thought began to evolve. New tendencies asserted themselves in literature and art. All this naturally made an impact on the Church and affected its position.

## Church and State

In the period under consideration, relations between Church and state fall into three basic periods: the first quarter, the mid-1720s through the 1750s, and the 1760s through the 1790s. Each of these stages was highly important, each had specific features of its own and needs special consideration.

At the end of the 17th century, when Peter I ascended to the throne, no particular changes occurred in the position of the Church. The government continued essentially the same policy in relation to the Church as before, endeavouring to curb the growth of its estates, depriving it of some fiscal immunities, and extensively drawing on its financial wealth through non-repayable loans and grants.

The only new elements in Peter's policy of those times were the government's attempts to establish control over the incomes and expenditures of the monasteries and hierarchs' houses, by restricting, in particular, the building of new churches, etc. At the same time a lively discussion of church matters went on in the highest governmental circles, and plans were evolved for more drastic measures in regard to the Church. One of the signs of these changes was the appointment, after Patriarch Adrian's death, of Metropolitan Stefan Yavorsky of Ryazan Patriarchal Locum Tenens in December 1700. In contravention of the well-established tradition prescribing the appointment of the authoritative metropolitan of Krutitsy to that position, this time a person little known among the higher clergy was given that office. The latter circumstance seemed to be the decisive factor in Yavorsky's appointment. Such a person could become an obedient instrument in the implementation of the serious reforms in the church sphere. Even more important was the fact that Stefan Yavorsky was entrusted with ecclesiastical administration only, while the economic and some judicial affairs, also in contravention of the tradition, were withdrawn from his jurisdiction. Soon, even more significant events were to follow.

An edict signed by Peter I on January 24, 1701, instituted the Monastery Department headed by Boyar Ivan Musin-Pushkin who was entrusted with the administration of the house of His Holiness the Patriarch, the houses of the hierarchs and monasteries and convents.[1] Thus a purely secular institution headed

---

[1] PSZ-I, Vol. 4, No. 1829, p. 133.

by a boyar was set up to govern the clergy. In the same year, several more edicts were promulgated, clearly defining the functions and prerogatives of the Monastery Department.[1] That was the beginning of Peter I's famous church reform, whose first stage lasted until c. 1705.

At this stage, the entire administration of the estates of the patriarch, the hierarchs and the monasteries with their population passed into the hands of the Monastery Department and its local representatives. Besides, the Monastery Department was given the right of collecting all revenues from church estates and disposal of them. Part of these revenues was spent on maintaining the clergy, while another part went to the exchequer. To all intents and purposes the Church thus lost its landed estates, and they passed into the hands of the state. In other words, church estates were thus factually secularised. Let us emphasise the word *factually*, since legally the estates still belonged to the clergy: there was no law yet abolishing the clergy's right to possess lands and peasants, while in actual fact the lands were already controlled by the state.

Stefan Yavorsky, Patriarchal Locum Tenens was entirely barred from the control of the patriarchal estates; he even had to ask the czar's special permission to enter them. He could not dispose of patriarchal property, and could only receive anything from the patriarchal treasury or the stores by permission of the Monastery Department. This shows that all the Church's income from its estates went into the hands of the Monastery Department. The clergy could not spend even small sums without the permission of the czar and the Department.

The fact that the government freely disposed of the former church estates was an important indication that they were factually secularised at the first stage of the church reform. In 1702-1704, some 1800 peasant homesteads formerly in the possession of the clergy and vast tracts of unpopulated land were granted, by the czar's edicts, to various persons in their "eternal possession", sold, distributed for quit-rent farming, and

---

[1] Ibid., No. 1834, pp. 134-140; No. 1886, pp. 181-182 ff.

attached to various departments.¹ Another indication was the fact that all quit-rent possessions of the clergy, such as fisheries, mills, bridges, ferries, etc. were simply confiscated in 1704, which brought the state some 54,000 roubles per annum in revenue.²

The reforms also affected the everyday life of the clergy and especially of the black clergy or the monastics. Monks were forbidden to move from one monastery to another. Such transfers were only permitted in exceptional cases, where the reason was pressing, with the monk having to have a written authorisation to leave from his former father superior. That measure was aimed against monks' vagrancy, widespread in those times; it was intended to make the number of monastics in the cloisters more stable, which would facilitate their management. It was ordered to remove from the monasteries all laymen living in them: sextons, readers, choristers, scribes, and so on. Their duties were to be performed by the monks themselves, in order to save the monasteries' money. Monks were forbidden to write in their cells or to keep paper and ink there; they could only write in special corner of the refectory, only in cases of absolute necessity, and only by permission of their superiors—"openly, not secretely".³ These orders were prompted by the suspicion that monks wrote and circulated all sorts of seditious letters against the government and against Peter, and the new measures were intended to put an end to these activities. A new feature of the life of the white clergy was the duty, imposed by the April 14, 1702, edict on parish priests, to hand in every week a list of all newborn babies and deceased to the Patriarchal Spiritual Department; from the latter, a summary of these data were passed on to the Monastery Department.⁴

Such was the first stage of Peter I's church reform. Explaining the causes for and the necessity of the reform, the government wrote in one of the edicts of

---

¹ I. A. Bulygin. *Monastyrskiye krestyane Rossii v pervoy chetverty XVIII veka* (Monastery Peasants of Russia in the First Quarter of the 18th Century), Moscow, 1977, pp. 92-95.
² Ibid., pp. 95-99.
³ PSZ-I, Vol. 4, No. 1834, pp. 139-140.
⁴ PSZ-I, Vol. 4, No. 1908, p. 192.

1701 that the purpose of the reform was not "the ruin of the monasteries" but a "better fulfilment of monastic vows". In antiquity, said the document, monks "living in communities industriously worked to earn their living and fed many destitute people with the labour of their hands, while the monks of today not only failed to feed destitute people with their labour but themselves fed on other people's labour". Besides, church estates were the cause of "strife and murder, and numerous wrongs and hurts".[1] But the causes of the reform listed here cannot be regarded as entirely true to fact.

Of course, the government endeavoured to regulate the internal life of the clergy, and especially of the monastics, in order to make their ideological influence on the masses more effective. But the factual data on the implementation of the reform show that its real purpose was quite different; that purpose was the use of the Church's wealth for the state's needs. That issue arose already at the end of the 17th century, but now, in view of the beginning of the Northern War, which required vast sums of money, it became especially vital, and was solved practically. It was with this objective in view that the factual secularisation of all the clergy's estates and revenues was implemented. After an allowance was handed out to the monasteries and hierarchs' houses, a sum of about 50,000 roubles remained which was appropriated by the exchequer. Besides, the government, as has been pointed out above, received some 54,000 roubles in revenue from the secularised quit-rent possessions of the Church. Therefore already in the first years after the reform the state began to receive some 100,000 roubles a year in revenue from the church possessions. Actually, the state's income in those years was even higher, for the exchequer also received certain sums from the sale and quit-rent of church lands, and also from various extraordinary confiscations of the funds and treasures of monasteries and hierarchs' houses.

There are therefore no grounds for the view, held by some scholars, that the primary objective of the church

---

[1] PSZ-I, Vol. 4, No. 1886, pp. 181-182.

reforms was the creation of economic premises for the abolition of the patriarchate.[1] Materials from 1701-1705 provide no data, not even indirect ones, on the government's intentions at the time to abolish the patriarchate or in general to reform the higher church administration in any way. The views of some other historians on this score are also not without interest. "We do not feel entitled to think," wrote Sergei Solovyov, "that the idea of complete abolition of the patriarchate had already grown ripe in Peter's mind by the year 1700; it is more probable that that idea grew ripe in the course of time, when the patriarch's absence caused no inconvenience, when the corporate form was recognised as the best form in all aspects of administration, when, finally, the case of Czarevich Aleksey aroused strong doubts in Peter's soul as to the sympathetic attitude of the majority of the higher clergy towards the new order."[2] P. V. Verkhovskoy believes that the idea itself of instituting an Ecclesiastical Collegium (and therefore, let us add, of the abolition of the patriarchate) occurred to Peter only at the end of 1718, and it was "unexpected and novel".[3] Rejecting the possibility that Peter intended to abolish the office of patriarch already at the beginning of his church reforms, we must admit, however, that objectively the reform, once it began, facilitated both the conception of this idea and its practical implementation.

The second stage of the church reform covered the years between 1705 and 1720. The most important innovations fell on the beginning of that stage. The first of these changes apparently took place in 1705—a critical year in the whole of the church reform. In that

---

[1] Yu. Ya. Kogan, Ye. F. Grekulov, V. F. Milovidov. "Tserkov i russkiy absolyutizm v XVIII v." In: *Tserkov v istorii Rossii (IX v.—1917). Criticheskiye Ocherki* [The Church and Russian Absolutism in the 18th Century. In: The Church in the History of Russia (9th century-1917). Critical Essays], Moscow, 1967, p. 166.

[2] S. M. Solovyov. Op. cit., Moscow, 1967, Book VIII (Vols. 15-16), p. 91.

[3] P. V. Verkhovskoy. *Uchrezhdeniye Dukhovnoy kollegii i Dukhovnyi reglament* (The Institution of the Ecclesiastical Collegium and the Ecclesiastical Regulations), Rostov-on-Don, 1916, p. 255.

year, the Novgorod, Pskov, Kiev, Astrakhan and Siberian dioceses were exempted from the control of the Monastery Department, and all the church estates within their boundaries reverted to the state that existed before the reform. One of the principal causes for going back on the reform already in progress was, evidently, the fact that most of the monasteries' estates in these dioceses were small, and the incomes from them, were small, too—barely sufficient, and that not always, for satisfying the monasteries' own needs. Some of these monasteries had neither peasants nor any kind of income at all, their only source of livelihood being a state subsidy (*ruga*). Naturally, the government could therefore derive but little income from the church estates in these dioceses. But there were also major landowners among them; thus the Novgorod hierarch possessed one of the largest and richest estates. However, they too were exempted from the Monastery Department's control and the reform. There were also other weighty reasons for that move.

For example, we cannot fail to notice that all of the five dioceses mentioned were located close to or along the borders. The dioceses of Novgorod, Pskov and Kiev were actually frontline ones, their territory being the scene of military operations, and the government of Peter I naturally had an interest in the aid and support of the clergy precisely in these areas. But the secularisation of their estates had aroused considerable discontent among the clergy, of course, and the government could no longer rely on their unconditional and vigorous support in the frontline dioceses. Besides, the population of these areas, including church peasants, bore a greater burden than the peasants of the inner provinces, being ruined by hostilities, various dues connected with the movements and billeting of troops, etc. It should be assumed, therefore, that Peter I took all this into account and returned the lands and independence in other questions to the clergy of these dioceses. Other circumstances were apparently also taken into account. Thus the diocese of Kiev had comparatively recently, only in the second half of the 17th century, passed under the control of the patriarch, and was still hoping to uphold its independence.

It was therefore unwise to complicate the relations with the Ukrainian clergy. As for Siberian monasteries, the czar obviously took into account their remote location and the consequent difficulty of their administration. Thus, in 1705, the Monastery Department's sphere of control was significantly reduced; it now included the Patriarchal Region and 15 of the 20 existing dioceses: those of Krutitsy, Rostov, Vologda, Ustyug, Kholmogory, Suzdal, Nizhniy Novgorod, Kazan, Vyatka, Kolomna, Ryazan, Belgorod, Voronezh, Tver and Smolensk.[1]

At approximately the same time, in 1705 and 1706, other changes also began, which were indicative of a reversal of the actually implemented secularisation of church possessions. All the hierarchs' houses and monasteries, which were left under the control of the Monastery Department were divided into two large groups. The more numerous of these consisted of owners to whom their estates were returned and who were to administer them as of old, and also to dispose of the income from the lands. In other words, these monasteries and hierarchs' houses were exempted from the reform; they were termed unassigned. In a letter to Peter I, I. A. Musin-Pushkin described them as small monasteries with small incomes, so that "no profit could be extracted from them".[2] Apart from their direct meaning, the reasons given in the letter had a broader significance, revealing the more general objectives of the church reform. Four hierarchs' houses were included among the unassigned owners—those of Ryazan, Kazan, Voronezh and Ustyug, and 238 monasteries. Indeed, most of them were owners of very small estates, with incomes that barely sufficed for their own upkeep. But we also find among them several major church feudals: the houses of the hierarchs of Ryazan (which had 1,636 peasant homesteads) and Kazan (1,126 homesteads), the Trinity-St. Sergiy Monastery (20,131 homesteads) and the Novodevichiy Convent (2,346 homesteads).[3] The causes for this strange situation must apparently be sought for in the fact that

---

[1] I. A. Bulygin. Op. cit., pp. 103-109.
[2] TsGADA, reg. 9, section II, Book 5, sheets 514-514 (reverse).
[3] I. A. Bulygin. Op. cit., pp. 120-122, 202-215.

Peter I decided to protect some major lords of the Church from the blow that would undoubtedly have been inflicted on them by the reform. The house of the hierarch of Ryazan must have been granted the privilege because its head, Stefan Yavorsky, was simultaneously Patriarchal Locum Tenens, and Peter I did not therefore wish to hurt his interests thereby setting him against himself. The house of the hierarch of Kazan must have been exempted from the reform because much of its income was spent on the spreading of Christianity among the peoples of the Volga region. In the case of the Trinity-St. Sergiy Monastery an exception was apparently made for its great services to the czar, particularly for the vast sums of money it gave to Peter. Thus, in 1703 alone it gave the czar a gift of 10,000 roubles, and another 7,500 roubles were spent on various state tasks.[1] The Novodevichiy Convent must have been exempted from the reform because Czarevna Sofia was incarcerated there until 1704.

The second group consisted of hierarchs' houses and monasteries to which allowance was assigned in the form of grain, money and lands. The assignment proceeded in the following fashion. The overall sum of the income of a monastery or a hierarch's house was divided into two parts; one part, in the form of money, quit-rent grain and arable land tithe was handed over to the house or monastery as allowance, while the other, in the same form, went to the Monastery Department, that is, to the state. Accordingly, the estates of most of the owners of this group were divided into two parts; the income from one part of the estates became the assigned allowance of a monastery or a hierarch's house; these estates and incomes from them came to be called *opredelyonnye* ("assigned" ones), and direct management of these estates was returned to their owners; the revenue from the other part of the possessions went to the Monastery Department. These revenues and possessions were termed *zaopredelyonnye* (estates whose income went to the state.— *Ed.*) and their direct management continued to be in the hands of the

---

[1] TsGADA, reg. 237, case 1, Section II, file 911, sheets 197-239 reverse.

Monastery Department. The estates of a few *opredelyonnye* owners were not divided into these two parts, and the *zaopredelyonnye* sums were exacted directly from the total income. The assignment continued until 1710; in all, it involved 11 hierarchs' houses and 60 monasteries; most of these hierarchs' houses and two-thirds of the monasteries were in the centre of the country. In terms of the size of their estates, they were among the major feudal landowners. Let us mention some of them. Among the hierarchs' houses, especially prominent were the house of the metropolitan of Rostov which owned 4,376 peasant homesteads, of Suzdal (1,602 homesteads), and of Vologda (1,213 homesteads). Of the monasteries, assignment involved such giant landowners as the Moscow monasteries—the Chudov Monastery, which had 3,026 homesteads, the Monastery of Our Saviour (2,638 homesteads), and St. Simon's (2,493 homesteads); the Monastery of the Resurrection on the Istra (2,297 homesteads) and the Monastery of St. Savva of Strozbvi in Zvenigorod (2,054). Of the monasteries in the outlying regions, mention may be made of the Byeloye Ozero Monastery of St. Kirill which owned 5,250 homesteads, and others.[1]

Thus at the second stage of the reform, the sphere controlled by the Monastery Department sharply decreased in size. It lost control of all the church estates of the outlying dioceses; and in the other dioceses, of monasteries, owning small estates, hierarchs' houses, and of the *opredelyonnye* possessions. It now had direct control only of the *zaopredelyonnye* possessions of assigned monasteries and hierarchical houses. Thus the government gave up the policy of complete secularisation of church possessions, restricting itself to partial secularisation. The main reason for this reorientation was the realisation by the government that it was impossible to draw any income from the owners of small estates. Just as in the first years of the reform, the income from church lands amounted to about 100,000 roubles per annum.

At the end of the second stage of the reform, Peter I

---

[1] I. A. Bulygin. Op. cit., pp. 160-181, 113-120.

realised the need for a reform of the higher church administration or, to be more precise, for the abolition of the patriarchate and its replacement by an Ecclesiastical Collegium, In 1718, the czar entrusted Archbishop Feofan Prokopovich of Pskov, a prominent church figure, to prepare a special document, later entitled *Dukhovnyi reglament* (Ecclesiastical Regulations), which set out the reasons for the reforms and at the same time outlined the functions and tasks of the new organ of the highest church authority.

1720-1721 saw the third stage of the church reform. The czar's *ukase* of 17 August 1720 closed down the Monastery Department, all its affairs being handed over to the new, recently established institutions: Chamber Collegium (*Kamer-kollegiya*), State Office Collegium (*Shtats-kontor-kollegiya*) and Justice Collegium (*Yustits-kollegiya*).[1]

The abolition of the Monastery Department and the restoration to the clergy of those estates that were still under the Department's control is usually explained by the fact that there was no room for the Department in the new system of local and central state bodies set up at that time which simply made it superfluous.[2] Of course, this fact had some significance, and it has to be taken into account, but other factors must have played a role as well. It was precisely at that time that Peter I got the higher hierarchs to sign the *Dukhovnyi reglament,* that is to say, to approve the reform of the high-level church administration—which they had opposed. We can therefore assume that the abolition of the Monastery Department was meant to assuage the opposition of the clergy to the intended abolition of the patriarchate.

In February 1720, Feofan Prokopovich completed the *Dukhovnyi reglament* and handed it over to Peter I.

---

[1] M. Gorchakov. *Monastyrskiy prikaz (1649-1725)* [The Monastery Department (1649-1725)], St. Petersburg, 1868, pp. 127-128.

[2] B. G. Slitsan. "Reforma tserkovnogo upravleniya". In: *Ocherki istorii SSSR: Period Feodalisma: Rossiya v pervoy chetverti XVIII v. Preobrazovaniya Petra I* (Reform of the Church Administration. In: Essays in the History of the USSR: The Period of Feudalism: Russia in the First Quarter of the 18th Century. Peter I's Reforms), Moscow, 1954, pp. 375-376.

The czar demanded that it be fully approved and signed by the senators and the higher church hierarchs. When this was done in the capital, Lieutenant-Colonel S. Davydov was sent on a tour of the country to collect the signatures of the church hierarchs and the fathers superior of major monasteries and convents. Carrying out that assignment, he returned in January 1721 to St. Petersburg.

On January 25, 1721, Peter I issued a manifesto on the abolition of the patriarchate and the setting up of the Ecclesiastical Collegium, and on the confirmation of the *Dukhovnyi reglament*.[1] Just as the other Collegiums, the Ecclesiastical Collegium consisted of 11 members: the president (an office to which Stefan Yavorsky, former Patriarchal Locum Tenens, was appointed), two vice-presidents (these offices were filled by Feodosiy Yanovsky, the Archbishop of Novgorod, and the Bishop Feofan Prokopovich of Pskov, four counsellors and four assessors. All the members of the Collegium had to be church dignitaries. Two days later all of them, just like any other state officials, took an oath of allegiance and obedience to the czar, recognising him as the "ultimate judge of this Ecclesiastical Collegium"—and, consequently, their complete subjection to the monarch.

The manifesto and the introduction to the *Dukhovnyi reglament* outlined the reasons for reforming the higher bodies of church administration. The explanation began with general statements concerning the advantages of corporate administration introduced in all the officies of the state. Next the principal reason why individual administration of the Church was regarded as dangerous to the state was expounded. The common people, amazed at the "honour and glory" surrounding the "spiritual ruler", i.e., the patriarch, might think that he was "a second czar equal to the autocrat", and that "the spiritual order" was "another and better state". Matters were quite different when the church administration was instituted "by the monarch's decree and the Senate's approval", when the title itself of president of the collegium "was not proud", and no

---

[1] PSZ-I, Vol. 6, No. 3718, pp. 314-346.

one, the president not excluded, "placed it high in their thoughts", while the "supreme pastor" of Orthodoxy was the monarch himself".[1] Thus we see that the primary objective of the reform was the strengthening of the absolutist autocratic power that would make the clergy a docile instrument of the czar's will.

On February 14, 1721, on the day of the opening of the Ecclesiastical Collegium, Peter I renamed it the "Holy Governing Synod". On the same day he entrusted the Synod with the management of church estates.[2] These changes made the Synod, the highest body of church administration, a more representative institution than the Ecclesiastical Collegium had been intended to be, and equated it, to some extent, with the Senate. On the other hand, a year later, in 1722, a Chief Procurator was appointed to the Synod—an officer who was meant to be "like our eye and caretaker of the affairs of state".[3] The Chief Procurator was responsible directly to the czar and had complete control of the Synod. In the same year, the office of the president of the Synod was abolished after the death of Stefan Yavorsky.

The Synod became the highest government body administering the affairs of the Orthodox Church. It made appointments to ecclesiastical posts, interpreted Christian dogma, fought various heresies and deviations from the official church dogma, and had the powers of a court of law in matters of faith, marriage and some crimes committed by members of the clergy. It was also entrusted with the important task of "reforming the *spiritual* ecclesiastical estate" in order to enhance its prestige and thus strengthen the Church's ideological influence on the people.

Of great significance was the April 22, 1722, edict instituting the obligatory oath of allegiance of the

---

[1] PSZ-I, Vol. 6, No. 3718, pp. 317-318.
[2] PSZ-I, Vol. 6, No. 3749, No 3749, pp. 366-367. For the management of the estates, the Synod asked the czar to restore the Monastery Department, which was done in 1721; however, this time it was a secondary institution fully subordinated to the Synod, and in 1725 it was renamed Chamber Office of the Synodal Board.
[3] PSZ-I, Vol. 6, No. 4001, p. 676.

clergy to the emperor, which made the Church subordinate to secular authority.[1]

The view is widely current in literature that the establishment of the Synod marked the end of the church reforms. But, as was suggested recently, that view was wrong, and the reform continued.[2] We share this opinion, and we believe that the years 1722-1725 marked the fourth stage of the reforms. Characteristic of this fourth stage was Peter I's intention to set strictly defined limits to the staff of monasteries and hierarchs' houses. Extensive work was done preparatory to the implementation of this measure, new data on the economic state of church estates were gathered, and some instructions were issued on the size of the staff. However, because of the death of Peter I in January 1725, none of these plans were carried out.[3]

Such were the content and stages of the church reform implemented by Peter I in 1701-1725. It was designed as a means of using the wealth of the Church in the interests of the state. Church estates were, in actual fact completely secularised during the initial period of the reform. It turned out, however, that a considerable number of ecclesiastical landowners received but small incomes. That was why the government soon switched to the policy of partial secularisation of church possessions. The reform ended in the state restoring to the clergy the control of practically all its possessions; it may thus be said to have ended in partial secularisation of church incomes. This result was important in itself, since it was the first real secularisation of the Church's wealth since the issue had arisen some two hundred years previously, late in the 15th and early in the 16th centuries. But it had an even greater significance in that the Church never recovered from the blow; all the subsequent governments had to deal with the issue of *zaopredelyonnye* estates, and generally of churchmen's peasants in one way or another, until it was finally resolved through their

---

[1] N. M. Nikolsky. *Istoriya russkoy tserkvi* (A History of the Russian Church), Moscow, 1983, 3rd ed., p. 220.

[2] T. Maykova. "Pyotr I i pravoslavnaya tserkov" (Peter I and the Orthodox Church). In: *Nauka i religiya*, 1972, No. 7, p. 46.

[3] I. A. Bulygin. Op. cit., p. 132.

complete secularisation in 1764. Another important result of the reform was the reorganisation of the top-level of church administration, the abolition of the patriarchate and its replacement by the Synod, which was actually a state body. All this undoubtedly seriously undermined the Church's economic and political positions, placing it into a more subordinate position in relation to the absolutist government than before.

The second half of the 1720s was marked by a fresh aggravation of the struggle between secular authority and the clergy. It flared up immediately after Peter I's death, on January 26, 1725. Feodosiy Yanovsky, one of the heads of the Synod, its vice-president and the archbishop of Novgorod, openly opposed the church reform, demanding a return to the old order, in particular, to the Church's complete control of its finances. Undoubtedly he expressed the mood of a considerable part of the clergy, especially the hierarchs. But this outbreak of protest was quickly suppressed, Feodosiy was divested of his archbishopric, demoted to mere monk and sent to the Karelian Monastery.

Simultaneously the government took measures to make the clergy even more subordinate to secular authority, and to tighten state control over church estates. With that aim in view, the Supreme Privy Council, by its edict of July 12, 1726, divided the Synod into two departments. The first department, which was named the Ecclesiastical Sobornoye Government, but mostly continued to be called the Synod, was to manage religious affairs only (questions of dogma, Christian morality, etc.). On all questions within its cognizance it could communicate directly with the Supreme Privy Council, and was expected to submit to it monthly reports of all resolved and outstanding issues, and also financial reports. The second department was named the Collegium of the Economy of Synodal Government; its functions were the management of the clergy's estates and the settlement of judicial issues. It had to report to the Senate on cases within its jurisdiction.[1]

This reorganisation indubitably undermined the posi-

---

[1] PSZ-I, Vol. 7, No. 4919, pp. 675-676; No. 4959, pp. 697-698.

tion of the Synod and therefore of the clergy. Previously, the Synod had the right to communicate directly with the monarch and was subordinated to the monarch alone, while now the Synod was subordinated to the Supreme Privy Council—a deliberative organ at the czar. Although the Collegium of the Economy, which dealt with economic matters, was formally part of the Synod, it was practically more within the cognizance of the Senate. Thus secular authority tightened its hold on the Church.

But that was not the end of the struggle. In 1726-1730, the Church took part in the confrontation between the new aristocracy, which had risen to power under Peter I and expressed the interests of the bulk of the gentry and the nobility, and the old aristocracy endeavouring to establish an oligarchic form of government and to restrict absolutist power. The Church took the side of this second party.

The supporters of the old ecclesiastical order began an open struggle against Feofan Prokopovich as the most fierce proponent of the church reform in the first quarter of the 18th century. They accused him of Protestant heresy alleged to be contained in his works substantiating the church reforms carried out under Peter I. One of the most important instruments used in the persecution of Feofan Prokopovich was the work of Stefan Yavorsky *The Rock of Faith,* first published in 1728 and mostly aimed against the heresy imputed to Feofan. In the Synod, the same kind of changes took place as in the Supreme Privy Council. In the latter, the old aristocracy gained ascendancy; in the same way, the Synod was now dominated by churchmen aspiring to restore the old prereform state of affairs in the Church. Georgiy Dashkov, Metropolitan of Rostov, seen as a candidate to the patriarchal throne, was appointed member of the Synod. At this stage, the interests of the old secular and ecclesiastical aristocracy coincided, as both fought against absolutist autocratic power. That was why their historical destinies became so closely interwoven.

Peter II's unexpected death in January 1730 and the failure of the designs of the Supreme Privy Council members connected with the election of Anna Ioannovna to the imperial throne led to the fall of the Dolgorukiy-Golitsyn group, and with it, of their followers among the clergy. Feofan Prokopovich's group came out on top, and Prokopovich again became a leader of the Synod. Although there was no direct evidence of the involvement of the higher clergy in the designs of the Supreme Privy Council, they were also subjected to repressions, and Prokopovich naturally had a hand in that.

Later, Anna Ioannovna's government dealt yet another blow to the Church. Using as a pretext the fact that church-owned peasants were a long way in arrears, it accused the Synod of negligence and, taking in 1738 the Collegium of the Economy from the hands of the Synod, transferred it entirely within the cognizance of the Senate.[1]

In 1741, Elizabeth, Peter's daughter, renowned for her piety, ascended to the throne. To please the clergy, she abolished in 1744 the Collegium of the Economy and handed control of church estates back to the Synod. But she, too, had to change her policy in this sphere. The arrears of the church-owned peasants again began to grow. Besides, a broad peasant movement was launched on the lands of the clergy. In 1751, the peasants of the St. Trifon Monastery of the Dormition rose in rebellion; in 1752, those of the Khutyn Monastery; in 1753, the peasants of the Moscow Monastery of the Transfiguration, and so on. All this, as well as the need for money, made the empress choose the policy of secularising church estates, justifying it by the well-used argument: "so that the ecclesiastical orders might not be burdened with mundane cares". The edict of September 30, 1757, ordered the Senate and the Synod to change the mode of management of church-owned peasants, entrusting it to retired officers. However, the clergy succeeded in delaying the implementation of the edict[2].

In this period, the Church's subjection to secular autocratic power increased despite its resistance to the process. The Synod's role in the system of state

---

[1] PSZ-I, Vol. 10, No. 7558, p. 458.
[2] N. M. Nikolsky. Op. cit., p. 199.

administration fell, and at the end of that period the issue of complete secularisation of church estates became really acute.

As we have said, the Church succeeded in delaying the implementation of secularisation planned by Empress Elizabeth. But it was no longer capable of averting the final solution of that issue, which could no longer be put off. The peasants' position on the Church's estates continued to deteriorate, and their rebellions and disturbances assumed an ever greater scope.

On March 21, 1762, Peter III issued an edict on the secularisation of church estates. All the peasants owned by the hierarchs and monasteries were transferred under the control of the newly established Collegium of the Economy subordinated to the Senate, and were given the usufruct of land. Apart from the poll-tax, they had to pay the state a rouble in quit-rent. The clergy, especially the hierarchs, were extremely disgruntled at that measure. That is why Catherine II, who soon ascended to the throne, abolished secularisation by her edict of August 12, 1762, in an attempt to win the sympathies of the clergy.

But that was a temporary measure. Catherine II soon realised that the positions of the Church in the state were weakened, that the Church was not supported by the nobility or the gentry, and that there was no threat from this quarter. At the same time the peasant unrest on the ecclesiastics' estates grew. Somewhat later she wrote to Voltaire that at her enthronement the disturbances involved more than a hundred thousand church-owned peasants who rose in arms because they were tyrannically oppressed.[1]

On February 26, 1764, Catherine II announced in a special manifesto the secularisation of church estates. On this occasion she made a speech in the Synod. The empress stated outright that the estates of the Church had been "stolen from the state", and that ecclesiastics could not "own them" without being "unjust" towards the state. Their business was not the possession of earthly riches but interpretation of Christian dogma and the spreading of Christianity. "If you obey the

---
[1] RIO, St. Petersburg, 1872, Vol. 10, p. 37.

laws," she enjoined the clergy, "if you are my most loyal subjects, you will promptly return to the state that which you unjustly own."[1]

All church-owned lands and peasants were transferred under the control of the Collegium of the Economy, and the peasants were now called "economic". In all, about a million peasants and more than eight million *dessiatinas* of land were handed over to the Collegium. Apart from the poll-tax, the peasants were now obliged to pay a rouble and a half in quit-rent, not a rouble as stipulated by the 1762 edict, the total coming to about 1.5 million roubles. Out of this sum, about one-third was to be expended on the upkeep of hierarchs' houses and monasteries, while the rest went to the treasury. The number of monasteries and convents was cut by half, from 814 to 396; the rest of the monasteries and convents, mostly small ones, were closed down. The law on secularisation was only effective in Great Russia and Siberia; in the Ukraine, the secularisation was only implemented in 1786.

Most of the clergy did not resist the secularisation. Only Metropolitan Arseniy (Matseyevich) of Rostov opposed it openly and resolutely. The reason for this nonresistance lay in the fact that the secularisation did not at all ruin the Church, as clerical historians insist. Apart from the money allowance, the clergy received land as a means of livelihood: up to 30 *dessiatinas* per monastery and from six to nine *dessiatinas* per hierarchical house. In 1797 their staffs were considerably increased. They now received about one million roubles, that is, twice as much as before, and the land allotments grew in size—up to 60 *dessiatinas* to monasteries and 30 *dessiatinas* to hierarchs' houses; apart from this, they were now given forests, too.

That was the end of the struggle, which had lasted for nearly three hundred years, between secular authority and the clergy over the Church's land possessions. The Church suffered a defeat in this struggle and was deprived of its estates, but that did not undermine its class alliance with the feudal state. On the contrary, it began to serve the state with an

---

[1] ChOIDR, 1862, Book 2, pp. 187-188.

even greater zeal. The reason for this was that, secularisation or no secularisation, the material position of the clergy deteriorated insignificantly, if at all; Orthodox Christianity retained its positions as a state religion; and the Church as a whole continued to play a great role in the country's life.

## The Church and Popular Movements

Despite her engagement in the political Fronde and even, at times, open opposition to the state, the Church invariably and resolutely supported it in the matter of suppression of popular movements that threatened the prevailing feudal system. This position of the Church was determined not only by its function of ideologically sanctifying the feudal system—the Church itself, as we have seen, was a major feudal landowner. At the same time there were individuals and even whole groups, especially among the lower-ranking clergy, who sympathised with the people and openly took their side in the struggle for liberation. These facts, however, did not alter the Church's general position, and besides, the ecclesiastical authorities made short work of these rebellious pastors.

Let us consider the attitude of the Church to the major antifeudal mass movements of the 18th century, such as the Astrakhan uprising of 1705 and 1706. In that period, Astrakhan was a major commercial and handicrafts' city as well as a military-administrative centre in the country's south-eastern border area. The bulk of the city's population consisted of working people and non-estate landless people who worked at fisheries and salt-works. Billeted here were several regiments of the *streltsy* and regular army. Driven to desperation by the endless extortions and the abuses of the local administration, especially of the governor, Timofey Rzhevsky, the citizens rose in rebellion on the night of July 29, 1705, and seized power. Soon the township of Krasnyi Yar, Chornyi Yar, Guryev and Terki joined the rebels. A large contingent of the rebels moved up the Volga, intending to seize Tsaritsyn and go as far as Moscow. To suppress the rebellion, the government dispatched a considerable task force under Field Marshal B. Sheremetyev. The city bosses abandoned the movement and began agitation for giving up to the czar. They were actively aided by the local clergy, in particular by the metropolitan of Astrakhan, who was in secret correspondence with Sheremetyev. On approaching Astrakhan, the government troops were welcomed by the rich citizens and the clergy headed by the metropolitan; soon after, in March 1706, the city fell. The subversive and splitting activities of the local clergy undoubtedly were a great help in the suppression of the Astrakhan uprising.

No sooner had the government suppressed this outbreak of popular unrest than the peasant war of 1707 began, in which the people were led by the Don Cossack Kondratiy Bulavin. It swept through the Don and the Volga regions, the central districts and part of the Ukraine. Despite the peasants' heroic struggle, their movement was defeated in 1708. The rebels' primary goal was liberation from serfdom, and religious motives did not play a great role in the movement. Still, one of Bulavin's slogans was defence of ancient piety. It was therefore no accident that the Old Believers living along the Khopyor, the Buzuluk and the Medveditsa, took a most active part in the uprising.

It was highly significant that precisely in the spring of 1708, i.e., at the height of the Bulavin uprising, a secret *ukase* of the czar enjoined the clergy to violate the secrecy of the confession thus making them the government's political informers. The purpose of the edict was, beyond all doubt, to make more active and wider use of the Church in suppressing the popular movement. It instructed the clergy "to diligently question their spiritual children, people of all ranks, during confession, whether they were going to rebel or had evil intentions or conspired with any one to rebel or to do harm to the state, or made plans with anyone to commit brigandage or murder". If any such "evil intention" was discovered, and it was established that there were plans to "put it later into effect", the clergy were obliged to report immediately to "Metropolitan Stefan of Ryazan and Murom, for which information those priests would have the honour of the czar's favour".[1] At the same time the edict bound the priests and deacons to keep the flock under their continual surveillance.[2]

Later, the function of the Church as political informant, involving, among others, the use of confessions, was confirmed by the above-mentioned edict of April 22, 1722, concerning the clergy's taking the oath of allegiance to the emperor. It ended with the obligation to inform the authorities of any "treason or rebellion against the czar" discovered during confession.[3]

The Church played a particularly active part in the suppression of the most powerful of the peasant wars—the war of 1773-1775 led by Yemelyan Pugachov. It swept through a vast territory, and the demands for peasants' liberation from serfdom and for abolishing their sale were voiced in that movement with particular force. The government used all possible means, including the clergy, to suppress it.

As early as October 15, 1773, almost immediately after the beginning of the uprising, Catherine II issued an "admonitory" *ukase* which was read in all the churches. The edict called on the people to "remain unshakeably in the Orthodox faith and in obedience to the most wise divine law". The *ukase* threatened the rebels with infernal torment in the next world and punishment on the earth. While reading it, the priests had to tell the population that the rebellion was "God's punishment for the people's sins", and that its participants would be damned.

The Synod as the highest body of church administration issued in April 1774 a special appeal to the people's masses, in which Pugachov was declared to be "a devil attacking the flock of Christ, an enemy of the motherland and of the Church who trampled faith and law". The appeal anathematised all who took part in the movement. Some time later, in August 1774, the Synod issued a fresh appeal enjoining the clergy to arouse in the people "a fervent zeal for the destruction

---

[1] *Istoricheskiy arkhiv*, 1955, No. 4, p. 198.
[2] Ibid., p. 199.
[3] N. M. Nikolsky. Op. cit., p. 220.

of the evil-doer's impious and pernicious undertakings", threatening at the same time to divest priests of their dignity and punish them in other ways if they were to render homage to Pugachov.

Local hierarchs took an active part in the suppression of the peasant war. In response to a special letter by Catherine II, Archbishop Veniamin (Putsek-Grigorovich) of Kazan circulated his "admonition" throughout his diocese, in which he branded the rebels. Retreating from Kazan, the rebels burnt down in revenge Veniamin's country residence, while the authorities promoted him to metropolitan and made him the gift of a *klobuk*[1] with a cross of diamonds. Other hierarchs showed the same hatred as they stigmatised the peasants, who rose to fight for their liberation. Thus Bishop Varfolomey of Vyatka presented Yemelyan Pugachov as "the scum of the earth, a fierce beast and all-poisonous... enemy and disturber of universal peace and quiet, and an obvious perjurer".

Most of the rank-and-file parish priests obediently carried out the will of the higher secular and ecclesiastical powers. Thus D. I. Chicherin, Governor of Siberia, asked Bishop Varlaam of Tobolsk to reward priest Vasily Udintsev, who managed to keep the population of Irbit "from participation in the rebellion" and helped to catch Pugachov's men. Priests were also used as spies and informers, reporting to the authorities on the mood of the peasants and factory workers, the movements of Pugachov's troops, etc. Thus the sexton of the Ocher Works reported the situation in the Pugachov detachment after it seized the township. The priest of the village of Tazovskoye informed the authorities of Perm on the kind of arms that the Tatars had. The monks of the Sarov Monastery reported to the government troops of the intention of the rebel detachment led by Ivan Ivanov to seize Pensa, as a result of which the insurgents failed to carry out their plan.

Frequently, the clergy directly participated in military operations against Pugachov's troops.

The rebels naturally gave short shrift to the ecclesias-

---

[1] *Klobuk*—headgear of an Orthodox hierarch or monk.

tics who opposed them. Where churches were used by the punitive forces as their strong points, they were sometimes destroyed. In all, some 200 priests, deacons and other parish church servants were executed and 63 churches destroyed by the rebels, according to official sources.

Using these facts, the government and the Church spread the rumours that the rebels were enemies of the Orthodox faith, thus attempting to sow religious strife and to set the popular masses against the rebels. These accusations were false, of course, and failed to achieve their purpose. The bulk of the rebels were believers, and their leaders declared this on numerous occasions. In many of his manifestos Pugachov insisted that he acted "by the grace of God", explaining his successes by "the power of the hand of God". The reason he gave for his appeal to the people "to catch, punish and hang" the landowners was that they tormented and ruined the peasants, "having no Christian spirit in them". A close associate of Pugachov, Ivan Gryaznov, wrote thus in one of his appeals for the liberation of the peasants from the landowners' oppression: "The Scripture says that the landowners must keep their peasants as children, and yet they treat the peasants worse than dogs". "We don't want Orthodox blood," he stated further, "we are the same as you, of the Christian faith".

Generally speaking, the religious element did not play any substantial role in the programme of the Pugachov uprising. Probably the most significant slogan in this respect was the appeal for the freedom of the Old Belief. In his manifestos Pugachov declared, on more than one occasion, that he granted the peasants not only land and freedom but also "the ancient cross and prayer, their heads and beards". On the whole, characteristic of the movement were religious tolerance and respect for religion and the Church.

Although the Church as a whole took an active part in the suppression of the movement, in some cases members of the lower-ranking parish clergy fought on the side of the rebels. They were close to the exploited popular masses in their position, they had a sincere sympathy for them and therefore supported them in their struggle for the liberation from serfdom. For example, Danila Shitov, the priest of the village of Kosevo, Ufa Province, took part in the storming of the town of Sarapul, for which feat he was promoted to the rank of lieutenant-colonel by Pugachov. The priest of the village of Beryozovka-Kamskaya headed a detachment of local rebels. The priest of the Rozhdestvensky Works wrote the community's resolution recognising Pugachov as emperor, and authenticated the resolution by signing it. On many occasions local priests greeted the arrival of Pugachov's troops with bell-ringing, icons and crosses, as was the case in Alatyr, Saransk, Krasnoslobodsk and some other towns and villages. However, the reason for this lay mostly in the fear of being punished by the rebels rather than in any sympathy for them.

Pugachov's arrest and the defeat of the uprising were greeted by the clergy with jubilation. Count Panin, Commander of the government task force, wrote in a letter informing Bishop Samuil of Krutitsy of the capture of Pugachov: "accept... my congratulations, and share the universal joy with me". The court that tried Pugachov included Samuil mentioned here, Bishop Gennadiy of Suzdal, Archimandrite Ioann of the Moscow Monastery of the Transfiguration, and two archpriests. The Synod confirmed the court's sentence to quarter Pugachov, and then damned the names of Pugachov and of his closest associates in all eternity. Thus the Church sanctified with its authority the cruel punishment meted out to the leaders of the Peasant War of 1773-1775.

The Church was an important stronghold of the autocracy in the fight against the people's antifeudal movement.

### The Church and the Development of Culture

Just as in the previous epochs, the Church played a controversial role in the development of 18th-century culture. In many respects, the Church acted as a conservative and even a reactionary force. At the same time there is no gainsaying the positive significance of some of the aspects of the Church's activity in this sphere.

In its very essence, the religious world outlook was unscientific, and it is therefore no accident that the Church especially persecuted everything that contradicted the religious views of Nature and man. As late as the first half of the 18th century, the Synod demanded that the authors of works aimed against Church doctrines be sent to them for interrogation and inquiry. Even the Academy of Sciences was under the Synod's surveillance. The clericals censored its publications and demanded confiscation whenever they found doubtful passages or those contrary to Christian laws and the government. For instance, it was at the clerics' insistence that in 1743 the astronomical calendar published by the Academy of Science was banned on the grounds that it contained data about the planets "which could be a temptation to the people". The clerical censors also opposed the publication by the Academy of Sciences of such a remarkable monument of our culture as the Russian chronicles on the pretext that there were many falsehoods in them.

The scientific and literary activities of Mikhail Lomonosov, the great Russian scholar, also aroused the clericals' spite and hatred. His works undermined the basis of the religious doctrine on the creation of man and Nature by God, and on their immutability. Lomonosov did not hesitate to criticise the clergy openly and sharply and to ridicule them. Widely known was his satirical poem *A Hymn to the Beard* written in 1757 of which handwritten copies were circulated in St. Petersburg. The poem showed that the priests' respectable beards concealed ignorance, fraud and dull wits. For this, Lomonosov was summoned to the Synod for interrogation, where he boldly admitted authorship of the free-thinking poem. The Synod then addressed a special report to the empress, insisting that this sort of poems by Lomonosov or anyone else must be destroyed and publicly burnt, and Lomonosov himself sent to the Synod "for proper admonition and correction". However, these attempts of the clericals met with no success, and Lomonosov continued his attacks on them.

In 1759, D. S. Anichkov, Professor of Moscow

University and prominent progressive scholar, published a dissertation entitled *Discourse from Natural Theology on the Beginnings and Origin of Worshipping Gods, Especially Among Ignorant Peoples*. The *Discourse* rejected the divine origin of religion and denounced the ignorance and charlatanism of the clergy. Metropolitan Amvrosiy of Moscow described it as "pernicious and seductive". The book was destroyed.

N. I. Novikov, the prominent Russian enlightener, made a great contribution to the development of Russian culture, in the first place through publication of a great number of books and historical sources in various fields. Some of them contained a critique of religion and the Church, as well as of serfdom. Informed on by Pyotr Alekseyev, an archpriest of the Moscow Monastery of Michael the Archangel, Novikov was arrested and put into the Shlisselburg Fortress for 15 years.

The Church also fiercely persecuted Alexander Radishchev, the outstanding Russian writer and pioneer of the revolutionary-democratic thought, author of the famous *Journey from St. Petersburg to Moscow*. In this and other works he openly advocated the abolition of serfdom and autocracy, and criticised the Church's views of the immortality of the soul and various religious prejudices. Radishchev was accused of his views which were said to be contrary to "the ten commandments, Holy Scripture, Orthodoxy and civil law", and sentenced to death, the sentence later commuted to ten years' hard labour. Even a hundred years later, in 1903, ecclesiastical censorship regarded Radishchev's book dangerous to the Church, and practically all the copies of the book were burnt.

The Church was hostile to foreign works written from the natural-scientific positions. Thus in 1740, the book by the French Academician, Fontenelle, *Entretiens sur la pluralité des mondes* (Discourse on the Plurality of Worlds) was published on Lomonosov's suggestion; the origin of the world was treated in it in terms of scientific astronomy. The book was confiscated and destroyed. The Synod described it as "contrary to faith and morality". The same fate befell Alexander Pope's *Essay on Man*, a philosophical poem which appeared in

1756. It was found to contain "Copernicus's pernicious ideas ... contrary to Holy Scripture". The Church put every obstacle in the way of the publication and distribution of the works of the French materialist enlighteners Voltaire, Diderot, Holbach, and others.

Significantly, it was at this time that even those young people who grew up in an ecclesiastic environment showed a desire to obtain truly scientific knowledge. Thus in 1771, Nikita Kryukov, a pupil of the Krutitsy Seminary, begged to be permitted to study medicine, citing his lack of ability for theological instruction as a reason. Pavel Pomerantsev, a student of the Moscow Theological Academy, submitted in 1772 a request to be transferred to "Moscow University in order to continue the study of science", and later graduated from that university with honours.

All this shows beyond any doubt that in the 18th century the Church hampered the development of progressive scientific and social thought.

It must be said, though, that some aspects of the activities of the ecclesiastics objectively promoted the development of certain spheres of culture. Thus most of the system of primary education in the country was in the hands of the Church, and although the pupils were instructed in the spirit of Orthodoxy and autocracy, the schools spread literacy among the people. The pupils also received some elements of secular knowledge. That activity was of especially great significance for the non-Russian population of the outlying provinces, where schools were founded by the Church in the course of its missionary activities. Some of the cultic buildings intended for the assertion of the religious ideology were at the same time outstanding monuments of Russian architecture, and that is, above all, what makes them dear to us now. Church composers made a great contribution to the country's music culture.

A summary of church history in the 18th century can be formulated as follows. Despite its rather resolute resistance, the Church suffered a defeat in the struggle against secular power. The abolition of the Patriarchate and the secularisation of the Church's estates made the Church utterly dependent on and subordinated to the state. The secularisation of the estates belonging to the clergy also had a more general significance for the country's socio-economic development. "The property of the church," wrote Karl Marx, "formed the religious bulwark of the traditional conditions of landed property. With its fall these were no longer tenable."[1] In Russia, secularisation did not lead to a breakdown of the relations of feudal serfdom, but it undoubtedly precipitated the disintegration of feudalism begun a long time before, thereby contributing to the triumph of the new, bourgeois relations. The Church lost its monopoly in the field of culture, becoming more and more a drag on the development of progressive scientific thought, education and art. Its role as an important weapon of the czars in the struggle against popular antifeudal movements was also becoming more apparent.

---

[1] K. Marx. *Capital*, Vol. I, Progress Publishers, Moscow, 1978, p. 676.

*Chapter VI*

# THE ORTHODOX CHURCH IN THE 19TH CENTURY

Right up to the overthrow of the autocracy, the position of the Russian Orthodox Church was mostly determined by the legislative acts passed in the times of Peter I. The most important articles of the *Dukhovnyi reglament* (Ecclesiastical Statute), along with the subsequent legislation complementing it, were codified in the first half of the 19th century in the *Code of the Russian Empire*. The first article of the Code contained a religious substantiation of the czar's power, sealing the age-long alliance between the Orthodox Church and the autocratic state. "The Emperor of All Russia," read the law, "is an autocratic and absolute monarch. God himself ordains that we obey his supreme power not for wrath but also for conscience sake."[1]

Article 40 of the Code declared Orthodoxy the "primary and dominant" faith in Russia, and the next two articles defined the emperor's relation to the Orthodox Church. He was obliged to adhere to the Orthodox faith only, and was declared to be the "supreme protector and custodian of the dogmata of the established Church, the guardian of Orthodoxy and of all order and decorum in the Church". This gave the autocracy the right to run church affairs without any hindrance, including even questions of dogma, and to persecute other confessions.

---

[1] *Svod zakonov Rossiyskoy imperii* (The Code of the Russian Empire), Vol. I, Part I, St. Petersburg, 1842.

Formally, the law permitted profession of other religions in Russia provided they were loyal to the autocracy and gave their blessing to the "reign of the Russian monarchs"; there was even a mention of the "freedom of faith" (Art. 45). What the law did not recognise was the right of individuals to stay outside the confessions.

And then, a footnote to Article 46 contained a reservation concerning the "limits" of religious tolerance and a reference to the Statute on the Prevention and Suppression of Crime.

It was this Statute that factually determined the position of the various confessions in the empire. Christian denominations had advantages over non-Christian ones, and Orthodoxy, over all the others. The law did not prohibit the conversion of persons of non-Christian faiths to Christian ones or of non-Orthodox Christians to Orthodoxy, but abandonment of Orthodoxy, as well as going over from non-Orthodox Christian denominations to non-Christian ones was absolutely forbidden. Apostates were sent to their former ecclesiastical superiors "for admonition and instruction", and in cases of conversion to a non-Christian faith deprived of the rights to their property, which was placed under trusteeship. Persons found guilty of "seducing" people away from the Christian faiths (including Orthodoxy) to non-Christian ones were sentenced to 8 to 10 years' hard labour. "Leading astray" from Orthodoxy to other Christian faiths was punishable by penal servitude from one to one and a half years. Old Believers, termed *raskolniki* (schismatics) in the law, were specially forbidden to "challenge the Orthodox Church or its clergy in any way".[1]

The law imposed on the Church the functions of registry offices and required that Orthodox subjects go to confession and communion regularly, at least once a year. Cases of persistent evasion were to be reported by the clergy to the secular authorities. All these and other privileges of the Orthodox Church created in the

---

[1] Ibid., Vol. XIV, Art. 36, 37, 45; Vol. XV, Art. 184-188.

country a regime of religious serfdom. Lenin wrote that "Russian citizens lived in feudal dependence on the established church."[1]

As an estate, the clergy had a number of privileges. The czar's edicts of 1796 and 1802 exempted the clergy from corporal punishment. The lower-ranking clerics (deacons and sextons) were exempted from corporal punishment much later, in the 1860s, yet even that was a privilege, for peasants were flogged by court decision and without trial as late as the beginning of the 20th century.

The Orthodox hierarchs received a salary from the state. In 1842, the white clergy of some dioceses also began to receive salaries. However, most of the white clergy continued to "earn their living from the altar", the source of their main income being the performance of religious rites (baptism, weddings, etc.) and various collections among the parishioners. Another major source of the clergy's income was church lands.

At the beginning of the 19th century, there were some 27,000 Orthodox churches and 447 cloisters (monasteries and convents) in Russia. We have no precise data on the numbers of the white clergy; the number of monastics was in the neighbourhood of 5,000. The secularisation carried out in the 18th century sharply limited monastic landownership, but later it began to grow again. Emperor Paul's edict of December 18, 1797, allotted 30 *dessiatinas* of land to each monastery. Under Nicholas I, cloisters received forest allotments of 50 to 150 *dessiatinas*. The growth of the monasteries' estates was restricted by legislation: any acquisition of real property (gifts included) by a monastery had to have emperial sanction. These restrictions did not apply to monetary donations. Thousands of pilgrims flocking to cloisters brought them incomes far beyond those of the white (parish) clergy. Another manifestation of the black clergy's privileged position was the fact that it was from their numbers that the Church hierarchs were traditionally recruited.

---

[1] See V. I. Lenin, "Socialism and Religion", *Collected Works*, Vol. 10, Progress Publishers, Moscow, 1978, p. 84.

In the early 19th century the great majority of the Orthodox clergy were ignorant and unenlightened. The rural priest's way of life was hardly different from that of a peasant. Metropolitan Platon (Levshin), who occupied the Moscow see in the late 18th and in the early 19th centuries, noted with regret that he had "found his clergy in bast shoes but did not have the time to make them wear boots and introduce them to drawing-rooms".[1] The Orthodox priest stayed outside the noblemen's drawing-rooms, where French, quite unfamiliar to him, was spoken.

At the beginning of the 19th century, a unified system of theological education did not exist in Russia; various educational establishments were run by diocesan hierarchs. Under Alexander I, theological schools and academies formed a system under centralised control. Later the curricula of educational establishments of the same type were standardised, and identical textbooks were introduced. An active role in the reforms was played by Mikhail Speransky and Archimandrite Yevgeniy (Bolkhovitinov), the well-known historian.[2]

In the first quarter of the 19th century, three theological academies functioned in Russia—those of Kiev (founded in 1701 on the basis of the Kiev Collegium), St. Petersburg (until 1809, the Alexander-Nevsky Academy), and Moscow (until 1814, the Slavonic-Greek-Latin Academy). Later, in 1842, a theological academy was opened in Kazan. That academy was seen as a strong point in the struggle against Islam and an instrument of spreading Orthodoxy among the peoples of the Volga region.

In 1852, some 54,000 students attended four theological academies, 48 seminaries and 300 district and parish schools. There were seven schools for girls

---

[1] S. S. Dmitriev. "Pravoslavnaya tserkov i gosudarstvo v predreformennoy Rossii" (The Orthodox Church and the State in Russia before the Reform). In: *Istoriya SSSR* (A History of the USSR), 1966, No. 4, p. 52.

[2] N. P. Yeroshkin. *Krepostnicheskoye samoderzhaviye i yego politicheskiye instituty (pervaya polovina XIX v.)* [Serfdom-Based Autocracy and Its Political Institutions (The First Half of the 19th Century)], Moscow, 1981, p. 125.

from clerical families. The educational level of the Orthodox clergy gradually rose.

But theological academies did not restrict their activities to the spreading of church learning. They also played a major role in the government's policy of suppressing progressive social and scientific thought. In 1808, ecclesiastical censorship committees were set up at theological academies. During the reaction in Nicholas I's reign, ecclesiastical censors began to interfere actively in secular publishing, a process for which a legal basis was later provided by the Ecclesiastical Censorship Statute of 1828. Ecclesiastical censorship was even harsher than the secular one. In 1840-1841, a third of all the books banned in Russia was stopped from publication by ecclesiastical censors. Their victims included works by the French materialist philosophers of the 18th century, Utopian socialists, and the classics of Russian and world literature.

Administratively, the Church was divided into dioceses, deaneries and parishes. Dioceses were the principle units in local church administration. In 1825, there were 37 Orthodox dioceses in Russia (together with the dioceses of the Georgian Exarchate, added to the Church early in the century). Later some of the larger dioceses were subdivided, and new ones were established on lands added to Russia. In 1861, the number of dioceses rose to 58.

The dioceses were headed by diocesan hierarchs (metropolitans, archbishops or bishops). In some dioceses, the office of vicar-bishop, or deputy of the diocesan hierarch, was instituted. The church hierarchy was closely linked with the upper echelons of the ruling classes and, as a rule, remote not only from the bulk of the believers but also from the rank-and-file clergy. It was not for nothing that diocesan hierarchs were ironically called "spiritual governors" or "spiritual generals".

In the reign of Nicholas I, the government made attempts to curb the hierarchs' abuses of power. In 1841, a new Statute of Ecclesiastical Consistories was introduced. A hierarch had to administer his diocese through a consistory whose members were clergymen elected by the hierarch and approved by the Synod. In actual fact, though, the management of all affairs was concentrated in the hands of the consistory's secretary, a secular official appointed by the Synod on the Chief Procurator's recommendation and entirely subordinated to him.[1] The new order did little to curb the hierarchs' arbitrariness while the introduction of secular officials into local church administration increased bribery.

In the unanimous opinion of Soviet historians, the Synod, the highest body of church administration, virtually became just another ministry in the 19th century. The law said that "in church administration autocratic power acted through the Holy Governing Synod instituded by it".[2] This stressed the derivative character of the highest church administration from autocratic power. The alliance of Church and state formed a long time before and given legal status in the 17th-19th centuries, was not an alliance of equals. Autocracy played the leading role in that alliance, and the Church, a subordinated one. This was also expressed in the fact that the Synod members were appointed by the emperor. The Synod's powers were not great (the granting of pensions, benefits, and bonuses, the hearing of complaints against diocesan superiors, etc.). All decisions on other, more important matters had to be sanctioned by the emperor.[3] In 1822, the Synod's right to appoint diocesan hierarchs was considerably restricted. From then on, the Synod merely nominated three candidates, one of which was appointed by the czar to a vacant see. In actual fact, though, the appointments were made by the synodal Chief Procurator.

The higher hierarchs and the Church as a whole never expressed discontent at the fact that the emperors appropriated the rights of the highest church

---

[1] *Sbornik deistvuyushchikh i rukovodstvennykh tserkovnykh i tserkovnograzhdanskikh postanovleniy po vedomstvu pravoslavnogo veroispovedaniya* (A Collection of Guiding Decisions on Church and Civil Matters Effective in the Orthodox Faith Department), compiled by T. Barsov, Vol. I, St. Petersburg, 1885, pp. 101-139.

[2] *Svod zakonov...*, Vol. I, Part I, Art. 43.

[3] *Sbornik deistvuyushchikh i rukovodstvennykh tserkovnykh i tserkovnograzhdanskikh postanovleniy...*, pp. 7-8.

administration. In a sense, the Orthodox Church became part of the autocratic state mechanism. But a complete merger was not achieved. The Church remained a separate part of the state machine.

The alliance of Church and state was not without its internal contradictions. The higher hierarchs felt the burden of secular officialdom pressing on them. The friction between the Synod and the Chief Procurator practically never ended. In all these conflicts the ecclesiastics invariably appealed to the emperor, seeking direct contacts with him and sending him pleas and petitions. The czar frequently lent a sympathetic ear to these complaints. Thus Emperor Pavel dismissed, on the insistence of the Synod's primary member Metropolitan Amvrosiy (Podobedov) of St. Petersburg, the Chief Procurator of the Synod Prince Khovansky. Senator Dmitry Khvostov, a dull poet specialising in heavy-footed odes, became the new Chief Procurator who was selected out of three candidates nominated by the Synod. Amvrosiy paid little attention to him, and often reported directly on church matters to the czar without consultation with the Procurator, afterwards informing the Synod on the decisions taken.[1] The right of reporting directly to the emperor, lost soon after the enthronement of Alexander I, later remained an unattainable dream for the synodal hierarchs for more than a hundred years. Khvostov's successor Alexander Yakovlev (Alexander Herzen's uncle) could not get on with the members of the Synod and was removed from the office, which he held for nine months, by their efforts. But Prince Alexander Golitsyn, a personal friend of the czar who replaced Yakovlev, held on to the office of chief procurator during many years.

Alexander I's church policy, closely linked with the name of Golitsyn, is a complex and insufficiently studied subject. "Alexander I's special interest for Catholicism, then for mysticism, Protestantism, and for Quakers was a matter of common knowledge...", writes S. S. Dmitriyev. "It is also known, though, that he always found time and money for the Orthodox

---

[1] N. P. Yeroshkin. Op. cit., p. 124.

Church. The variety of Alexander I's interest in religion and cults was, in our opinion, an indication of his search for the best means of implementing his policy, and not of his religious indifference. Orthodoxy and the Russian Orthodox Church were precisely such an instrument, which the czar, despite his flexibility, never lost sight of"[1].

Of course, there can be no question at all of Alexander's religious indifference. (Despite the fact that that emperor had greater religious tolerance than his successors.) There can be no question either of the emperor's desire to "replace" Russian Orthodoxy by some other religion, say, Catholicism, if only in the upper strata of society. No action was taken, either, which might be interpreted with certainty as an intention to prepare the merging of Orthodoxy with one of the Western confessions.

The patronage of Catholicism and the Jesuits at the beginning of Alexander I's reign was partly due to foreign policy considerations. The czar's government widely opened the doors of Russia to all opponents of Napoleonic France, including the Jesuits. After the victory over Napoleon there was no longer any need for the Jesuits. Besides, during the 1812 Patriotic War, many members of the Catholic clergy actively collaborated with the Napoleonic invaders.[2] After the war, Catholicism therefore went out of fashion, and the Jesuits were banished. The war against Napoleonic France coincided with the brief period of "enlightened absolutism". New universities, lyceums, and gymnasiums were opened. The Orthodox clergy, never distinguished for a high level of education, came to be regarded as a bearer of stagnation and ignorance. In the salons of high society, Orthodoxy was slighted as a religion of the common people.

After the defeat of Napoleon, the czarist government saw the fight against the revolutionary movement and the spreading of progressive ideas as its primary task. Religion was the principal ideological weapon in that struggle. However, many political figures of the

---

[1] S. S. Dmitriyev. Op. cit., p. 27.
[2] Ibid., p. 31.

Alexandrine epoch believed that Orthodoxy was not quite suitable for such purposes. There were no mass popular movements in Russia at that time. Revolutionary ideas were mostly spread among educated society, on which the Orthodox Church had but a negligible influence. The government therefore tried to bring Orthodoxy up to the level of the West European religions, to make it more "cultured" and refined. Along with the personal inclinations of Alexander I and Golitsyn, these were the main factors explaining the government's special attention for the Protestants, mystics, Quakers, etc. December 1812 saw the beginning of the functioning in St. Petersburg of the Russian Bible Society, modelled on the British Bible Society. The emperor, many courtiers, and the Church's top hierarchs became members of the new society. Golitsyn was elected its president. Representatives of almost all European religions took part in the sittings of the society.

In pursuance of the same policy, the Ministry for Ecclesiastical Affairs and Public Education was set up in 1817 through a merger of three departments: the Ministry of the Public Education, the Synod and the Chief Office for Interconfessional Affairs. The principal goal of establishing this combined ministry was to impart a religious character to public education. But there was also another objective here—to bring Orthodoxy still closer to the Western religions. This cumbersome and absurd office was also headed by Alexander Golitsyn.

In the meantime, the higher hierarchs resolutely opposed these attempts to europeanise Orthodoxy. The Church opposition was headed by Metropolitan Serafim (Glagolevsky) of St. Petersburg. The all-powerful Alexei Arakcheyev was in alliance with Serafim. After numerous delations, the czar's confidence in Golitsyn was undermined, and in May 1824 the latter retired from his post. Golitsyn's ministry was dissolved.

Despite its inertness, the Orthodox Church began to take part in the struggle against the dissemination of revolutionary ideas, seeing them as a threat both to itself and to autocracy.

In 1823, *Catechism* compiled by Metropolitan Filaret of Moscow (and revised, with additions, by the Synod in 1839) was published; it became an obligatory textbook for many years to come. In accordance with the author's political views, the Fifth Commandment (on respect for parents) was given a broader interpretation, one's superiors being added to father and mother, while the Sixth Commandment ("Thou shalt not kill") was interpreted in a narrower sense, the killing at war and capital punishment being excluded from it.[1]

The Church did the autocracy a great service in the struggle against the Decembrists. On December 14, 1825, Metropolitan Serafim and Metropolitan Yevgeniy (Bolkhovitinov) of Kiev went to the Senate Square, on Nicholas I's instructions, to admonish the insurgents. In the words of the Decembrist Andrei Rosen, the soldiers "did not waver when faced by the metropolitan".[2]

To mete out punishment to the rebels, the Supreme Criminal Court was set up. Traditionally, it included three representatives of the Synod. The clerical members of the court did not sign the death sentence, although they expressed their agreement with it. In accordance with this position, members of the Synod, Metropolitans Serafim and Yevgeniy and Archbishop Avraam made this statement at the conclusion of the court proceedings: "Having heard in the Supreme Criminal Court the investigation of the case of the state criminals Pestel, Ryleyev and other accomplices, who planned regicide and the introduction of republican rule in Russia, and seeing their admission of guilt and absolute exposure, we agree that these state criminals deserve the harshest punishment, and we thus will not reject any sentence whatever it may be; but, inasmuch as we are in Holy orders, we cannot undertake to sign the sentence."[3]

The ecclesiastics role in the reprisals against the Decembrists was not restricted to their participation in

---

[1] N. M. Nikolsky. *Istoriya Russkoy tserkvi* (A History of the Russian Church), p. 232.

[2] M. V. Nechkina. *Dvizheniye dekabristov* (The Decembrist Movement), Vol. 2, Moscow, 1955, pp. 300, 301.

[3] *Dekabristy i tainye obshchestva v Rossii* (The Decembrists and Secret Societies in Russia), Moscow, 1906, p. 75.

the Supreme Criminal Court. Another fact can also be pointed out in this connection: in 1829, the Decembrist F. P. Shakhovskoy spent his last days in the Suzdal Monastery of the Saviour and St. Euphimius.[1]

Nicholas I apparently highly appreciated the services of the Orthodox clergy to autocracy. The re-orientation towards traditional Orthodoxy at the end of Alexander I's reign developed into a stable religious policy under Nicholas I. The history of the Orthodox Church in the dark times of the Nicholas reaction is characterised by the activities of four persons, not counting the emperor himself. Two of these were laymen (N. A. Protasov and S. S. Uvarov), and the other two, clergymen (Serafim and Filaret).

Colonel Protasov of the hussars, an aide-de-camp, took up the post of chief procurator of the Synod in 1836 and occupied it until his death in 1855, earning the title of count and the rank of aide-de-camp-general. In accordance with the general spirit of Nicholas's reign, Protasov surrounded himself with a swarm of secular officials, making the Synod an ordinary bureaucratic department and reducing the collegium of synodal hierarchs to the position of a dumb deliberative body; the "rattle of his hussar sabre inspired awe" not only in the Synod members but also in all the other "princes of the church".[2]

For many years to come, Golitsyn's religious tolerance was completely forgotten. After the 1830-1831 uprising in Poland, the government pursued course of abolishing in Russia of the Uniate (Graeco-Catholic) Church. That Church was established at the end of the 16th century with the aid of Polish feudals and was thrust on the Orthodox (Byelorussian and Ukrainian) population of Rzecz Pospolita, as Poland was then called. Later, the territories inhabited by members of the Uniate Church were incorporated into Russia, but by that time Uniate Christianity had become well-established, and in the 19th century most of the

---

[1] See A. Prugavin. "Dekabrist knyaz F. P. Shakhovskoy v Spaso-Yevfimievskom monastyre" (The Decembrist Prince F. P. Shakhovskoy at the Monastery of the Saviour and St. Euphimius). In: *Russkoye bogatstvo* (Russian Wealth), 1911, No. 1, pp. 55-83.

[2] See S. S. Dmitriyev. Op. cit., p. 39.

rank-and-file believers had no wish to embrace a different faith (tradition, as we know, plays an enormous role in religious matters). Disregarding this fact, the government passed several successive acts "reuniting" the Uniate Church with the Russian one. Orthodox divine services and rites were introduced in Uniate churches, recalcitrant priests were removed, and believers' protests suppressed.[1] However, many Uniate members persisted in their opposition, rejecting Orthodox priests and remaining Orthodox on paper only.

Simultaneously the government, aided by the Church, mounted a large-scale campaign against Old Believers, resorting both to exhortation and to military and police measures. One of the forms of assault on the Old Belief was *Yedinoveriye* (One Belief) established in 1800 according to a plan evolved by Metropolitan Platon of Moscow. Old Believers who accepted the One-Belief compromise retained their rites but were subordinate to the official Church in terms of organisation. In the first quarter of the 19th century there were only a few One-Belief parishes, but later their number grew sharply. Between 1828 and 1855, 164,604 persons embraced the One-Belief denomination—very rarely of their own free will.[2]

Since Old Believers' ecclesiastics were mostly recruited from Orthodox priests, an edict was passed in 1832 forbidding Old Believers to accept runaway priests. At the same time the destruction began of Old Believers' monasteries on the Bolshoy Irgiz River in Saratov Province, where runaway priests went through a period of "correction" before being sent to Old Believers' communities. In 1841, the last of the Irgiz monasteries was closed down. The Old Believers' clergy noticeably began to dwindle.

A church hierarchy of its own soon established itself among Old Believers recognising priesthood. In 1846, Metropolitan Ambrose of Bosnia embraced Old Belief and became the metropolitan of Byelaya Krinitsa (a

---

[1] See *Tserkov v istorii Rossii* (The Church in the History of Russia), pp. 220-221.

[2] V. F. Milovidov. *Staroobryadchestvo v proshlom i nastoyashchem* (Old Belief in the Past and Present), Moscow, 1969, p. 46.

village in Bucovina, then within the confines of Austria). The "Austrian Accord", which had metropolitans, bishops and priests of its own, became, as it were, a second Orthodox Church in Russia. The number of its followers grew despite the fact that the principal organisers of the new Church were soon thrown into monastery dungeons. The number of supporters of the Byelaya Krinitsa hierarchy in Moscow and the Province of Moscow reached 120,000.[1] Thus Protasov's persecution of the Uniate and Old Believers' Churches ran into strong opposition.

The activity of the government and the Orthodox clergy in suppressing various branches of the Orthodox Church and bringing them back into the fold of Orthodoxy was a form of the asserting religious serfdom. This serfdom took on a harsher aspect under Nicholas I because in that period Orthodoxy began to play a greater role in the official ideology of autocracy.

Protasov was a man of practical action. The role of the ideologue was assumed by another servant of the czar, Count Sergei Uvarov, Minister of Education (1833-1849). Indifferent towards religion (according to Solovyov), remote from the Church and even more remote from the people but close to the throne, he became well-known as the author of the "theory of official narodnost, i.e. populism" ("Orthodoxy, autocracy and *narodnost*"). The purport of that demagogic and completely false "theory" was to set the revolutionary spirit of the gentry and intellectuals in opposition to the inertia and passivity which were characteristic of the people's masses in the first decades of the 19th century. Revolutionary ideas were declared to be something extraneous and widespread only among the "spoilt" part of educated society. The peasants' passivity, their patriarchal piety and faith in the czar, explained by their ignorance and down-troddenness, were presented as the people's "primordial" features, their "invariable loyalty" to the throne and profound religiosity.

The link connecting autocracy and the people in Uvarov's formula was the Orthodox Church, entirely

---

[1] Ibid., p. 52.

devoted to autocracy, inert, patriarchal, never renowned for the learning of its clergy but possessing a considerable influence on the more ignorant strata of the people. The times of "enlightened absolutism" had sunk into oblivion, and the sluggishness and ignorance of the Orthodox clergy were now seen as signs of its "affinity with people", Uvarov's formula became part and parcel of the ideological arsenal of the Orthodox Church. The clergy refused to see the falsity of that formula even in the light of the events of 1905, which dealt a crushing blow to the legend of the "czar-loving Orthodox people".

A typical representative of the Orthodox clergy of the first half of the 19th century was Metropolitan Serafim, who did such a great service to the government in the Decembrists' case. Talentless and inactive, he occupied the St. Petersburg see for 22 years, well into his old age, and was, *ex officio,* the leading member of the Synod. Chief Procurator S. D. Nechayev said of Serafim and his associates that "in the Synod chambers they talked more of their ailments than of church affairs, and mostly spent their time chattering". This deadly description reached the ears of the "spiritual lord", and he pressed the resignation of the uncautious Chief Procurator. It was then that Protasov was appointed to that post and took all the affairs in his hands, while all that remained to the synodal hierarchs was talk about their ailments.

The Moscow see was occupied for more than 40 years by Archbishop (since 1826, Metropolitan) Filaret (Drozdov). A gifted and well-educated man, he delivered brilliant sermons and wrote poems on religious topics. In the days of his youth, Filaret was close to Golitsyn and the Masons, he even had the reputation of a liberal. But times changed, and Filaret changed with the times. In the Synod, he could not get along with Protasov. Filaret was removed from the Synod, and when Serafim died, the see of St. Petersburg, in contravention of the custom, did not pass on to the metropolitan of Moscow. It was occupied by Antoniy (Rafalsky), a hierarch of a secondary see. Later, Filaret was passed over a second time: after Antoniy, Metropolitan Nikanor of Warsaw was promoted to the St.

Petersburg (in 1848) see. It was believed at first that Filaret would join the opposition, but he began to work his way forward by flattery. He "distinguished himself" during the 25th anniversary of Nicholas I's reign, winning back the "monarch's grace". In his see, Filaret practised despotic methods of administration. Extremely touchy, he intentionally surrounded himself by talentless people and persecuted talented ones. Gifted Theological Academy teachers were simply martyred there. That hierarch, considered a holy man by many of Moscow's society ladies, took little care of the morals of his clergy, requiring only absolute obedience.

The inert and ever satisfied Serafim and the dry, dogmatic Filaret personified, as it were, two aspects of the mid 19th-century Orthodoxy, when the Church sanctified by its authority the absolutist regime and fought against the revolutionary movement, asserting religious serfdom throughout the country.

\* \* \*

Preparations for the 1861 reform proceeded in the context of acute political struggle. Some of the higher hierarchs of the Orthodox Church were among the vehement champions of serfdom who openly tried to sabotage peasant liberation. Bishop Afanasiy of Kazan stated in a speech before the nobility of his province that "the Church found no reasons to use its influence in the cause of the emancipation of the peasants". Bishop Ignatiy (Bryanchaninov) of Stavropol, whose brother was the governor of the province, expressed much the same views.

The opponents of the reform sought support from Metropolitan Filaret. The Moscow metropolitan was no longer in disfavour, although he still never went beyond the confines of his see. He maintained a lively business correspondence with Chief Procurator Count A. P. Tolstoy, and the young czar heeded his advice. In actual fact Filaret was the primate of the entire Russian Orthodox Church. Metropolitan Isidor of St. Petersburg did not have much authority.

The conservative views of the Moscow metropolitan were widely known. It was no accident that a certain gentleman (whom Filaret preferred not to name) came to Filaret in the autumn or winter of 1858 proposing that Filaret point out to the government "the inconvenience of the measures concerning the peasants". "I said that it was outside my competence," wrote Filaret in a letter to his vicar Antoniy. The metropolitan continued to adhere to this wait-and-see policy until the most decisive moment. The fear of annoying the government and falling into disfavour again kept Filaret from active interference in the debate on the peasant reform. As we shall see, Filaret's attitude towards the reform was, on the whole, unsympathetic.

Most of the Orthodox hierarchy adhered to similar views and tactics. The New Ritualists' Church, wrote Alexander Herzen with indignation, "showed stony indifference to the People's cause, the same disgraceful, criminal callousness with which it had looked for two centuries, from under its *klobuks,* fingering its rosary, at the villainy of the landowners, their violence, fornication and murder ... without finding a single word of indignation or damnation in its empty soul!"[1]

That was the position of the Church as a whole. But some of its clergy spoke out in defence of the reform. In 1858, Bishop Grigoriy of Kaluga stated in his speech at the opening of a Nobles' Assembly that "improving the peasants lot was a cause pleasing unto God". The *Pravoslavnyi sobesednik* (Orthodox Interlocutor), the journal of the Kazan Theological Academy, published the articles "A Word on the Liberation of Peasants" by Archimandrite Ioann (Sokolov), rector of the academy, and "The Voice of the Ancient Russian Church in Defence of the Non-Free Estate" by A. P. Shchapov. The free-thinking tendencies of the Kazan journal roused discontent among the higher hierarchs of the Church. The *Pravoslavnyi sobesednik* was withdrawn from the cognizance of the censorship committee of the Kazan Theological Academy and transferred to that of the Moscow committee.[2]

---

[1] A. I. Herzen. *Sochineniya* (Works), Moscow, 1958, Vol. 15, p. 136.

[2] See Filaret, mitropolit. *Sobraniye mneniy i otzyvov Filareta, mitropolita moskovskogo i kolomenskogo, po uchebnym i tserkovno-gosudarstvennym voprosam* (Metropolitan Filaret. A Collection of the

Despite Filaret's attempts to evade involvement in the peasant reform, he too was eventually carried along by the torrent of the events. Fearing peasant unrest, the government called the Church to its aid. Count Panin, Minister of Justice, stressed in a letter to Chief Procurator Tolstoy in November 1860 that "the primary duty of the clergy was impressing on the peasants the need for further diligent and constant performance of their duties to the czar and the authorities ... and persuading the peasants of the need to fulfil their duties to the landowners". The chief procurator sent in an inquiry on this matter to Filaret, who wrote a long memo, recapitulating the main propositions of Panin's letter. Filaret's statement was included in special instructions published by the Synod and circulated among parish priests.

Early in 1861, projects for a peasant reform assumed the final shape, and the question arose of compiling a manifesto in which abolition of serfdom would be announced and the principal propositions of the reform explained. The first version of the manifesto was rejected as lacking in solemnity and abounding in superfluous detail. With the emperor's permission, Panin turned for help to the Moscow metropolitan renowned for his eloquence. In a letter dated January 31, 1861, the minister asked the metropolitan to make the necessary changes and additions in the draft of the manifesto.

Senator M. I. Tapilsky was sent to Moscow to conduct negotiations with the metropolitan. In trying to talk the hierarch into accepting the commission, the senator used quite a lot of "flattering words", as he later admitted himself, while the metropolitan pleaded the fact that the "subject of the commission" was remote from his ordinary range of occupations. It transpired during the conversation, though, that the secrets of the St. Petersburg offices were well known to the metropolitan. "We know a great deal of this,"

---

Opinions and Statements by Metropolitan Filaret of Moscow and Kolomna on Educational, Church and State Matters), Moscow, 1887, Vol. 5, Part I, p. 38.

stated Filaret, calling the reform a "fragile undertaking".[1]

Having given his consent to carry out the imperial commission, the metropolitan acted quickly enough. Most of the work was done in one day, February 4. On the following day Filaret sent a letter to Panin with explanations of the revised text. Filaret wrote that he "decided not to feel bound" by the draft he had received. Rather than confine himself to certain changes and additions, he rewrote the entire text. "The manifesto must be read to the peasants," explained Filaret. "Their mind is not accustomed to long uninterrupted concentration." At the end of the letter the metropolitan stressed that he had "merely carried out his duty of obedience" and prayed that "shrewd wisdom and straightforward zeal"[2] might be bestowed upon statesmen. That was a flowery hint that the authors of the reform lacked in these qualities.

On the following day, February 6, Filaret discarded circumlocution, deciding, at long last, to state his views on the substance of the matter. "Only men of theoretical progress," he wrote in a new letter to Panin, "greet the planned extensive reform, while many loyal persons await this with puzzlement, foreseeing difficulties." As the letter showed, Filaret recognised but two "reliable" measures, "a declaration of renunciation by the landowners of their right to serfs, and a persistent endeavour to induce both landowners and peasants to conclude a decisive agreement on the land question". Filaret was decidedly against detaching part of the landowners' estates and handing that land over to the peasants as their permanent possession. This, he believed, "would form a basis for the peasants' obstinacy, which they display even without a legitimate basis". On learning of their right to permanent allotment, the peasants would grow even more recalcitrant, and the landowners would find it even more

---

[1] S. P. Melgunov. "Mitropolit Filaret—deyatel krestyanskoy reformy". In: *Velikaya reforma. Russkoye obshchestvo i krestyanskiy vopros v proshlom i nastoyashchem* (Metropolitan Filaret and the Peasant Reform. In: The Great Reform. Russian Society and the Peasant Question in the Past and Present), Moscow, 1911, Vol. 5, p. 161.

[2] Filaret. Op. cit., p. 8.

difficult to conclude agreements with them. At the same time, wrote Filaret, the alienation of part of the landowners' land "without their consent" could adversely affect "their devotion to the government".

The letter was couched in cautious phraseology, but since the author's greatest objections were aroused by the intention to hand land over to the peasants for permanent use, it may be taken that Filaret favoured liberation of the peasants without land, so that they would have to rent the land from the landowners. In actual fact Filaret proposed, to please the landowners, to rob the peasants on an even greater scale than was envisaged in the draft reform. In its present form, Filaret believed, the reform might undermine the landowners' "devotion" to the government and shake the autocracy. That was what the metropolitan of Moscow was afraid of more than anything else.

The rest of the letter was devoted to listing the technical difficulties that might arise in the implementation of the reform. Its writer pointed out to the absence, in a number of cases, of detailed plans and descriptions of estates, and to the enormous amount of work involved in the implementation of the reform, etc.[1] In a word, Filaret tried to intimidate the government, hoping to delay the reform, to make it even more gradual, curtailed and convenient to the serf-owners.

Filaret's belated interference did not have any practical consequences. But the metropolitan had to weather quite a few uneasy days. Intimidating the government, he feared the reform himself. "Lord, save the czar and have mercy on all of us," he wrote on February 16. "At present, they write to me from St. Petersburg of their apprehensions, fearing among other things that the first blow would be dealt to the higher clergy, the monasteries and churches." "The people are awaiting the 19th, but that day will hardly bring what they expect."[2]

On February 19, 1861, the czar signed the laws on the peasant reform, and on March 5 Filaret's version of

---

[1] Ibid., pp. 16-17.
[2] S. P. Melgunov. Op. cit., pp. 162-163.

the manifesto with insignificant amendments, was published. Unaware of who the real author of the manifesto's text was, the contemporaries showed little admiration for its literary merits.

Written in solemn bombastic style, consisting of long sentences whose meaning was hard to grasp by ear even to an educated person, the manifesto was all but incomprehensible to the peasants. Only the mentioning of "free labour" in the concluding phrase were remembered and imprinted on the hearers' minds. But that was precisely where the main falsehood was concealed. "The 'free labour '," wrote Lenin, "for which the manifesto drawn up by a jesuitical priest called upon the peasantry to ask the 'blessing of God' turned out to be nothing more nor less than labour-service and bondage."[1]

Just as the secular and ecclesiastical authorities feared, the peasants in many cases did not believe the manifesto, deciding that the "true" manifesto was concealed from the people by their oppressors. As many as 1,176 peasant disturbances occurred in 1861. The most widely rumoured of these were the uprising in the village of Bezdna, Kazan Province, and the village of Kandeyevka, Penza Province. In suppressing the rebellion in Bezdna, the punitive force killed 91 peasants and wounded 87. The leader of the uprising Anton Petrov (A. P. Sidorov) was executed by a firing squad.

The reprisals in Bezdna gave rise to a profound indignation among the democratically minded sections of society. On April 16, students of Kazan University and the Theological Academy organised a *panikhida* for the murdered peasants. A speech was delivered by A. P. Shchapov, Bachelor of the Theological Academy. According to the governor's report, he said that "Christ's teaching was a democratic one, that He died for freedom just as our toiling brethren were dying now, and that soon the time of Russia's liberation would come". The *panikhida* was said by the students of the academy, priest Yakhontov and hierodeacon

---

[1] V. I. Lenin. "The Workers' Party and the Peasantry", *Collected Works*, Vol. 4, Progress Publishers, Moscow, 1977, p. 421.

Meletiy. During the service, Yakhontov remembered in the prayer "those killed for freedom and love for the Motherland".[1]

Having read the governor's report of Shchapov's speech and of the participation in the *panikhida* of "two monks", Alexander II appended these instructions in his bold hand: "Shchapov to be arrested, the two monks gaoled at the Solovki Monastery." [2]

Shchapov, who was arrested, wrote a letter to the emperor outlining his plan for state reforms. Shchapov's memo was handed over to Filaret, who was irritated by it.

Filaret regarded Shchapov as the main culprit; his speech, in Filaret's view, "contained, on the one hand, an inappropriate and outrageous protest against the actions of the government's organs of justice, and on the other, distortions of Christ's teaching". For these reasons, the metropolitan proposed to remove Shchapov from the academy and to "bring him to his senses at a monastery". In accordance with the imperial orders, Filaret believed it necessary to banish the priest Yakhontov to the Solovki Monastery. As for Hierodeacon Meletiy, Filaret suggested sending him "to a monastery in some close-lying diocese". Besides, the metropolitan suggested the replacement of Rector Ioann and the tightening of discipline at the Kazan Academy.

Yakhontov remained on the Solovki Islands until the autumn of 1863, but Shchapov, despite Filaret's suggestion, was not incarcerated at a monastery. The many months he spent in prison during the investigation were accounted towards his punishment, so he was dismissed from the academy and fined.[3]

The archpastor of Moscow, who lived in the seclusion of his chambers, who saw the people only during solemn services and processions (and that only at a distance), and who valued so highly the favours coming

---

[1] Filaret. Op. cit., p. 98.
[2] Ibid., p. 55.
[3] Ibid., pp. 95-106, 475; Ye. F. Grekulov. *Tserkov, samoderzhavie, narod* (The Church, Autocracy, the People), Moscow, 1969, pp. 39-40.

from St. Petersburg, realised of course that the "democratic element" threatened not only autocracy but also the dominant Church. He therefore openly approved of the harshest punitive actions of czarism. When General Mikhail Muravyov was sent in 1863 to suppress the uprising in Poland, Lithuania and Byelorussia, Filaret gave him an icon of St. Michael the Archangel ("let it precede you with its fiery sword, and let it cover you with a heavenly shield").[1] Later, too, Filaret watched the actions of Muravyov the Hangman with sympathy and approval.

It was no accident that numerous memoranda and other documents, which did not always have a direct bearing in church affairs, were sent to Filaret from St. Petersburg. As we have noted, Filaret was in those years the actual primate of the Russian Orthodox Church. Having begun the struggle against the revolutionary movement in the times of the Decembrists, Filaret continued it in the 1860s. At the same time the example of Shchapov and Yakhontov shows that under the impact of the revolutionary democratic movement in the country, democratically-minded figures began to appear in the 1860s within the Orthodox Church itself. Some churchmen (such as the Archimandrite Ioann mentioned above) gravitated towards liberalism.

The re-emergence of Orthodox clericalism, at first in fairly modest forms, was also connected with Filaret's activities. In 1861, Pyotr Valuyev, Minister for the Interior, raised the question of appointing Orthodox bishops to the State Council. The metropolitan's of Moscow reaction was negative. He believed that, without proper training, bishops could not usefully participate in handling state problems. (Much later, when the clergy were admitted to the State Council, this supposition was largely borne out). Besides, Filaret feared that the State Council, using the presence of bishops in it, as a pretext, would begin to interfere in church affairs and decide on them, instead of the Synod. It was necessary for the "grandees and noble men" themselves to come to the bishop, surrounding the altar together with him and thus "embellishing the

---

[1] Filaret. Op. cit., p. 444.

Church and its feasts". Here, in his native element, Filaret believed, the bishop would be able to exert a much greater influence on state affairs.

Filaret apparently had no particular illusions about the "grandees" flocking to the bishop as at a word of command; he therefore put forward one concrete demand as well—the handing over of primary education to the clergy. In that sphere, which was closer to the clergy, as Filaret thought, they would be able to render an important service in the fight against the spreading "plague of atheism, materialism, and immorality".[1]

On January 18, 1862, an imperial decree was passed leaving the people's schools already established or being set up by the Church under its control, whereas the Ministry of Public Education had to build its own network of primary schools.[2]

This act of the government aroused open displeasure of the Moscow metropolitan, who feared a rapid development of secular primary education. "Russia has lived a thousand years, it has grown and become stronger and expanded, it has considerably advanced and improved—all despite the people's limited literacy; so would it matter much if Russia were to be made literate gradually, in fifty or a hundred years, instead of five or ten?" The population, Filaret held, were not yet ready for universal education. Education therefore had to be introduced gradually. Thus Filaret not only strove for a transfer of primary education into the hands of the clergy—he also rejected the social need for and significance of rapid development of education, favouring gradual introduction of universal literacy among the people over 50 or 100 years.

The fall of serfdom caused a change in "the entire system of the Russian state", and "that change was a step in the transformation of feudal monarchy into a bourgeois monarchy".[3] Filaret, who greatly feared lest bourgeois reforms should affect the Church as well,

---

[1] Filaret. Op. cit., Vol. V, Part I, pp. 174-179.
[2] PSZ-II, Vol. 37, No. 37873.
[3] V. I. Lenin. "Apropos of an Anniversary", *Collected Works*, Vol. 17, Progress Publishers, Moscow, 1974, p. 114.

stressed on many occasions that various "special conferences" and committees consisting of secular officials must not interfere in intra-Church matters, and that the internal order of the Church "must especially be protected against upheavals in this time of upheavals".[1] Filaret's ideal was an immutable Church frozen in the splendour of its ceremonies and relying on the autocratic state and the immobile and semi-literate people. But the people were not immobile. They had thrown off the fetters of serfdom, went to work in factories and plants, learned to read and write, and there were complex social processes taking place in them. That meant that Filaret's ideals were not destined to outlive their creator by many years, and that a severe downfall awaited the Church which ceased to develop.

Filaret failed to delay the abolition of serfdom and the subsequent bourgeois transformations in the state system, but the 1860s reforms, through the efforts of Filaret and his associates, left the Orthodox Church virtually untouched.

In the early 1860s, an "office for the affairs of the Orthodox clergy" was established by an imperial edict; the office was headed by Grand Duke Konstantin, known for his Slavophile views. Intending to "revive" the Orthodox parish of the pre-Petrine times, the office worked out a draft statute on church parish boards of guardians which were to have control of the local clerical-economic affairs and even elect the priest. This last suggestion caused Filaret's protest. He wrote that if an appropriate law were to be passed, it would mean "a restriction of a most important prerogative of diocesan administration".[2]

On Filaret's insistence the relevant propositions were withdrawn from the draft, and the significance of the reform was largely undermined. The statute on church parish boards of guardians was approved on August 2, 1864.[3]

According to the law, the boards, elected from

---

[1] Filaret. Op. cit., Vol. V, Part I, pp. 178, 474.
[2] Ibid., pp. 179, 462-474.
[3] PSZ-II, Vol. 39, Section I, No. 41144.

among the parishioners, were obliged to take care of the well-being of the parish clergy and of the "splendour" of the parish church, to support the parish schools and practise charity. Besides, in some areas the boards saw to it that the parishioners regularly attended church, fought against the survivals of pagan rites among the peasants, and were used by the clergy in the struggle against Old Believers and sectarians.

In 1867, boards of guardians (more than 5,000 of them) were opened in most dioceses, primarily in rural areas. In 1890, there were 13,424 such boards, which collected upwards of two million roubles in donations. By that time, the rate of the growth of the number of boards had dropped considerably. Some of them showed signs of lively activity, others existed on paper only. From some dioceses came satisfactory reports of the state of the boards, in others, the hierarchs disapproved of them. The latter category included several Great Russian dioceses. The hierarch of Astrakhan complained that some boards of guardians "existed merely on paper, and were opened only as a result of persistent demands of the superiors, while others did not function properly and sometimes were even harmful". The "harm" lay in the fact that the boards endeavoured to control the spending of church funds.[1]

In 1868, the Synod explained in a special decree that the boards of guardians had not been set up for "encroaching" on church property.[2] However, conflicts over the expenditure of parish money occurred later, too.

In some places, assemblies of villagers continued to insist on their right to elect members of the parish clergy, petitioning for the removal of certain priests and appointment of candidates nominated by the assemblies. In 1887, a decree was passed forbidding the

---

[1] I. V. Preobrazhensky. *Otechestvennaya tserkov po statisticheskim dannym s 1840-1841 po 1890-1891 gg.* (The Church in Russia from Statistical Data Between 1840-1841 and 1890-1891), St. Petersburg, 1897, pp. 138-142.

[2] *Sbornik deistvuyuschchikh i rukovodstvennykh tserkovnykh i tserkovnograzhdanskikh postanovleniy* (Collection of Guiding Church and Ecclesiastical Civil Decisions), p. 385.

peasants to decide on the removal of priests, to bring complaints against them, or to elect new priests.[1]

The setting up of parish boards of guardians was the only church reform of the 1860s. In 1865, Count Dmitriy Tolstoy was appointed to the post of chief procurator. Indifferent to religion, cruel and arrogant, the new chief procurator, who often mixed up evangelical texts with French proverbs, had no rational programme of action except for the conviction that "any hierarch dreams at heart of becoming a Pope". Under Tolstoy, it looked as if the Synodal Department had gone back to Protasov's times. Soon, Tolstoy became also Minister of Public Education. As P. A. Zayonchkovsky remarked, "during the term of his office, Tolstoy managed to earn the unanimous hatred of all the strata of society".[2]

In 1880, Mikhail Loris-Melikov, then dictator *de facto*, succeeded in removing Tolstoy from both of his offices. That was one of the liberal gestures of the short-lived "dictatorship of the heart". Konstantin Pobedonostsev, senator and professor of civil law, former tutor of the Grand Dukes, became the new chief procurator. The "liberal gesture" meant in effect that one reactionary was replaced by another, more sophisticated, calculating, and "solid" in his reactionary views; not a mere man of practical action but also a theoretician of the reaction.

Pobedonostsev was a confirmed supporter of "pure" autocracy. Only that kind of autocracy, he believed, could oppose the revolution. In his view, the concessions and semi-concessions, reforms and semi-reforms of impractical reformers could only shatter the building of the autocratic state.

Church and state in Russia, in Pobedonostsev's opinion, had to form an indivisible union. Under such an order, the state "rests on the firm foundations of faith", which is to it "indubitable advantage". The break-up of that link would be disastrous for both

---

[1] *Tserkov v istorii Rossii*, p. 235.
[2] P. A. Zayonchkovsky. *Rossiyskoye samoderzhaviye v kontse XIX stoletiya* (Russian Autocracy at the End of the 19th Century), Moscow, 1970, p. 63.

Church and state. A "faithless" state, Pobedonostsev insisted, "is nothing but an unrealisable Utopia, for faithlessness is a direct negation of the state."[1]

If the state protects the "true" Church against its enemies and ensures the material basis of its activity, the Church too, according to Pobedonostsev, had to conform with the existing state order and heed the "opinions of competent persons".

Stating these "opinions" meant complete and unconditional control. That was Pobedonostsev's constant objective. In their private conversations, the synodal hierarchs complained of his despotism and sometimes showed signs of refractoriness. At first, the chief procurator had to resort therefore to a simple subterfuge: in summer time he sent the permanent members of the Synod to their dioceses, summoned especially chosen "extras" and had all the previously blocked decisions passed.[2] However, the need for summer "extras" later disappeared, for the permanent members of the Synod assumed that role, the more so since the principal directions of Pobedonostsev's policy were shared both by the hierarchy and the overwhelming majority of the rank-and-file clergy.

There were two such directions. The first of these had been prompted to the government by Filaret. A great deal had changed since those times, secular education had made progress, *zemskiye* schools had been set up, and clericalisation of primary education was thus a more difficult task now. And yet Pobedonostsev undertook that task.

On June 13, 1884, a Statute on Parish Schools was published.[3] Considerable funds were assigned for the establishment and maintenance of synodal schools. Later, "literacy schools" maintained by rural communities and previously controlled by Zemstvos [district councils.—*Ed.*] were also transferred to the ecclesiastical department.

In 1884, that department controlled slightly over

---

[1] K. P. Pobedonostsev. *Moskovskiy sbornik* (The Moscow Collection), Moscow, 1896, pp. 14, 15, 18.

[2] See P. A. Zayonchkovsky. Op. cit., p. 107.

[3] PSZ-III, Vol. 4, No. 2318.

4,000 primary schools. In the ten years that followed, their number grew manifold, reaching in 1894 the figure 31,835, while the number of pupils rose to about a million. In 1896, the state allotted 3.4 million roubles to parish schools and 1.5 million roubles to primary secular ones. Church authorities showed a tendency towards the ousting out of secular primary schools: in many provinces, the heads of dioceses did all they could to hinder the opening of new *zemskiye* schools.

The Scripture, Church Slavonic, and church singing were the principal subjects at parish schools. Only the most elementary skills in reading, writing and arithmetic were taught.

A great deal of activity in the development of parish schools was strictly for show. Many of the schools reported by diocesan heads as opened existed on paper only. There is no doubt, though, that during the reaction the Church made the first real steps towards the clericalisation of primary education in Russia. And yet it failed to abolish primary secular schools.[1]

In the Pobedonostsev times, the missionary activities of the Church were considerably expanded. A traditional trend in church policy, it temporarily declined when the revolutionary movement was on the rise, and grew stronger in the years of the reaction. The Church mission was divided into internal and external. The latter had as its goal the conversion to Christianity of peoples of other creeds, while the former was aimed at suppression of Old Believers and various sects.

The spreading of Orthodoxy among Moslems and pagans was in the hands of the All-Russia Orthodox Missionary Society founded in Moscow in 1870, which intensified its activity in the years of the reaction. A number of Orthodox brotherhoods were also engaged in missionary activities. The missionaries often turned to the administration, the police and the judicial bodies for help. In the 1880s, the "seducers" and the "seduced" were persecuted in accordance with the

---

[1] See P. A. Zayonchkovsky. Op. cit., pp. 363-365; Ye. F. Grekulov. Op. cit., pp. 45-46; B. B. Veselovsky, *Istoriya zemstva za 40 let* (The History of Zemstvos Over 40 Years), St. Petersburg 1909, Vol. I, p. 493.

harsh laws of the times. The "seducers" often included ecclesiastics of various creeds.[1]

The partial liberalisation of government policy with regard to Old Believers in the 1870s continued for some time under Alexander III as well. The law of May 3, 1883, permitted Old Believers to conduct divine services in the open.[2] In actual fact, though, the law was never implemented. The principal Old Believers' churches in Moscow still stood sealed up. Under pressure from Pobedonostsev and the entire ecclesiastical department the persecution of Old Believers was soon intensified again. Leaders of Old Believers were arrested and exiled, Old Believers' icons, church-plate and vestments were taken away from them and handed over to One-Belief churches.[3]

In 1887, the First All-Russia Missionary Congress was held in Moscow. Militant missionaries went as far as to demand that the children of refractory Old Believers and sectarians be taken away from the parents, and the parents themselves be deprived of citizenship.[4]

In 1900, the czarist government, with Pobedonostsev's direct participation, prepared a new series of measures against Old Believers. It was intended to press Old Believers' ecclesiastics into renouncing their status of persons in holy orders and their right to conduct divine services. Refractory churchmen were to be sent into exile.[5] Only a sharp rise of the revolutionary movement in the early 20th century made the government refrain from the implementation of these measures. The second missionary congress, held in 1891, laid primary stress on the struggle against sectarianism. Administrative measures were needed to put an end to it, emphasised the congress.[6] Reliance on the administration and the police were the distinguishing feature of the Orthodox mission. Without them, it would be helpless.

---

[1] See P. A. Zayonchkovsky. Op. cit., pp. 128-129; Ye. F. Grekulov. Op. cit., pp. 52-58.
[2] PSZ-III, Vol. 3, No. 1545.
[3] See V. F. Milovidov. Op. cit., p. 63.
[4] See *Tserkov v istorii Rossii*, p. 282.
[5] See V. F. Milovidov. Op. cit., p. 63.
[6] See *Tserkov v istorii Rossii*, pp. 282-283.

The rapid development of capitalist relations in the second half of the 19th century affected the Orthodox clergy, too. They willingly used the new sources of income made available under capitalism. Consider this striking example. More than 20 hierarchs came in 1899 to celebrate the jubilee of Metropolitan Ioannikiy of Kiev. After a *moleben*, they gathered in the refectory. According to an eyewitness' account, "not a single fresh idea was expressed, not a single fervent word was said on the position of the Church and the decline of faith", but there were competent "discussions of the rate of railway shares and the best way of investing capital".[1]

Major monasteries became rentiers. The Pererva Monastery of St. Nicholas in Moscow had deposits at the State Bank; it granted loans to the clergy and gained considerable profit in interest.[2] The Moscow clergy used monastery loans to build on church lands tenement houses whose ground floors were taken up by shops and stores. Some priests and deacons secretly practised usury, bought railway shares and bonds, and built summer houses for rent.[3]

The clergy's use of capitalist sources of income was by no means evidence of "embourgeoisement" of the church organisation. It was church property that was involved in capitalist circulation; the profit was spent entirely on consumption, and not for restructuring the Church.

The church organisation and doctrine retained the form they assumed in the times of Nicholas I and Filaret. The Church defended autocracy and landownership, calling on the people to be obedient and relying on the patriarchal peasants.

The revolutionary movement against which the Church had fought since the Decembrists' times was limited, in the clericals' view, to a relatively narrow circle of young people who had read too many foreign books. Increasing the role of religion in the life of society and enhancing the Church's social significance, clericalisation of primary education, rejection of

---

[1] *Tserkovnyi vestnik* (Church Bulletin), 1 June 1906, p. 717.
[2] RO GBL, reg. 250 (N. P. Rozanov), folder 2, file 1, sheets 7, 8.
[3] Ibid., sheets 7, 8, 68, 69.

"foreign influences" in politics, philosophy, morals and ethics were, in the clericals' view, the most reliable methods of combatting the revolutionary movement. That was the common opinion of such widely different figures as Filaret and Pobedonostsev.

The Church largely underestimated the scope of the revolutionary movement in the country, which at the end of the 19th century entered a new, proletarian stage in its history. In those years, the Church did next to nothing to win the masses of the urban population. Although the Church never interrupted its struggle against the revolutionary movement, the main emphasis in its policy of that period was on preserving its dominant position, on suppressing the movements of Old Believers, sectarianism, and other creeds. To achieve these goals, the Church widely used the state machine of autocracy.

The whole of the 19th century was a time of merging of the church and state mechanisms, of the bureaucratisation of the Church. The role of secular officialdom in church affairs grew. At the beginning of the 19th century, the masterful Amvrosiy replaced chief procurators at his will. At the end of the 19th century, Pobedonostsev, just as masterful, replaced Synod members also at his will. However, in contrast to autocracy, which made a step towards bourgeois monarchy, the Church did not take a single step towards bourgeois reformation. The setting up of parish councils of guardians was too timid an experiment (which failed precisely because of its timidity) to be regarded as such a step.

Under capitalism, the Church performs important political, ideological, propagandist and organisational functions, directing its efforts towards protecting the interests of the classes dominating bourgeois society. Striving for a partial smoothing out of the contradictions of bourgeois society, and creating the appearance of "unity" of the rich and the poor on a religious basis, the Church in bourgeois society serves as an instrument of stabilising the existing system. The Orthodox Russian Church, which still adhered to the notions of past centuries, was far from performing such functions. It did not try too hard to smooth out and dampen the social contradictions that were growing more and more acute under capitalism. This led to disappointment in the Church both among the poor, who turned to it in vain for protection, and among the rich, who saw its inability to extinguish the fire of class struggle.

At the end of the 19th century, the Orthodox Church was in a state of crisis and on the threshold of great upheavals. The people began to leave the Church. The peasants' patriarchal piety was giving way to religious indifference and even atheism among progressive workers. A great role in this process was played by the spreading among workers of the ideas of socialism as a result of the propaganda work of the first Marxist circles.

In the countryside, the drifting away from the Church was much more slow to come. But the peasants also began to see that the Church was on the side of their oppressors. An indirect proof of the drifting away of the peasants from the Church was the intense spreading of sectarian doctrines in the post-reform Russian countryside.

We must also take into account, however, the slow rate and complexity of the people's departure from the Church. The objective causes underlaying this departure slowly penetrated to the people's consciousness. Even in the grip of a profound crisis, the Church retained its great attraction. The fact that the people's masses, especially the peasants, were ignorant and down-trodden, played a role here. The historical tradition was still a great force. Orthodoxy was the religion of one's fathers and grandfathers, the Orthodox Church had become a well-established institution. It was not so simple to part company from it. "Tradition," wrote Engels, "is a great retarding force, is the *vis inertiae* of history."[1] That is why the falling away from the Church was not always conscious and mostly took no outward definite form. At the end of the 19th century, the Church still exerted a great influence on the people and was a serious political force.

---

[1] F. Engels. "Socialism: Utopian and Scientific", Karl Marx and Frederick Engels, *Selected Works* in three volumes, Vol. Three, Progress Publishers, Moscow, 1976, p. 113.

*Chapter VII*

# THE ORTHODOX CHURCH IN THE EARLY 20TH CENTURY

In the early 20th century, the Orthodox Church was a numerous and highly ramified organisation. Orthodoxy was the most widespread faith in Russia. In 1897, Orthodox believers numbered 87.3 million, accounting for 69.5 per cent of the empire's population.[1] Of course, the census only registered formal coherence to the religion, ignoring the level of religiosity and rejecting the non-confessional state. There is no doubt, though, that in the early 20th century the Orthodox Church had the greatest mass audience in the country.

In 1905, there were 66 dioceses in Russia (one Russian Orthodox diocese was abroad, in North America), and 48,375 Orthodox churches. The white clergy (including lower-ranking ecclesiastics) numbered 103,437.[2] In some areas, especially rural ones, the church retained its significance as the primary source of information about all the most important events. Governmental manifestoes were read at churches and explained in the official spirit.

There were 267 Orthodox monasteries and widernesses in the country, and 208 convents and communities

---

[1] See: *Raspredeleniye naseleniya imperii po glavnym veroispovedaniyam* (The Distribution of the Empire's Population among the Principal Confessions), St. Petersburg, 1901, pp. 2-3.

[2] See: *Vsepoddaneyshiy otchyot ober-prokurora Sv. Sinoda po vedomstvu pravoslavnogo ispovedaniya za 1905-1907 gody* (A Most Humble Report of the Chief Procurator of the Holy Synod, Orthodox Faith Department, for 1905-1907), St. Petersburg, 1910, p. 7; *Appendices*, pp. 9, 26-29.

of nuns. The black clergy numbered 20,199. Ecclesiastics were trained at four theological academies, 57 seminaries (with 19,348 students), and 184 theological schools for boys. Besides, the Synod ran a network of primary schools for the masses, which included "literacy schools", and parish and teachers' schools. In 1905, there were 25,478 parish schools alone.[1]

The church had considerable typographical and publishing facilities. *Tserkovnye vedomosti* (Church Gazette), the Synod's official organ distributed in all the parishes, appeared in 42 to 46 thousand copies—which was considerable for those times.[2] Religious publications were brought out in mass editions.

The established Church with its numerous and multinational clergy, hierarchy, academies, seminaries and schools appeared to be a well-ordered, unified and strong organisation—but only at first sight. The Orthodox Church was in a state of crisis, its social doctrine and organisation decrepit and archaic.

The cornerstone of the Church's entire social doctrine was the view that the division of society into the rich and the poor was eternal. The Church called on the poor to toil "in the sweat of their brow", while the rich were enjoined not to plume themselves on their riches and to practise charity.

The Church condemned, in principle, those rich people who refused to be charitable. However, much stronger condemnation was reserved for any sort of social protest on the part of the people's masses. According to the Church doctrine, the lower strata of the people had no right to struggle for transforming society or even to protest against violations of the *status quo* by the rich and the powers that be. The plebs was expected to be always passive and to rely on the mediating role of the pastors. The Church limited its activity to preaching patience and submission.

The social doctrine of the Orthodox Church was adapted to relations devoid of dynamism or acuteness

---

[1] *Appendices*, pp. 100, 155, 173, 210.
[2] See *Bibliografiya periodicheskikh izdaniy Rossii. 1901-1916* (A Bibliography of Russia's Periodical Publications. 1901-1916), Leningrad, 1960, Vol. 3, p. 584.

of class conflicts. Retarded social development and adherence to the traditional style was seen by the leading figures of the Church as a source of strength and firmness of countries and peoples.

The patriarchal way of life in villages unaffected by stratification and in small out-of-the-way towns was the social ideal which the Orthodox clergy aspired to support. That ideal also accorded with their political views. Monarchist views were shared by the entire hierarchy and most rank-and-file clergy. During the 1905-1907 revolution, the Synod called upon all Orthodox believers to "rise as a strong, indestructible wall to protect our czar, the Russian land, and its old Christian way of life".[1]

In upholding the patriarchal way of life, the clerics realised, of course, that the "wall" of the old way of life was growing less and less "indestructible". They could not fail to notice the growth of cities with their social contrasts and class conflicts, the stratification of the peasantry, the disintegration of large peasant families, the collapse of the patriarchal way of life, and the people's mounting struggle for their social and political liberation. They saw it all, but they had no inkling of the scope and irreversibility of these processes.

The whole of the social doctrine of Orthodoxy was a reactionary Utopia from beginning to end. Neglect for the "spirit of the present age" became the official Church's main principle. This meant breaking with the present in the name of the past. Perpetuation of czarist autocracy, preservation of the social *status quo* with its inequality and different forms of exploitation, including "patriarchal" ones, with its serf-owning survivals, restoration of survivals of old times in everyday life, in the family, and in the life of society, were the main content of the Orthodox Church's socio-political doctrine in the early 20th century. In preaching that doctrine, the Church joined the most reactionary forces of society.

The church hierarchy came from the black clergy, concentrated mostly at monasteries, where church wealth was accumulated. In 1905, the monasteries

---

[1] A free supplement to *Tserkovnye vedomosti*, 1905, No. 5.

owned 739,777 *dessiatinas* of land in the 50 provinces of European Russia. Some of the monasteries were real latifundia owners. The Solovki Monastery owned 66,000 *dessiatinas* of arable land, the Temnikov Men's Wilderness had 24,000 *dessiatinas*; the St. Alexander Nevskiy Lavra, 13,000; the Trinity-St. Sergiy Lavra, 2,000.[1] Cloisters were also major timber traders, houseowners, and usurers.

In most cloisters, consumption and accumulation were the primary concerns. Their economic structure was much the same as that of landowners' estates, which were going through a slow and drawn-out process of capitalist evolution. Politically, monastics were the most reactionary part of the clergy.

On the whole, the white clergy were not as well provided for as the black. Still, there was a considerable stratum of well-to-do ecclesiastics among the parish clergy as well. In the 50 provinces of European Russia, persons of the ecclesiastical estate owned 337,000 *dessiatinas* of land in 1905.[2] The urban white clergy were the most prosperous. As an illustration we can cite the data on the income of the St. Petersburg clergy. The dean of the Cathedral of the Kazan Icon of the Mother of God had an annual income of 5,700 roubles, that of St. Isaac's Cathedral, 3,300 roubles; the archpriest of the same cathedral, 3,200 roubles; the third priest, the same sum; and the fourth, 2,200 roubles. In all, 368 priests and other ecclesiastics in the St. Petersburg diocese received an income between 1,000 and 2,000 roubles; 201, between 2,000 and 5,000; and three, more than 5,000 roubles.

In terms of income, the white clergy as a whole were in the same bracket as the top bourgeois intellectuals. Suffice it to say that a fully tenured professor received a salary of 3,000 roubles per annum; an assistant

---

[1] See: *Statistika zemlevladeniya 1905 g. Svod dannykh po 50 guberniyam Yevropeiskoy Rossii* (Landownership Statistics for 1905. A Summary of Data on 50 Provinces of European Russia), St. Petersburg, 1907, pp. 132-133; V. F. Zybkovets. *Natsionalizatsiya monastyrskikh imushchestv v Sovetskoy Rossii (1917-1921)* [The Nationalisation of Monastery Property in Soviet Russia (1917-1921)], Moscow, 1975, pp. 113, 120, 132, 178.

[2] See *Statistika zemlevladeniya 1905 g. ...* p. 147.

professor, 1,200 roubles, an average attorney at law earned between two and five thousand roubles,[1] whereas the annual average wage of a St. Petersburg worker in 1904 was 366 roubles.[2] Thus an average priest had an income nearly ten times as great as that of his parishioner.

The virtual merging of the urban clergy and bourgeois intellectuals imposed its imprint on the conduct of the former during the 1905-1907 revolution. Members of the urban clergy took almost no part at all in the democratic movement. Popular among them were the ideas of "renovation" of the Church, ideas that echoed the theories of liberal-bourgeois intellectuals and reflected the desire of some clerical circles to find a way out of the crisis in which the Church found itself.

The rural clergy were not as well provided for as their urban counterparts. The reasons for this were the modest size or complete absence of the salary, the poverty of the peasants and the growing landlessness.

Land was one of the primary sources of the rural clergy's income. In the 50 provinces of European Russia, there were 1,871,858 *dessiatinas* of church land.[3] (Taking into account monastery lands and private estates of the ecclesiastics, the latter controlled some three million *dessiatinas* in these provinces.)

The average size of church land property ranged from 64.8 *dessiatinas* in the St. Petersburg diocese to 37.7 *dessiatinas* in the Georgian Exarchate.[4] Land was divided among the members of the parish clergy in such a way that the bulk of it was owned by the priest. The land was mostly tilled by hired labour or rented

---

[1] See V. R. Leikina-Svirskaya. *Intelligentsiya v Rossii vo vtoroy polovine XIX v.* (The Russian Intelligentsia in the Second Half of the 19th Century), Moscow, 1971, p. 184.

[2] See Yu. I. Kiryanov. *Zhiznennyi uroven rabochykh Rossii (konets XIX-nachalo XX v.),* [The Living Standards of Workers in Russia (The End of the 19th C.—Early 20th C.)], Moscow 1979, p. 108.

[3] *See Statistika zemlevladeniya 1905 g. ...,* pp. 132, 133.

[4] See N. A. Lyubinetsky. *Zemlevladeniye tserkvey i monastyrey v Rossiyskoy imperii* (Landownership of Churches and Monasteries in the Russian Empire), St. Petersburg, 1900, p. 15.

out; sometimes the members of the parish clergy tilled the land themselves.

The lower rural clerics (deacons and sextons)—the poorest stratum of the clergy—were approximately in the same income bracket as the middle peasants; rural priests belonged among the well-to-do peasants. On the whole, rural ecclesiastics were closer to their flock than urban ones. That was why some rural priests became involved in the general peasant movement during the first Russian revolution. It must be noted at the same time that as the countryside increasingly stratified those rural priests whose incomes were close to those of the richer peasants drifted further and further away from the bulk of the parishioners.

Considerable differences in the legal and property status of different rungs of the clergy gave rise to conflicts. The greatest of these conflicts were between the black and the white clergy, between the hierarchs and the rank-and-file priests. Within the white clergy there were contradictions between the priests and the lower clerics. The traditional structure of the Orthodox Church became affected by disintegration processes, which were a manifestation of its crisis under capitalist conditions.

At the same time, certain uniting factors in the Church were still very strong. The entire clergy—white and black, rural and urban—were united by the fact that most of their income depended on the office they held, i.e., on their membership in the church organisation. The Orthodox Russian Church was in a sense part of the state machine of autocracy. That was why the bulk of the clergy were on the side of the autocracy. The alliance with the autocracy concealed to some extent the elements of the crisis in the Church. But, retarding the reformist tendencies, that alliance led to accumulation of these elements rather than to their overcoming.

The network of theological educational establishments was also in a state of deep crisis. In some remote areas the authorities could not find men to priests to fill vacancies, while the seminaries turned out fewer and fewer priests. Graduates of seminaries gravitated towards secular professions. "Religious enthusiasm in the seminaries went out," recalled Metropolitan Evlogiy, "young people preferred the civil service, mining, the industries".[1]

The level of education at parish schools was far below that of secular schools. Even inspectors from the ecclesiastical department admitted that progress in the study of Holy Scripture at parish schools "could be called only satisfactory", while progress in arithmetic was, as before, "not quite satisfactory".[2] Parish schools were obviously below contemporary standards; in particular, they did not meet the demands of the bourgeois relations developing in the country.

The process of the mass drifting away from the Church, begun in the 19th century, continued. On the eve of the first Russian revolution the Church still underestimated the scope of the liberation movement in the country. The ecclesiastics laid the main stress on spreading the ideas of Orthodoxy and autocracy through schools for the people, on persecuting Old Believers and sectarians, and on suppressing various forms of religious heterodoxy. The ecclesiastical authorities persecuted Lev Tolstoy as well. The great Russian writer and thinker was a believer, but his faith had little in common with official Orthodoxy. Tolstoy evolved a religious doctrine of his own; regarding himself as standing outside the established Church. He was critical of the clergy and outraged by the fact that they virtually reduced religion to performance of established rites, ascribing supernatural significance to them, and thus implanting superstition in the people and exploiting them. Tolstoy denounced the autocratic order, police violence, and militarism. Many of Tolstoy's works did a great deal to dispel the people's illusions about the czar.

The established Church and the autocratic state regarded Tolstoy as their common enemy. Publication of many of his works was banned. Demands to "nip the

---

[1] Evlogiy, mitropolit. *Putj moyey zhizni. Vospominaniya mitropolita Yevlogiya, izlozhennye po yego rasskazam T. Manukhinoy* (Metropolitan Yevlogiy. The Path of My Life. Reminiscences of Metropolitan Yevlogiy Written Down by T. Manukhina), Paris, 1947, p. 199.

[2] The State Archives of Tula Province, reg. 31. (The Tula Diocesan Educational Council), case 1, file 1045, sheets 2, 5.

evil in the bud" were heard more and more often among the clergy. As early as 1888, Archbishop Nikanor of Kherson wrote this in a private letter about the intentions of the Orthodox Church's hierarchs: "We are not joking in preparing to solemnly anathematise ... Tolstoy."[1]

At the end of the 1880s, the idea was mooted in the church and government circles of incarcerating Tolstoy in the Suzdal Monastery of the Saviour and St. Ephimius. One of the higher officials told the czar, though, that such a step would only enhance Tolstoy's fame. Since that day, Alexander III kept repeating that he did not want "to add a martyr's halo to Tolstoy's fame".[2] It was then that the idea of excommunication came: while police reprisals against Tolstoy were dangerous, it was necessary at least to stop the spreading of Tolstoy's denunciatory works among the people. After all, this was more important for both the secular and ecclesiastical authorities.

The excommunication was to be accompanied by a noisy campaign of denunciation. The authorities wanted to create an atmosphere in which the common people, religious and superstitious, would be afraid even of touching a book by the outcast writer. On the other hand, excommunication could also be seen as persecution, which would enhance Tolstoy's renown. That was why the authorities vacillated for a long time.

Pobedonostsev firmly insisted on excommunication. "It is awful to think even of Lev Tolstoy," he wrote in a letter in 1896. "He spreads the terrible plague of anarchy and disbelief throughout Russia... Obviously, he is an enemy of the Church, of any government and any civil order. There is a view in the Synod that he must be excommunicated, to avoid any doubts and misunderstandings in the people..."[3]

The year 1899 saw the appearance of Tolstoy's novel *Resurrection* depicting the clergy mechanically performing the rites. Everyone recognised Pobedonostsev as the

---

[1] G. I. Petrov. *Otlucheniye Lva Tolstogo ot tserkvi* (The Excommunication of Tolstoy), Moscow, 1978, p. 22.

[2] Ibid., pp. 21-23.

[3] S. I. Pozoysky. *K istorii otlucheniya Lva Tolstogo ot tserkvi* (On the History of Tolstoy's Excommunication), Moscow, 1979, p. 82.

prototype of Toporov, the high dignitary that figured in the novel. The novel's publication precipitated the Church's reprisals of its author.

On February 11, 1901, the first member of the Synod Metropolitan Antoniy (Vadkovsky) of St. Petersburg wrote to Pobedonostsev: "Everyone in the Synod now agrees about the need to publish in *Tserkovnye vedomosti* a synodal judgement on Count Tolstoy. This should be done as soon as possible. It is desirable to publish a well-edited synodal judgement on Tolstoy in the issue of *Tserkovnye vedomosti* for the coming Saturday, February 17, on the eve of the Week of Orthodoxy". That would not be, the metropolitan added, "condemnation without hearing a justification".[1]

On the first Sunday of Lent (in 1901 it fell on February 18), all heretics and "apostates" were traditionally anathematised in the churches. Since 1869, this had been done in general form rather than name by name. For example, anathema was pronounced on all who rejected the doctrine of the Trinity. Since Tolstoy did not recognise that dogma, the announcement in church on that day of this "well-edited" synodal judgement would show clearly that Tolstoy was also anathematised.

Later Antoniy gained the reputation of a "liberal" alien to "backward ecclesiastical conservatism", as B. V. Titlinov, a well-known writer favouring renovation of the Church, believed.[2] But Antoniy played an active role in the excommunication of Tolstoy. By way of explaining this fact, the synodal official V. M. Skvortsov referred to the St. Petersburg metropolitan's "weak will". Even Pobedonostsev said of him at a moment of vexation (according to Skvortsov): "Anyone who will take our metropolitan in his hands like (a broom) will be the sweeper."[3]

It is hard to accept the opinions of Titlinov and Skvortsov, Antoniy was not a liberal. He was a moderate ecclesiastical conservative, a cautious and

---

[1] G. I. Petrov. Op. cit., pp. 28, 29.

[2] B. V. Titlinov. *Tserkov vo vremya revolyutsii* (The Church During the Revolution), Petrograd, 1924, pp. 8-9.

[3] G. I. Petrov. Op. cit., pp. 31, 32.

clever politician and not at all a blind instrument or toy in someone's hands. On the issue of Tolstoy, Antoniy allied himself with Pobedonostsev.

However, the chief procurator missed the dates suggested by the metropolitan. The reasons for the delay are not yet clear. Skvortsov later recalled that only on February 18 or thereabout was he summoned by Deputy Chief Procurator V. K. Sabler, who instructed him to prepare a report on the system of Tolstoy's religious views.[1] The original text of the synodal decision was written by Pobedonostsev. This text was revised by Metropolitan Antoniy and other members of the Synod, who considered it during their sessions of February 20 and 22.

G. I. Petrov expresses the view that the Synod could not have taken such a responsible step without Nicholas II's knowledge.[2] Indeed, on February 22, Pobedonostsev went to see the czar in the Winter Palace. The conversation lasted about an hour.[3] The chief procurator apparently came there straight from the Synod with a prepared decision.

On February 24, 1901, the synodal decision was published in *Tserkovnye vedomosti*. Apart from Antoniy, it was signed by the metropolitans Vladimir of Moscow and Feognost of Kiev, by Archbishop Ieronim of Kholm and Warsaw, Bishop Iakov of Kishinev, and Bishops Markell and Boris.[4]

As reported by Skvortsov, the amendments made by the members of the Synod were intended to "soften the tone and the content" of the decision to make it look a statement of Tolstoy's defection from the Church rather than an excommunication.[5]

Indeed, there are signs of such an intention in the text of the decision. It says, among other things, that Tolstoy "cut himself off from any communication with the Orthodox Church", and there is a reference to his "defection". But the key sentence states that "the

---

[1] G. I. Petrov. Op. cit., p. 32.//
[2] Ibid., p. 33.//
[3] TsGIA of the USSR, reg. 516, case 2, file 136, sheets 56 (reverse)-57.//
[4] *Tserkovnye vedomosti*, 24 February, 1901, pp. 45-47.//
[5] G. I. Petrov. Op. cit., p. 32.

Church does not regard him as its member, neither can it regard him as such until he repents and re-establishes his communication with it". It was thus a matter of excommunication, after all.

The decision did not expound the content of Tolstoy's religious doctrine. The authors of the decision, concerned only with presenting the doctrine and its author in as ugly light as possible, merely listed the church dogmas and rites rejected by Tolstoy. That was indeed "condemnation without hearing a justification".

The synodal decision was read out from the ambo. Because the date set beforehand was missed, the effect of the announcement was not so great as the clergy had expected. Still, they used the excommunication as a pretext for launching a fierce campaign against Tolstoy. The church press published "denunciations" couched in the most primitive terms. The most vicious attacks on Tolstoy came from the well-known preacher Ioann Sergiyev (Kronshtadtsky), the dean of St. Andrew's Cathedral in Kronstadt.[1] The baiting of Tolstoy by the clerics continued unceasingly for many years.

And yet the secular and ecclesiastical authorities failed to denigrate the great writer or to reduce the attraction of his books. The synodal decision aroused indignation among the progressive public. Tolstoy received countless letters and telegrams with expressions of sympathy.

In April 1901, Lenin's *Iskra* wrote this on the subject of Tolstoy's excommunication and the sending of students to the army: "To both of these crazy escapades by the government ... the proletariat responded with loud expressions of its solidarity with the 'rebellious' students and the excommunicated writer."[2]

\* \* \*

At the beginning of the 20th century, the revolutionary movement in Russia took a fresh step forward. The working people's strikes assumed an unprecedented scope. The uprising at the Obukhov Factory

---

[1] G. I. Petrov. Op. cit., pp. 34, 69.
[2] *Iskra*, December 1900-November 1903, No. 1, Leningrad, 1925, p. 47.

in St. Petersburg, the general strike in the south of Russia and other actions of the proletariat were evidence of its growing strength, political consciousness and revolutionary potential. Under the impact of the working class movement, the peasants showed greater signs of activity.

In 1903, the Bolshevik trend in the Russian social-democratic movement emerged at the Second Congress of the Russian Social-Democratic Labour Party. Standing at the head of the proletarian movement, the Bolshevik Party set itself the objective of rallying the broad masses of the peasants around the proletariat and of overthrowing the autocratic system.

The programmatic principles of a workers' party with regard to religion and Church were worked out in Lenin's writings. "There should be no '*established*' religion or church," Lenin explained. "All religions and all churches should have an equal status in law. The clergy of the various religions should be paid salaries by those who belong to their religions, but the state should not use state money to support any religion whatever, should not grant money to maintain any clergy, Orthodox, schismatic, sectarian or any other."[1]

The party of the working class, Lenin stressed, "must be the ideological leader in the struggle against all attributes of medievalism, including the old official religion and every attempt to refurbish it or make out a new or different case for it, etc."[2] At the same time Lenin rejected the appeals to declare an immediate "war on religion". That would mean that "the religious question ought to be advanced to first place, where it does not belong at all". On the contrary, wrote Lenin, "we do not and should not prohibit proletarians who still retain vestiges of their old prejudices from associating themselves with our Party". "No number of pamphlets and no amount of preaching can enlighten the proletariat, if it is not enlightened by its own

---

[1] V. I. Lenin. "To the Rural Poor", *Collected Works*, Vol. 6, Progress Publishers, Moscow, 1977, p. 402.

[2] V. I. Lenin. "The Attitude of the Workers' Party to Religion", *Collected Works*, Vol. 15, Progress Publishers, Moscow, 1977, p. 411.

struggle against the dark forces of capitalism. Unity in this really revolutionary struggle of the oppressed class for the creation of a paradise on earth is more important to us than unity of proletarian opinion on paradise in heaven."[1]

The party, Lenin pointed out, must direct its struggle in the first place against the social roots of religion. "Does this mean that educational books against religion are harmful or unneccesary?" asked Lenin, and answered that question as follows: "No... It means that Social-Democracy's atheist propaganda must be *subordinated* to its basic task—the development of the class struggle of the exploited *masses* against the exploiters."[2]

Lenin's propositions formed the basis of the Party's programmatic slogans on the question of religion and the Church adopted by the Second Congress. The main slogan among these was separation of the church from the state and of the school from the Church. Besides, the RSDLP programme envisaged confiscation of the property of monasteries and churches and the use of this property as one of the sources of returning to the peasants of redemption money and quit-rent payments.[3]

The impending revolution raised the issue of the overthrow of autocracy. In an attempt to avoid the revolution, the government tried to gain control over the working-class movement. With that aim in view, police-controlled organisations were implanted in the proletarian environment, which conducted religious-monarchist propaganda and endeavoured to restrict the working-class movement to partial economic improvements. Police authorities were actively aided by certain members of the clergy.

Early in 1904, the Association of Russian Factory

---

[1] V. I. Lenin. "Socialism and Religion", *Collected Works*, Vol. 10, pp. 86-87.

[2] V. I. Lenin. "The Attitude of the Workers' Party to Religion", *Collected Works*, Vol. 15, p. 406.

[3] *KPSS v rezolyutsiyakh i resheniyakh syezdov, konferentsiy i Plenumov TsK* (The CPSU in the Resolutions and Decisions of Its Congresses, Conferences and Plenary Sessions of the Central Committee), Vol. 1, Moscow, 1970, pp. 63, 65.

Workers of St. Petersburg was organised by the priest Georgiy Gapon, a police agent. Gapon was not a well-educated man, but he had the gift of the gab and the talent for organisation; he showed interest in the workers' life, which attracted many of them to him.

Beginning with the autumn of 1904, the organisation began to grow quickly. At a time of hardships caused by the Russo-Japanese war and increased exploitation, the workers' discontent had to find an outlet, so Gapon's 10,000-strong organisation became, regardless of the will of its founders, the channel through which that discontent burst out. Late in December 1904, a conflict erupted at the Putilov Plant over the sacking of several workers who were members of the Gapon organisation. On January 3, 1905, workers of the Putilov Plant declared a strike. By January 8, the strike had spread through all the factories of the capital.

There are different opinions as to how the idea of a petition-carrying procession emerged. Two main causes are obvious here: the general impact of the exacerbating revolutionary situation (in particular, the unbearable conditions of the working class, wartime hardships, etc.), and the persisting naive monarchist illusions shared by a considerable section of workers, illusions that were fortified by Gapon's propaganda. "Comrades! You must go to the czar!" said Gapon. "The czar is the truth! You must always go towards the truth!"[1]

The petition which the workers wanted to hand in to the czar was also imbued with naive monarchic sentiments. This strikingly dramatic document expressed the extreme desperation to which the workers were driven by poverty and lack of any rights. At the same time, owing to the spontaneously democratic spirit of the working class and the propaganda of the Social-Democrats, in the first place of the Bolsheviks, the petition included the demands of the social-democratic minimum programme, even the demand for convening a Constituent Assembly. Some of the versions of the petition mentioned separation of the Church from the

---

[1] N. Simbirsky. *Pravda o Gapone i 9-m yanvare* (The Truth about Gapon and the 9th of January), St. Petersburg, 1906, pp. 67-68.

state,[1] others demanded freedom "in religious matters".[2]

The ecclesiastical authorities grew worried over Gapon's activities; on January 7 he was summoned to Metropolitan Antoniy, but ignored the summons.[3] Carried away by the general movement, Gapon became arrogant and got out of the police and ecclesiastical authorities' control. Still, the church authorities tried to interfere in the events, strengthening monarchist propaganda to counterbalance the activities of the Social-Democrats. On January 8 *Tserkovnye vedomosti* published the exhortation of Bishop Makariy of Tomsk "On Preserving the Behests of Old Times". The exhortation sought to prove that the best way to eliminate all troubles was moral self-perfection. "My good Russian man!" appealed the bishop. "Hold fast to the behests of old times, and do not forget the wise dictum that the land in which the foundations are being undermined will collapse. Guard your immutable loyalty to the czar, knowing that God is in heaven, and on earth, the czar anointed by God."[4] The exhortations published by *Tserkovnye vedomosti* were intended as material for sermons. It was assumed that on Sunday, January 9, Makariy's exhortation would be read in the churches of St. Petersburg.

On January 9, the czar's troops opened fire at the workers' peaceful procession. After that bloody lesson, the workers gave up their naive faith in the czar. On that very day, the first barricades were raised and fighting broke out in St. Petersburg. January 9 became the first day of the first Russian revolution.

---

[1] *Revolyutsiya 1905-1907 gg. v Rossii: Dokumenty i materialy: Nachalo pervoy russkoy revolyutsii, yanvar-mart 1905* (The 1905-1907 Revolution in Russia. Documents and Materials. The Beginning of the First Russian Revolution, January-March 1905), Moscow, 1955, p. 30.

[2] N. Simbirsky. Op. cit., p. 73.

[3] S. F. Platonov. "Pravoslavnaya tserkov v borbe s revolyutsionnym dvizheniyem v Rossii (1900-1917)" [The Orthodox Church in the Struggle against the Revolutionary Movement in Russia (1900-1917)]. In: *Yezhegodnik MIRA*, Vol. IV, Moscow-Leningrad, 1960, p. 127.

[4] Additions to *Tserkovnye vedomosti* (Hereafter: *Additions.—Ed.*), January 8, 1905, pp. 51-54.

The scope of the tragedy, the active participation of an ecclesiastic in it, and the religious-monarchist paraphernalia of the procession—all of this compelled the Church to express its attitude to the events. On January 15, the Synod published a message to "the beloved children of the Holy Orthodox Church". On January 9, the message explained, there was "unrest" in the capital, attempts "to regain allegedly violated rights by violence and rebellion". The Synod blamed the "unrest" on "ill-intentioned elements" which had "an unworthy clergyman in their midst". The unrest was caused by "bribery on the part of the enemies of Russia and of all social order" who, it was alleged, had contributed "considerable sums of money". "Our enemies," the synodal hierarchs elaborated on their version of the events, "want to undermine our foundations—the Orthodox faith and the autocratic power of the czar. Russia lives by them, it has grown on them, and without them it will perish." This was followed by appeals to revere the czar and obey the authorities. The message was signed by the Synod members: three metropolitans—Antoniy of St. Petersburg, Vladimir (Bogoyavlensky) of Moscow, and Flavian (Gorodetsky) of Kiev; Archbishop Nikolai of Finland and Bishop Kliment of Vinnitsa.[1] The Church thus declared its unreserved support for the government, joining the ranks of the most reactionary forces. The churchmen went so far in their attempts to justify czarism's bloody action as to put forward an obviously slanderous suggestion of "bribery".

Gapon was resolutely condemned by the ecclesiastical authorities, although previously he enjoyed the patronage of Metropolitan Antoniy.[2] On January 19, 1905, the disgraced priest, who had by that time escaped abroad, was defrocked by the St. Petersburg Ecclesiastical Consistory.

On January 19, Nicholas II received at Tsarskoye Selo a workers' "deputation" organised by the police. That was an attempt to play the recent events over

---

[1] *Tserkovnye vedomosti*, 1905, No. 3 (Supplement).

[2] D. N. Lyubimov. "Gapon i 9 yanvarya" (Gapon and January 9). In: *Voprosy istorii* (Problems of History), 1965, No. 8, p. 125.

again. The czar "graciously" forgave the workers and advised them to go back to "peaceful labour" as soon as possible.¹ On this occasion the Synod issued a Hierarch's Exhortation before the Reading of the Experor's Gracious Words to the Workers, in which the people were enjoined to adhere firmly "to the holy faith and the Orthodox Czar".²

The appeal of the synodal hierarchs found a response among parish priests. The Church continued its propaganda of autocratic monarchist principles, persecuting revolutionaries and progressive intellectuals. The synodal message of January 15, 1905, was a landmark in the expansion of the activities of the clergy aimed directly against the revolutionary movement. The fight against schismatics and sectarians gradually receded into the background. The process, however, was not without internal friction in the bureaucratic apparatus of the Church.

The anxiety and uncertainty experienced by the St. Petersburg clergy after the events of January 9 were expressed at their meetings on January 11, 14 and 21. "The arguments were heated, but the conclusions irresolute," wrote *Tserkovnyi vestnik* in this connection.³ The people at these meetings could only agree as to the "need for strengthening the pastors' activities among the working population of the capital". The idea was expressed that a priest should always be on the staff of every major enterprise.

At the same meetings, a small circle of "young elements" was formed and isolated itself from the rest.⁴ Of the numerous clergy of the capital, only 32 priests became members of the group. N. P. Aksakov, a layman and hereditary Slavophile, played a prominent, if not the leading, role in that group. Reflecting its mood, the priest M. Cheltsov wrote in *Tserkovnyi vestnik* on February 10 that the causes of the "deplorable events" did not rest in the intrigues of England and Japan but in the fact that there was a "great deal of

---

¹ *Additions*, 22 January, 1905, pp. 171-172.
² Free supplement to *Tserkovnye vedomosti*, 1905, No. 5.
³ *Tserkovnyi vestnik*, 12 January, 1906, p. 40.
⁴ Ibid., p. 40.

injustice" with regard to the people. "We do not denounce those that perpetrate the injustice," wrote the priest, "but merely call upon the people to be patient... If this goes on, we shall be left completely alone: part of the flock will go to sectarianism, others, to the socialist parties."[1]

The ruling bureaucracy felt even greater uncertainty and fear in the face of the revolution in that period. Having no clear plan for dealing with the crisis, the government resorted to clumsy manoeuvres, combining the policy of reprisals with the tactics of limited concessions. First of all, the czarist government tried to conclude an armistice with its old enemies—Old Believers, sectarians and followers of other creeds. In January, the Committee of Ministers took measures to release the persons exiled or arrested by the administration for "religious delusions". The heads of the departments on whose initiative the relevant imperial edicts were promulgated in the past now had to request a decree on "amnesty". Among these was the "department of the Orthodox faith". On January 26-28, 1905, the Synod passed a decision according to which six prisoners of the Suzdal Monastery of the Saviour and St. Ephimius and one from the Solovki Monastery were to be freed. Peasant Pyotr Leontyev, arrested for spreading a "false doctrine" directed against "the supreme authority and the Orthodox clergy", spent 33 years on the Solovki Islands[2].

On January 25, 1905, the Committee of Ministers began discussing measures for introducing the principle of religious tolerance. Metropolitan Antoniy was invited to take part in the work of the committee. There was a strong opposition against religious tolerance among the Orthodox clergy. And yet the metropolitan, in keeping with his far-reaching political calculations, did not protest against these measures. In his turn, however, he raised the question of the position of the Orthodox Church. The Committee of

---

[1] *Tserkovnyi vestnik,* 10 February, 1906, pp. 169-171.

[2] *Vsepoddaneishiy otchot ober-prokurora Sv. Sinoda za 1905-1907 gody* (A Most Humble Report of the Chief Procurator of the Holy Synod for the Years 1905-1907), pp. 21-23.

Ministers, having prepared the materials necessary for the tolerance edict, proceeded therefore to the consideration of that question.

During an audience with the czar, Sergei Witte, Chairman of the Committee of Ministers, got the permission to discuss the question of church reforms in the Committee.[1] After that, a special document was presented on behalf of the metropolitan, entitled "Questions of the Desirable Reforms in Our Orthodox Church".[2] The document alleged that, as a result of the planned reforms, Old Believers and sectarians would be in a more advantageous position than the established Church. In this connection the question was raised of revising the status of the Orthodox Church in order "not to deprive it of its authority among the people". This was followed by a number of demands of Orthodox hierarchs formulated as questions.

First of all, the demand was stated for a relaxation of "too vigilant a control exercised by secular authority"; this would permit the Church to make "the Church's restored moral authority an irreplaceable support of the Orthodox state". Then the questions were raised of restoring parishes, of permitting the Church to acquire property freely, and of participation of the higher hierarchs in the work of the State Council and the Committee of Ministers. To draft these reforms, it was suggested to call a "special conference of representatives of the church hierarchy and the laity".

The memorandum compiled under the guidance of the St. Petersburg metropolitan was contradictory. Some of the points (such as the relaxation of state tutelage, restoration of the parishes) indeed seemed to be timid steps towards a bourgeois restructuring of the Church. On the whole, however, the memorandum was dominated by quite different demands, which indicated the desire of the Church to consolidate its position in the framework of the autocratic system and to augment its wealth. Church leaders apparently did not realise the entire extent of the crisis of their organisation,

---

[1] *Krasnyi arkhiv*, 1928, No. 5 (30), p. 111.

[2] *Istoricheskaya perepiska o sudbakh pravoslavnoy tserkvi* (Historical Correspondence on the Fate of the Orthodox Church), Moscow, 1912, pp. 26-31.

while the difficult position in which the autocracy found itself compelled them to speak out. It is also possible that the authors of the memorandum believed that, by moving closer to the throne, the Church would increase its influence not only on the government but also on the people.

The "Questions" apparently failed to satisfy Witte, and the Committee of Ministers received another memorandum sent in on his behalf and entitled "On the Present Condition of the Orthodox Church".

The memorandum discussed the "stagnation in internal church affairs", the decline of parishes, the gap between the parishioners and the clergy, the ecclesiastics' indifference to "the interests of society", and the "narrow bureaucratic character of the activities" of the entire church administration. Witte's special displeasure was aroused by the clergy's unpreparedness "for fighting the intellectual and moral trends in present-day culture unfavourable to the Church". "Our clergy believe in the superiority of our state system over the forms of West European social life," the memorandum noted, "but that belief is merely childlike ... whereas the state needs a conscious, well-considered protection of its interests by the clergy..."

The authors of the memorandum saw their primary task in achieving a real, rather than formal, unity of believers by restoring the parish intended to eliminate the "split" which existed, as the memorandum stated, between the people and the intellectuals. This statement echoed the characteristic illusions of Witte: the people were regarded as the foundation of the regime—a foundation subject to temporary waverings but nevertheless solid enough, whereas intellectuals were seen as the main source of trouble. Rightist politicians, including many clerics, intended to suppress "sedition" by harassing the intellectuals, while Witte wanted to initiate them into the "popular element".

The memorandum raised the question of a general church reform and the convocation of a Local Council of bishops, members of the white clergy and laity. "The Church needs an alliance with the state, the state also needs the support of the Church, the memorandum stressed, "but the terms of the alliance of the two sides must be formulated in such a way as not to weaken the independence of either the church or the state organism."[1]

Witte's plan was not realistic, either. His desire to achieve within parishes a unity of the bourgeoisie and the workers, of the peasantry and the landowners was Utopian, as was the plan for suppressing "sedition" through attracting intellectuals to church parishes. At the same time the convening of a Local Council could hinder the involvement in the revolutionary movement of backward sections of workers and peasants who retained their religious mode of thinking, and could distract them from social and political issues.

Pobedonostsev did not take part in the work of the Committee of Ministers, being ill at the time or, as Witte said, declaring himself ill in order to avoid participating in the discussion of an edict on religious tolerance.[2] However, on reading Antoniy's "Questions" and Witte's memorandum, the chief procurator wrote a countermemorandum entitled "State Secretary Pobedonostsev's Considerations on Desirable Reforms of the State of the Orthodox Church in the Country".

In fact, Pobedonostsev did not mention a single "desirable" reform, describing all proposals of the metropolitan and Witte not only as undesirable but dangerous. "Until now, the unbreakable link between state and Church has been regarded as the mainstay of both state and church," wrote the chief procurator. "The memorandum ... apparently tends to weaken this link under the pretext of the liberation of the Church; the result poses a great threat to church and state."

Pobedonostsev was fairly sceptical about the idea of restoring the parish, pointing out, not without reason, that "we will not be able to go back from this new world to the 16th or the 17th century", and he was just as sceptical about the proposal "to arm the clergy with a knowledge of 'negative cultural trends'".[3]

---

[1] *Historical Correspondence...*, pp. 7-25.

[2] S. Yu. Witte. *Vospominaniya* (Memoirs), Vol. 2, Moscow, 1960, p. 362.

[3] *Historical Correspondence...*, pp. 32-48.

On Pobedonostsev's insistence, the question of church reforms was transferred to the Synod, and Witte was debarred from further participation in this case. However, it was then given a new twist quite unexpected by the chief procurator. On March 16, 19 and 22, the Synod discussed the issue. The discussion resulted in "A Most Humble Report of the Holy Synod on the Reorganisation of the Administration of the Russian Church on the Principle of *Sobornost*". The Synod requested the emperor's permission for the convocation in Moscow, "at a suitable time", of a Local Council of diocesan bishops for the election of a patriarch. Besides, the Council was expected to consider the questions of parishes, acquisition of church property, and participation of hierarchs in the sessions of the State Council and the Committee of Ministers.[1]

Metropolitan Antoniy's "Questions" were apparently used in drafting that programme, but the Synod's report displayed clericalist tendencies even more clearly. Some time before, Filaret had rejected the suggestion that bishops take part in the State Council, but he had insisted on the transfer of people's schools under the control of the clergy, and cautiously advocated convening a Local Council.[2] Now that primary education was largely in the hands of the Church, the hierarchs themselves laid a claim to participation in the higher state bodies. "The Russian Narodniks and liberals," wrote Lenin, "have long been comforting themselves, or rather deceiving themselves, with the 'theory' that in Russia there is no basis for militant clericalism, for a struggle of 'the princes of the Church' with the temporal power, and so forth. Our revolution has dispelled this illusion, as it did a number of other Narodnik and liberal illusions. Clericalism existed in a hidden form, so long as autocracy existed intact and inviolate. The all-powerful police and bureaucracy concealed from the gaze of 'society' and the people the class struggle in general, and the struggle waged by the 'feudalists in cassocks' against the 'base rabble' in

---

[1] TsGIA SSSR, reg. 796 (The Synod Office), case 209, file 2241, sheets 420-421.

[2] *Additions*, 16 June, 1907, p. 956.

particular. But the first breach which the revolutionary proletariat and peasantry made in the feudalist autocratic regime laid bare what had been hidden."[1]

The rumours concerning the preparations for a church reform reached the press. On March 17, *Tserkovnyi vestnik* published the sensation-making "opinion of a group of St. Petersburg clergymen" ("the 32-man group") "On the Need for Changes in Russian Church Administration". "It is necessary, it is absolutely necessary," the authors insisted, "that the Church should regain its entire force of fruitful influence on all sides of human life and the entire power of its voice." The memorandum spoke of the planned reform of diocesan administration in accordance with the *sobornost* principle, of participation of parish churchmen and laity in the election of bishops, of development of parishes and periodic Local Councils under the chairmanship of the patriarch.[2] In its content, the "memorandum of the 32" differed but little from the synodal report. It entirely passed over the question of the composition of the Local Council. There were also familiar clerical echoes in it. Even Witte's memorandum treated the whole issue on a broader and more substantial basis.

The actions of the Synod compelled Pobedonostsev to recover from his illness completely. On March 31, the czar wrote the following on the synodal report, on Pobedonostsev's presentation: "I hold it impossible to carry out this great undertaking in these troubled times... I reserve the right to set this great cause in motion when favourable times come, following the ancient examples of Orthodox emperors..."[3]

The struggle around church reforms largely involved factions within the reactionary governmental camp. At that time the adherents of church renovation were in that camp, too. In raising the issue of the reforms, Witte and the synodal hierarchs endeavoured to increase the Church's influence on the people, and to

---

[1] V. I. Lenin. "Classes and Parties in Their Attitude to Religion and the Church", *Collected Works*, Vol. 15, pp. 416-417.

[2] *Tserkovnyi vestnik*, 17 March, 1905, pp. 321-325.

[3] *Tserkovnye vedomosti*, 2 April, 1905.

consolidate the alliance of church and state. The hierarchs believed that they could achieve this by purely external changes. Witte and some "renovationists" attempted to introduce certain internal changes, to achieve the desired effect by a more active involvement of the white clergy and the laity in church life. The measures suggested by Witte were undoubtedly a step towards bourgeois reformation.

The steps taken by Witte and other "reformers" were prompted in the first place by their fear of the revolution. By pushing the religious question into the foreground, they tried to distract the people from revolutionary struggle. However, in the revolutionary situation of that time their actions merely introduced disorganisation and confusion in the governmental camp. "The irony of history has punished the autocracy in that even friendly social forces, such as clericalism, must organise against it to some extent, thereby breaking down or widening the framework of the bureaucratic police regime."[1]

\* \* \*

In the autumn of 1905 the revolution reached its climax. On the eve of the October All-Russia political strike, the system of the central church administration was in a state of complete collapse. The Synod, its membership almost entirely altered by Pobedonostsev after the March events, was virtually inactive. *Tserkovnye vedomosti* published lists of the "sins" of the Orthodox people ("rejection of all true principles of faith", "failure to obey the superiors", "incomprehensible autonomy", "inauthorised strikes harmful to all") and kept saying about the "righteous wrath of God".[2]

News came from the outlying provinces of mass defections from the Orthodox faith, which began after the religious tolerance edict of April 17, 1905. In all, more than 170,000 former members of the Uniate Church defected from Orthodoxy to Catholicism;

---

[1] V. I. Lenin. "The Third Congress", *Collected Works*, Vol. 8, Progress Publishers, Moscow, 1977, p. 448.

[2] *Additions*, 8 October, 1905, p. 1746.

36,000 forcibly baptised Tatars and Bashkirs reverted to Islam, and some 10,000 embraced Protestantism.[1] Conversions to Old Belief and sectarianism became more frequent.

"Telegrams bring nothing but news of destructive nature," wrote Metropolitan Antoniy in a letter to Pobedonostsev in the autumn of 1905. "It's all going to wrack and ruin. One is gripped by fear. Life is becoming completely incomprehensible."[2] The mood of Pobedonostsev himself was reflected in his correspondence with Witte. The chairman of the Committee of Ministers asked the heads of all the departments to send in information about "all the major events of political nature". Pobedonostsev's reply dated October 18 indicated his total perplexity. The chief procurator wrote that he found it difficult to single out "major events in the entire series of daily major events of political nature in which the general unrest was and is expressed". Pobedonostsev complained about priests "preaching the ideas of socialism and anarchism", seminarians on strike, a group of "agitators and trouble-makers", and a metropolitan who refused to report the names of those priests. Pobedonostsev promised to provide the same kind of information "in the future as well".[3] However, on October 19 he was dismissed from the post which he had occupied for 25 years.[4] Having failed to mobilise the Church to fight the revolution quick enough, Pobedonostsev no longer suited the czarist government. In those days he wrote to Bishop Yevlogiy of Kholm: "The situation has become unbearable... In the Church itself wolves have appeared which do not spare the sheep. The time of darkness and the power of darkness have come, and I am leaving..."[5]

While the Synod was virtually inactive in October 1905, many members of high-ranking and rank-and-file clergy were very active indeed. During the October

---

[1] *A Most Humble Report of the Chief Procurator...*, pp. 29-31.

[2] TsGIA SSSR, reg. 797, case 75, 2nd section, 3rd table, file 461. sheet I.

[3] Ibid., file 439, sheets 6, 7 rev.

[4] See *Tserkovnye vedomosti*, 22 October, 1905, p. 487.

[5] Metropolitan Yevlogiy, *The Path of My Life...*, p. 166.

strike in Moscow, a joint action by the ecclesiastical and secular Black-Hundreders[1] took place. The Union of the Russian People issued an appeal to set up parish "committees of order" to fight "unrest". In some of the parishes the committees were elected, in others protests were voiced by priests. Metropolitan Vladimir and his assistant, Bishop Nikon of Serpukhov, then circulated an "exhortation" round the churches, instructing the priests to read it during the divine service on October 16. The "exhortation" was directed against strikers and revolutionaries, who were called "the scum of the earth". An appeal was made to the parishioners "to rouse themselves, to wake up" and be ready "to die for the Czar and Rus".[2] In effect it was a call for political *pogroms*.

Realising the danger of such calls in the tense political situation of those days, some priests read an abridged version of the "exhortation", others did not read it at all.[3] Seventy-six priests published a statement expressing their "complete lack of solidarity" with the "exhortation" inciting to *pogroms*. However, it was read at some of the churches, and clashes began immediately right in the churches, followed by the *pogroms* throughout the city.[4]

Moscow was not an isolated case. On October 20 a *pogrom* took place in Tomsk. After a *moleben* and speech by Bishop Makariy, a crowd of Black-Hundreders set fire to the theatre, where some 3,000 workingmen gathered for a meeting.[5]

The Black Hundred agitation of Bishop Ghermoghen of Saratov went too far even in the view of the local governor, who delayed by several days the publication of several issues of the newspaper patron-

---

[1] Black-Hundreders—members of the *pogrom*-monarchist organisations, such as the League of the Russian People and "Black Hundreds", armed detachments of declassé elements for struggle against the revolutionary movement in 1905-1907.— *Ed.*

[2] See *Tserkovnyi vestnik*, 27 October, 1905, pp. 1350-1351.

[3] See *Listovki moskovskikh bolshevikov v period pervoy russkoi revolyutsii* (Leaflets of the Moscow Bolsheviks During the First Russian Revolution), Moscow, 1955, p. 317.

[4] *Tserkovnyi vestnik*, 27 October, 1905, p. 1351.

[5] *Yezhegodnik MIRA*, Vol. IV, p. 140.

ised by Ghermoghen".[1] In his reminiscences, Yevlogiy pointed to Ghermoghen's certain "oddities": "He hated intellectuals, and he wished all revolutionaries were hanged."[2]

Rank-and-file priests, too, were engaged in Black-Hundred-type agitation. The role of some clergymen as inciters to *pogroms* was so obvious that in its decision of October 22, the Synod was compelled to express censure of the Moscow "exhortation" without naming its authors.[3] Archbishop Dmitriy of Kherson condemned the Odessa *pogrom* after the event, describing it as yet another manifestation of "unrest" and "disorder".

Thus by no means all the clergy, not even the majority of them, were engaged in *pogrom* agitation, but the political division within the Church became quite obvious. Earlier, the group of "renovationists" was formed, while now the right wing emerged, connected with the Black-Hundred movement.

Despite the help from secular and ecclesiastical Black-Hundreders, the czarist government had to make a number of important concessions under pressure from the revolutionary forces. On October 17 a manifesto was published which contained promises to convoke the legislative Duma and to introduce a regime of civil liberties. On October 28, the Synod published a message on the manifesto. The synodal hierarchs called on the Orthodox "to be worthy of the Czar's grace" and to use the "gift of freedom ... for the peaceful and fruitful feat of free state labour" rather than for engaging in "wilful and seditious rebellion". "Remember, Christian," the hierarchs enjoined, "that the heart of the Czar is in the hand of God, and that the Most High directs him, and that your duty is to obey the Czar not only out of fear but also for conscience's sake."[4] The synodal message not only repeated the ambiguities of the manifesto (in speaking of "liberties", it passed over in silence the question of the constitu-

---

[1] TsGIA SSSR, reg. 797, case 75, 3rd section, 5th table, file 177, sheets 7, 8 rev.
[2] Metropolitan Yevlogiy. Op. cit., p. 198.
[3] *Tserkovnye vedomosti*, 29 October, 1905 p. 499.
[4] Ibid., pp. 489-491.

tion)—it pursued the same goals; extinguishing the revolution, reviving the czarist illusions, and bringing the peasants and workingmen into submission. Later the official organ of the Synod stated that the power of the czar remained autocratic, and that the Church was not going to renounce any of the elements of the Uvarov formula—"Orthodoxy, autocracy and *narodnost*".[1]

In the meantime, the church administration was reorganised. On October 20, Prince A. D. Obolensky, Witte's personal friend and admirer of Vladimir Solovyov's philosophy, was appointed chief procurator. The hierarchs appointed by Pobedonostsev in the spring and summer of 1905 were removed from the Synod, and two representatives of the white clergy introduced: A. A. Zhelobovsky, protopresbyter of the military clergy, and I. L. Yanyshev, protopresbyter of the court department. Their appointment was not just a liberal gesture on the part of the new chief procurator but reflected the growing role of the army and the court in the home policy of czarism.

On November 4 the members of the new Synod were received by Nicholas II. "I firmly hope," said the czar, "that all the clergy, especially rural clergy, will demonstrate sincere and Christian zeal in establishing peace and quiet among their flocks, and in the fulfilment by everyone of his duties..."[2] Thus the church hierarchs were given political instructions by the czar himself. From that moment, the counter-revolutionary activities of individual clericals, numerous though they might have been, gave way to planned activities of the entire church apparatus conducted on a wide scale.

In that period, the strategic directions and the tactics of the Church's fight against the revolution took definite shape. They differed considerably from those practised by the Western Churches. True, in the West, too, the Church largely relied on the support among the most inert sections of the population. Nowhere in Italy were the positions of the clergy as strong as in the agrarian south. But even in those times the Catholic

---

[1] *Additions*, 17 December, 1905, pp. 2232-2238.

[2] Free supplement to *Tserkovnye vedomosti*, 1905, No. 45.

Church tried to bring the proletarian movement under its control directing it along reformist channels. To achieve that goal, the Catholic trade unions were also used.[1]

The Orthodox clergy had little experience in working among the proletarian masses. Many ecclesiastics regarded factory workers as "lost". The strategy of the Orthodox clergy was to attack the revolutionary movement from the rear, gradually separating from it more or less backward sections. Considerable effort was made to remove the peasants from the revolutionary struggle. Towards the end of 1905 the ecclesiastics realised that the agrarian movement had a socio-economic basis. In their sermons they admitted already that the peasants had no or little land and were oppressed by the landowners. And yet the primary cause of the agrarian movement was, according to the clergy, the activities of revolutionary agitators who were termed in the sermons the "seducers of the people", "false teachers", etc.

The preachers endeavoured to capitalise on the peasants' religiosity. "We must believe and profess," taught the Serpukhov missionary F. O. Silin, "that God gave our land the Czar, in whom all power is vested, after the model of His omnipotence; the autocratic Czar, after the model of His own autocracy; the hereditary Czar, after the model of his kingdom that lives everlasting from age to age."[2]

The tactical instrument used in the propaganda against revolution was the coming convocation of the Duma. "Have faith that your needs are close to the Czar's heart..." proclaimed the synodal organ. "Your needs will be paramount in the future State Duma."[3] The clergy tried to inspire hopes for the Duma in the peasants, to persuade them to wait passively. That accorded with the goals of the autocratic government at the time when the revolution reached its climax.

---

[1] N. N. Potashinskaya. *Katolicheskaya tserkov i rabocheye dvizheniye v Italii* (The Catholic Church and the Working-Class Movement in Italy), Moscow, 1979, pp. 63, 64.

[2] RO GBL, reg. 234 (of I. V. Polyansky), folder 7, file 1, sheet 76 rev.

[3] *Additions,* 3 December, 1905, p. 2115.

In the autumn of 1905, the struggle against the revolution became finally established as the principal direction of church policy. That struggle can hardly be described as successful, although the Church undoubtedly contributed to the spreading of hopes for the Duma among the peasants. At the same time the clergy's sermons during the revolution clearly showed that the Church defended the interests of autocracy, and this was a factor in the further fall of the clergy's authority in the eyes of the people.

The revolution continued, urgently compelling the authorities to invent new means and methods of influencing the people in order to distract them from the struggle. The issue of church reforms was again raised in the ruling circles. Chief Procurator Obolensky attributed great significance to the convocation of a Local Council and restoration of the parish.

Not daring to implement these reforms immediately, the church leaders decided to set up parish councils, as a temporary measure. According to the synodal decision of November 18, 1905, these councils, elected by general meeting of parishioners and functioning under the guidance of the priest, were called upon to practise charity and arouse among the parishioners zeal for "the affairs and the issues of faith". The members of parish councils could be invited by the clerics of the parish and the churchwarden to take part in running the economic affairs of the church. It was assumed that church councils would first be introduced where councils of guardians did not exist.[1] The Synod's official organ called the decision of November 18 "a great initiative" which would probably "sober and morally improve our wavering generation".[2]

Great hopes were placed in the convocation of the Local Council. On December 17, Nicholas II received three Orthodox metropolitans (Antoniy of St. Petersburg, Vladimir of Moscow and Flavian of Kiev). The emperor stated that "at the present time, when the shakiness of religious beliefs and moral principles have come to light, the improvement of the order within the

---

[1] *Tserkovnye vedomosti*, 26 November, 1905, pp. 523-525.
[2] *Additions*, 26 November, 1905, pp. 2045-2047.

Orthodox Russian Church ... is a pressing matter". The hierarchs were instructed to prepare for the convocation of the Council "at the earliest possible date". On December 27, a rescript was issued to Metropolitan Antoniy. The three metropolitans were told to set the date of the convocation of the Council.[1]

When Nicholas received the metropolitans, an armed uprising was still in progress in Moscow. The coincidence was not entirely accidental. For autocracy, the Church was still a most important weapon of ideological brainwashing of the people's masses. According to the government's plans, the Council would revive the effect of the church sermon, introduce new methods of preaching and again bring under the control of the Church those strata of the population that had escaped such control. Czarism hoped to enlist the support of the Council and to consolidate its position in the struggle against the revolution.

Despite the acute differences on the question of the Council's composition, all the principal groups of the clergy advocated its convocation. As pointed out earlier, the hierarchs declared in March 1905 in favour of convening a council of bishops. The "renovationists" objected to that. In May 1905, "the group of 32" published a second memorandum to the effect that a council of bishops would not result in greater unity of the clergy and the laity. The bishops had no close links with the "flock", and the latter could disagree with the decisions of the Council. "In order to avoid a very natural and very dangerous split in the Church," the "renovationists" warned, participation in the Council of the white clergy and the laity was necessary.[2]

At the highest point of the revolution, the contradictions between the church conservatives and the "renovationists" were somewhat smoothed out. Both groups were united by a hostile attitude to the revolutionary movement. *Tserkovnyi vestnik,* the "renovationists" unofficial organ, repeatedly stressed that "the direct duty of every Russian was helping the government by all legal means, in its endeavour to

---

[1] *Tserkovnye vedomosti,* 7 January, 1906, pp. 1-2.
[2] *Tserkovnyi vestnik,* 26 May, 1905, pp. 641-648.

restore order and the strength of the law in the troubled country".[1]

In the autumn of 1905 "the group of 32" formed the Union of Zealous Supporters of Church Renovationism. It now comprised 60 persons, both laymen and ecclesiastics.[2] Small circles of "renovationists" existed in Moscow, Kharkov, Yalta and other cities. The renovation movement of 1905 was numerically weak and divided. In the church "liberals'" programme, the search for new organisational forms far outstripped the renovation of the socio-economic and political doctrine.

Late in 1905, under the impact of the revolution, political split among the clergy became more pronounced. Along with the emergence of the Black Hundred wing as a separate group, differentiation began among the "leftist" ecclesiastics. Bishop Antonin (Granovsky) of Narva joined the liberal-constitutional movement, omitting from the formula of remembering the czar the title of "the most autocratic".[3] Some rural priests became involved in the peasant movement.

The cases of police persecution of the clergy were fairly frequent, but there was not always much sense in them. On one occasion a priest was arrested for spreading non-political rumours; on another, a policeman misunderstood a church sermon; on a third, a priest was informed on by his personal enemy, etc.[4]

A few priests went over to the democratic camp at the cost of complete breakaway from the Church's official principles. That was yet another manifestation of its crisis.

Lenin thus evaluated this situation: "Discontent among the clergy, the striving among them after new forms of life, the emergence of clericals as a separate group, the appearance of Christian Socialists and Christian Democrats, the resentment of the 'heterodox', sectarians, etc.—this all serves the purpose of the revolution and creates exceedingly favourable condi-

---

[1] *Tserkovnyi vestnik*, 10 November, 1905, p. 1432.

[2] *Slovo*, 24 November, 1905.

[3] *Yezhegodnik MIRA*, Vol. IV, p. 142.

[4] TsGIA SSSR, reg. 797, case 75, 3rd section, 5th table, file 28, sheets 12-23, 32-33, 51-55, 72-80.

tions for agitation for the complete separation of the Church from the State."[1]

The leaders of the Church primarily looked to administrative measures as a way out of the crisis. Recovering from the confusion caused by the October strike, the Synod launched a campaign of repressions and "purges". On December 20, 1905, a decision was passed on the "Reprehensible Conduct of Certain Priests during Popular Unrest". Pointing out that such cases were infrequent, the Synod enjoined that resolute measures be taken against such persons, including suspension from conducting divine services and the handing them over to the proper authorities for investigation.[2] This decision foreran a wave of repressions that swept through the ecclesiastical department in the period that followed.

It was obvious, however, that the crisis could not be overcome by repressions. It was a general crisis of the established Church under the conditions of capitalism to which neither its obsolete internal organisation nor the reactionary autocratic and patriarchal ideology were adapted.

\* \* \*

In 1906-1907, the struggle against the revolutionary movement featured more prominently than anything else in the activities of the Church. The clergy began to expand their counter-revolutionary propaganda with all the means at their disposal. On September 9, a circular letter of Metropolitan Antoniy to the diocesan hierarchs was published. In the name and on behalf of the Synod the metropolitan called on the hierarchs to hinder in every way the spreading of "pernicious doctrines" inciting to "defection from the Church, rejection of faith, oblivion of Christian love, enmity between the estates and rebellion against the lawful authorities and the state order".[3]

---

[1] V. I. Lenin. "The Third Congress", *Collected Works,* Vol. 8. p. 448.

[2] *Tserkovnye vedomosti,* 7 January, 1906, pp. 6, 7.

[3] Ibid., 9 September, 1906, p. 397, 398.

Earlier, the main form of church propaganda was the sermon from the ambo, whereas now it was supplemented by literature for the masses. *Tserkovnye vedomosti* continued to publish materials directed against the revolutionary movement and intended for use as sermons. Similar materials were published by local "diocesan bulletins". Some of them published leaflets for "popular reading" as supplements.[1] On September 1, 1906, the first issue of the daily *Pochayevskiye izvestiya,* published by the Pochayev Lavra, appeared. Books for "popular reading" were published at the Trinity-St. Sergiy Lavra.[2]

A stream of religious and monarchist literature also came from private publishing houses closely connected with the Church. The Vernost publishers of Moscow produced a whole series of counter-revolutionary low-priced propaganda pamphlets. The leading author here was Archpriest Vostorgov, a well-known reactionary.

In order to distribute this sort of literature more widely, libraries were opened at parish churches. In 1906, 328 such libraries were opened, and in 1907, 336. In all there were 30,323 libraries in 1907 at churches and deaneries (apart from the Georgian Exarchate).[3] The ecclesiastical authorities saw to it that there was nothing "undesirable" on the shelves of those libraries.

Church construction was also largely subordinated to the goals of disseminating monarchist ideology. Each new church became a new centre of preaching and a new strong point in the struggle against the revolution. It was no accident that the building of churches in those years assumed a great scope. In 1905, 508 churches were built; in 1906, 575; and in 1907, 525.[4]

In 1906, church construction in working districts began to expand. Sums deducted from workers' wages and employees' salaries at the Putilov Plant were spent on the construction of a church of Nicholas the Miracle

---

[1] *Additions,* 18 February, 1906, p. 342; 31 March, 1907, pp. 599, 600.

[2] Ibid., 2 June, 1907, p. 889.

[3] *A Most Humble Report of the Chief Procurator...,* pp. 98, 99.

[4] Ibid., pp. 95-98.

Worker and St. Czarina Alexandra—in honour of Nichalas II and his spouse. With the building of that church, the Putilov plant would emerge as a separate parish in its own right, according to the decision of the St. Petersburg Consistory of January 12, 1907.[1]

In Moscow, ecclesiastical propaganda among the proletariat also assumed greater scope. Here it was headed by Metropolitan Vladimir, who addressed workers on numerous occasions. In his lectures the metropolitan intentionally distorted the socialist teaching, attacked the Social-Democrats, and called for the restoration and cultivation of the customs of the peasant patriarchal families of old in the workingmen environment—a structure that was disintegrating at that time even in the village. Asserting that factory owners and officials were "toilers" just as the workingmen, the metropolitan attempted to gloss away the class differences between the exploiters and the exploited. The main content of his exhortations was expressed by Vladimir in the following three points: "(1) everyone must work; (2) every worker must receive his reward; (3) he who has this reward must be content with it".[2] It is easy to see that the third point of that "doctrine" was spearheaded against any action by the workers, even if they were most ruthlessly exploited.

In 1906 and 1907, the Church sharply intensified its antisocialist propaganda. *Tserkovnye vedomosti* regularly published articles directed against the socialist teaching. Similar materials were published in local church periodicals. In 1907, the synodal organ published a detailed review of antisocialist literature, which mentioned more than 20 major works, original and translated ones, published in 1905 and 1906. The author of the review, Professor Bronzov, called for a "vigorous all-out struggle against the socialist bane".[3]

After the failure of Gapon's experiments, the ecclesiastics of St. Petersburg did not give up their attempts to set up workingmen's organisations under their guidance. Gapon had established a unified and

---

[1] TsGIA SSSR, reg. 19, case 97, file 8, sheets 2, 15, 21, 22.
[2] *Additions*, 30 June 1907, p. 1024.
[3] *Ibid.*, 10 February 1907, pp. 277-280.

centralised organisation in the capital, whereas now the Church endeavoured to spread a network of parish "brotherhoods" unconnected directly with one another. The Rules of the first such "brotherhood", that of St. Sampson's Church in the Vyborg district of St. Petersburg, was approved in March 1906. The "brotherhood" held talks "of religious-moral nature", distributed corresponding literature, arranged charity festivals on New Year's Day, and took part in the temperance movement,[1] which camouflaged to some extent its clerical-monarchist propaganda. In November 1906, the Rules of the Gatchina parish fraternity were approved.

In rural areas, the clergy's organisational activities were connected with attempts to establish parish councils in accordance with the synodal decision of November 18, 1905, which met with an active support of many diocesan hierarchs. Particularly active was Bishop Serafim (Chichagov) of Oryol, who was believed to be the author of the idea itself of setting up such councils.[2]

However, some of the rank-and-file clergy, who were closer to the people than the hierarchs, were rather sceptical about the synodal decision. At some assemblies of the clergy in the Kiev diocese the view was expressed that the measures suggested were premature. Objections to the setting up of parish councils were also raised by the clergy of the St. Petersburg and Novgorod dioceses.[3] Parish councils became centres of monarchist propaganda endeavouring to distract the peasants from the struggle for a radical improvement of their position.

At the second stage of the revolution the Church came in close contact with rightist and Black Hundred organisations. Religious Black-Hundreders, along with laymen, spent a great deal of effort to mould the mixed crowd of *pogrom*-makers into Black Hundred

---

[1] TsGIA SSSR, reg. 19, case 98, file 20, sheets 31, 116; case 99, file 3, sheets 5-7.

[2] See A. B. Petrishchev. "Khronika vnutrenney zhizni" (A Chronicle of Internal Life). In: *Russkoye bogatstvo*, 1909, No. 6, p. 66.

[3] *Additions*, 18 March, 1906, p. 586; 7 October 1906, p. 2690.

parties and "leagues". Early in 1906, a Monarchist Party was founded in Saratov with Bishop Ghermoghen's blessing. Also with his blessing, it was transformed into a local League of the Russian People. During the Christmas festivities of 1906, the grateful Black-Hundreders presented to their preceptor a solemn statement of greetings.[1]

The centre of the Black Hundred movement in Volynia became the Pochayev Lavra, where a local department of the League of the Russian People was active. In January 1907, a congress of the Black Hundreders of the entire province was held in Pochayev with the blessing of Antoniy of Volynia.[2]

In other places, too, there were close links between the Black Hundreders and the clergy. On April 6, 1906, the First Monarchist Congress was convened in Moscow by the leaders of the League of the Russian People. Before the congress, Metropolitan Vladimir with three vicar bishops concelebrated a *moleben*. In his speech at the congress Archpriest Vostorgov called for defending autocracy.[3]

The closer contacts between the official church leadership and the ecclesiastical and secular Black-Hundreders was a result of the general shift to the right of the entire hierarchy and the bulk of the rank-and-file clergy.

One of the reasons for this were the Church's own defeats in the struggle against the revolution. The traditional preaching again proved its poor effectiveness. This circumstance increased the desire of the clergy to use more drastic means, furnished by the Black-Hundreders. It was no accident that in some areas diocesan hierarchs distributed Black Hundreds' leaflets and advised the priests to attend the meetings of the League.

The law on elections to the State Duma gave the clergy extensive electoral rights. Before the elections to the Duma the Synod published a special appeal to the

---

[1] *Bratskiy listok* (Fraternal Bulletin) (Saratov), 6 January, 1907.

[2] TsGAOR SSSR, reg. 102 (Police Department), O.O., case 236, 1906, file 13, part 21, sheet 27.

[3] *Slovo*, (The Word), 7 April, 1906.

Orthodox clergy. The clergy, the authors of the appeal stated, must not campaign for any single party. "May all that follows the path of peace, love and order, all that defends the true faith and the Orthodox Czar—may all that be blessed," the Synod expostulated. "All that is against this, all that calls for violence and rebellion rather than follow the path of peace and love, may it be rejected by you in the name of God." The "path of peace and love" as the Synod understood it, meant the cessation of class struggle and the preservation of the social and political *status quo*. The clergy were expected to support monarchist candidates and take an active part in the voting, besides persuading the Orthodox to vote.[1]

The "renovationists" in St. Petersburg also joined the election campaign. In March 1906, the Union of Zealous Supporters of Church Renovationism published a special memorandum, which said: "We must maintain in the people the faith in a better and brighter future, insisting that they choose the path of peace, goodwill agreement, mutual concessions and respect for one another, renouncing all violence". Just as the synodal hierarchs, the "renovationists" called for a cessation of revolutionary struggle. However, while the hierarchs advocated maintaining the *status quo*, the "renovationists" suggested the path of "goodwill agreement". The memorandum attempted even to outline such an agreement in very general terms.

Its authors pointed out that protection of "indigent and oppressed labourers" was the task of the Church. The memorandum spoke of the workingman's right to rest and "certain leisure", to an existence worthy of man. It was stressed in this connection that the "working hours must be regulated without offence, without humiliating constraints for the labourers". In the view of the authors of the memorandum, a concrete solution of that question would be achieved by the social sciences, legislation and practice". On the agrarian question, the authors restricted themselves to vague wishes for providing the peasants with "land and

---

[1] Supplement to No. 7 of *Tserkovnye vedomosti*, 1906.

cultural and educational facilities for an existence worthy of man".

In its programmatic memorandum, the Union of Zealous Supporters of Church Renovationism resolved "not to tie itself down to any particular political party and its programme to an extent that would require joining the ranks of its fighters subject to party discipline".[1] Despite the vagueness and lack of concreteness of the theses outlined here, we can notice that they come fairly close to the programme of the Constitutional Democrats (Cadets).[2]

The clergy took a fairly active part in the elections to the First Duma, but their campaign ended in failure. Only six priests were elected. Three of them were close to the Cadets, the other three, to the Octobrists[3] and the extreme right. The composition and activities of the First Duma gave rise to disappointment and growing discontent among the secular and ecclesiastical bureaucrats. But, since the Duma was a state body, *Tserkovnye vedomosti* refrained from criticising it. The clergy used other periodicals, including *Tserkovnyi vestnik,* for their attacks against the Duma, although that journal was on the whole well-disposed towards it. Archpriest Akvilonov was highly indignant at the "impudent" tone of the speeches of some deputies, and also at the spate of foreign words in the Duma's stenographic reports. Under the pretext of fighting for the purity of the language, the archpriest suggested the elimination of such words as "social revolution", "social-democrat", "agrarian project", "proletariat", "nationalisation", "secularisation", "bureaucrat", "provocation", etc. He also disliked neologisms like "Bolsheviks" and "Mensheviks", "politically conscious workers" and "self-determining nationalities". The archpriest suggested that the deputies take as the model for their speeches

---

[1] *Tserkovnyi vestnik,* 16 March, 1906, pp. 321-331.

[2] The Cadets (The Constitutional-Democratic Party)—the main party of the liberal-monarchist bourgeoisie in Russia in 1905-1917.

[3] The Octobrists (The October 17 Union)—a counter-revolutionary party of big landowners and the commercial and industrial bourgeoisie in Russia in 1905-1917.

the czar's address to the First Duma, which contained none of these words and expressions.[1]

Having no hopes for bringing about the church reforms on their own and disappointed in the chief procurator's "renewal", church liberals attempted to stake on an alliance with the Constitutional Democrats. This appeared all the more tempting as the Constitutional Democrats constituted the most numerous faction in the Duma.

The only difference between the "renovationists" and the Constitutional Democrats was on the issue of church and monastery landownership. The "renovationists" of St. Petersburg were against the handing over of church lands to the peasants even on condition of payment of redemption money. As for monastery landed estates, *Tserkovnyi vestnik* consented to alienation and redemption of that part of land which was rented out.[2]

Late in June and early in July 1906 the conflict between the Duma and the government reached a critical point. On July 9 the Duma was dissolved. That moment marked the beginning of a gradual shift of the "renovationists" away from the Constitutional Democrats to the right. Soon the clergy joined in the new election campaign. Diocesan hierarchs now acted more vigorously than during the elections to the First Duma.

On December 12, the Synod distributed a circular message whose objective was to coordinate the activities of the local ecclesiastical authorities in preparing for the elections. The Synod instructed that no effort should be spared "to elect to the college of electors and later to the Duma the greatest possible number of clergymen enjoying the trust of their brethren and not the trust of the enemies of religion".[3]

Thirteen representatives of the Orthodox clergy were elected to the Second Duma. Four of them were rightists, including Bishop Yevlogiy of Kholm and Bishop Platon of Chigirin. Four priests were close to the liberal parties, among them the well-known

---

[1] *Tserkovnyi vestnik*, 18 May, 1906, pp. 642-643.

[2] Ibid., 1 June, 1906, pp. 701-703.

[3] *Tserkovnye vedomosti*, 16 December, 1906, pp. 530-531.

preacher G. S. Petrov, who was then serving a penance at a monastery. Five priests found seats on leftists' benches. A. V. Arkhipov, A. G. Grinevich, Ye. A. Kolokolnikov and F. V. Tikhvinsky joined the Trudoviks[1] faction. A. Brilliantov was a Socialist-Revolutionary.[2]

The results of the elections made a new conflict between the government and the Duma inevitable. In the spring of 1907 the government launched a series of provocations in a search for a pretext for dissolving the undesirable chamber.

In May, the government published a report on the arrest "of an association within the Socialist-Revolutionaries[3] which set itself the goal of making attempts on the life of the august person, the emperor, and of perpetrating terrorist acts directed against Grand Duke Nikolai and the Chairman of the Council of Ministers".[4] After the publication of the communique about that "terrible" association which was preparing several attempts on the life of the czar at once but failed to get inside the palace even, rightist deputies of the Duma, apparently acting according to a prepared scenario, made an interpellation to the Duma. The plan was to make the Duma condemn the revolutionaries, and in case of a refusal to do so, to use it as a pretext for dissolving the Duma.

The provocative "interpellation" was discussed on May 7; the left-wing factions boycotted the session. The Constitutional Democrats, however, resolved to "save" the Duma at any cost, formed a block with the Black-Hundreders. As a result, the Duma accepted a formula for passing on to the current affairs, in which it stated its "profound indignation at the criminal design that came to light".[5] The Duma gained a short

---

[1] The Trudoviks (the Labour Group)—a petty-bourgeois-democratic faction of peasant deputies and of the Narodniks in the 1st and 4th State Dumas of Russia (1906-1917).

[2] See *Chleny II Gosudarstvennoy Dumy* (Members of the Second State Duma), St. Petersburg, 1907.

[3] The Socialist-Revolutionaries—the biggest petty-bourgeois party in Russia in 1901-1923.

[4] *Tserkovnye vedomosti*, 12 May, 1907, p. 198.

[5] *Additions*, 12 May, 1907, pp. 792-793

respite, but the Constitutional Democrats harmed their own reputation considerably by making a deal with the Black Hundreders.

The church leadership caught at the chance offered by the government's provocation. On May 9, fourteen hierarchs that came to the capital celebrated a *moleben* at the Trinity Cathedral of the Alexander Nevskiy Lavra "on the occasion of the saving of the precious life of the Emperor from the seditious attempt on it". Metropolitan Antoniy made a speech in which he expressed his "unlimited joy" at the timely exposure of the "hellish design".[1]

The provincial clergy also joined in the campaign launched by the Synod. Prayers of thanks were said at churches, and telegrams of greetings were sent to the emperor "on behalf of the parishioners". In the Warsaw diocese alone, such *molebens* were celebrated at two hundred churches. Telegrams were sent on behalf of diocesan congresses of the clergy, church fraternities and societies of church banner bearers.[2]

In this situation the hierarchs decided that it was time to institute proceedings against those clergymen whose presence in the Duma displeased the Synod. The Synodal decision of May 12 blamed democratic priests for "permitting themselves to be conspicuously absent" at the May 7 session, "thereby obviously evading their duty of censuring the designs of regicide". The synodal hierarchs insisted that a clergyman could not belong to parties "striving for the overthrow of the state and social system and even the Czar's power". The Synod instructed the metropolitan of St. Petersburg to summon all the priests elected to the Duma who absented themselves from the May 7 session and demand that they publicly announce their withdrawal from the parties of which they were members. In case of refusal, the synod warned, they would either have to be defrocked or called to account before their diocesan superiors.[3]

---

[1] *Additions*, 12 May, 1907, pp. 777-778.

[2] *Tserkovnye vedomosti*, 16 June, 1907, pp. 266, 267; 30 June, 1907, pp. 275-277.

[3] Ibid., 19 May, 1907, pp. 200, 201.

In view of the fact that the Synod was obviously violating the deputies' rights, the Duma interpollated the Chairman of the Council of Ministers and the chief procurator of the Synod. The actions of the hierarchs were described as "a gross violation of the freedom of opinion of the State Duma's members". According to the law, the interpollation stated, "hindering the performance of duties by a Duma member through threats or abuse of power" was punishable by several months of imprisonment.[1] Thus a conflict arose between the Duma and the Synod.

On May 19, the Synod passed a decision on several Duma members—the priests Grinevich, Brilliantov, Arkhipov, Kolokolnikov, and Tikhvinsky. The first of these stated that he had left the Trudoviks and had been present at the session of May 7, and so no punishment was meted out to him. Brilliantov, Arkhipov, Kolokolnikov and Tikhvinsky were handed over for trial by their diocesan superiors.[2] As expected, the latter defrocked them. The same fate soon fell to the lot of priest G. S. Petrov.[3] The church leadership strove to cleanse the Church from leftist and, partly, even liberal priests, hoping to restore in this way the unity of the church organisation shaken during the revolution.

On June 3, 1907, the government dissolved the Duma and changed the electoral law, thus virtually effecting a *coup d'etat*, as it is generally seen. The Synod, which had only recently illegally persecuted the Duma members, found it easy to approve the czarist government's unlawful action. The synodal decision of June 3, 1907, instructed the manifesto to be read in all churches on Whitsunday, June 10.[4]

The St. Petersburg "renovationists", losing by that time almost entirely their former spirit of opposition, supported the dissolution of the Second Duma. "The Second Duma," wrote *Tserkovnyi vestnik*, "did not

---

[1] *Additions*, 26 May, 1907, p. 835.

[2] *Tserkovnye vedomosti*, 2 June, 1907, pp. 220-221.

[3] A. V. Rumyanov. *Svyashchennik G. S. Petrov, chlen Gosudarstvennoy dumy* (The Priest G. S. Petrov, Deputy of the State Duma). Moscow, 1907, p. 53.

[4] *Tserkovnye vedomosti*, 9 June, 1907, p. 264.

justify the main hope pinned on it—the hope of pacifying the country exhausted by the revolutionary nightmare..."[1] The conclusion may thus be drawn that not only the church leaders but also many members of the rank-and-file clergy were well-disposed to the June 3 coup. That was determined by the Church's general strategy of fighting the revolutionary movement and preserving the alliance with the czarist monarchy.

\* \* \*

On January 14, 1906 the Synod decided to set up a special committee chaired by Metropolitan Antoniy whose task it would be to prepare the Local Council. The membership of the Pre-Council Committee included the chief procurator, a number of hierarchs, clerical professors and Laymen close to the court.[2] The Pre-Council Committee represented all the trends within the Church except for democratic clergymen.

On the eve of the opening of the Pre-Council Committee, the Union of Zealous Supporters of Church Renovationism published its programme. "Everything that does not accord with the principle of *sobornost*," stated the Union, must be eliminated from the Church: the synodal form of administration, dependence on the state, "excessive development of episcopal power", the obligatory connection between monkhood and the bishop's order. The members of the Union believed it necessary to introduce elections to all ecclesiastical offices, from bottom to top, under obligatory supervision of the elections from the top.

The platform of the episcopal "party" was outlined during the work of the Pre-Council Committee. Some members of the Office were politically close to the Black-Hundreders.

What united all the members of the Committee was the desire to use the "spiritual sword" of the Orthodox Church to fight against the continuing revolution. There were differences, though, among the members

---

[1] *Tserkovnyi vestnik*, 7 June, 1907, p. 732.
[2] See *Tserkovnye vedomosti*, 21 January, 1906, pp. 38-39. March 4, 1906, p. 117.

of the Committee as to the methods of achieving their objectives—the struggle against the revolution, reviving religiosity among the people, and strengthening the positions of the Church.

Between March and May the work of the Committee continued in the sections. In that period the Witte cabinet fell. Obolensky resigned. On April 26, Prince A. A. Shirinsky-Shikhmatov, Pobedonostsev's deputy who had been dismissed together with his chief, was appointed chief procurator. Just as Pobedonostsev, the new chief procurator saw no special need to convene a Council.

On May 5, 1906, the question of the Council's composition was raised at a sitting of the Pre-Council Committee. The Committee resolved that members of the white clergy and laity, along with bishops, should participate in the Council. The hierarchs demanded, however, that the bishops be given the deciding vote and the rest, the deliberative one. Members of the Church, declared Metropolitan Antoniy, are divided into "two classes: administrative and the administered, the teachers and the taught, the pastors and the flock". "Opponents of this view adopt the Protestant point of view," stressed the Metropolitan. For his part, Professor Zaozersky described these views as ultramontanist, accusing the metropolitan, in fact, of Catholic tendencies.[1] (In Catholicism, the ultramontanes are adherents of secular papal power, or extreme clericals.)

The hierarchs also demanded that each bishop be given the right to choose the clerics and laymen in his diocese from among elected candidates for participation in the Council. The "renovationists" sharply objected to that, but the majority of the Committee, headed by metropolitans Antoniy and Vladimir, supported the procedure of episcopal approval of clerics and laity.

Summing up the work of the spring session of the Pre-Council Committee, *Tserkovnyi vestnik* wrote that it was mainly concerned with "restoration" of the Church

---

[1] *Zhurnaly i protokoly vysochaishe uchrezhdyonnogo Predsobornogo prisutstviya* (The Journals and Minutes of the Imperially Established Pre-Council Committee), Vol. 2, pp. 432, 511.

in the spirit of the pre-Petrine times rather than with reform.[1]

However, the "renovationists" were not as ardent adherents of church reforms as one might think after reading the materials of the Pre-Council Committee. On April 24, 1906, a petition was submitted to the St. Petersburg consistory for confirming the Rules of the Fraternity of Zealous Supporters of Church Renovationism. Its purpose was legalisation of the Union, and to achieve that the "renovationists" were ready to make substantial concessions. The Rules, just as the previously published programme, stated the need to free the Church "from subordination to the state" and to adhere consistently to the principle of *sobornost,* but the point on "excessive development of episcopal power" disappeared. The fraternity pledged that it would submit to the metropolitan of St. Petersburg all their minutes, resolutions and decisions. By decision of the St. Petersburg diocesan superiors of May 24-31, the Rules were approved "by way of an experiment", which was to last three years. The St. Petersburg "renovationists" thus hid under the wing of the local diocesan authorities, becoming fully dependent on them.

When the revolution began to ebb away, the church hierarchs launched a decisive offensive against the "renovation" movement among the clergy. Even before the Pre-Council Committee began its work Bishop Antoniy of Volynia wrote in his sensation-making memorandum, referring to the secular and ecclesiastical "renovationists", that "even if any hard-labour prison were to be invited to take part in the Council, it would not disgrace our holy faith and rouse God's anger to such an extent as this kind of candidates for the membership of the Local Council".[2]

On November 18-25, 1906, the Synod approved the Rules Determining the Attitude of Church Authorities to Societies and Unions Emerging Within the Orthodox Church and Outside It, and to the Social, Political and Literary Activities of Church Officials. The previously

---

[1] *Tserkovnyi vestnik,* 15 July, 1906, pp. 773, 774.
[2] *Additions,* 11 February, 1906, pp. 268, 269.

approved Rules of the St. Petersburg fraternity were used in the compilation of this document. All church societies and circles were brought under control, of the local bishop, who could dissolve them at any moment. The publication of "church and social organs" also needed the sanction and surveillance of the hierarch. Ecclesiastics, the decision said, could not take part in "anti-state and anti-Church parties". Those who disobeyed the rules were subject to church trial.[1]

Metropolitan Vladimir of Moscow used that decision to launch an attack against the Society of Friends of Church Education, where Moscow "renovationist" forgathered. They were ousted out of the Society's presidium, many of them were subjected to administrative punishment, others lured away from the movement by all kinds of promises. The "migration" of priests from the "liberal" camp to the conservative one were fairly frequent in those days.[2] Towards the end of 1906 the hierarchs succeeded in bringing the "renovationists'" movement under their control.

The autumn session of the Pre-Council Committee (November 1-December 15, 1906) passed "almost unnoticed both in society and in the press", as *Tserkovnyi vestnik* noted,[3] although the session debated the parish issue, which usually aroused considerable interest in bourgeois-liberal circles. This time, though, when the hierarchs strengthened their positions and the "renovationist" movement was on the decline, it did not attract much attention. Even many rank-and-file priests did not follow the proceedings of the Pre-Council Committee closely. As for the bulk of the parishioners, they heard nothing about the Council, and their wishes on the church question did not go beyond confiscation of church lands, state salaries for priests and cancellation of all extortinate church taxes.[4]

The Pre-Council Committee, rejecting the very moderate programme of bourgeois reforms proposed by the "renovationists", failed to work out any new

---

[1] *Tserkovnye vedomosti,* 2 December, 1906, pp. 505-507.
[2] RO GBL, reg. 250, folder 2, file 1, sheets 198, 271.
[3] *Tserkovnyi vestnik,* January 4, 1907, p. 10.
[4] *Additions,* 23 June, 1907, pp. 1000-1004.

formulas for consolidating the church organisation. The victorious "party" of the hierarchs reduced all wishes to strengthening the position of the church top dignitaries in the existing political system and to partial reform of church administration.

The government's policy in relation to the Orthodox Church in 1906 and 1907 was not consistent. Frequent replacement of chief procurators was a contributing factor here. Shirinsky-Shikhmatov, the heir of Pobedonostsev's bankrupt policy, resigned when Pyotr Stolypin became head of government. On July 27, 1906, P. P. Izvolsky was appointed to the post of chief procurator. His term of office lasted longer than the previous two procurators', but his position was not much stronger. Pobedonostsev had been regarded as one of the pillars of the regime, while Izvolsky was a mere official. During his office, the prestige of the chief procurator's authority declined, while the role of the hierarchs grew.

The government acceded to some of the hierarchs' claims. Representatives of the Orthodox clergy—three white clergymen and three black—became members of the reformed State Council. Instead of being elected, the white clergymen were actually appointed by the Synod, while the black clergy's representatives were chosen by diocesan bishops, from their midst.

The conflicts that came to light even in the carefully selected Pre-Council Committee made the government revise its attitude to the question of the Council. A freely elected Council could become a new source of trouble for the government. On the other hand, a Council elected on the hierarchs' instructions, and enjoying no prestige among the people, would hardly be of any use to the government. Restoration of the patriarchate, on which the hierarchs insisted, would undoubtedly hinder the government's control over church affairs, and that consideration did not prompt secular bureaucrats to hasten the convocation of the Council, either. So it was not convened until autocracy fell.

The Church was in a state of deep inner crisis caused by the discrepancy between its obsolete socio-political doctrines and the mood of the broad masses of believers. The principal manifestation of that crisis was the breaking away from the official Church of the broad people's masses, and the anticlerical movement launched during the 1905-1907 revolution.

The tireless propaganda activities of the Bolshevik Party among the proletarians, its denunciation of all the forces of the old regime, the spreading of the ideas of socialism, and the work of explaining the foundations of a scientific worldview made the Russian working-class extremely unreceptive to church preaching. It was precisely the workers, the chief procurator's report stated, who "now constituted the main body of the followers of socialism".[1]

The anti-clerical movement spread in the rural areas as well. The peasants seized church and monastery lands, drove away reactionary priests, and established lower prices for church rites.

The first Russian revolution shook the autocratic regime to its very foundations. It also dealt a heavy blow to the system of religious serfdom. The working masses were throwing off the fetters of the established Church.

\* \* \*

In the period that followed the defeat of the first Russian revolution, the Church continued its struggle against the revolutionary movement and socialist ideas. The stream of low-grade anti-socialist literature never ran dry. The ideas of socialism and materialism were criticised in such books as I. Vostorgov's *Sotsialism pri svete khristianstva* (Socialism in the Light of Christianity), V. Kozhevnikov's *O Feyerbakhe* (On Feuerbach), V. Nesmelov's *Vera i znaniye* (Faith and Knowledge), N. Stelletsky's *Lektsii po pravoslavnomu bogosloviyu* (Lectures of Orthodox Theology), and others. Just as before, church publications were actively engaged in propaganda against democracy and socialism.

The Orthodox clergy encouraged the counter-revolutionary feelings and attitudes that spread among bourgeois intellectuals after the defeat of the revolu-

---

[1] *A Most Humble Report of the Chief Procurator...*, p. 123

tion. An indication of these attitudes and feelings was the miscellanea called *Vekhi* (Landmarks) published in 1909 and calling for consolidation of the autocratic power which "alone protects us, with its bayonets and prisons, against the fury of the people". Bishop Antoniy of Volynia, who always felt free to use the most abusive language about liberal intellectuals, published a letter of greeting to the *Vekhi* authors.

The Church actively supported the government in the new election campaign. Chief Procurator Izvolsky was in lively correspondence with diocesan hierarchs, sounding the mood of the rank-and-file clergy and making sure that not a single "leftist" priest was elected to the Duma.

The electoral law of June 3 actually handed over to the clergy the preliminary electoral conventions of petty landowners. In 71 districts of European Russia the clergy played a decisive role at these conventions, getting their candidates elected to the district electoral meetings. An unprecedented number of deputies from the Orthodox clergy were elected to the Third Duma: two bishops and 46 priests. Reactionary hierarchs now set the fashion among the Duma clergy. Thirty-one clergymen belonged to the rightist and nationalist factions, four priests were right-wing Octobrists, five were Octobrists, six said they belonged to the Progressists,[1] and two called themselves non-party. There were several leftist priests among the Progressists, whose views were close to those of the Trudoviks. However, the experiences of the Second Duma and the fear of divestment kept them from joining that faction.

The overwhelming majority of the Third Duma clergy supported the government's punitive policy, using the Duma rostrum for the propaganda of monarchist ideas.

The Third Duma sanctioned Stolypin's *ukase* on the dissolution of the village commune. The Duma clergy (Bishop Mitrofan, the priests V. F. Golynets and F. I. Nikonovich) also supported that measure. But Stolypin's agrarian reform was not supported by the

---

[1] The Progressists—a "progressive party" of the big bourgeoisie in Russia in 1912-1917.

whole of the clergy. Leftist priests (such as Duma members I. V. Titov and A. A. Popov) were against the plunder of the commune and against robbing the peasants of their lands on a mass scale. The extreme rightists among the clergy also objected to the reform, seeing it as a threat to the patriarchal relations in the countryside and refusing to see their inevitable and irreversible disintegration.

Bishop Ghermoghen of Saratov held approximately the same positions. The rural clergy of his diocese frequently voiced their support for the peasants' complaints about the abuses of Stolypin's land-tenure regulators, and appealed to various offices at the request of village communities. The clergy of Saratov failed to achieve close contacts with the flock, but Ghermoghen's activity was noticed in the ruling circles. Apart from everything else, his demagogy knew no bounds. He interfered in the work of the local administration, and his behaviour vis-á-vis the government was often defiant. For these reasons he was soon deprived of his see and sent to a monastery.

In 1911 and 1912, some village priests tried to organise aid to the famine-stricken peasantry, but they ran into opposition from the police. The authorities only permitted aid under their own control and along established channels.

In their turn, the higher church dignitaries resisted the government's attempts to bring the laws then in force into agreement with the April 17, 1905, manifesto, to regulate the position of various creeds and to achieve a partial solution of the issue of denominations. The government submitted to the Third Duma bills on Old Believers' (Ritualists) communities, on the lifting of some restrictions on the rights of defrocked persons, and on changes in the laws regulating the conversion from one creed to another. These bills were discussed in the Duma in May 1909.

The first of these was a replica of the October 17, 1906, *ukase* issued after the dissolution of the First Duma according to Article 87 of the Fundamental Laws. Now the Statute on Old Believers' Communities needed the sanction of the legislative chambers. In 1909 the position of Stolypin's government was strong enough, so that the clericals in the Duma did not dare to openly oppose the *ukase* that had already been implemented. Their critique was mostly directed against the liberal Duma amendments, one of which recognised the Old Believers' right to conduct religious propaganda. Stressing that in some of Old Believers' communities there were strong socio-political tendencies, the ecclesiastics tried to instill in the Duma the fear that the Old Believers' right to preaching could be used by the Socialist-Revolutionaries and Anarchists.

When the bill was considered by the State Council a year later, in May 1910, Archbishop Arseniy of Pskov, a member of the upper chamber, objected strongest to the Duma amendment that indirectly opened the way to an official recognition of the Belaya Krinitsa hierarchy. The archbishop declared that that would be "an insult to the Orthodox Church". Another member of the State Council representing the clergy, Archpriest D. N. Belikov, also stated that the bill proposed by the Duma "deprived time-honoured Orthodoxy of its position of the established Church standing above the other creeds and denominations".[1]

The reactionary majority of the State Council willingly met halfway the demands of representatives of the established Church. Not only were all the amendments proposed by the Duma struck out—even the government's bill was altered.[2] The putting of the new bill into effect would make the Old Believers' position even worse.

To bring the positions of the two chambers into agreement, a conciliation commission was formed. It presented a report to the Duma which was not considered during the term of the third convocation. Because of this, the *ukase* passed in 1906 under emergency powers remained in force.

The bill "On Changes in the Legislation Pertaining to the Conversion from One Creed to Another" was intended to bring into agreement the April 17, 1905,

---

[1] *Gosudarstvennyi sovet. Stenograficheskiye otchoty: Sessiya 5* (The State Council. Stenographic Records: Session 5). St. Petersburg, 1910, pp. 2852, 2870.

[2] Ibid., pp. 3083-3085, 3113, 3530-3531.

*ukase* on religious tolerance with the legislation then in force. In itself, the bill did not introduce anything new compared to the *ukase* which permitted freedom of conversion from one Christian creed to another but kept the restrictions on the conversion from the Christian creeds to non-Christian ones. The Duma commission lifted these restrictions but refused to give legal recognition to the extraconfessional state.[1] Protesting against the attempts to expand the scope of the April 17 *ukase*, Bishop Yevlogiy of Kholm stated that "this expansion introduces in our legislation the idea of equality, of equal value of Christianity and non-Christianity, in fact, the idea of religious indifference". When the Duma accepted the commission's amendments, Yevlogiy, on behalf of the entire rightist clergy, refused to participate in any further discussion of the bill.[2] On October 30, 1909, the bill was passed by the Duma and submitted to the State Council.[3]

Representatives of the Orthodox clergy in the "upper chamber" launched a vigorous campaign against the bill submitted by the Duma. Archbishops Nikolai and Arseniy, Bishop Nikon, and member of the State Council V. K. Sabler made a separate statement insisting on the bill's rejection.[4]

But the State Council's majority acted differently. Not content with deleting all of the Duma's amendments, it introduced amendments of its own. In particular, the new version of the bill did not provide for conversion from Christian faiths to non-Christian ones. Adoption of the law in this new wording would seriously restrict the 1905 *ukase* on religious tolerance. In November 1911 the bill was returned to the Duma and buried in the Duma commissions, as had previously happened to the bill on Old Believers' communities.

The fate of the bill On the Abolition of Political and

---

[1] *Gosudarstvennaya Duma. Stenograficheskiye otchoty. Sozyv III, Sessiya 2* (The State Duma. Stenographic Records. Third Convocation, Session 2), Part 4, pp. 1745-1749.

[2] Ibid., pp. 1766, 2103.

[3] Ibid., Session 3, Part 1, p. 1024.

[4] *Gosudarstvennyi sovet. Stenograficheskiye otchoty: Sessiya 7* (The State Council. Stenographic Records. Session 7), St. Petersburg, 1912, p. 149.

Civil Restrictions Connected with Divestment or Voluntary Renunciation of Holy Orders and Title was somewhat different. According to the law then in effect, priests renouncing their holy orders had no right to enter state service for 10 years, those divested by court decision also lost that right for 20 years, and, besides, they were forbidden to come to the capitals during seven years. Restrictions on the rights of former monks became tougher still.

Reaching an agreement with the Synod, the government proposed to lift most of these restrictions in the bill submitted for consideration, with one exception: persons who renounced their holy orders or were divested, were prohibited to enter state service in the provinces where they had served in holy orders. The Duma commission proposed to lift that restriction, too. A. P. Rogovich, deputy chief procurator, in a statement in the Duma on May 5, 1909, called for not going beyond the framework of the resolutions agreed upon with the Synod. He was supported by a Duma member, priest F. I. Nikonovich, while another priest, K. N. Dobromyslov, demanded that the bill be rejected. However, despite the opposition of the rightist clergy, the Duma passed the bill in the wording suggested by the commission.

The commission of the State Council took a different view of the bill; in that commission, a prominent role was played by V. K. Sabler, who had held the office of deputy chief procurator for several years in the times of Pobedonostsev. The commission virtually rejected the Duma's bill and proposed one of its own, which did little to improve the position of former priests and monks. However, Sabler failed to win the support of the majority of the "upper chamber". He was opposed by Witte and Obolensky (the former chief procurator), and the State Council passed the Duma bill with insignificant amendments. That was a fairly rare case in the history of the June 3 monarchy. Sabler, who made the report on the bill, was among the nays.[1]

---

[1] *Gosudarstvennyi sovet. Stenograficheskiye otchoty: Sessiya 6* (The State Council. Stenographic Records. Session 6), St. Petersburg, 1911, pp. 674-676.

And yet the bill was not implemented. On May 26, 1911, it was submitted for approval to the czar, who refused to sign it. The influence of the court camarilla and of its creature, the new chief procurator Sabler, undoubtedly played a role here. His appointment was linked in the press with the rumour that the idea of reverting to Pobedonostsev's views was beginning to prevail in the ruling circles.

The Orthodox Church persistently and systematically resisted all plans for asserting the principles of religious tolerance in the country. (Only a very small group of Duma liberal priests supported these plans). Running into an opposition from the clericals and other reactionaries, the government gave up the reforms on religions.

Encouraged by their success, the clericals assumed the offensive and renewed an active struggle against the secular school, hindering the development of public education and fighting for control of it. In 1911, differences arose between the Duma and the State Council in connection with the bill on the introduction of universal primary education. A conciliation commission failed to reach a definite agreement, working out instead two different bills (one for the majority and one for the minority).

The first version envisaged the growing role of the Synod in public education, handing over to it a tenth of all the funds provided for by the bill. According to the second version, the funds were only assigned by the Ministry of Public Education and only for schools incorporated in the educational network by the decision of Zemstvos and of educational councils. The ecclesiastical department now had to coordinate its activity with representatives of secular schools or else lose the funds provided for by the bill. Believing that the State Council would not dare to kill such an important bill, the Duma accepted the minority's version.

Returned from the Duma, the bill was received in a very hostile manner especially by representatives of the Orthodox clergy. In June 1912 it was rejected by the State Council.

Fighting against real and imaginary attempts to affect the dominant position of the Orthodox Church, its clergy realised on the whole that the Church was going through a crisis, that the people were turning away from it. Attempts were continued to achieve closer contacts with the flock, to revive church propaganda. Despite the defeat of the revolution, these attempts were as unsuccessful as before.

Acute differences arose between the hierarchs on the issue of parish councils. As newspapers reported, Bishop Serafim of Kishinev (formerly of Oryol) continued to defend that undertaking, while Bishop Antoniy of Volynia insisted that parish councils would make the priest a "public clerk", that they would "impose requests on him and hold him accountable", that they would "bait him like an animal". The archbishop of Volynia called for an immediate end to experiments with parish councils.

Parish brotherhoods that existed in the cities did not occasion so violent disputes as the councils, but they fell into decay.

Just as before the 1905-1907 revolution, attempts were made to remedy the growing indifference towards religion by a spate of canonisations. In 1903, solemn festivities were held on the occasion of the canonisation of Serafim of Sarov. In 1909, Princess Anna Kashinskaya was glorified, and in 1911, Bishop Ioasaf (Gorlenko) of Belgorod, who lived in the 18th century, was canonised.

An important instrument of reviving religiosity was, in the hierarchs' view, the convocation of a Local Council. At one time suggestions were made to time the Council to the celebrations of the 300th anniversary of the House of the Romanovs. In this connection, the sittings of the Pre-Council Committee were resumed in 1912 under the chairmanship of Archbishop Sergiy of Finland. Later, though, the Council was put off again.

Instead of the Council, several congresses were convened—those of monastics and Holy Writ teachers. The leaders of the Church held these congresses in order to mobilise the clergy to the struggle against the revolutionary movement, to strengthen the influence of church preaching on the younger generation. But these congresses did not have much effect on the public.

After the revolution, conventions of missionaries, just

as militant as before, were resumed. It was openly stated at the convention in Nizhniy Novgorod in 1907 that the introduction of the principle of religious tolerance posed a "great danger" to the Orthodox Church. Lev Tolstoy was still in the missionaries' "field of vision". In 1908, one of the sections of the missionary convention in Kiev resolved to appeal to the Synod to issue a statement prohibiting participation in the celebration of the great writer's jubilee. The Synod called on "all the true sons of the Church" to refrain from participation in the celebration.[1]

Not content with persecution of Tolstoy, the missionaries launched an offensive against "literary paganism". In 1910 diocesan convention of missionaries in Kazan set up a special department to discuss this question. As the missionaries stated, Maxim Gorky, Leonid Andreyev and other "literary pagans" had "already created and continue to spread an atmosphere of godlessness in society". The department appealed for setting up a special committee at the Synod to watch over the whole of ecclesiastical and secular press.[2] In other words, the demand was put forward for the restoration of ecclesiastical censorship in a somewhat different form. Going beyond the relatively narrow framework of the struggle against Old Believers, "heterodoxy" and sectarianism, the missionaries began to interfere in the general questions of politics and culture.

The intensified activity of the missionaries was yet another proof that the Church leadership and the clergy as a whole were now dominated by the most reactionary forces thirsting for revenge for the retreat during the first Russian revolution. The situation was unfavourable for the activities of church "renovationists". In 1908, the Synod conducted a purge in the theological academies, getting rid of liberal professors. That was yet another blow at the "renovationist" movement. Bishop Antonin (Granovsky), renowned for his liberalism, was banished from St. Petersburg. In the

---

[1] *Russkoye bogatstvo* (Russian Wealth), 1908, No. 8, p. 119; No. 9, p. 51.

[2] Ibid., 1910, No. 11, pp. 147, 148.

period between the revolutions, the liberal "renovationist" movement almost petered out although the discontent with the hierarchs among the white clergy, which fed this movement, continued to exist.

More prominent in that period was the movement of the so-called "free" or "non-church" Christians, or "Christian socialists". In the first years after the defeat of the revolution, some workers, who had previously taken an active part in the revolutionary struggle, succumbed to the feelings of tiredness, of disappointment and apathy, breaking away from social-democracy and embarking on religious quests. As these workers were not satisfied with the official religion, they joined the "free" Christians, which explains the temporary revival of their circles.

There were three principal trends among the "free" Christians. The first of these, headed by I. M. Tregubov and mostly limited to St. Petersburg, was based on Tolstoy's precepts. The adherents of this trend preached non-resistance to evil by violence, which aroused a sharp protest from other groups of "free" Christians.

The second trend took shape through the merging of the circles of V. Sventsitsky, I. Brikhnichev and Archimandrite Mikhail. Sventsitsky organised the Christian Brotherhood of Struggle as early as 1905. In the same year, priest Brikhnichev published in Tiflis a leftist radical magazine *Sleeper, Arise.* Archimandrite Mikhail (Semyonov), Professor of the St. Petersburg Theological Academy, declared himself a "People's Socialist" during the revolution (although in all probability he was not a member of that party). At the end of 1906 he was forbidden to teach and banished to a monastery. Later the archimandrite joined the Old Believers and even was promoted to bishop by them, although he had little in common with Old Believers, since he paid little attention to rites. Circles of Christian socialists of this type were active in Simbirsk, Tiflis, Tsaritsyn, and other cities.

The third trend, the most diffuse, existed for a while among the Moscow workers. It was headed by V. M. Sokolov and A. A. Musatov. There were differences between the adherents of this trend in their understanding of religion. Some said that "Orthodoxy would be the real faith" if only the "money-seeking clergy were replaced by a better one". Others resolutely stated: "No more rites, no clergy, no church!" The element that united the "free" Christians of Moscow was their critical attitude to the established Church. They appeared at anti-sectarian conversations and greatly annoyed the official missionaries. That trend was so closely connected with the anticlerical movement among the people's masses that it may be seen as one of its branches which assumed an unusual form at a time of the reaction. Later, in the years when the revolutionary movement began to swell, the believers among the workers were drawn into the general flow of the proletarian movement, while Christian socialism lost its followers.

In the period between the revolutions, church "liberals" kept a very low profile, whereas the opposite wing, the Black Hundreds, consolidated their position in the established Church. The League of the Russian People successfully recruited new members among the clergy. Of the priests elected to the Third Duma, seven proved to be members of that League.

Under pressure from the League, which attempted to turn the Church into one of its departments, the Synod had to deviate from the principle of non-party monarchism adhered to in its previous messages. In 1908, clergymen were officially permitted to become members of the League of the Russian People. True, the Synod found it impossible to satisfy another of the Black-Hundreders' demands—on taking up collections for the benefit of that organisation. However, later, in 1903, the Synod permitted the placing of the League of the Russian People's banners in churches. In 1909, there were 32 Orthodox bishops who were members of the League.[1]

Many prominent members of the Black Hundreds' movement belonging to the clergy played a role in the Church's internal life that by far did not correspond to their modest position in the church hierarchy. The Moscow archpriest Vostorgov was sent in 1909 on an

---

[1] *Russkoye bogatstvo,* 1909, No. 5, p. 106.

inspection tour of the Siberian dioceses. That tour, for which the Synod allocated considerable sums, was used by that clergyman for agitation in favour of the Black Hundreds and the setting up of local bodies of yet another organisation—the Archangel Michael League.

Another well-known figure was Hieromonk Iliodor, who attacked in his sermons not only revolutionaries and heterodoxy but also the government which, in his words, largely consisted of non-Russians and spongers.[1]

Iliodor was the most outstanding representative of series of Black Hundred monks and priests whose *pogrom* agitation went far beyond the established framework, and who recognised no control over them. Glorifying the czar's power, they reviled not only the enemies of autocracy but also the ministers, the synodal chief procurators and other administrators who for some reason fell into disfavour with the Black-Hundreders. The activities of these demagogues sometimes raised serious problems for the Synod, which was not always able to cope with them.

In the Synod itself, the role of hierarchs close to the Black Hundreds grew. In 1912, Metropolitan Antoniy died. Vladimir, the "specialist" on the workers' question who had a long-standing friendship with the Black-Hundreders, occupied Antoniy's post. Vladimir's place in Moscow was occupied by Bishop Makariy of Tomsk, well-known for his *pogrom*-mongering in 1905.

Lay and ecclesiastical Black-Hundreders undermined church discipline and the Church, compromising it in the eyes of the believers. But the Black-Hundreders themselves were split into several rival factions, they acted chaotically and in the final analysis failed to establish their control over the church organisation.

The attempts to establish control over the Church on the part of the court camarilla, which gradually took the affairs of the Church in their hands, were more successful. In 1909, newspapers reported that the question of church reforms was being dealt with "in the salon of some countess".[2] The author of the article

---

[1] TsGAOR SSSR, reg. 102 (Police Department), case 236, 1906, file 13, part 21, sheet 28.

[2] *Russkoye bogatstvo*, 1909, No. 6, p. 67.

Moscow.
The Kremlin.
View from
the Spasskaya Tower

Novgorod.
St. George's Monastery.
An architectural ensemble
of the 12th-17th centuries

Novgorod. The Church of St. Parasceve (Pyatnitsa) **"na torgu"**. 1207.

Novgorod.
St. Vlasiy's Church. 1407

Moscow.
The Ascension Church
in the village
of Kolomenskoye. 1530-1532

Moscow. The Cathedral of the Protecting Veil (St. Basil's Cathedral) in Red Square. 1555-1560

"Christ Appears before Maries",
a miniature from a 9th-10th-century Gospel.
The Greek Collection
of the State Public Library,
Leningrad

A page from Fyodor Koshka's Gospel,
1392. The State Lenin Library
of the USSR

St. Demetrios of Thessaloniki, an icon of the second half of the 12th century. The State Tretyakov Art Gallery in Moscow

Andrei Rublev. St. Paul the Apostle from the Deisis row, the 1420s. The State Tretyakov Art Gallery, Moscow.

Andrei Rublev.
The Trinity, c. 1411.
The State Tretyakov Art Gallery,
Moscow

St. Michael the Archangel with a Life.
An icon of the early 15th century.
The Cathedral of St. Michael
the Archangel, Moscow

Metropolitan Photius' sakkos (Detail). Old Russian face embroidery, 1409-1417. The State Armoury, Moscow

*The Burial of St. Anne.*
Old Russian face embroidery,
the last quarter of the 15th century.
State Museum of History and Art,
Zagorsk

Dmitriy Ivanovich Donskoy, Grand Duke of Muscovy. 1666 wall painting. The Cathedral of St. Michael the Archangel, Moscow

Vladimir Svyatoslavich,
Grand Duke of Kiev.
From the 1672 **Titulyarnik**

Czar Alexey Mikhailovich.
From the 1672
**Titulyarnik**

Patriarch Ghermoghen,
of All Russia.
From the 1672 **Titulyarnik**

Patriarch Filaret of All Russia. From the 1672 **Titulyarnik**

Patriarch Nikon of All Russia. From the 1672 **Titulyarnik**

Feofan Prokopovich (1681-1736), church and public figure, scholar and writer. From an 18th-century print

Metropolitan Arseniy Matseyevich (1697-1772), opponent of the church reform. From an 18th-century print

Archbishop Filaret (1805-1866), church historian and theologian. From a 19th-century print

Metropolitan Makariy (1816-1882), church historian. From a 19th-century lithograph

Ye. Ye. Golubinsky (1834-1912), historian of the Russian Church

A. P. Shchapov (1830-1876),
Russian historian
and democrat,
student
of the people's religious life

World Congress
of Peace Forces.
Moscow, 1973.
Patriarch Pimen is third from right

Participants
in the Round Table Conference on Prohibiting
the Use of Outer Space
for Military Purposes.
Moscow, 1984

More than 270 representatives of the US Christian circles came in 1984 to the USSR to study the life and activity of the Russian Orthodox Church and the life of Soviet people. Religious figures of the USSR and the USA met at the Theological Academy in Zagorsk

A delegation
of religious leaders from
the USSR at an ecumenical peace-makers'
conference in India

had in mind Countess S. S. Ignatyeva, hostess of a high society salon in which church questions were mostly discussed.[1] In various periods, the Ignatyeva circle comprised Ghermoghen of Saratov, Antoniy of Volynia, Ioann of Kronshtadt, as well as such highly placed bureaucrats as V. Sabler, A. Shirinsky-Shikhmatov, B. Sturmer, and others. "Religious conversations" were also held in the salons of Baroness Korf, Kammerherr Ye. Schwartz, A. Bryanchaninov, F. Pistolkors, and others. To these salons came metropolitans and bishops, members of the State Council and senators, writers and journalists, courtiers and grand dukes. These gatherings were not confined to man-of-the-world chatter and exchange of gossip; the company often heard some specially prepared report or paper.[2]

The groups that gathered in the salons comprised men of more or less similar views. Secular and spiritual princes, ex-ministers, excitable court ladies—they were all afraid of losing a single particle of their wealth, their power and its trappings, and they grieved for the times when they had more of all this. However rightist the official government might be, the court camarilla was always even further to the right. In the course of time it began to remove and appoint synodal chief procurators. Thus Sabler was an obvious creature of that camarilla. Its influence, however, came to be fully felt only during the war.

\* \* \*

The crisis of autocracy, which grew extremely acute in the years of the First World War, brought total confusion in the central church administration.

Because of the desire to shift the burden of responsibility for the military defeats on one another, the forces on which the government formerly relied were now divided into sharply opposed groups. Power became the bone of contention between the Duma, the

---

[1] *Russkoye bogatstvo,* 1911, No. 7, p. 140.

[2] N. D. Zhevakhov. *Vospominaniya tovarishcha ober-prokurora Sv. Sinoda kn. N. D. Zhevakhova* (Memoirs of Prince N. D. Zhevakhov, Deputy Chief Procurator of the Holy Synod), Munich, 1923, Vol. 1, p. 248.

generals, and the court camarilla. The latter emerged more and more often the top dog in that fight. Becoming the object of general hatred, it grew more and more embittered itself. As the official government was being engulfed by the court camarilla, ever fresh forces, even rightist nobles and gentry, even the clergy, joined the opposition.

The court camarilla was headed by Empress Alexandra Fyodorovna, whose incompetent meddling in state affairs was becoming more and more persistent. The empress's closest advisers were A. Vyrubova, a lady-in-waiting, and the *"starets"* Grigoriy Rasputin. The former controlled many appointments to the highest posts, while the latter assumed the functions of the chief procurator.[1]

During his stay in the capital Rasputin made the acquaintance of a number of synodal officials and regarded himself as a true master of the "department of the Orthodox faith". The ambitious Sabler failed to take into account this circumstance: he ruled his subordinates with an autocratic hand. The subordinates complained to Rasputin, and in 1915 Sabler was compelled to resign.

The political games took such a turn that Sabler's successor, A. D. Samarin, was not Rasputin's protégé. The former marshal of Moscow's nobility, Samarin was connected with conservative circles of the aristocracy and the gentry; he was a close acquaintance, since their Moscow days, of Metropolitan Vladimir, the first member of the Synod, and had support in the Duma. The conflict between the new chief procurator and the camarilla arose over the canonisation of Ioann of Tobolsk. The canonisation was an idea of Rasputin's friend, Bishop Varnava (Nakropin) of Tobolsk. That hierarch, who did not even have a seminary education, was in a hurry to make his career while Rasputin was in power; a canonisation in his diocese would promote him to archbishop. The Synod, which was against Varnava's promotion, did its best to delay the proceedings. The synodal hierarchs were apparently vexed by

---

[1] S. P. Beletsky. "Grigoriy Rasputin", In: *Byloye* (The Past), No. 20, Petrograd, 1922, p. 216.

the fact that the court camarilla now furnished not only bishops and chief procurators but also saints for the Church. The Synod's intentional go-slow tactics aroused the empress's indignation. In the end, Varnava got the permission (circumventing the Synod) to start the "glorification" of Ioann of Tobolsk (that was a step towards canonisation). An open conflict erupted between the bishop of Tobolsk and the Synod; Samarin, who took the side of the Synod, had to resign after a mere ten weeks in office, and Varnava became archbishop despite everything.[1]

The two chief procurators that followed, A. N. Volzhin and N. I. Rayev, were protégés of the camarilla. Under them the prestige of the chief procurator's office dropped to zero. In 1916, the Synod even received the right to report directly to the czar on church matters, but in the situation of utter chaos in church administration that no longer had any significance.

Having disposed of Samarin, the camarilla decided to make some changes in the Synod. The empress was critical of the hierarchy. "I know many of them," she said, "but they are all somewhat odd, they have little education but great ambitions... They are religious officials of sorts... The people follow righteous men, not officials..." As for the restoration of the patriarchate, which was the hierarchs' objective, the empress did not like the idea at all.[2]

The search for "righteous men", as we know, led the czarina to Rasputin. That "holy devil", as Iliodor called him, did not care much for bishops either. Neither did he care for church renovationism, although some persons tried to rouse his interest for these problems. His rantings contained no definite positive programme, and yet in the last year of his life Rasputin was the actual chief procurator.

In 1915, Metropolitan Flavian of Kiev died. On orders from the court camarilla, Metropolitan Vladimir of Petrograd was translated to the see of Kiev, while

---

[1] *Byloye,* 1922, No. 20, pp. 207, 220, 222; see also N. D. Zhevakhov. Op. cit., p. 86.

[2] N. D. Zhevakhov. Op. cit., pp. 85, 87.

that of Petrograd went over to Exarch Pitirim (Oknov) of Georgia, patronised by Vyrubova and Rasputin.

These off-handed replacements caused indignation in the Synod. Pitirim, who immediately occupied a prominent place in the camarilla, was boycotted by the synodal hierarchs. Vladimir, as the senior of the metropolitans (in terms of the time of his elevation to that office), remained the first member of the Synod.

On his appointment to the Synod, Prince N. D. Zhevakhov, Deputy Chief Procurator, also a creature of the camarilla, found the situation as follows. Chief Procurator Rayev was supported only by Pitirim and the aged Metropolitan Makariy of Moscow. All the other members of the Synod—the first member Vladimir, Archbishop Arseniy of Novgorod (formerly of Pskov), Archbishop Sergiy of Finland, Bishop Tikhon of Lithuania, Bishop Iakov of Nizhniy Novgorod, and Bishop Mikhail of Grodno, as well as the Protopresbyter of the military clergy G. I. Shavelsky—were in opposition, as was the Protopresbyter of the court clergy A. Dernov, also a Synod member. All suggestions coming from the chief procurator were doomed to failure. Of the 30 or 40 cases intended for consideration at each session, only three or four were dealt with, others were put off.[1] The central church administration was completely paralysed.

Striking evidence of this was the last session of the Synod under the old regime, on February 26, 1917. By that time, Chief Procurator Rayev had already disappeared. Some hierarchs failed to come because of street jams. Deputy Chief Procurator Zhevakhov declared to the Synod members who attended the session that the Church could not stand aside from the events then taking place. He proposed to issue an appeal to the population: it was to be a "stern warning of the Church which, in the case of disobedience, would entail a church punishment". The suggestion was received without enthusiasm. "That's the way things always are," said the first member Vladimir. "When there's no need for us, they don't even notice us, and at a moment of danger we are the first to whom they turn for help".

---

[1] N. D. Zhevakhov. Op. cit., pp. 131, 181-183.

The young, hot-headed prince continued to insist, but the hierarchs baulked, and nothing came of the appeal.

"...It was, of course, impossible to assume," wrote the extremely annoyed Zhevakhov, "that the metropolitan could have given such an answer if he had fully realised what exactly was taking place. Like many others, the metropolitan was unaware of what happened in reality, and his refusal was not a refusal of the higher church hierarchs to help the state at a moment of danger but a routine manifestation of the Synod's opposition to the chief procuratorship."[1]

Could it be that none of the hierarchs realised that what was taking place was the overthrow of autocracy? The frictions between the Synod and the chief procurator's office were a usual thing, but previously they had taken place in a framework of cooperation. But on the eve of the February revolution the crisis of the autocratic system was so acute that the mechanism of that cooperation was largely in disarray.

\* \* \*

The bourgeois Provisional Government that came to power after the February revolution proclaimed the abolition of all the "estate, denominational and national restrictions".[2] In actual fact, however, as Soviet historians stress, the Provisional Government did not implement the freedom of conscience—it did not go beyond religious tolerance.[3] Neither the secularisation of church and monastery lands nor the separation of church from state were effected. The Orthodox Church continued in fact to retain its dominant position. The bourgeois and landowners' government was conscious of the shakiness of its positions and was therefore afraid of alienating the Church, hoping to recruit its help in the fight against the revolutionary movement. "Until new fundamental laws are worked

---

[1] Ibid., pp. 374, 375.
[2] See Ye. S. Osipova. "Tserkov i Vremennoye pravitelstvo" (The Church and the Provisional Government). In: *Voprosy istorii*, 1964, No. 6, p. 66.
[3] Ibid., p. 67; Ye. F. Grekulov. Op. cit., p. 166.

out by the Constituent Assembly," stated an official governmental document, "the Provisional Government regards itself as standing close to the affairs and interests of the Orthodox Church."[1]

In an attempt to establish control over the Church, the Provisional Government preserved the chief procurator's office in its old form. The post of chief procurator was given to V. N. Lvov, a landowner from Samara and chairman of the Duma Commission on the Affairs of the Orthodox Church. In the Duma he belonged to a small centrist faction that stood further to the right than the Constitutional Democrats and the Octobrists.

Early in March, the relations between the new authorities and the Church were normalised. On March 6, the Synod published a message calling on the "faithful children of the Orthodox Church" to support the Provisional Government. The synodal decision of March 7-8 cancelled the mentioning of the deposed emperor's name during divine services; it was resolved "to offer prayers for the pious Provisional Government".[2]

In the very first days of his office Lvov removed from the Synod Rasputin's protégés, Pitirim and Varnava. Metropolitan Makariy of Moscow, who supported them, was only compelled to retire at the end of March. The Moscow see was occupied by Archbishop Tikhon. But Metropolitan Vladimir of Kiev, a monarchist and a Black-Hundreder, retained his position as the first member of the Synod. The chief procurator, himself an inveterate monarchist at heart, was in no hurry to part with the Synod members who were close to him in spirit.

The revolutionary process in the country continued to develop, the old order was collapsing. In some places the peasants drove the priests away from their parishes, where they were known for their monarchist views and links with the police. Under pressure from the workers, soldiers, peasants and democratically minded intellectuals, various bourgeois organisations that sprang up in

---

[1] Ye. S. Osipova. Op. cit., p. 66.
[2] Ibid.

the provinces sent telegrams to Petrograd requesting the removal of diocesan hierarchs who had compromised themselves under the czarist regime.

In April, the peasants' actions against church and monastery landownership began. Between April and October, this movement involved 51 provinces; it was especially intense in central Russia, the Ukraine, and in the south.

The rank-and-file clergy could not fail to take into account the changed situation. As we have said above, during the period of the reaction church liberals had kept a very low profile, while now it was the turn of monarchists and Black-Hundreders to do so. Previously, there were quite a few liberals turning conservative, while now there was a mass and hurried movement in the opposite direction. Diocesan conventions (in Moscow, Kiev, Oryol, Tambov, Penza and other cities) adopted resolutions in the Constitutional Democrats' spirit. Thus the Voronezh diocese recognised as the "only acceptable" the basic principles of the Cadet programme.[1]

The representation of the laity and lower parish clergy at diocesan conventions increased.

In March, a group of Petrograd priests and intellectuals formed the Union of the Democratic Clergy and Laity. Its branches soon appeared in other cities as well. The Union advocated the democratisation of the Church, while politically it was close to the Socialist-Revolutionaries. The Union's policy was conciliatory by nature, its objective being to slow down the development of the revolution.

Towards mid-April a situation arose when the Synod as an instrument of the old regime, far from enjoying some influence in the country, could not control even the processes in the Church itself. The Provisional Government was obliged to reorganise it. Of the members of the old Synod, only Archbishop Sergiy of Finland remained in it—a relatively young hierarch, formerly a learned monk, a disciple of Metropolitan Antoniy of St. Petersburg, a moderate conservative, a cautious and flexible politician. Archbishop Agafanghel

---

[1] Ye. S. Osipova. Op. cit., p. 67.

of Yaroslavl (formerly of Riga) was not above social demagoguery. Under the old regime he had been a member of the Synod, but he incurred the Black-Hundreders' displeasure and fell into disfavour. Another of the new members of the Synod was Bishop Andrey (secular name, Prince Ukhtomsky) of Ufa; he was close to Constitutional Democrats. Besides, the Synod now included Exarch Platon of Georgia, Bishop Mikhail of Samara, N. Lyubimov, Protopresbyter of the Dormition Cathedral, and the archpriests A. Smirnov, A. Rozhdestvensky (former editor of *Tserkovnyi vestnik*), and F. D. Filonenko (member of the Fourth Duma, who belonged to the nationalists' faction). Formally, Vladimir was regarded as the first member of the Synod, but he no longer took part in its work; neither did he sign the synodal documents. In general, the Synod was somewhat further to the left and more liberal than most of the Orthodox hierarchy. However, as the revolution developed and the class forces became clearly delimited, the Synod increasingly shifted to the right, and the hierarchy consolidated its positions in the Church.

On April 29, the Synod published a message to the "archpastors, pastors and all the faithful children of the Russian Orthodox Church" which was read in all the churches. It was, in fact, a programmatic document of the new Synod. The Synod declared its principal objective to be the convocation of the All-Russian Local Council at the earliest possible date. Just as during the first Russian revolution, the top hierarchs intended, by raising the issue of the Council, to push the church question into the foreground of political life, to distract the people's masses from the revolutionary struggle and to bring them back into the "bosom" of the Church.

Other tasks set by the Synod were also prompted by the same desire. The message said that "under the changed state system the Russian Orthodox Church could not preserve the order that has outlived its usefulness", and that the "elective principle must be introduced in all the forms of church administration amenable to it". In speaking of the "amenable forms", the Synod implied that the democratisation of the

Church must not go beyond certain limits. The same idea was stressed more openly in the call to the rank-and-file clergy to introduce the necessary changes in the local church life "only in agreement with church authorities", for "everything in the Church of Christ must conform to the rules of propriety". In conclusion, the Synod appealed to the faithful: "Adhere to law and order in your mutual relations, for neither the church nor the state system can be consolidated without respect for the rights of others."[1] The Synod thus called for an end to the revolution, for the preservation of the old social order.

On the same day, April 29, the Synod passed the decision on setting up a Pre-Council Board, on the model of the Pre-Council Committee which functioned in 1906.

The Synod, both the former and the new one, conducted its activities in line with the policy of the Provisional Government. The Synod supported the government's policy of continuing the war, and helped to collect the Loan of Freedom.[2] During the July crisis, the Church supported the government in every way. On July 12, the Synod adopted a special message concerning the July events. The higher ecclesiastics endeavoured to prove that the Bolsheviks were crushing the "shoots of desirable freedom", sowing "theft, plunder, brigandage, and violence". The church press launched a fierce anti-Bolshevik propaganda campaign.[3]

After the events of July 1917, when the counter-revolution assumed the offensive, lay and ecclesiastical monarchists raised their heads.

That was the situation in which the last preparations for the Council were rounded off. On July 5, the Synod approved the Statute on the Convocation of the Local Council of the Orthodox All-Russian Church.

On the eve of the opening of the Council, the

---

[1] *Svyashchennyi Sobor Pravoslavnoy Rossiyskoy Tserkvi: Deyaniya. Kniga 1: deyaniya I-XVI* (The Holy Council of the Orthodox Russian Church: Acts. Book 1: Acts I-XVI), Moscow, 1918, pp. 3-5.

[2] See Ye. S. Osipova. Op. cit., pp. 71-73.

[3] Ibid., p. 74.

Provisional Government abolished the office of the chief procurator and set up the Ministry for Confessions.

The Council was solemnly opened on August 15 in Moscow in the presence of the members of the Provisional Government: Minister-Chairman Alexander Kerensky; Minister for the Interior Nikolai Avksentyev, a Socialist-Revolutionary; and Minister for Confessions A. V. Kartashev, a Constitutional Democrat.

Of the 569 members of the Council, 80 belonged to the top hierarchy; there were also 20 archimandrites, hegumens and hieromonks, 127 archpriests and priests; the lower parish clerics had 36 representatives, and 299 members belonged to the laity. There were well-known rightist politicians among the latter, such as V. A. Bobrinsky, S. I. Zubchaninov, A. D. Samarin (the former chief procurator). Octobrists' leaders—A. I. Guchkov, M. V. Rodzyanko, S. I. Shidlovsky—were also present. The Constitutional-Democratic Party, which became the core of counter-revolution, had its representatives, too—S. N. Bulgakov, S. A. Kotlyarevsky, Ye. N. Trubetskoy, and others. The majority of the Council consisted of traditionalists, the "renovationists" did not play too great a role. Eleven members of the Council belonged to titled aristocracy, 130 were officials, 20, factory-owners, while the bourgeois intelligentsia was represented by 69 members. Only 20 peasants were present at the Council, and not a single worker.[1] The Council was dominated by the hierarchs, who relied on the reactionary part of the white clergy and the laity.

The first sessions of the Council were devoted to hearing messages of greeting and organisational issues. On August 18, Metropolitan Tikhon (Belavin) of Moscow was elected chairman of the Council. Metropolitan Vladimir became its honorary chairman.

On August 21, a statement, signed by 184 members, was considered by the Council's Board, which insisted on the "need to free the printing-works of the Synod and the lavras seized by the Soviets of soldiers' and workers' deputies and other class and revolutionary

---

[1] Ye. S. Osipova. Op. cit., p. 75.

organisations which printed in them publications inappropriate to their purpose". After discussing this statement, the Council resolved to request the Synod and the minister for confessions to inform the Council "what measures they intended to take in order to restore the disrupted order".[1] In other words, the Council demanded that the government use force to return to the church authorities the confiscated printing-works previously used to turn out counter-revolutionary monarchist literature. That was the first open attack of the Council against the Soviets and other revolutionary organisations.

On August 25, General Kornilov's mutiny began. Putting aside the current affairs, the Council devoted two of its sessions (on August 30 and 31) to discussion of the political situation in the country. The debate was not reflected in the *Acts*. Apparently there were quite a few supporters of the rebellious Commander-in-Chief among the Council deputies. In the meantime, the mutiny failed. After that the Council appealed to the government to "spare the lives of the vanquished".[2]

That move was commented on in a leaflet produced by the Moscow and Petrograd committees of the Russian Social-Democratic Labour Party (Bolsheviks): "When capital punishment for soldiers was introduced at the insistence of General Kornilov, they were silent, they even approved of it ... and they did not rise in the name of Christ against the floods of the people's blood shed in the past three years and more. And now that General Kornilov betrayed the whole people, when he was ready to slaughter it, the Church Council says, 'Thou shalt not kill.' That is the deception that we expose, and the fact that they have always helped to hold the people in the dark and under a yoke."[3]

In the autumn, the Council began to discuss the question of the highest church administration. At a time of the mounting Bolshevik influence and the declining prestige and power of the Provisional Gov-

---

[1] *Deyaniya* (Acts), Book 1, Issue 3, Petrograd, 1918, pp. 78, 79.
[2] Ibid., p. 158.
[3] *Tserkov v istorii Rossii* (The Church in the History of Russia), p. 325.

ernment, the clericals were in a hurry to constitute themselves as an independent political force which was to occupy a prominent position in the camp of the revolution's opponents.

Counter to the hopes of the clericals, the Council failed to make the religious question the focus of the country's social life and to distract the masses from the revolution, from the solution of the pressing socio-economic and political issues. Workers, peasants and soldiers, led by the Bolshevik Party, were preparing for a new revolution, rallying their ranks, overcoming the opposition of the forces of the old regime, including the resistance of the established, dominant Church.

*Chapter VIII*

# THE CHURCH IN THE YEARS OF THE SOCIALIST REVOLUTION AND CIVIL WAR

The socialist revolution, to which the ideologists of the Russian Orthodoxy always referred with unconcealed hatred, became a fact on October 25 (November 7), 1917. Owing to circumstances beyond its control, the Russian Orthodox Church found itself in a new historical situation, the epoch of socialist construction.

How did the Church, as represented by its episcopate and the rest of the clergy, behave under the new social conditions?

## The Restoration of the Patriarchate. The Church's Support for the Counter-Revolution and the Foreign Armed Intervention

The Russian Orthodox Church took a sharply negative attitude to the Great October Socialist Revolution of 1917. The church newspapers and journals, both national and diocesan, which appeared soon after the October armed uprising, unanimously condemned the socialist revolution and declared their refusal to recognise the new government—Soviet power. The malicious and slanderous statements intended to incite the believers to oppose the socialist revolution and the triumphant Soviet power, were obviously the response of an enemy—political as well as ideological.

The Local Council of the Russian Orthodox Church also reacted very promptly to the October armed uprising. Three days after the fall of the Provisional Government, the Council held a session to discuss purely political rather than religious and church problems. Among others, the question was discussed of the mobilisation of all the church forces in Russia to fight the victorious revolution.

The restoration of the patriarchal form of administration in the Russian Orthodoxy was recognised as the most urgent and primary task and all debate on that item of the agenda was discontinued immediately. The Council's leaders did not even bother to conceal from the rank-and-file believers that the clergy and the dispossessed classes they represented needed a patriarch as a spiritual head of the counter-revolution, as a champion and defender of the old regime.

In November 1917, a sortition was arranged at the Moscow Church of Christ Our Saviour, where the Local Council sat. In this way Metropolitan Tikhon, a well-known monarchist and an active figure in the *pogrom*-mongering League of the Russian People, Became Patriarch of Moscow and of All Russia. The newly elected patriarch fully justified the hopes of the counter-revolutionaries in cassocks.

Apart from the patriarch, the Council elected several so-called Patriarchal Locum Tenens and their deputies (in case of unforeseen disruption of the patriarch's office). To aid the patriarch, the Council set up two auxiliary bodies of church administration: the Synod, consisting of hierarchs, and the Higher Church Council, which included both priests and laymen.

Thus, after two centuries of the rule of the Holy Governing Synod, the patriarchate was restored in the Russian Orthodox Church, and a patriarch was elected. By doing so, the Local Council of 1917-1919 undertook not so much a religious as a political move prompted by counter-revolutionary, anti-Soviet considerations. Explaining these considerations, Pavel Milyukov, former Cadet leader, Minister for Foreign Affairs in the bourgeois Provisional Government, and later a White emigrant, wrote that the question of restoration of the patriarchate "was solved by the October 25 revolution. The Council, frightened by the Bolsheviks' victory and awaiting a forced interruption of its proceedings, decided to leave behind it a reminder of its activities in the form of a 'strong power' capable of opposing state authority and of influencing it."[1]

That was precisely the way in which the newly elected Patriarch Tikhon interpreted his goal, as was demonstrated by his very first actions in his capacity of head of the Russian Orthodox Church—actions that were political in their essence and anti-Soviet in their social orientation and class content.

Soon after the patriarch's election the Local Council officially stated its rejection of the new state system. The Church published a special message of the Council "to all the children of the Orthodox Russian Church" containing various insinuations about the atheist Bolsheviks and foretelling the imminent downfall of the "Godless power" established by them.[2]

That was merely a beginning. Not content with public expression of their rejection of the Soviet power, the Council's leaders and the clergy undertook various moves aimed at undermining the prestige of the socialist state and its policy in the eyes of believers, at sabotaging the measures implemented by the Soviet government, finally, at organising political demonstrations and military operations against the young Soviet Republic.

The church press declared the plan for the construction of the foundations of socialist economy worked out by Lenin and outlined in his work *The Immediate Tasks of the Soviet Government* to be impracticable, subjecting Lenin's work to arrogant and malicious critique.[3]

However, the Church did much more than denigrate Soviet power. It called on believers to sabotage the Soviet state's moves (especially those that threatened to undermine, in one way or another, the Church's economic power), and actively joined in the sabotage itself. A striking example of this kind of provocation was the opposition of the Petrograd clergy

---

[1] P. N. Milyukov. *Ocherki po istorii russkoy kultury* (Essays on the History of Russian Culture), Paris, 1931, Vol. 2, Part 1, p. 222.

[2] *Tserkovnye vedomosti*, 1917, Nos 46-47, p. 417.

[3] *Tserkovnye vedomosti*, 1918, Nos 11-12, *Additions*, p. 396; Nos 17-18, *Additions*.

to the requisition of part of the empty premises of the Alexander Nevskiy Lavra by the People's Commissariat for State Charity. The conflict between religious fanatics and other elements and the representatives of Soviet power who came to the Lavra was later exaggerated by the church press out of all proportion for clearly anti-Soviet purposes.

Soon the Council decided to direct such actions; at one of its sittings, it specially considered the question of the most effective ways and means of counteracting the decrees of Soviet power.[1]

It was decided that the most effective means of rousing the animosity of believers for the new government and its local representatives would be the anathematising of Soviet power by the patriarch—which he did in his message of January 19, 1918. The message contained the Church's damnation of representatives of Soviet power. It ended with a call for the clergy and the believers to actively resist the Soviet government.[2]

The patriarch's message, full of the most malicious attacks on Soviet power, was received with enthusiasm by the Local Council and the church press. It was clear from the Council leaders' speeches that they interpreted Tikhon's démarche as an open call for political struggle against the new state system, stating their complete support for the head of the Church on that issue.[3] The Council passed a special resolution approving Tikhon's message and calling on the bishops, the clergy and the believers to lend their support to the head of the Church through concrete acts.

Lenin's decree "On the Separation of the Church from the State and the School from the Church", published on January 23, 1918, stung the church leadership into yet another burst of counter-revolutionary activity. The Council passed a special decision on that decree, distorting Lenin's document and containing more threats against Soviet power.[4]

---

[1] *Tserkovnye vedomosti*, 1918, Nos 23-24, *Additions*, p. 669.
[2] *Acts...*, Book 6, Issue I, pp. 4-5.
[3] Ibid., pp. 6, 11; *Tserkovnost*, 1918, No. 348, pp. 11, 13.
[4] *Acts...*, Book 6; Issue I, p. 72.

The Council also made an appeal to members of the Church, openly inciting them to the most extreme steps of anti-Soviet nature. The appeal called on them: "Unite, ye Orthodox people, round your churches and pastors, unite all, men and women, old and young, form unions for the protection of our shrines... It is better to shed our blood and gain a martyr's crown than to let the Orthodox faith be desecrated by the enemies. Take heart, holy Russia! Go to thy Golgotha!"[1]

Following that appeal, the clergy were given a concrete programme of action outlined in the letter of January 30, 1918, from Patriarch Tikhon to the priest N. Troitsky. In that letter, reprinted by the whole of the church press, the head of the Church thus instructed the priests: "Do not waste time, gather your flock round you... Summon them to pastoral conversations, one or two at a time, read to them the Word of God, especially the writings of the prophets, in which you will find many references to evil times of trouble and unrest like the present one. Choose at first the best men, do not neglect to talk with pious women, who often restrain their husbands and brothers from lawless acts and defend the Lord's Church. Unite pious parishioners in brotherhoods, unions, councils— whatever you find useful and suitable to the local conditions..."[2] A still more detailed programme of resistance to Lenin's decree was contained in the decision of the patriarch and the Synod of February 28, 1918.[3]

Following the instructions of the patriarch and the Council, the clergy began to organise mass anti-government actions. In particular, religious processions bearing the cross and church banners were organised, which were not so much religious as political in character and proclaimed anti-Soviet slogans.[4]

The processions, the participants of which were often provoked by the clergy to commit anti-government acts, often turned into *pogrom,* which led to serious conflicts

---

[1] *Tserkovnye vedomosti,* 1918, Nos 3-4, pp. 19, 20.
[2] Ibid., No. 5, p. 26.
[3] Ibid., Nos 7-8, pp. 32-34.
[4] *Tserkovnost,* 1918, No. 349, p. 16.

and bloody fighting. These violent acts were precisely what the clergy, and their leaders needed. The latter needed victims that could be passed off for martyrs who have suffered for their faith, and thus used both for fanning religious fanaticism and for anti-Soviet propaganda. But the Soviet Government and the local bodies of power did not give in to provocation and tried to avoid bloodshed wherever possible, using persuasion to influence the masses of the believers and the clergy, and only punishing those who consciously fought against the new system as implacable enemies of Soviet power.

These enemies, arrested or executed by the revolutionary people, were declared by the Church to be "confessors" and "martyrs" and it glorified them vigourously. Church authorities instructed priests to gather all the information about the executed and to send it to the Council and the editors of *Tserkovnye vedomosti*. The Council set up a special Commission on the Persecution of the Church, which suggested that the patriarch appoint a special day for "prayers in cathedrals for the executed for the faith and the Orthodox Church". On that day, the liturgy was used as a means of anti-Soviet political agitation.[1]

Somewhat later, one of the sessions of the Council passed a decision providing for a series of measures to glorify the alleged "sufferers for their faith": "1. To establish prayers at churches for those persecuted now for their Orthodox Church and for those who died as martyrs... 3. To establish throughout Russia an annual prayer of remembrance on January 25 or on the Sunday following it (in the evening) for all confessors and martyrs who have died in these evil times of persecution. 4. In all the parishes where confessors and martyrs lived who have given up their lives for their faith and Church, to hold, on the second day of the second week of Eastertide, processions with the cross and church banners to the places of their burial, and offices for the dead glorifying their memory. 5. To give the Holy Council's blessing to all the confessors."[2]

---

[1] *Tserkovnye vedomosti*, 1918, Nos 15-16, *Additions*, p. 503.
[2] Ibid., Nos 23-24, pp. 165, 166.

The Local Council of the Russian Orthodox Church thus became the centre of the "holy counter-revolution", its principal headquarters, and Patriarch Tikhon, elected by the Council, who directed the Council's activity after the Revolution, precisely the kind of "spiritual leader" which the anti-Soviet-minded bishops and clergy needed.

Not content with fighting against the implementation of Lenin's Decree "On the Separation of the Church from the State and of the School from the Church", the church leadership, actively supported by the episcopate and the clergy, launched an offensive against Soviet power on other fronts as well.

In particular, Patriarch Tikhon, unanimously supported by the Council, came out against the conclusion of the Peace Treaty of Brest-Litovsk, demanding the continuation of the war. He hoped that continuing war operations would drain the strength of the young Soviet Republic, get the soldiers' masses against it and thus precipitate its downfall. When the treaty was concluded, despite everything, on March 3, 1918, Patriarch Tikhon attacked that forced act of the Soviet Government, in order to discredit it in the eyes of the working people.[1]

The Church incited believers against all the new elements introduced by the victory of the socialist revolution. Thus it prohibited not only the clergy but also the laity to participate in the celebration of May Day, the day of international proletarian solidarity, under threat of church damnation in case of disobedience.[2] But the clergy failed to wreck the celebrations.

Even the introduction of the word "comrade" as a mode of address did not go unnoticed by the Church. The author of an article "Who Should the Common People Especially Listen to?" called on the believers not to listen to the "alien 'comrade' ", and not to use that mode of address under any circumstances.[3]

---

[1] *Tserkovnye vedomosti*, 1918, Nos 9-10, pp. 49, 50.

[2] *Vitebskaya tserkovno-obshchestvennaya zhizn* (Vitebsk Church and Public Life), 1918, No. 3, p. 8.

[3] *Golos svobodnoy tserkvi* (The Voice of Free Church), Ryazan, 1918, No. 3, p. 14.

The canonisation of new saints was also used by the Council as a means of influencing believers. In April 1918, the Local Council passed a decision on the canonisation of Bishop Sofroniy of Irkutsk (1703-1771) and Metropolitan Iosif of Astrakhan (1597-1671), both of them highly reactionary church figures of the past, whose glorification was intended by the clergy as an anti-Soviet political demonstration. In characterising Metropolitan Iosif, the church press especially stressed the fact that he "suffered as a martyr during the terrible rebellion of Stenka Razin".[1]

Neither the Local Council nor the clergy that followed its lead were going to stop at these actions. They realised that their political demonstrations, church damnation, and the bloody conflicts they had provoked—none of this was enough to overthrow Soviet power which enjoyed the full support of the people's masses, including the believers. That was why the church circles, which rallied their forces round Patriarch Tikhon, placed their main hope on the forces of the counter-revolution which had unleashed a civil war in the country, and on the help of interventionists.

The reactionary clergy regarded the White armies, which were attacking the Soviet Republic on all sides, as "liberators of Russia", doing everything they could to help these armies. The church circles even used the Local Council to express their solidarity with the armies of Denikin, Kolchak and other self-styled "saviours of Russia". Under the guise of appeals for "reconciliation", Patriarch Tikhon demanded in his messages that the Bolsheviks stop fighting against the White Guards, recognising them as their "brothers".[2]

Collaboration between the counter-revolution, the episcopate and the clergy was especially active in the areas seized by the White Guards. Thus General Krasnov was helped by Bishop Ghermoghen, while Metropolitan Yevlogiy was active in the region controlled by General Denikin. It is a well-known fact that Denikin recruited for his army priests, deacons and

---

[1] *Orlovskiye yeparkhialnye vedomosti* (The Oryol Diocese Gazette), 1918, No. 12, p. 312.

[2] *Tserkovnye vedomosti*, 1918, Nos 7-8, p. 31; Nos 9-10, p. 50.

even church watchmen. Near Stavropol he recruited a special force consisting of 700 clergymen.[1]

Metropolitan Antoniy (Khrapovitsky), who fled to the south to join the White Guards, Archbishop Anastasiy (Gribanovsky) and other hierarchs were also active in the south of the country. Towards the end of 1919, nearly a third of the bishops of the Russian Orthodox Church gathered in Denikin's army, not merely seeking protection in the "Volunteer Army" but also intending to vent their hatred of the Soviet power.

To consolidate the church forces and to work out a programme for a more active participation of the clergy in the White movement, a Council was convened in May 1919 in Stavropol, with General Denikin's sanction, which was attended by 11 hierarchs, 23 priests of various ranks and 22 laymen, including two princes, two counts, three generals, a colonel, and other representatives of the overthrown exploiter classes. The Stavropol Council formed the Provisional Higher Church Administration in the south of Russia (PHCA), whose purpose was to aid Denikin in retaining power on the territories he seized. Metropolitan Antoniy (Khrapovitsky), one of the most active leaders of the clerical counter-revolution, became honorary chairman of the PHCA, which acted as the church branch of Denikin's headquarters.

After the rout of Denikin's army, the PHCA moved to the Crimea, to Baron Wrangel's army; later it was evacuated, along with the remnants of Wrangel's army, to Constantinople (Istanbul), where it was renamed the Higher Russian Church Administration Abroad ("the HCA Abroad"), which proceeded to unite the forces of the Russian emigration.

The clergy also actively supported the bands of Admiral Kolchak and other candidates for military dictatorship. Thus after the taking of Simbirsk by the White Guards and Czechoslovak troops, Archbishop Veniamin of Simbirsk addressed a message to the faithful expressing his joy at the fall of Soviet power in

---

[1] *Revolyutsiya i tserkov* (The Revolution and the Church), Moscow, 1919, Nos 6-8, p. 96.

the city and calling on the population to render every assistance to the new rulers.[1]

In November 1918, the Siberian Church Conference was convened in Tomsk, attended by 13 hierarchs, 26 priests and laymen—mostly members of the 1917-1918 Local Council. In their appeal to the clergy and the believers, the participants in that Conference called for armed struggle against Soviet power and for support of Kolchak. A Provisional Higher Church Administration was instituted, whose authority extended over the dioceses of Siberia, the Ural region and other eastern provinces of the country occupied by Kolchak's troops.

In a few cases, the clergy and monks directly participated in military operations, joining "Jesus Regiments", "the Regiments of the Most Holy Mother of God" and other military units, although church canons strictly forbid clergymen and monks to take up arms.

The Russian Orthodox Church also placed great hopes in foreign intervention. The official church organ's item on "The Salvation of Russia" stated outright that Russia must rely in everything on the allies, letting them decide her fate. Among other things, it was suggested to set up, with the aid of the USA and Japan, New Russia in East Siberia and the Far East, protected by Japanese cordons—a refuge from "the German invasion and risky experiments in Utopian socialism".[2]

Soviet investigating agencies found out that Patriarch Tikhon had established contacts with official representatives of the Entente and blessed their intervention aimed at the annihilation of the Soviet Republic. In May-August 1918, official representatives of the French Government visited Tikhon several times. "During these conversations, the question was discussed of the overthrow of Soviet power, of the restoration of the Eastern Front with the aid of Czechoslovak troops, and of the landing of allied troops in the north. In answer

---

[1] *Izvestiya po Simbirskoy yeparkhii* (News from the Simbirsk Diocese), 1918, No. 12, p. 6.

[2] *Tserkovnye vedomosti*, 1918, Nos 13-14, *Additions*, p. 471.

to a direct question of Comte de Chevally, who informed the Patriarch of the beginning of a military intervention against Russia, Patriarch Tikhon ... replied that he 'blessed' the intervention, hoping that it would not end in failure as had 'the fruitless experiment of the Yaroslavl affair' [the reference was to the Left-wing Social-Revolutionaries' mutiny organised in Yaroslavl in July 1918 on instructions from Joseph Noulens, the French Ambassador to Russia, and crushed within two weeks of its beginning.— *Author*]. The news of Belavin-Tikhon's blessing was immediately reported to Grenard and telegraphed to Paris."[1]

Taking part in the internal counter-revolution and actively supporting the intervention, the church circles intended to overthrow Soviet power with their aid and to restore the prerevolutionary regime. Many members of the episcopate and clergy openly advocated the restoration of autocracy in the country, still regarding czarism as the most complete embodiment of the Christian ideal of state power. Patriarch Tikhon also remained a convinced monarchist. When czar Nicholas II and his family were executed on instructions from the Ural Regional Soviet, Tikhon delivered a sermon at one of Moscow's churches, in which he "called on the faithful, regardless of their political convictions, to publicly condemn the perpetrators of that unheard-of crime, even if they were to suffer for it".[2]

Such was the position adopted by the Russian Orthodox Church in the years of the socialist revolution and the Civil War—a position that was deeply reactionary in its social essence and anti-Soviet in its political orientation.

### The Fall of the Church's Prestige

Inciting the Russian Orthodox Church towards anti-Soviet activity and making it bulwark of counter-revolution and an advocate of the restoration of the

---

[1] *Yezhegodnik Muzeya istorii religii i ateizma* (Yearbook of the Museum of the History of Religion and Atheism), Leningrad, 1961, Vol. 5, p. 227.

[2] *Putj*, (The Way), Paris, 1925, No. 1, p. 120.

pre-revolutionary social and state system, Patriarch Tikhon and his followers hoped to enlist the support not only of the entire clergy and the classes overthrown by the revolution but also that of the bulk of the believers. They hoped that the religiosity of the masses, inculcated over the centuries and supported by the whole life style in pre-revolutionary Russia, would prove stronger than their political consciousness, which began to develop only through the participation of the masses in the revolutionary process, that it would outweigh their class feeling. They hoped that, by declaring the Soviet power to be "iconoclastic" and a "persecutor of the faith and the Church", they would be able to incite religious-minded workers and peasants against it, thus undermining its social basis, its support among the masses.

However, these hopes of the reactionary clergy proved to be untenable. The working people of Russia, including believers, quickly realised the social advantages offered by Soviet power and the historical perspectives opened up by the socialist system. That was why the lower social strata, despite their religiosity, supported Soviet power rather than the Church that opposed it.

Moreover, the Church's hostility towards the decrees of the Soviet power, which accorded with the basic interests of the working people, the opposition of the clergy to the elimination of the exploiting system and the oppression of man by man, the condemnation by the church circles of the Soviet government's efforts to put an end to the imperialist war and establish peace, and similar actions antagonised many parishioners from the worker and peasant environment. A crisis was brewing unprecedented in the history of the Russian Orthodoxy.

True, it was not so much a crisis of religious belief as a crisis of political trust in the Church—the realisation that the latter was a force socially hostile to the people, a mouthpiece and defender of the interests of antipopular forces. However, such a crisis also posed a real threat to the very being of the Russian Orthodoxy because it narrowed down the social basis of the Church and opened up the path for creating prerequisites for the emergence and development of mass atheism in the country.

One of the manifestations of this crisis was the movement for the unsealing of the relics of the Russian Orthodox saints, which the Church declared to be "unperishable", using the worshipping of these relics to enhance the religiosity of the masses, and also the reaction to this movement on the part of believers and the clergy. The movement was triggered off by an accident. In October 1918, during the stock-taking of the Church property of the Monastery of St. Alexandr of the Svir (Petrozavodsk Province) a wax doll was discovered instead of the "unperishable relics" of St. Alexandr of the Svir in a silver shrine weighing more than 20 *puds*.[1] This fact, widely publicised, caused obvious confusion among the clergy and deep indignation among the revolutionary masses. At the insistence of the latter, competent and representative commissions opened 63 relics in 14 provinces of Soviet Russia, in the presence of the clergy and the believers. No "unperishable relics" were discovered, and even mummified corpses were few. The contents of opened shrines were mostly described by commissions as "a heap of semidecayed bones". In some shrines such objects were found as (we quote here the documents based on the materials of the openings): "a cloth doll with pieces of bone" (the relic of Evfrosiniya of Suzdal), "a doll in human shape" (the relics of St. Kirill Novo-Ozersky), "a cottonwool doll" (the relics of St. Savva of Storozhi), "a metal doll with wax-covered bones inside" (the relics of St. Pitirim of Tambov), and even "several boards, old coins, a jar of the Brocard fixature, shavings, earth, chips, and bricks" (the relics of St. Pavel of the Obnora).[2]

Not only many of the believers were shocked—even some of the clergy and monastics condemned the church practice of falsifying "unperishable relics". The church leaders were also worried about the further fall

---

[1] One *pud* equals some 16 kilogrammes.— *Ed.*

[2] Complete data on the results of the opening of the shrines published in the journal *Revolyutsiya i tserkov* (1920, Nos 9-12, pp. 74-81) are cited in the collection *O svyatykh moshchakh* (On Holy Relics), Moscow 1961, pp. 57-67.

of the Church's prestige. In February 1919, Patriarch Tikhon addressed a special "confidential" letter to diocesan hierarchs, instructing them "to use their discretion in eliminating, with archpastoral care and reasoning, all causes for temptation in regard of holy relics in all cases where and when it will be deemed necessary".[1]

Fearing self-isolation, the church leadership was compelled to resort to a more careful camouflaging of its true designs and political calculations. In order to mislead both the believers among the working people and Soviet government and to dull the people's revolutionary vigilance, Patriarch Tikhon published in September 1919 a "Message on the Cessation of the Clergy's Struggle Against the Bolsheviks".

The whole of the subsequent activity of both the Patriarch and of the clergy he headed showed that the message was merely a tactical move on the part of the clerical schemers whose hostility towards Soviet power and hopes for its speedy fall remained unchanged. And yet there were obvious indications that the church circles began to realise that their open political enmity towards the new state and social structure found no support among the bulk of the religious working people which the reactionary clergy and their leaders originally hoped to find. That was why they took greater care to conceal their true goals and intentions and to await a more favourable situation for more active anti-Soviet actions.

---

[1] *O svyatykh moshchakh* (On Holy Relics), p. 52.

*Chapter IX*

# ON THE PATH
# OF POLITICAL REORIENTATION

The process of the political reorientation of the Russian Orthodox Church, ostensibly begun at the end of 1919 and reflected in Patriarch Tikhon's aforementioned message, did not only stop in the early 1920s but was even reversed for a while. This was confirmed by the events of 1921-1923, which demonstrated again the hostility of the ideological and practical activity of the Russian Orthodox Church to the interests of the people.

## The Church and Famine

The drought of 1921 destroyed the crops in 34 provinces with a total population of 30 million. The catastrophe struck hardest in the Volga region, where some 14 million people were doomed to starvation. To help the famine-stricken population, the Soviet Government decided to buy grain abroad. To do that, though, it needed hard currency. But the Soviet Republic's gold reserves were virtually exhausted.

True, there were valuables in the country which could be converted into hard currency—a great many valuables: diamond-studded gold and silver settings of icons, silver shrines for relics weighing many *puds,* gold and silver cups, candlesticks, expensive chandeliers, and so on. According to Lenin's decree "On the Separation of the Church from the State and the School from the Church", all this was the property of the whole people, property which the Church used but did not possess. However, the clergy continued to regard the treasures at the Churches' disposal as their property and were not going to part with them.

The idea took shape in the popular consciousness that church treasures could be used to buy grain to help the famine-stricken population. It was sympathetically received by considerable sections of the believers, and by some of the clergy, who believed that, by using the wealth at the disposal of the Church to help the people in their hour of need, it would rehabilitate itself in the eyes of the people and raise its prestige in all strata of society.

Carrying out the will of the people, the Presidium of the All-Russia Central Executive Committee decided on February 16, 1922, to begin collecting church valuables to aid the famine victims, explaining to the believers that that measure "could not affect the interests of the cult itself". The decision was so obviously prompted by humane considerations that Patriarch Tikhon did not dare either to ignore or to challenge it. But neither was he going to support the action of Soviet Government, deciding on a tactic of covert opposition. On February 19, 1922, he published an appeal to the clergy and believers permitting them to donate only those objects to the relief fund that had no liturgical function. It was in fact, a call to sabotage the collection of valuables, for the clergy could easily declare any of the precious objects in the churches to be absolutely necessary for services and thus not subject to requisition. And that was indeed the course of action they opted for, bringing the campaign of collecting valuables on the verge of collapse.

This situation compelled the Soviet Government to take more drastic action in order to nip the possibility of sabotage in the bud. On February 23, 1922, the All-Russia Central Executive Committee passed a decree of which the first point read: "...To suggest that local Soviets should requisition, within a month of the publication of the present decision, all the objects of gold, silver and precious stones that are part of the church property handed over to groups of believers of all religions according to inventories and contracts, provided this requisition does not considerably affect the interests of the cult itself; and should hand these objects over to the agencies of the People's Commissariat of Finances to be passed on to the fund of the Central Commission for Famine Relief." The decree especially stressed that "the requisitioned property ... is to be used exclusively to aid famine victims".[1]

This time Patriarch Tikhon "forgot" all about his message of September 1919 promising not to interfere in politics and not to oppose Soviet power. In response to the decree, he issued a message of February 28, 1922, to the effect that "the requisitioning of all precious objects from the churches, including sacred vessels and other liturgical objects, is an act of sacrilege". "We cannot," said the patriarch's message, "approve of removal from churches, not even through voluntary donation, of sacred objects whose use for purposes other than liturgical is forbidden by the laws of the Ecumenical Church and is punished by it as sacrilege — laymen by excommunication, the clergy, by divestiture (Apost. Canon 73; Twice-Held Ecumenical Council. 10).[2]

It was clear that the patriarch's references to Apostolic and Council canons allegedly forbidding the use of church valuables for non-religious purposes were intended to provoke discontent among the believers. It was a fact that these canons had been disregarded when the Russian Church had donated its valuables to the autocratic regime. Addressing the czar on the occasion of the beginning of the Russo-Japanese war, Metropolitan Antoniy (Vadkovsky) of St. Petersburg declared on the behalf of the Church: "We and our property are at your disposal. If need be, the churches and the cloisters will bring the precious ornaments of their shrines to the altar of our Motherland."[3] And so they did — more than 2.5 million roubles worth.[4] The same happened during the First World War. "We dare say," wrote Archpriest I. Vostor-

---

[1] *Izvestiya VTsIK*, 26 February, 1922.

[2] *Tserkovnye vedomosti*, 1922, Nos 6-7, p. 2.

[3] *Tserkovnyi vestnik* (Church Bulletin), 1905, No. 1, p. 4.

[4] See *Tserkovnye vedomosti*, 1906, No. 8, *Additions*, p. 26.

gov, expressing the loyalty of the clergy and monks to the czar, "that, if the authorities of the state and the Church invite it, if they permit or order it, the churches and the cloisters will give away, without delay or regret, the copper of the bells, the gold and silver of church-plate, the precious settings of the icons, the ornaments of the crosses and vestments, provided this does not affect the religious feeling but prompts others, those who can, to give away silver and gold to meet the needs of the war."[1] And so they did again. Suffice it to say that the Kiev-Pechery Lavra alone contributed to the Nicholas II fund 33,073 roubles and 23 kopecks; 12 pounds 55 *zolotniks*[2] of gold; 45 *puds* 37 pounds 62 *zolotniks* of silver, and 65 puds in copper coin.[3]

The patriarch's message was seen by the clergy and religious fanatics as a call to anti-Soviet action. In some areas, their provocations led to clashes between believers and members of commissions requisitioning church valuables. The press even mentioned the number of such bloody conflicts provoked by Patriarch Tikhon's appeal: 1,414. That figure was later quoted by church historians, too.[4]

Now, what objectives did the patriarch pursue in embarking on a confrontation with the Soviet Government?

The first goal lay on the surface, one might say; it was stated quite plainly: preventing the Soviet state from coping with the difficulties caused by the drought and famine, and thus pushing it to the brink of collapse. The article "Holy Counter-Revolution" published in *Izvestiya VTsIK* pointed out that "the Church was interested in the 'bony hand of famine' strangling Soviet power".[5] The interests of the emigré circles were very much the same. "Famine," a certain church leader later admitted, "roused the Russian emigration's hopes for a speedy fall of the Bolsheviks, as it appeared that

---

[1] *Tserkovnost*, 1917, No. 337, p. 7.

[2] *Zolotnik* equals 1/96 of Russian pound.

[3] *Svet pecherskiy* (The Light of Pechery), 1917, Nos 21-22, p. 41.

[4] S. Troitsky. *O nepravde karlovatskogo raskola* (On the Falsehoods of the Karlovci Schism), Paris, 1960, p. 24.

[5] *Izvestiya VTsIK* (News of the All-Russia Central Executive Committee), 28 March, 1922.

the power in Russia would not be able to cope with that calamity, that it would therefore never survive it."[1]

The second objective was at the back of the clergy's mind, and it was not much talked about in Patriarch Tikhon's entourage. But the emigrant press, convinced that the days of Soviet power were numbered and that there was no longer any need for secrecy, let the cat out of the bag. *Russkaya mysl* (Russian Thought), the emigrant journal printed in Paris, published an item which said that "church valuables must be preserved for financing the struggle against Soviet power".[2] The anti-Soviet counter-revolutionaries wishfully hoped that Patriarch Tikhon would "soon take power in his hands to transfer it to the lawful carrier of that power whom he himself would name". That would be the time, they believed, when "the treasures of churches and monasteries would be of major financial significance during the transition period".[3]

Thus the church canons to which Patriarch Tikhon referred were merely an instrument in the hands of the patriarch himself and his followers for camouflaging a new burst of counter-revolutionary activity aimed at overthrowing the power of the people. However, the church counter-revolutionaries' designs were doomed to failure. The republic of the Soviets withstood all hardships, and at the same time all the working people of the country, including believers, could once again see for themselves how reactionary and hostile to the people the church policy pursued by Patriarch Tikhon and his adherents was. The most rabid of the saboteurs in cassocks were tried by the people's courts and deservedly punished for their anti-Soviet activities of concealing the valuables that were subject to requisitioning and for organising violent opposition to Soviet Government bodies.

Although the clergy and the emigrant press of those times referred to these trials as acts of "persecuting the Church", their purely political character was so obvious

---

[1] I. Stratonov. *Russkaya tserkovnaya smuta* (Unrest in the Russian Church), Berlin, 1932, p. 43.

[2] S. Troitsky. Op. cit., p. 24.

[3] I. Stratonov. Op. cit., p. 43.

that in the end the leaders of the Russian Orthodox Church themselves admitted the fact. "In the years after the October Revolution," says an official publication of the Russian Orthodox Church, "there were numerous trials of churchmen. What were they tried for? Exclusively for their anti-Soviet activities under the cover of their cassocks and the church banner. These were political trials which had nothing to do with the purely church life of religious organisations and the purely church work of the individual clergymen."[1]

At one of the trials in Moscow in 1922, Patriarch Tikhon himself was called as a witness; he tried to disclaim any responsibility for the bloody excesses that had been organised by the clergy in accordance with his instructions. However, the facts and the documents presented to the court proved beyond a shadow of a doubt that the openly counter-revolutionary subversion of the measures taken by Soviet power to fight famine was carried out by the episcopate and the clergy on direct instructions from the patriarch. All this served as the grounds for taking Tikhon into custody and for instituting proceedings against him. The head of the Church was given a chance to analyse all the consequences of his activity and to assess the results of the political orientation which he and his followers adhered to.

## Tikhonians and Renovationists

Although Tikhon's followers comprised the overwhelming majority of the episcopate and the clergy, he never had complete and unequivocal support among the clergy. In particular, the members of the liberal-Renovationist trend in the Russian Orthodoxy did not approve either the Tikhonians' monarchist attitudes, their reliance on the most frenzied political reaction, or their direct support for the counter-revolution and foreign intervention, all of which, in their view, deprived the Church of the support of the broad

---

[1] *Pravda o religii v Rossii* (The Truth about Religion in Russia), The Moscow Patriarchate Publishers, Moscow, 1942, p. 26.

masses of the believers, thereby dooming it to gradual degeneration. This part of the clergy condemned Patriarch Tikhon's anathematising Soviet power and saw no danger for the Church in the decree "On the Separation of the Church from the State and the School from the Church".[1]

Taking these attitudes into account and intending to suppress them, the Local Council passed a decision on April 19, 1918, which said, in particular, that the clergymen who "promoted the implementation of the provisions of the decree on the freedom of conscience and similar acts hostile to the Church were to be banned from conducting services and, in case of failure to repent, divested of holy orders".[2]

These threats, however, had none of the desired effect. The opposition, who termed themselves a "group of progressive clergymen and laymen", were merely awaiting an opportune moment for removing Tikhon from power and changing the church policy which doomed the clerics to isolation. That moment, in the view of the group, came with the beginning of the investigation of Patriarch Tikhon's anti-Soviet activities, which made the head of the Church legally incapable and justified the raising of the issue of transference of patriarchal authority to other persons, as envisaged by the decisions of the 1917-1918 Local Council.

On May 12, 1922, several members of that group— the priests Vvedensky, Krasnitsky, Kalinovsky and Belikov, and sexton Stadnik—visited Tikhon, who was at that time under house arrest, and held conversations with him concerning further management of church affairs. Two days later, *Izvestiya VTsIK* published an appeal to the believers. The authors of the appeal condemned the clergy's meddling in politics and raised the issue of convening a new Local Council for the "pacification of the Church". "We believe it necessary," they wrote, "to convene immediately a Local Council to try those who are to blame for the disarray within the Church, to settle the issue of church administration and to establish normal relations between the Church and

---

[1] *Pravda bozhiya* (God's Truth), 1918, No. 1.
[2] *Tserkovnye vedomosti*, 1918, Nos 17-18, p. 96.

Soviet power. The anti-state civil war of the Church led by the top hierarchs must stop."[1]

On May 18, 1922, Tikhon was visited by Vvedensky, Kalinovsky and Belkov, who took over the Church's affairs later to be handed over to Metropolitan Agafanghel of Yaroslavl as Patriarchal Locum Tenens. But Agafanghel failed to arrive in Moscow. This suited the patriarch's opponents quite well, for it gave them a chance for taking independent decisions. By that time they had assumed a definite organisational shape, forming a group called the Living Church, which comprised not only clergymen but also laymen.

The constituent assembly of the Living Church was held on May 16, 1922, at the Trinity *podvorye* in Moscow. According to the programme adopted there, the group pursued the following goals: "(a) Revision of the existing laws on church administration with a view to finding out which of them have been made null and void by life itself and are even harmful to the Church. (b) Revision of church dogmas with a view to identifying the features that were introduced in them by Russia's former regime. (c) Revision of church liturgics ... and ensuring freedom of the pastors' creativity in liturgy, without violation of the rites and sacraments. (d) Revision of the statute on parishes in connection with the present-day conditions of church life. (e) Revision of church ethics and the elaboration of a doctrine of Christian public life suited to the social tasks posed by the present moment. (f) In general, revision and alteration of all the aspects of church life which are imperatively demanded by life today."[2]

The adherents of the Living Church formed the Higher Church Board (HCB) with Archbishop Antonin (Granovsky) at the head, although the latter was not a member of the group; they soon won the approval of their activity by the clergy of the central dioceses—first of the Moscow diocese and later of that of Petrograd. Following the example of Moscow and Petrograd, groups of the Living Church were formed at other

---

[1] *Izvestiya VTsIK*, 14 May, 1922.

[2] *Zhivaya tserkov* (The Living Church), Moscow, 1922, No. 3, pp. 11, 12.

dioceses as well. Many hierarchs also declared their support for the Board. One of the first to recognise the new church authority was Metropolitan Sergiy (Stargorodsky) of Vladimir, who soon became a member of the Board.

The organisers of the Living Church launched a vigorous campaign for involving the clergy in the movement they headed, which they described as "ecclesiastical-revolutionary" whose primary tasks were, in their view, the removal of bishops who were former monks from the administration of the Church, the abolition of monasteries, the introduction of a married episcopate, the opening of the way to church government for the white clergy, which would hold in their hands the church treasury, and only after that, the implementation of their radical church reforms.

The question arose of the convocation of a new Local Council which would sanction the changes in the Church and determine its position in the new social environment. Without awaiting for the convocation of a Council, members of the Living Church convened in late July and early August 1922 an All-Russia congress of their association, at which the institution of monasticism was criticised and a resolution was passed on the introduction of a married episcopate and reorganisation of church administration. As for the renovation of dogmas, ethics and liturgy, the solution of these problems was put off until the coming Council.

The Living Church's radical programme, which began to be implemented without any preparation, and the unaccustomed phraseology of the leaders of that group alarmed the moderate adherents of the renewal of the Russian Orthodoxy, who decided that the Living-Church group had gone too far to the left. This part of the clergy and of the laity supporting them came to be headed by Archbishop Antonin, Chairman of the Higher Church Board, who founded and led the League for Church Revival. The Petrograd committee of the Living Church headed by Vvedensky and Belkov also announced their rupture with the Living Church and declared their support for Antonin's group.

In the programme of the League for Church Revival, the main emphasis was on the social aspect of

Orthodoxy, while changes in dogmas and canons were virtually ignored. "Following the basic democratic equalitarian principle," the programme stated, "the group sets itself the goals: realisation of the interests of believers from among broad lower-strata people and the masses, their religious enlightenment through science and moral improvement, enhancement of spirituality of the cult, simplification of the external ritual and ceremonial aspects, prevention from the inclination towards pagan magic and the mechanics of the cult, and elimination of religious exploitation"[1].

The programme of the League for Church Revival appeared too moderate and insufficiently clearcut to Vvedensky and his followers. They broke off with Antonin and founded an independent group—the Association of Communities of the Ancient Apostolic Church, which took up a position intermediate between the other two groups. The Association advocated fairly radical changes in the Orthodox ideology and church organisation, but its adherents avoided leftist phraseology and extreme wordings for which the Living Church members had a propensity. Neither did they approve of the caste-type exclusiveness characteristic of the Living Church.

The Association's programme envisaged "the cleansing of Christianity of all pagan elements accumulated over its almost two-millennium-long existence; the struggle against belief in the rites and against prejudices; the struggle against ignorance; explaining to believers of the causes of the natural phenomena that gave rise to many superstitions and rites... A revision of the dogmas and ethics by a Council to clarify the true evangelical and apostolic principles of faith and morality obscured by medieval scholastics and school theology... Purification and simplification of the liturgy and its greater accessibility to the people's understanding: revision of liturgical books and calendars, introduction of ancient apostolic simplicity in the liturgy, in particular in the furnishings of churches and the vestments of the clergy, the native tongue instead of the obligatory

---

[1] *Zhizn i religiya* (Life and Religion), Kazan, 1923, No. 7, p. 8.

Slavonic, the institution of deaconesses, etc.... election of all pastors... Abolition of all awards... Elimination of religious professionalism... The closing down of all urban and rural cloisters... A white episcopate... Revision of all church canons and abrogation of those of them which have lost their vitality... The Church must be absolutely apolitical"[1].

Immediately after its establishment, the Association sent its representatives to the Higher Church Board, where they were given a third of the places. All three groups were recognised as equal Renovation associations willing to pool their efforts in reforming church life and adapting it to the new social conditions. True, several other Renovationist type groups evolved at that time, such as the Puritan Party of the Revolutionary Clergy and Laity, the Free Working Church, and others, but the Higher Church Board declared them to be "non-church associations" and did not include them in the sphere of its activity.

The Higher Church Board published a "Statute on the Organisation of the Zealous Supporters of Church Renovationism", which said, among other things: "The purpose of the union is actual renovation of the church life of the masses of the believers, Christian enlightenment, moral improvement through the implementation of the programmes of the Renovationist organisations which head the movement".[2] From the moment of publication of the Statute, members of all these groups came to be known everywhere as "renovationists" *(obnovlentsy)*, and their church organisation as the Renovationist Church.

April 1923 was chosen as the time of the convocation of a Local Council, which had to sanction the reorganisation of church life planned by the Renovationist groups. The "Statute on the Convocation of the Local Council of the Orthodox Russian Church" said: "The Local Council of 1923 will review all aspects of the life of the Church—matters of doctrine and ethics, liturgy, parish administration—with a view to eradicating all the extraneous elements that were introduced in the

---

[1] *Za Khristom* (Following Christ), 1922, Nos. 1/2, pp. 23, 24.

[2] *Zhizn i religiya*, Kazan, 1923, No. 7, p. 6.

life of the Church by the period of the Church's subordination to and alliance with the capitalist state, and to revealing the treasury of apostolic traditions in the life of the Church which it has retained"[1].

The programmes of the three Renovationist groups, the "Theses for the Coming Reforms of the Orthodox Church at the Local Council" drafted by Vvedensky on the basis of the programme of the Association of Communities of the Ancient Apostolic Church and approved by the Higher Church Board, and finally the statute on the Local Council itself—all these documents testified to a fairly substantive modernisation of the Russian Orthodoxy. The supporters of the Board intended to implement, under the new social conditions, the programme of church reforms which representatives of the liberal Renovationist movement in the Russian Orthodoxy began to work out as early as the first Russian revolution. Judging from the statements of their leaders, the Renovationist groups intended to reform the Church within a very short period of time. However, their very first practical actions showed that it would not be all that simple to achieve the results they desired.

The political platform of the Renovationist groups, which was based on recognition of Soviet power and approval of the socialist revolution, was welcomed by the overwhelming majority of the believers, who saw the socialist state as the defender of the people's interests and therefore condemned the counter-revolutionary anti-Soviet activities of the Tikhonians. That platform was also adopted by the main body of the clergy who, by the moment of the formation of the Renovationist Church, had had time enough to realise that the Soviet system was strong and that it was supported by the broad masses of the people. All this ensured a wide support of the clergy and laity for the political re-orientation of the Russian Orthodox Church, which was effected by that Renovationists, although there were numerous elements among them,

---

[1] *Tserkovnaya zarya* (Church Dawn), Vologda, 1923, No. 1, pp. 1, 2.

of course, that were hostile to the new regime and continued to hope for a restoration of the prerevolutionary system.

But the situation was quite different as far as the Renovationists' reformist tendencies were concerned — i.e., their demand for a radical modernisation of the Russian Orthodoxy, for a fundamental reorganisation of church life. True, their desire to give more scope to the white clergy by removing the monastic-episcopal hierarchy from the leadership of the Church, their attempts to democratise the administration of church parishes and to find new solutions to the problem of material security for the clergy were supported not only by rank-and-file clerics and laymen but also by part of the episcopate. As for the draft of reforms in the sphere of dogmas, canons and liturgical order proposed by the Renovationists, they found little support among the great mass of the clergy and the laity, and still less among the hierarchs. There were good reasons for that.

The idea of a radical renovation of Orthodoxy, beginning with the rites and ending with dogmatic matters, was not supported by the rank-and-file parishioners of Orthodox churches because the bulk of the remaining parishioners were satisfied by their religion precisely in its traditional form. Those believers who were dissatisfied with the traditional Orthodoxy for some reason or other, and who had, before the Revolution, to remain in the state Church, had ample opportunity to express their discontent in the years after the Revolution. And they did express it — by leaving the Church.

Under the impact of the revolutionary changes in the country and the socialist construction, under the influence of the emerging system of scientific and atheistic education, most of these malcontents finally broke off with religion in general, not just with the Orthodox Church.

Thus only those people remained in the Church who were content with the Orthodoxy in its properly religious aspects — as a confessional system satisfying their religious needs exactly in the form which it assumed historically and in which it had existed in pre-revolutionary times. The majority of them were socially passive individuals, besides, they were mostly middle-aged. They were more accustomed to the traditional Orthodoxy, while all kinds of religious innovations were seen as "departure from the faith of our fathers", as "corruption of the faith".

The rank-and-file parish clergy also treated the modernisation of the Orthodoxy, especially of the dogmas and the standards of church life, with greater reserve than the Renovationist leaders would have liked. Even those of the clerics who had no objection in principle to the freeing of the Russian Orthodoxy from obvious anachronisms took a cautious attitude towards the headlong pace of radical changes suggested by the renovationists. Moderate adherents of church Renovationism were especially worried about the decisions of the First All-Russia Congress of the "Living Church". "At the congress of the Living Church," wrote one of the Renovationist journals, "the church innovationists made a tactical error; they ignored the fact that convictions are different from institutions; institutions are easy to pull down and rebuild, while convictions must be changed through education, which requires time and a certain amount of caution; that is why noble thoughts and a noble attempt have brought nothing but hostility and division"[1].

As for the episcopate of the Russian Orthodox Church, they were worried lest the extreme radicalism of the Reformists should deprive the hierarchs of their former leading position and lead to the removal of monastic bishops from church administration. That was why the traditional Orthodoxy, which envisaged concentration of church power in the hands of the top hierarchs, suited the bishops better.

Thus the political reorientation of the Church implemented by the Renovationists found broad support among the believers and the clergy, whereas their programme of modernising the Orthodoxy did not have that support. Evidence of this came quite soon—as early as the 1923 Local Council, i.e., merely a year

---

[1] *Po stopam Khrista* (In Christ's Footsteps), Kaluga, 1925, No. 5, pp. 4, 5.

after the beginning of the organisational institutionalisation of the Renovationist movement.

At the Local Council of the Russian Orthodox Church, which took place in Moscow between April 29 and May 9, 1923, each of the Renovationist groups hoped to implement its own church reform programme, but the Council took a course quite different from the one the adherents of the modernisation of the Orthodoxy hoped for. The first seven items on the agenda were considered and resolved by the participants practically unanimously.

The resolution on the first item ("On the Orthodox Church, the Social Revolution, Soviet Power, and Patriarch Tikhon") expressed approval of the social revolution, condemned capitalism, annulled the anathematisation of Soviet power, and expressed support for the policy of the Soviet government; Tikhon's counter-revolutionary activity was condemned, and he himself was divested of his patriarchal dignity and monkhood.

Having considered the second item on the agenda (on a married episcopate), the Council "found it absolutely necessary to introduce a white married episcopate, side by side with unmarried persons".

The third item concerned second marriages for the clergy; this question was also resolved positively.

On the issue of relics, the Council expressed itself against falsification of relics and resolved to leave unsealed shrines open.

After that the Council considered the question of monasteries, resolving to "close down monasteries and convents keeping to a way of life that has been condemned", i.e., situated in the cities, but to "bless" unions and brotherhoods of "Christian toiling communities" formed on the basis of monasteries remote from the cities. That was an attempt to preserve the monasteries and convents by somewhat changing the form of their existence.

The sixth question was that of a calendar reform: it was decided to go over to the New Style beginning with June 12, 1923.

Finally, háving considered the question of the ecclesiastical emigration, the Council excommunicated those of its leaders who continued an open anti-Soviet activity[1].

There was a hitch during the discussion of the eighth item ("On Church Reforms") which, as we know, was central to the programmes of each of the three principal Renovationist groups. On this issue the Council passed a decision which virtually ruined the hopes of church reformers for a speedy realisation of their programmes. "The Holy Council of the Orthodox Russian Church," read the decision, "... deems it necessary to call on all workers in church renovation, without introducing any dogmatic or liturgical obligatory reforms, to do everything to preserve the unity of the church; it blesses the creative initiative and the start made in arousing the religious feeling, church consciousness and social morality"[2].

This resolution of the Council was an obvious step backwards in the Renovationist movement; in fact it doomed Renovationism as a reformist movement in the Russian Orthodoxy. Blessing the "creative initiative" of the Renovationists, it actually withheld its blessing from the ultimate results of that initiative—draft reforms of the dogmas, the canonical structure of the church life, and liturgical practice. Without the Council's sanction, all the drafts of church reforms outlined by Renovationist groups had no weight at all in the eyes of the clergy and the laity.

The positive attitude of the 1923 Council to Soviet power and its factual condemnation of innovations in the sphere of dogma and liturgy won over many Tikhonians, whom this position of the Church suited very well. The number of ex-Patriarch Tikhon's followers began to swindle—the Renovationist Church now controlled about half of all the parishes. The Renovationists anticipated easy victory, the more so that not only more and more members of the white clergy but even bishops went over to their side. As the

---

[1] *Pomestnyi sobor rossiyskoy pravoslavnoy tserkvi 1923 (Byulleteni)* (The Local Council of the Russian Orthodox Church of 1923 [Bulletins]), pp. 14-17.
[2] Ibid., p. 22.

Renovationist press reported, 73 hierarchs took part in the 1923 Council[1].

In the meantime, Patriarch Tikhon, deposed by the 1923 Renovationists-dominated Council, was far from going to surrender his positions. Realising that his counter-revolutionary activity merely isolated him from the believers and, moreover, made them adherents of the Renovationists, Tikhon took a step that confused and disarmed his opponents in the struggle for church power. On June 16, 1923, he sent a letter to the Supreme Court of the Russian Federation of which the facsimile was published in the *Izvestiya VTsIK*. "Being educated in a monarchist society," said the letter among other things, "and being influenced right up to my arrest by anti-Soviet-minded persons, I was indeed hostile to Soviet power, and this passive hostility sometimes developed into vigorous action, such as the appeal in connection with the Peace Treaty of Brest-Litovsk in 1918, the anathematising of the government in the same year, and, finally, the appeal against the decree on the requisition of church valuables in 1922... Conceding the correctness of the court decision on instituting legal proceedings against me on the counts listed in the bill of indictment (several articles of the Criminal Code pertaining to anti-Soviet activities), I repent of these my offences against the state system and beg the Supreme Court to change punishment, i.e., to release me from custody. I assure the Supreme Court that from now on I am no enemy to Soviet power. I finally and resolutely dissociate myself from both the foreign and the internal monarchist-White Guards counter-revolution"[2].

July 4, 1923, saw the publication of Tikhon's address to the episcopate, the clergy and the laity, developing the ideas of his letter to the Supreme Court. Calling on the clergy and the flock to "show examples of obedience to the existing civil power, in accordance with God's commandments," Tikhon took away the Renovationists' trump card — their monopoly to politi-

---

[1] *Vestnik sv. Sinoda* (Bulletin of the Holy Synod), 1923, No. 1, p. 3.

[2] *Izvestiya VTsIK*, 1923, July 1.

cal loyalty to the socialist state. "As for my attitude to Soviet power," said Tikhon's address, "I have defined it already in my statement to the Supreme Court.... The crime to which I plead guilty must in fact be blamed on the society which kept inciting me as the head of the Orthodox Church to active opposition to Soviet power. I now state quite definitely that I resolutely condemn any encroachments on Soviet power whatever their source might be. Let all foreign and internal monarchists and White Guards realise that I am no enemy to Soviet power. I have understood all the falsehoods and slander directed against Soviet power by its compatriots and foreign enemies, which they spread in oral and printed form throughout the world".

Having regulated his relations with Soviet power and regained freedom, Tikhon launched a resolute offensive against the Renovationists. To forestall that offensive, the Renovationist groups that were at loggerheads with each other decided to join their efforts in opposing the former patriarch in order to prevent his return to church power. On July 2, 1923, a joint session of the central committees of the Living Church and the Association of Communities of the Ancient Apostolic Church passed a resolution instructing all the Renovationist organisations of the Living Church and the Association of Communities of the Ancient Apostolic Church to concentrate all their attention on the elimination of "Tikhonianism" as politically and ecclesiastically counter-revolutionary organisation; to discontinue all public argument within the movement and to commit everyone to mutal and all-out support"[1].

In his message of July 15, 1923, Patriarch Tikhon declared that he was taking back in his hands the ecclesiastical authority which he had handed over a year before to Metropolitan Agafangel. He declared the 1923 Council to be incompetent, and its decisions devoid of canonical validity. Playing on the conservative inclinations of the bulk of the believers, who held fast to the traditional forms of religion and rejected

---

[1] *Izvestiya VTsIK*, 1923, July 4.

experiments in this area as "profanation of the faith of our fathers and grandfathers", on the monks' fear of losing their privileged position in the Church, and on the clergy's suspicious attitude to the overly sudden and speedy breaking of the routine of church life and of the Orthodox dogmas, proposed by the Renovationists, Patriarch Tikhon launched a large-scale campaign of discrediting the Renovationist movement.

The leaders of that movement were accused of destroying the unity of the Church, of "rebelling" against the "legal ecclesiastical power" in the person of Patriarch Tikhon. In July 1923 Tikhon anathematised them.

But the main emphasis of Tikhonian agitation was on something different—on the content and modernising character of the Renovationists' reformist activity, which were subjected to public condemnation and discredited.

The anti-Renovationism campaign resolutely waged by the Tikhonians led, within a relatively short period, to tangible results. Many hierarchs and clergymen, who had previously identified themselves with the Renovationists and even participated in the 1923 Council, began to return to Patriarch Tikhon, repenting of their apostasy. The Renovationist Church lost one parish after another.

Seeing that their policy of modernising the Orthodoxy found no support among the bulk of the clergy and laity, merely giving cause to the Tikhonians for accusing the Renovationists of "heretical" designs, the leaders of the Renovationist movement decided to change their tactics. Once again they went back on their original plans.

In August 1923, a plenary session of the Higher Church Council elected by the 1923 Local Council in place of the Higher Church Governing Board, took place. It was decided to dissolve the Living Church, the League for Church Revival, and the Association of Communities of the Ancient Apostolic Church, and to unite the Renovationist movement within a "single, holy, *sobornaya* Apostolic church", which was to be named the Russian Orthodox Church (and not the Renovationist Church as before).

As for the Higher Church Council itself, it was reorganised as the Holy Synod, traditional in the Russian Orthodoxy; Metropolitan Yevdokim (Meshchersky) became its head. Since February 1925, the office of chairman of the Holy Synod was held by Metropolitan Veniamin (Muratovsky), and since May 1930, by Metropolitan Vitaly (Vvedensky). During the reorganisation of the governing body of the Renovationist Church, one significant reservation was made. The Synod declared itself "not responsible for the actions and instructions of the Higher Church Governing Board and the Higher Church Council, and disclaimed any responsibility for their instructions"[1]. Such a decision gave the new leadership of the Renovationist Church full scope for manoeuvre.

Of the leaders of the three Renovationist associations, only the head of the Association of Communities of the Ancient Apostolic Church Vvedensky, who was promoted to archbishop by the 1923 Council, obeyed the Synod's decision and remained a member of that highest church body. The other two—Protopresbyter Krasnitsky and Metropolitan Antonin—refused to disband their groups and continued to act independently, opposing both the Tikhonian group and the Renovationist Synod.

Metropolitan Antonin demonstratively rejected the title of Metropolitan of Moscow and All Russia given to him by the Renovationist Church, and called himself a bishop of the League for Church Revival. The League comprised some 40 members and disintegrated right after the death of its founder in 1927.

The Living Church was more numerous and influential. After secession from the Renovationist Church, it existed as a narrow group within the white clergy estate, and its members continued to pretentiously call themselves "church revolutionaries".

The Synod set up at the August plenary session deemed it necessary to put an end to all talk of "renovation of the Orthodoxy" and the "new Church". It instructed the episcopate and clergy within its jurisdiction to suggest to the believers that the innova-

---

[1] *Vestnik sv. Sinoda*, 1923, No. 1, p. 14.

tion of the Renovationist organisations and groups was a thing of the past and that now the Renovationist movement firmly stood on the positions of the Orthodoxy in its traditional form. The Synod's letter circulated in February 1925 in all the diocesan departments stated: "The Orthodoxy must be the motto and symbol of the ideological workers of the Holy Church. The Renovationist movement is not a group, party, or new Church. The Renovationism is the Orthodoxy... It must be explained to the parishioners that Tikhonianism is a rupture with the Orthodoxy, that it is a sectarian schism that has nothing in common with the Orthodoxy... The Holy Synod ... stands on guard of the Orthodoxy." The letter then recommended the Synod's adherents to substitute, once and for all, the word "orthodoxy" for "Renovationism"[1].

The Renovationists openly declared that they regarded the Christian dogma as immutable and did not intend to revise the dogmas of the Orthodoxy. In his report on "An Apologetic Substantiation of Renovationism" delivered at a plenary session of the Synod in January 1925, Vvedensky, promoted by that time to metropolitan, emphasised that "the Renovationist movement resolutely accepts the dogmas of the Church, not daring to revise that which lies in the light of absolute reliability"[2] There was thus not a trace left of the demands for modernisation of the dogmatic foundations of the Orthodoxy which the Renovationists had put forward at the very beginning of their movement.

As for the reforms of the church order, the Synod handled that issue very cautiously, too, promising to reduce their number to an absolute minimum. "We recognise the need," said the Holy Synod's Appeal to the Orthodox People, "for changes in the everyday church life that have long been outlined by our best and oldest archpastors, learned professors, theologians and pre-Council conferences, changes that were implemented by the 1917 and 1923 Local Councils. But

---

[1] *Po stopam Khrista*, 1925, Nos. 1-4, p. 5.

[2] *Tulskiye yeparkhialnye vedomosti* (Tula Diocese Gazette), 1925, No. 6, p. 17.

we guard sacredly, firmly and staunchly, and will guard to the end of our life the purity of the teaching of the Orthodox faith, its sacraments and dogmata"[1].

The same ideas were expressed in Holy Synod's Message to All the Eastern Patriarchs[2].

The Renovationists made several attempts at achieving a reconciliation with Tikhon and his adherents so as to join their efforts in overcoming the split in the Church that weakened the Russian Orthodoxy. In its address to the Tikhonian episcopate, the Renovationist Synod wrote: "What divides us? If you are disturbed by the revolutionary impulses of the Renovationist groups, by their headlong breaking of the church-administrative apparatus, their plans for future reformation, their internal strife and divisions, you should know that the 1923 Local Council put an end to their reformist tendencies, leaving the dogmata, the sacraments and the liturgical order intact"[3].

To achieve an agreement with the Tikhonians, the leaders of the Renovationist Church even went as far as to revise those few reforms which were sanctioned by the 1923 Council. Demonstrating their spirit of reconciliation, the Renovationists reduced to a minimum the consecration of married bishops, practically ceased to give permissions to a second marriage, objected to the use of the New Style, etc. All this was done in order to convince Tikhon and his adherents that the so-called Renovationists were no longer innovators and reformists, that it was therefore quite possible to come to terms with them.

That was a complete and unconditional surrender by the Renovationists of their ideological positions, their capitulation as church reformers, a final rejection of any attempts to modernise the Russian Orthodoxy and its ideology. The Renovationist leaders had just one concern now—retaining the leadership of the Church at any price by sharing it with the Tikhonians.

But Patriarch Tikhon and his entourage rejected compromises. Sensing the weakness of the Renovation-

---

[1] *Vestnik sv. Sinoda*, 1923, No. 1, p. 5.

[2] Ibid., p. 2.

[3] *Tulskiye yeparkhialnye vedomosti*, 1924, Nos. 4/5, p. 1.

ists' position, the Tikhonians resolutely refused to recognise them as a church organisation. A conference of loyal bishops called by Tikhon in July 1923 declared the Renovationists to be "schismatics" and asked the patriarch not to retire until the Local Council. Refusing to negotiate with the Renovationists' Synod, Tikhon established contacts with the Living Church leaders, intending to use the conflict between that group and the Renovationist Church for his own purposes. Krasnitsky was even made a member of the Tikhonian Higher Church Council, which existed as a body attached to the patriarchal Synod in accordance with the decision of the 1917/1918 Council. However, the Tikhonians did not give any concrete work to the Living Church leader in their governing body, keeping him there merely as a bait for the Renovationists. On realising that, Krasnitsky broke off with Patriarch Tikhon and continued his separatist activity.

At the very height of his struggle against the Renovationist movement, Patriarch Tikhon died, leaving a testament that was published on April 5, 1925, in the *Izvestiya VTsIK*. "In the years of the civic collapse," said the testament, "Soviet power became, by the will of God without which nothing occurs in the world, head of the Russian state, taking upon itself the heavy burden of eliminating the horrible consequences of the war and dire famine... Without transgressing against our faith or our Church, without allowing any concessions and compromises in the matter of faith, we must be sincere as citizens in our attitude to the Soviet government and to work for the common good, bringing the Church's external life and activity in accordance with the new state system, condemning any association with the enemies of Soviet power and any agitation, overt or covert, against it." The testament showed that the decision to reorientate the Church taken by Tikhon in 1923 was not a purely tactical move but reflected his new conviction that the acceptance of the new social reality by the Russian Orthodoxy was historically inevitable. He realised, indeed, that without a political reorientation he would be unable to defeat the Renovationists or restore church unity.

## The Decline of the Renovationist Church

Patriarch Tikhon's death was seen by the leaders of the Renovationist Church as the disappearance of the main obstacle to the restoration of the Church's unity. This death, as the Renovationists later acknowledged themselves, "revived the Synod's hopes for a reconciliation..."[1] The Renovationist Synod therefore immediately called on the late patriarch's adherents to forget their past differences and to begin joint preparations for a new Local Council which would overcome the split in the Church.

The programme of the coming Council was drawn up in such a way as to satisfy both the Renovationists and the Tikhonians and thus to facilitate the "pacification of the hostile parties". It included the following items: (1) On peace within the Church (the liquidation of the division of the Church and the ways of pacifying the strife within the Church; the 1923 Local Council; the grace of the clergy); (2) On order within the Church (the ordering of church life under present statehood, the organisation of the central and local church administration; (3) On the participation of the Russian Church in the Ecumenical Council; (4) Elections of the highest, central administrative body of the Orthodox Church on the territory of the USSR.

In persuading the Tikhonians to take part in the preparation for and implementation of the coming Council, the Renovationist leaders expressed in advance their readiness to revise those decisions of the 1923 Council which were unacceptable to Patriarch Tikhon's followers.

However, even after the death of their head, the Tikhonians did not seek for ways of achieving a reconciliation with the Renovationists. With most of the parishes on their side, and with the number of such parishes growing from year to year[2], they hoped to win over the rest as well.

---

[1] *Vestnik sv. Sinoda,* 1926, No. 6, p. 15.

[2] According to the Renovationists themselves, there were 15,000 parishes on their side in 1924, 9,039 in 1925, and only 6,245 out of

Metropolitan Pyotr (Polyansky), Patriarch Tikhon's successor, categorically refused to conduct negotiations with the Renovationist leaders on joint preparations for a new Local Council. In a message of July 28, 1925, he called on the clergy and the believers to "obey the existing civil power in accordance with God's commandments", and expressed a sharply negative attitude both to the past Council (that of 1923) and to the future one. Both of these councils were called unauthorised, and the laity were instructed to ignore them.

The Renovationist Synod was not idle in that period, either. Having failed to reach an agreement with the leaders of the Tikhonian Church, it appealed directly to the clergy and the laity of Tikhonian orientation, inviting them to participate both in the preparations for the Local Council and in the work of the Council itself. But that invitation failed to achieve any significant results; only 15 delegates, ignoring Metropolitan Pyotr's interdiction, came to the Council from Tikhonian dioceses[1]. However, their presence hardly affected the character and content of the Council's work, neither did it make the decisions of the Council more palatable to the Tikhonian clergy, still less to the episcopate.

The Local Council convened by the Renovationists took place in Moscow on October 1-10, 1925. Some 400 persons participated in its work, half of them laymen.

The report "On the Position of the Orthodoxy Today" was made by Metropolitan Vvedensky, who began by stating the fact that in recent times there had been a distinct turning away of the masses from religion and a growth of atheism, especially among the young[2]. The speaker used this fact to substantiate his thesis on the need for joining all church forces in resisting the onslaught of atheism. This was followed by an account of the numerous but fruitless attempts of the Renovationist Synod to achieve a unity of action

---

28,743 in 1926 (*Vestnik sv. Sinoda*, 1926, No. 6, p. 15; 1927, No. 2, pp. 9, 17).

[1] *Tserkovnyi vestnik*, Irkutsk, 1925, No. 11, p. 2.

[2] *Vestnik sv. Sinoda*, 1926, No. 6, p. 9.

with the Tikhonians, of the Tikhonian hierarchs' refusal to come to an agreement with the Renovationists on a compromise basis.

A resolution passed by the Council on Vvedensky's report stated that "any further appeals to the Tikhonian hierarchy are useless", and called on the Renovationist clergy and laity to step up work among the ordinary parishioners of the Tikhonian orientation, explaining Renovationist positions in order to win them over to the Renovationists' side [1].

The second report (On the Activities of the Holy Synod and on Measures for Achieving a Reconciliation in the Church's Split), read by Archpriest Krasotin was devoted to analysis of the evolution of the Renovationist movement beginning with May 1922 and ending with its state at the time of the convocation of the Third Local Council. One of the main objectives of the report, which the speaker himself preferred to pass over in silence, was to present in the most favourable light the hasty retreat of the Renovationist leaders from their original ideological positions, the unconditional abandonment of their earlier much vaunted programme of church reforms.

In its resolution on Krasotin's report, the Council approved of his evaluation of the first stage of the Renovationist movement providing for sharp condemnation of the activities of Krasnitsky and Bishop Antonin. Appreciating the "caution with which the Holy Synod ... implemented the decisions of the 1923 Council", the Local Council resolved to restrict to a minimum the ordination of married bishops and the permission for priests to marry a second time. The clergy were allowed to use both the New and the Old Styles. The final decision on these last two issues was to be taken by the coming Ecumenical Council of the Orthodox Churches which the Eastern patriarchs intended to hold in the second half of the 1920s.

Thus, the Local Council of 1925 officially sanctioned the Renovationist Church's abandonment of proposed reforms not only in the field of dogma, canonical system and liturgical order (these had been given up by

---

[1] Ibid., p. 14.

the Renovationists already at the 1923 Council) but even in the sphere of everyday life, which the previous Council did not object to. In practical terms that meant final self-liquidation of Renovationism as a reformist movement called upon to modernise the Russian Orthodoxy to suit the new conditions of its social being. The Renovationist Church lost all of its specificity.

True, the Third Local Council did not reject in principle the idea itself of modernising religion and the Church, but its decisions oriented "church Renovationism" toward slow and imperceptible changes over many years and decades. As distinct from the original view of the Renovationist movement as a "revolution in the Church", as "a Russian edition of the Reformation", the 1925 Council declared that "the task of church Renovationism is a task of long organic work"[1].

The new interpretation of the essence of the Renovationism and its tasks compelled the Renovationist ideologists to work out new tactics. That was taken into account by the 1925 Council, which suggested that the episcopate and clergy of the Renovationist Church adhere in their work to the following tactical principles. Inasmuch as the bulk of clerics and laity did not approve of the changes planned by the Renovationists (even most insignificant ones, which are of no fundamental character), it was deemed expedient to publicly abandon the intention to change anything in the Russian Orthodoxy in the foreseeable future. All talk of innovations and reforms was to be stopped, and the Renovationist clergy's attention was to be focussed on a gradual and cautious preparation of the flock for future reforms—on replacing the traditional faith in the rites by a "conscious faith", on explaining to the parishioners of the content of Orthodox dogmas, and on developing in the believers the view of the Orthodoxy as a "dynamic religion" in a state of perpetual development and renewal.

The new programmatic and tactical principles of the 1925 Council were most clearly expounded in the theses of the Renovationist ideologist B. Titlinov, which

---

[1] *Vestnik sv. Sinoda*, 1927, No. 4, pp. 17, 18.

were circulated by the Holy Synod throughout the dioceses "for conversations and public readings on questions of Renovationist ideology". "Renovationist reformism," said the theses, "is not an innovation but restoration of the primary Christian tradition, revival of the creative process in the Church that stopped during the period of church stagnation. Church reformism must set church consciousness in motion, overcoming the inertia of rite-oriented religiosity deadening the living faith. But no church reforms can be fruitful unless they meet the mood of the believing masses halfway. The development in the masses of believers of living religious questions is therefore a necessary preparation for the realisation of the Renovationist reformist programme"[1].

Guided by the decisions of the 1925 Council, the Renovationist Synod decided to issue a special circular to dissociate itself publicly from the Living Church and other predecessors once again: "All articles which appeared in the journal *The Living Church* published in 1922 and early 1923, and which caused misunderstandings and doubts among the faithful, and also certain resolutions and Rules of groups imprudently touching on questions of dogma, must be seen as no more than the personal views of various authors or the private views of individual groups"[2].

In accordance with the instructions of the 1925 Council, the episcopate and the clergy of the Renovationist Church began working on the believers trying to persuade them through sermons, conversations, articles and reports, that the Renovationist movement was piously and unshakeably true to the Orthodoxy in its traditional forms, and that it could therefore never be identified with the Reformationism[3].

Attempts were made to convince the parishioners of Orthodox churches (above all those of the Tikhonian orientation) that innovations were of secondary importance to the Renovationist movement and had never

---

[1] *Vestnik sv. Sinoda,* 1927, No. 1, pp. 21, 22.
[2] Ibid., No. 3, p. 4.
[3] Ibid., No. 4, pp. 9, 10.

been in the foreground. Moreover, it was insisted that the Tikhonians had more innovations than the Renovationists. Thus, the All-Union missionary conference called by the leaders of the Renovationist Church early in February 1927, decided to publish a pamphlet *The Innovations of the Tikhonians or the So-Called Old Church Supporters"* [1].

The Renovationist leaders assumed that their new tactics of total negation of the reformist character of their movement would soon bring back to their Church those hierarchs, clerics and laymen who had abandoned them to join the Tikhonians because of the overly sudden and hasty changes of the old church traditions by Renovationists. But this was not the case. The ideologists of Renovationism were so much carried away by their own parallels between the Tikhonian and Renovationist Churches that they began to assure the flock that "there was in fact no difference between the old and the new church trend" [2]. That showed that even the Renovationist clergy let alone the rank-and-file members of the Renovationist parishes) no longer understood what the specific features and the prospects of their movement were. This situation suited the Tikhonians, who demonstrated their loyalty to the church traditions and won over ordinary believers by that loyalty; it facilitated the return of the Renovationist parishes to the jurisdiction of the Tikhonians.

Fairly soon, the Renovationist church leaders realised that the new tactic cost them more than it was worth. The Synod's plenary session held in April 1926 had to acknowledge "a fall in the morale in some dioceses" and "certain quantitative setbacks in the development of the Renovationist movement", the causes of which lay, in the Synod's view, in the "insufficiently profound implementation of the Renovationist principles".

The next plenary session of the Synod (at the end of January and early in February 1927) considered the question of the state of the Renovationist movement. It was pointed out there that a conciliatory attitude to the Tikhonians and the absence of a clearcut programme

---

[1] *Vestnik sv. Sinoda*, 1927, No. 3, p. 6.
[2] Ibid., No. 1, p. 20.

that would be convincing to the ordinary believers weakened the Renovationist movement.

Seeing that the tactics of smoothing out the differences between the church trends was to the Tikhonians' advantage, the Renovation leaders decided to step up their propaganda of the ideas of Renovationism, a practice that had virtually been discontinued after the 1925 Local Council. To infuse a fresh spirit in the Renovationist movement, it was decided to celebrate on a grand scale the fifth anniversary (in May 1927) of the emergence and organisational shaping of that movement, making that fairly modest jubilee a grandiose church festival. The Renovationist Church also took an active part in the preparations for the Eighth Ecumenical Council, intending to enlist the support of the Council's "fathers" in their strife with the Tikhonians. It was also planned to hold the next Local Council in 1928. But none of these plans of the Renovationists was realised.

Attempts to revive Renovationism as a reformist movement failed. Despite the vigorous propaganda by the leadership and ideologists of the Renovationist Church, their vague church slogans and vacuous ideological principles could not slow down, let alone stop, the disintegration of Renovationism as a movement for the modernisation of the Russian Orthodoxy. The unwillingness of the church Renovationists to take into account the psychology of the bulk of the believers, their excessive haste in the implementation of church reforms (especially at the first stage of the Renovationist movement)—all these factors contributed to the collapse of their reformist plans and programmes. Besides, the Renovationist leaders' plunging from one extreme to another disoriented the rank-and-file adherents of the "new Church", making it easier for Tikhon's supporters to win over the parishioners to their side.

True, the leaders of the Renovationist Church were still hoping for something to happen. The 1934 Renovationist Synod even formed a special commission to work out a programme of fighting the Tikhonian Old-Church Supporters (the commission was headed by Vvedensky). Special instructions were issued defining the terms for receiving the Tikhonians into the Renovationist Church. But all this was done merely for show. More and more Renovationists repented to the patriarchal Synod. With the death in 1946 of Vvedensky, the principal inspirer of the Renovationist movement, the last of the Renovationist parishes went over under the jurisdiction of Patriarch Tikhon's successor. The Renovationist movement became a thing of the historical past.

Despite the bankruptcy of the Renovationist Church, the Renovationism itself was not without effect. It has influenced and continues to influence the present-day Russian Orthodoxy. The emergence of the Renovationist movement, which accepted the new social realities, accelerated the rupture between the bulk of the clergy and church hierarchy, on the one hand, and the internal and external counter-revolution, on the other, thus forcing the transition of the entire Russian Orthodox Church to the positions of loyalty to Soviet power. It was precisely the Renovationist ideologists who worked out a programme for modernising the Orthodoxy to adapt it to the new conditions of the existence of the Church. Although that programme, far from finding support by the entire Church, gave rise to a schism, certain programmatic principles of the Renovationists were later favourably received by prominent hierarchs of the Moscow Patriarchate.

### Metropolitan Sergiy's "Declaration" and Its Consequences

According to Tikhon's last will and testament, the Patriarchal Locum Tenens was Metropolitan Pyotr (Polyansky), a reactionary and conservative hierarch. Owing to Tikhon's patronage, he had made a dizzy career, rising during several years from a second-rate synodal official to the rank of Metropolitan of Krutitsy, who traditionally supervised the Moscow diocese and was only inferior to the patriarch himself in the hierarchy of the Russian Orthodox Church.

Metropolitan Pyotr, who undertook to continue Patriarch Tikhon's political line, was supposed also to carry out the behest of his predecessor: "We envisage the setting up of a special commission, under our supervision, and entrusting it with the task of investigation and, where need be, removal from office, according to canonical procedure, of those archpastors who persist in their errors and refuse to repent of them before Soviet power, bringing such archpastors to the trial by an Orthodox Council... We charge the special commission with investigating the actions of archpastors and pastors who have fled abroad... and to appraise their activities without delay. Their refusal to obey our call will compel us to try them *in absentia*"[1]. But the Patriarchal Locum Tenens did nothing to set up such a commission. Moreover, he engaged in anti-Soviet activities, for which he was tried and sentenced.

The leadership of the Church was assumed by Metropolitan Sergiy (Stragorodsky) of Nizhniy Novgorod, deputy Locum Tenens of the patriarchal throne, but he encountered resistance from various enemies almost at once. A group of Tikhonian bishops then staying in Moscow held a conference at which a Provisional Higher Church Council was set up on December 12, 1925. It was headed by Archbishop Grigoriy (Yatskovsky) of Yekaterinburg.

The Provisional Council found support among those hierarchs and priests who recognised Soviet power in words but were in no hurry to give any real support to it. That was the beginning of the so-called "Grigorianism". Metropolitan Sergiy declared the Provisional Council to be "non-canonical" and forbade its members to conduct divine services. The latter in their turn challenged the canonicity of Sergiy's powers. A struggle for power began between "Sergians" and "Grigorians". Soon, Metropolitan Agafangel joined in the struggle, also claiming a right to be the Locum Tenens (in his testament Tikhon named him as a candidate for the office of Locum Tenens along with Metropolitans Pyotr and Kirill).

Metropolitan Sergiy's political and ecclesiastical experience, his energy and flexibility, and finally, his prestige as one of the oldest hierarchs who has the

---

[1] *Izvestiya VTsIK*, 1925, April 15.

reputation of a liberal before the Revolution—all this to some extent helped him to overcome the opposition. But the main thing was that Metropolitan Sergiy did not only declare his loyalty to Soviet power (statements of that sort were also made by "Grigorians") but also confirmed his words by practical moves, which won over to his side the bulk of the believers who had long insisted that their "spiritual pastors" fulfil their civil duties to the socialist state.

Restoring the order established under Patriarch Tikhon, Metropolitan Sergiy set up an auxiliary body— a Holy Synod consisting of six and later of eight hierarchs. That occurred in May 1927, and on July 29 of that year Sergiy worked out, together with the Synod, a programmatic document—an appeal to the clergy that came to be known as "Metropolitan Sergiy's Declaration" (published in *Izvestiya VTsIK* on August 19, 1927).

Announcing in the Declaration the establishment of a provisional ecclesiastical administration recognised by the bodies of Soviet power, and acknowledging the hostility of some of the clergy to the new social system, Sergiy called on the clergy to revise their attitude to Soviet reality. "We want to be Orthodox and at the same time to see the Soviet Union as our civic native land, whose joys and successes are our joys and successes, and whose failures are our failures. Any blow spearheaded against the Soviet Union, whether it be war, boycott, a social calamity or an assassination ... we feel as a blow spearheaded against ourselves. While remaining Orthodox Christians, we remember our duty to be the citizens of the Soviet Union 'not for wrath but also for conscience sake', as the Apostle taught". Then Metropolitan Sergiy informed his adherents of two moves that he and the Synod had found it necessary to make.

The Declaration ordered those hierarchs and clerics who still hoped for a restoration of the old social system to retire from church affairs, and all the rest, strictly to adhere to the principle of loyalty to the Soviet state in their activity.

Second, the Declaration demanded that the Orthodox clergy abroad, who had emigrated from this country but were in canonical communication with the patriarchal Church, make written statements that they would not take part in political activities directed against the Soviet Republic. Those who withheld such an obligation or violated it, the Declaration warned, would be excluded from the clergy in the jurisdiction of the Moscow Patriarchate. Indeed, seven years later, a joint decision of the deputy of the Patriarchal Locum Tenens and the Synod of June 22, 1934, brought the emigrant episcopate and clergy, who failed to comply with the demands of the Declaration, to church trial [1].

Metropolitan Sergiy's realistic position, which took into account the mood of the rank-and-file believers and their political sympathies, reflected changes in the mentality of most ministers of worship under the impact of the social reforms implemented in Soviet Russia in the ten years of the socialist state existence". This position was supported both by believers and by most of the clergy. It marked the beginning of a new stage in the attitude of the Russian Orthodox Church to the Soviet state: not just loyalty to the government, but support for its home and foreign policies although in the atmosphere of the emerging Stalin's personality cult in the late 1920s and early 1930s there were serious violations of the Leninist principles of the decree vis-a-vis religion, the Church and believers.[2]

But reactionary church elements hostile to the Soviet social and state system attacked the fundamental propositions of Metropolitan Sergiy's Declaration. It was first rejected by the Russian emigrant church circles who placed their hopes on a new foreign intervention against the USSR. It was also attacked by the remnants of the internal counter-revolution who cherished new hopes for the fall of Soviet power.[3]

These forces were merely awaiting a chance to manifest their hostility to the Church's political course which was proclaimed in Metropolitan Sergiy's Declara-

---

[1] *Zhurnal Moskovskoy patriarkhii* (Journal of the Moscow Patriarchate), 1934, No. 22, p. 1.

[2] "Socialism and Religion", *Kommunist,* 1988, No. 4, pp. 115-123.

[3] This question requires special examination.—*Ed.*

tion. That chance came early in 1928 when a conflict erupted between Metropolitan Sergiy and Iosif (Petrovykh), former Metropolitan of Leningrad, which resulted in the emergence of the so-called "Iosifism".

Iosif, one of the most reactionary church figures, did not adopt Metropolitan Sergiy's position. Disobeying the head of the Church, he refused to comply with Metropolitan Sergiy's order which translated him from Yaroslavl, his temporary abode, to Odessa. He and five other hierarchs of the Yaroslavl diocese published in February 1928 a message to the clergy and the flock in which he declared his refusal to obey Metropolitan Sergiy as a "usurper of power within the Church", and the establishment of an independent church district not subject to the deputy of the Patriarchal Locum Tenens.

Iosif was supported by that part of the clergy which opposed the establishment of normal relations between the Russian Orthodox Church and the socialist state. He also found support among the *kulak* and capitalist elements in town and country, religious fanatics, in a word all those forces which rejected the socialist system and cherished dreams of bringing it down.

But "Iosifism" failed to find any broad support among the bulk of the believers and the clergy, and in 1930 it was already defunct. The collapse of "Iosifism" again proved to the Russian Orthodox Church's episcopate and clergy that anti-Soviet activities, whatever their religious forms, would not find sympathy among the majority of believers who were citizens of a socialist society. The Church's loyalty to the new social and state system was no longer merely declared—it was demonstrated in real terms.

## Chapter X
# THE CHURCH UNDER THE NEW SOCIAL CONDITIONS

After the end of the Renovationism as a reformist movement and the concentration of ecclesiastical authority in the hands of Metropolitan Sergiy (Stragorodsky), Deputy Patriarchal Locum Tenens since 1925, the Russian Orthodoxy entered a period of stabilisation and thorough adaptation to existence in a socialist society. That process, begun in the 1930s, still continues.

### The Church on the Eve of and During the Great Patriotic War of 1941-1945

The development of mass atheism in the USSR, which made itself felt already in the 1930s, on the one hand, and the confrontation between the Renovationists and the Old Church adherents, on the other, did irreparable damage to the Russian Orthodox Church. The number of parishioners and the number of functioning churches diminished from year to year. Not only laymen but also priests, theologians and church figures abandoned the Church and religion. Many monasteries and convents—first in the centre and later in the outlying provinces—ceased to function.

There was a certain revival of religious and church activity in the Russian Orthodoxy in the later 1930s, when numerous parishes of the western regions of the Ukraine and Byelorussia, which became part of the Soviet Union, entered the Russian Orthodox Church. But that activity was on the whole local in character.

The war started by Hitlerite Germany against the Soviet people set off another wave of religious activity. War meant suffering for the masses, brought on by the barbarity of the enemy, the loss of one's near and dear, the loss of homes, etc. People's suffering has always provided a breeding-ground for religion.

Most citizens of the socialist society did not abandon their atheist convictions, growing stronger in spirit in the face of suffering. Some of those, however, who had only recently broke off with the Church and did not yet have firm atheist convictions, faltered as they were struck by an avalanche of grief. Parishes were restored, some churches previously closed down for lack of parishioners were reopened. Several monasteries and convents began to function again. The growth of religious and ecclesiastical activity was especially noticeable on enemy-occupied territory, where grief and privations were greatest, making people seek illusory consolation in religion.

In most cases the episcopate and clergy were unanimous in their attitude to the Hitlerite invaders. They followed Metropolitan Sergiy of Moscow (acting Patriarchal Locum Tenens since 1937), who, on the day of the Nazi attack against the Soviet Union—June 22, 1941, called on the believers to rise in defence of the Homeland, expressing his confidence in the victory of the Soviet people over the perfidious enemy. During the war years, Metropolitan (later Patriarch) Sergiy issued more than 20 such messages, all imbued with a noble patriotic spirit.

The conduct of the episcopate and clergy of the Russian Orthodox Church during the war varied. Some of the pontiffs and churchmen on the territories temporarily occupied by the enemy served the Nazis, choosing the path of betrayal of their Motherland, the path of treason. Others refused to cooperate with the invaders, sticking to purely ecclesiastical tasks. There were also those who took part in the Resistance, cooperating with the guerrillas.

Many priests of the Russian Orthodox Church did

much more than pray for the Red Army's victory; they made material contributions to the war effort. Just as all other citizens, they gave money and valuables to the defence Fund. Funds were collected at church parishes for a column of tanks to be named after Dmitry Donskoy and a squadron of planes to be named after Alexander Nevsky.

The patriotism of the Orthodox churchmen during the war was an expression of the maturity of their feelings as citizens. However, religious consciousness perceived it as conscientious performance of their religious duty. This restored the sympathy for the Orthodox Church of those Soviet citizens who had broken off with the Church at a time when it held counter-revolutionary, anti-Soviet positions; it enhanced the prestige of the church leadership and gave the latter a chance to take measures to consolidate the positions of the Church in a country engaged in a terrible war.

The intention grew strong in the leading circles of the Russian Orthodox Church to consolidate the bodies of church administration, to restore the church structures destroyed in the years of confrontation between the Renovationists and the Tikhonians, and to complete the process of reorganisation begun by Metropolitan Sergiy a few years back. As all anti-Sergiy groups had virtually disintegrated, the supporters of the Patriarchal Locum Tenens no longer faced any obstacles in the way of consolidation of the Church's forces.

On September 8, 1943, a council of bishops of the Russian Orthodox Church was held in Moscow, attended by 19 bishops. Metropolitan Sergiy as the Patriarchal Locum Tenens made a report on the Church's patriotic work in the time of war; then a new patriarch was elected. The election of Sergiy as the patriarch, the thirteenth since the establishment of the patriarchate in the Russian Orthodoxy, was unanimous.

The patriarch called on Christians throughout the world "to unite in the name of Christ, fraternally, strongly and powerfully, for a final victory over a common enemy in the world struggle for the ideals of Christianity trampled by Hitler, for the freedom of Christian Churches, for the freedom, happiness and culture of the whole mankind"[1]. The Council expressed the Church's condemnation for the traitors of the Motherland who collaborated with the Nazis.

The 1943 Council completed the post-revolutionary restructuring of the Russian Orthodoxy, the process of bringing it in accord with the new social conditions. The Russian Orthodox Church, which broke up in the early 1920s to form a number of groups and associations hostile to one another, torn apart by numerous schisms, again became a unified religious organisation headed by a patriarch.

After the 1943 Council, the activity of the Church became distinctly more energetic. The remaining Renovationist and Iosifite parishes returned to the bosom of the Patriarchate, the number of bishops increased, and contacts with other Orthodox Churches were renewed. *Zhurnal Moskovskoi patriarkhii* (The Journal of the Moscow Patriarchate),[2] published in the 1930s under the editorship of Metropolitan Sergiy, again began to appear, becoming the official organ of the Russian Orthodox Church. The question of reopening theological educational establishments was under advisement.

At the height of these activities, on May 15, 1944, Patriarch Sergiy died. In accordance with his last will and testament, Metropolitan Aleksiy (Simansky), Sergiy's longtime associate who actively implemented his religious-political principles, became the Patriarchal Locum Tenens.

On January 31, 1945, a Local Council of the Russian Orthodox Church was convened in Moscow; it was attended by several Eastern patriarchs, which enhanced the prestige of that ecclesiastical forum in the eyes of the clergy and believers. The Council elected Aleksiy (Simansky) Patriarch of Moscow and All Russia and adopted "The Enactment on the Government of the Russian Orthodox Church".

The organisational structure of the Russian Or-

---

[1] *Patriarkh Sergiy i yego dukhovnoye nasledstvo* (Patriarch Sergiy and His Spiritual Heritage), The Moscow Patriarchate Publishers, 1947, p. 45.

[2] Since the middle of 1971 it appears in English as well.— *Ed.*

thodox Church determined by this Enactment (discussed below) has on the whole been preserved up to the present, with some changes introduced by the Hierarchs' Council of 1961. The changes concerned only that part of the Enactment which dealt with parishes, of which the financial and economic activities were reorganised: according to the 1961 Council's decision, those activities formerly controlled by the church rector or dean, were handed over to the parish council consisting of the churchwarden, his assistant and a treasurer.

The stabilisation of church life continued. Secondary and higher theological schools were reopened. The publishing activities of the Moscow Patriarchate were expanded. The need to pay more attention to the sermons was pointed out to the parish clergy, for sermons were the live and comprehensible addresses which the parishioners heard in the church (the liturgy in the Russian Orthodox Church is still conducted in Old Church Slavonic).

The Russian Orthodox Church survived the organisational and structural crisis into which it had been plunged in the 1920s and 1930s. Its position was stabilised and even consolidated—a process facilitated by the deterioration of the Soviet people's living conditions due to the war, by multiplication of the factors that usually contribute to a growth of religiosity, and by the curtailment of the scientific-atheist propaganda among the masses during the war. Among the causes of the growth of the Russian Orthodoxy's prestige was the patriotic activities of the Orthodox clergy during the war years, motivated, first and foremost, by civic feelings.

As for the content of the Moscow Patriarchate's theological and liturgical activity, it largely remained traditional: the idea of immutability of Christian dogmata was still upheld, the immutability of the Orthodox canonical order of church life was proclaimed, and any innovations in liturgical practice were condemned. In other words, the Tikhonian policy of preserving the Orthodox dogmata and rituals in their traditional, historically developed forms was continued.

## Participation in the Peace Movement

During the war the Russian Orthodoxy's adaptation to new social conditions expressed itself, among other things, in the Church's support for the Soviet people's liberation struggle against the Nazi invaders. In the post-war years this adaptation was manifested in the Russian Orthodox Church's participation in the peace movement that involved the whole Soviet people. The Church's peace-making activity was its natural response to the desire of Soviet believers (including the Orthodox clergy, of course), who had gone through countless hardships of the war years, to do everything possible to avert the threat of a new war.

This activity was conditioned and stimulated by social factors—the civic duty of Soviet believers. But they themselves perceived it as performance of their religious duty, as the realisation by the Church of an initiative inspired by supernatural forces, by Divine Providence. Hence the references to the Bible and statements by the Church's Holy Fathers as the basis for the Church's peace-making role, which made up the content of the "theology of peace and reconciliation" worked out by the ideologists of Russian Orthodoxy endeavouring to give a theological interpretation of the need for the Church's participation in the peace movement[1].

Although the ideologists of Russian Orthodoxy put the religious motivation of the Church's peace-making activity to the forefront, they also invariably point out the exceptional importance of the social motivation which follows from the civic position of the clergy and the believers. "We, the episcopate, clergy and laity of the Russian Orthodox Church, citizens of the Soviet Union," emphasised Metropolitan Aleksiy, "are filled with patriotic sentiments for our Soviet Motherland that determine our relationship to the society of which we are an integral part and to that society's aspirations

---

[1] *The Local Council of the Russian Orthodox Church, May 30-June 2, 1971. Documents, Papers, Speeches, Proceedings*. Published by the Moscow Patriarchate, 1972, p. 80.

towards the establishment of peace and justice throughout the world."[1]

The same duality is characteristic of the theological understanding of the content of the Church's peace-making activity.

On the one hand, the ideologists of Russian Orthodoxy regard prayer for and sermons on peace as the principal manifestations of the Church's peace-making activity. Practically every service in the churches includes prayers for peace. Considerable parts of the parish clergy's sermons are devoted to the preservation of peace. Such sermons also often appear in church publications.

On the other hand, the leaders of the Russian Orthodox Church pay great attention to involving the episcopate, the clergy and the laity in direct participation in the country-wide peace movement at all levels. That aspect of the Church's peace-making activity goes beyond its framework, and its scope and effectiveness can be judged by its achievements.

The Russian Orthodox Church has participated in the peace movement since its inception in 1949. It is represented in the Soviet Peace Committee at the All-Union, republican and regional levels, and in the World Peace Council. The Church was also represented at all the all-Union conferences and world peace congresses.

The Church takes an active part in the activities of the Soviet Peace Fund, to which it renders financial assistance. Its hierarchs, the clergy and laity are members of commissions for assistance to the Soviet Peace Fund.

The Church is also represented in the Union of Soviet Societies for Friendship and Cultural Relations with Foreign Countries. Its pontiffs and clerics are among the leaders and members of many friendship societies.

The Russian Orthodox Church also initiates its own peace-making moves. Thus on the Church's initia-

---

[1] *The Local Council of the Russian Orthodox Church, May 30-June 2, 1971. Documents, Papers, Speeches, Proceedings.* Published by the Moscow Patriarchate, 1972, p. 97.

tive, conferences in defence of peace were held in 1952 and 1969, attended by representatives of all the Churches and religious associations existing in the USSR at the Trinity-St. Sergiy Lavra (Zagorsk, Moscow Region).

On two occasions, the Russian Orthodox Church acted as the initiator and organiser of international religious conferences in Moscow in defence of peace.

In June 1977, a world conference "Religious Workers for Lasting Peace, Disarmament and Just Relations Among Nations" was held. It was attended by 650 representatives of diverse religious creeds—Buddhism, Hinduism, Judaism, Islam, Shintoism, Sikhism and Christianity—coming from 107 countries of the world. The Conference was prepared and chaired by a representative of the Russian Orthodox Church, Metropolitan Yuvenaliy (Poyarkov).

In May 1982, the world conference "Religious Workers for Saving the Sacred Gift of Life from Nuclear Catastrophe" brought to Moscow 590 representatives of all the principal religions from 90 countries. Metropolitan Filaret (Vakhromeyev) was head of the International Preparatory Committee and chairman of the Conference itself. The main report, "To Save the Sacred Gift of Life from Nuclear Catastrophe—The Duty of Religious Workers", was delivered by Patriarch Pimen (Izvekov) of Moscow and All Russia, head of the Russian Orthodox Church.

The Church takes an active part in the work of inter-Christian peace-makers' associations.

The Russian Orthodox Church was one of the co-founders, in 1958, of the Christian Peace Conference (CPC). The Church is represented in the leading bodies of the CPC and has taken an active part in all the five congresses of that association. At present, Metropolitan Filaret (Denisenko), representative of the Russian Orthodox Church, is chairman of the CPC Continuation Committee.

Representatives of the Russian Orthodox Church invariably come up with peace-making initiatives at the general assemblies and conferences of the World Council of Churches (WCC) and at the forums of the Conference of European Churches (CEC), one of whose principal tasks is consolidation of peace on the European continent.

Since the Russian Orthodox Church joined the country-wide peace movement, the Church's peace-making efforts have been regularly discussed in the church press. Since May 1949, *Zhurnal Moskovskoy patriarkhii* has carried a special section on "Peace Movement", where information on the peace-making actions of the Russian Orthodox Church is published, as well as official documents, reports, speeches, articles and sermons on problems of international peace. Similar sections are to be found in other periodicals of the Moscow Patriarchate.

The theological substantiation of the Church's peace-making activity is intensively worked out; we have mentioned the emergence of the "theology of peace and reconciliation", the principal elements of which have been discussed in a number of publications. Let us mention only some of the articles and reports devoted to the Church's understanding of the conditions for preserving peace in the world today, which have been published in the Moscow Patriarchate's theoretical organ, the *Theological Studies:* Ass. Prof. V. D. Sarychev, "Essence of Reconciliation, and Its Grounds in Bible"; Dr. A. S. Buyevsky, "Reconciliation Through Christ, and the World Peace"; Rev. Prof. L. Voronov, "Implementation of Reconciliation in the Life and Activity of the Church"; Bishop Filaret (Vakhromeyev), "The Theological Basis of the Peace-making Activity of the Church"; Hieromonk Avgustin (Nikitin), "Orthodox Teaching on the Reconciliation between God and Man".

Special attention is paid to proofs of the desirability and permissibility of joint actions in defence of peace by Christians and non-Christians, of believers and non-believers.[1]

Many prominent hierarchs of the Russian Orthodox Church earned high government awards for their patriotic activities in defence of peace: Patriarch Aleksiy (Simansky) received four Orders of the Red Banner of

---

[1] *Pomestnyi sobor 1971,* pp. 84, 85; *Bogoslovskiye trudy* (Theological Studies), VI, pp. 173, 174.

Labour; Patriarch Pimen (Izvekov), two Orders of the Red Banner of Labour and one Order of Friendship between Peoples; metropolitans Filaret (Denisenko), Aleksiy (Ridiger), Filaret (Vakhromeyev), Antoniy (Melnikov), Yuvenaliy (Poyarkov) and Pitirim (Nechayev), an Order of Friendship between Peoples each.

Several leading workers of the Russian Orthodox Church were awarded the Gold and Jubilee medals of the World Peace Council, and many clerics and laymen received awards from the Peace Fund and the Soviet Peace Committee.

These are the principal aspects of the peace-making activity of the Russian Orthodox Church—an activity highly appreciated not only by Soviet believers but also by atheistically minded citizens of our socialist society.

## Modernisation of the Socio-Ethical Views, Dogmata and Rites

A characteristic feature of Orthodox theology in recent years has been its striving to substantiate the inexhaustible possibilities and viability of Christianity in today's world. Of the problems put forward by theologians, much attention is paid to social and political issues. Many theological problems are reviewed in the light of these issues.

The emphasis on new aspects in Orthodox theology is directly linked with the vast social changes characteristic of the modern times. In particular, the victory of the 1917 October Revolution was, in the view of theologians, a turning point "which demanded a reappraisal of the [Church's] attitude to society".[1] The successes of socialist construction in the USSR, the attraction of the ideas of socialism, and the radical social changes in the world no longer permit the Church to stick to its old positions. It has to change its political and social orientation.

In doing so, Orthodox theologians cannot find support in any of the earlier social doctrines. They

---

[1] *Zhurnal Moskovskoy patriarkhii* (The Journal of the Moscow Patriarchate), 1967, No. 9, p. 36.

are not content with the socio-political views of F. A. Golubinsky, N. V. Karpov, V. I. Nesmelov, M. M. Tareyev, V. S. Solovyov, N. A. Berdyaev, S. N. Bulgakov, or with the prerevolutionary social position of the Russian Orthodox Church as a whole.

Theologians point out that they must give their blessing to the social restructuring of the world, to the social revolution. "...The spirit of Gospel and biblical teachings and admonitions," they write, "calls upon all who would work for peace to give effective support to the efforts of men of good will whose aim is the radical 'transformation of social relationships'... The Church must see that its structure is not an obstacle to active Christian participation in the revolutionary developments..."[1]

New ideas are expressed in present-day Orthodox literature on the value of social life, on links between man's individual value orientations and those of society, of the collective. Political and social freedom, peaceful coexistence of states with different social systems, labour and creative activity, scientific knowledge and moral perfection are all declared to be Christian values by theologians.

But the axiological approach to various social phenomena in Orthodox theology entirely rests on the postulates of religion and accords with its basic worldview orientations. That means that social theology correlates social phenomena with the transcendental principle standing above man and the world rather than with society's material conditions of existence. It is in God that the theologians propose to look for the laws and causes of social phenomena conditioning the character and direction of social transformations. It is in religion that the significance of the specific changes for society and man are proposed to be looked for.

It follows that in considering various aspects of social phenomena social theology correlates them with illusory notions rather than with real ones, thereby including among the values of social life a system of views that interferes with the cognition and transformation of reality. In other words, divine determinism is

---

[1] *The Journal of the Moscow Patriarchate*, 1972, No. 1, pp. 38, 40.

substituted in theology for social determinism, and an illusory system of social values for a real one. In its axiological orientation, social theology substantiates and inculcates principles that follow from the illusory-compensatory function of religion.

The essence of the Orthodox conception of social values is revealed especially strikingly in the theological interpretation of human freedom and the ways of its attainment. In considering various aspects of social freedom, theologians correlate it with supernatural rather than natural necessity, always linking freedom with a dogmatic view of the predestination of an individual's deeds and acts. Man is regarded as a blind instrument in the implementation of divine predestination.

A distinctive feature of the theological interpretation of social values is the view that they directly depend on supernatural forces and on the degree to which they are correlated with the religious principles of man's life and activity. In actual fact, that means that the religious axiological aspect acquires fundamental significance in the distorted light of human vital activity presented only as an "image" and "likeness" of a deity, and not in a real system of relations between society and nature, between men in the process of their life activity.

Another specific feature of the theological interpretation of social phenomena consists in the fact that all social values are completely identified with and reduced to the level of purely moral values. In that way, the problem of freedom is transformed into a moral notion, a category of Christian ethics. Suffice it to say that it is reduced to the choice between good and evil, to an ideal state of the human spirit which enables man to acquire "holiness" in Christ. Orthodoxy regards freedom as a state of man characterised by an absence of any inclination towards sinful motives and by striving for a moral ideal. On the objective plane, it includes divine grace and predestination, on the subjective one, obligatory love for God, so that man "might gratefully accept life and the universe as the gifts of divine love".[1]

---

[1] *Bogoslovskiye trudy*, Moscow, 1972, VIII, p. 156.

Shifting the problem of social values into the illusory sphere of man's relations with God, theology thereby interferes with scientific cognition of the problem of real freedom and necessity, for man's true freedom is replaced by God's absolute will, and men's conscious activity by the freedom of choice.

Orthodox theologians today declare labour, working activity, man's creative activity, which ensure the improvement of the conditions of earthly life, to be among the highest Christian values. Nowadays, theologians call labour a source of social well-being, a means of achieving material security, a constant addition to the results of divine creation. Very rarely, mostly in their sermons on Old Testament topics, do churchmen refer to the biblical interpretation of labour as God's curse for original sin. It is more often stressed that Christianity has always respected labour, regarding it as a feat of creating material and spiritual values.

There is hardly any need to recall here that Christianity did not always regard labour as "pleasing unto God".[1] Forced labour was included among such "values" as suffering, martyrdom, poverty. Such a system of Christian views was the core of any social theology. That was the reason why Marx stressed that "the social principles of Christianity declare all the vile acts of the oppressors against the oppressed to be either a just punishment for original sin and other sins, or trials which the Lord, in his infinite wisdom, ordains for the redeemed"[2].

In socialist society, the character and essence of labour have radically changed, as have the incentives for it; the working people's attitude to labour is now fundamentally different. Labour has become the principal form of men's vital activity, their primary need.

Naturally, the ideologists of the Orthodox Church cannot but take into account the changes in the evaluation of labour that have occurred in socialist

---

[1] This question requires special examination.— *Ed.*

[2] Karl Marx. *"The Communism of the Rheinischer Beobachter,"* In: Karl Marx and Frederick Engels, *Collected Works*, Vol. 6, Progress Publishers, Moscow, 1984, p. 231.

society. They recognise that the new conditions of life pose before the Church the task of "going out to meet everything new and positive rather than locking itself up in the customary concepts of established norms". That means that Christianity must tackle the task of "creative revision of established traditions while remaining loyal to the foundations of the Christian faith, to religious views, world outlook, and attitude to the world"[1]. In this connection, labour is declared to be the "believer's sacred obligation", a "citizen's duty", a "Christian's feat", and a "universal necessity".

Does all this mean that Orthodox theology has completely reappraised the essence, character and significance of labour activity, of men rejecting, as a consequence of this, the familiar biblical notions? Can it be assumed that a new evaluation of labour activity by contemporary theologians has changed the Christian conception of social values, of which labour is among the most important?

In order to clarify the real significance of the new theological evaluation, we must first of all consider the interpretation of the essence of labour in Orthodoxy, and the attitude towards it formed under the impact of religious ideology.

It should be noted that the new theological evaluations of labour do not at all mean that Christianity now takes a different view of its essence. Labour in a theological interpretation is not expedient activity aimed at mastering nature or a natural condition of human existence but an inevitable necessity imposed on man by the Creator's absolute will. It offers man a God-given form of getting his daily bread—the means of subsistence. Even today theologians say, though not too often, that man was "doomed to lead his earthly life in the sweat of his brow, in an exhausting struggle for life from generation to generation".[2]

Nowadays, however, social theology concentrates on the assertion that labour is not so much punishment as commandment. If man toils well, he thereby follows the divine commandment to "fill the land", "possess it",

---

[1] *Zhurnal Moskovskoy patriarkhii*, 1968, No. 4, p. 34.
[2] *Zhurnal Moskovskoy patriarkhii*, 1971, No. 4, p. 36.

"improve on the results of creation". Moreover, through work man becomes, as it were, God's co-worker, participating in His creative designs.

Thus labour acquires an extrahistorical and extrasocial content in Orthodox theology. As a Christian commandment, it ultimately becomes a pure moral universal principle ensuring the individual's self-perfection.

In recent years, the Russian Orthodox Church has taken various measures to increase the topicality of its activity, extend the range of socio-political problems to be grappled with, raising issues that must provide answers to "all the questions of contemporary man's spiritual and practical life".[1] Its hierarchs now resort to such concepts as the "theology of the revolution", the "theology of peace", "social activation", "social service", all intended, as they themselves admit, to include theology in the orbit of social history. While pointing to the loss by religion of the right to call itself the decisive factor in improving social relations as an indubitable fact, they nevertheless continue to regard it as a most important condition of "positive aspirations" towards building "life on the principles of true justice".[2]

In their formulation and treatment of social and socio-political problems, theologians endeavour to stress not so much the dogmatic and canonical principles as the accord between the new church doctrine and the present-day views of the principal typological groups of believers and non-believers. In an article "The Main Problems of the Modern Theological Studies in Their Development Since the End of the 19th Century", Archbishop Pitirim, Chairman of the Publishing Department of the Moscow Patriarchate and Editor-in-Chief of *The Journal of the Moscow Patriarchate,* stresses that today "problems of Orthodox theology are not the dogmata of faith and morality themselves nor the foundations of the Church's graceful liturgical life preserved in the Church since the first days of its existence but rather a mode of their assimilation and

---

[1] Zhurnal Moskovskoy Patriarkhu, 1969, No. 9, p. 92.
[2] *Bogoslovskiye trudy,* 1970, V. p. 226.

implementation in the Life of Christians under definite historical conditions".[1]

It is noteworthy that theologians persistently endeavour to present their social conceptions as a new approach to the evaluation of all historical events. These conceptions are depicted as a logical outcome of an impartial study and interpretation of the results of the October Revolution in Russia and of the construction of social life on new foundations. In this connection the theologians also reject the social theory of V. S. Solovyov, who endeavoured to integrate the idea of the kingdom of God on earth and the establishment of the theocratic system; and the theory of M. M. Tareyev, a major theologian who demanded "the liberation of the human spirit's religious aspirations from any participation in man's concrete activity in the environment".[2] At present, theologians vigorously work to move to the "forefront" of serving mankind. The "theology of the revolution" is, even according to the biased bourgeois press, precisely this kind of progressive social aspect of Orthodoxy.

The "theology of the revolution" condemns the capitalist system, the system of exploitation and enslavement of peoples; it denounces wars of aggression, basically hostile to the people, and colonial plunder. At the same time the "theology of the revolution" calls on Christians to join the front ranks of the builders of a new social system, to perform their social duty, to take part in the revolution when all other means of fighting evil are exhausted, to "draw the sword against evil", and to realise the noblest aspirations of the progressive social forces in the struggle for a social revolution, for the victory of socialism. In other words, the "theology of the revolution", directed toward participants in the socialist transformations in the USSR, supports the practical programme of socialist construction and its general democratic principles.

But, while asserting the proposition that Christianity is in agreement with the economic and political foundations of socialist society, the "theology of the

---

[1] Ibid.
[2] Ibid., p. 224

revolution" regards the scientific-materialist worldview to be incompatible with religion. It also considers the doctrine of atheism and its convictions to be unacceptable. This aspect of the problems, however, has not been so widely discussed in the church press as, say, the practical realisation of the main socialist principles. The church press recognises the need for replacing old and obsolescent social structures by "new social forms".[1]

This position gave rise to all kinds of illusions about the essence of religious social doctrines in general. Some believers and non-believers have formed an erroneous conception of a radical change in the essence of religious ideology, which has manifested itself so clearly in the evaluation of the present-day social phenomena.

The point is that, apart from a general evaluation of social phenomena, the Orthodox social doctrine defines the causes of changes and the direction of social life, attempting to reduce the entire totality of social development to divine expediency. In the final analysis, religion and theology reduce the driving motives of the activity of man, social group or class to a purely external effect of transcendental causes. As for man himself, he, in the view of social theology, is an object rather than the subject of history, one that is guided towards a historical goal by the will of the Creator.

What are the distinctive features of the Orthodox social doctrine?

First, in the Orthodox interpretation of the life of society, the latter is considered in the light of dogmatic notions. The dogmata themselves may not be mentioned here, but the idea of predestination inevitably leads to transcendental conditioning of the character and direction of historical events.

The Orthodox Church today does not, of course, lay emphasis on the extreme forms of the interpretation of the predestination dogma. They have long given up the simplistic orthodox interpretation of this concept. But the renewed interpretation of predestination does not

---

[1] *Zhurnal Moskovskoy patriarkhii*, 1969, No. 11, p. 37.

go beyond the framework of a religious-theological evaluation of the life of society.

Second, a distinctive trait of Orthodox social theories is the assertion that the character of social relations directly depends on the strength of the belief in God and recognition of the Church's authority. All systems of social theology posit as a social ideal an organisation of people which retains a harmonious unity of God and Godlike human individual. From the standpoint of the Orthodox Church rejection of this harmony, which theologians refer to as individualism, opposing of the earthly to the heavenly, regarded as egoism, and the view of man as the product of social relations, which theologians describe as a collectivist Utopia, are all obstacles to social progress.

The third characteristic feature of the Orthodox interpretation of the historical process is substitution of moral problems for social ones. In the final analysis, it is the strictly defined moral law that determines moral consciousness and moral relations, according to the theological view, and not the socio-historical conditions. All the other forms of private and social life are determined in theology by various embodiments of eternal moral ideas. It is easy to see that this interpretation of social phenomena substitutes the consequence for the cause, a description of the principles of personal-religious creativity for an analysis of society's political organisation. It reduces the problem of transformation of social relations to direct dependence on various moral requirements.

The fourth characteristic feature of the religious conception of the life of society is the extension of eschatological ideas to the field of history. Here, too, modern theology has freed itself from all the eschatological notions of the past which are incompatible with the contemporary man's view of the world. It no longer bases its doctrine of the ultimate destiny of man and the world on the Revelation of St. John the Divine. But social theology continues to advise man to await a better future that will come about through some supernatural agency. Social theology thus sees the historical perspective as directly dependent on divine will.

Changes in the political and social orientation of the Orthodox Church are a new phenomenon in its ideology and activity. They are conditioned by the character of the social circumstances in which religion has found itself. To preserve its influence, and to consolidate its positions, the Church had to correlate its social orientation with the socio-political sympathies of the overwhelming majority of believers and non-believers. Historical experience has convinced the hierarchs of the Church that any other position will lead to inevitable loss of all influence on the masses, undermining first and foremost the Church's own position.

At a time of decline in the influence of religious ideology, church leaders are looking for devices and methods of its defence which would permit the adaptation of the system of doctrinal concepts to the level of consciousness of the modern man as a way out of the crisis of religion. In doing so, Orthodox apologetics take into account the existence of various categories and groups of believers with widely varying attitudes to the multiform devices and modes of interpretation of the main principles of the confessional doctrines. This, in its turn, gives rise to different tendencies in the ideology of modern Orthodoxy.

Most church hierarchs and rank-and-file priests are in favour of reinterpreting the present-day socio-economic and socio-political problems of a changing and developing society; they revise the old moral principles and norms of believers' life orientations, attitude to labour, science, culture, and civic duties. This approach has become predominant, as was pointed out at the 1971 Local Council of the Russian Orthodox Church and also, on numerous occasions, by the Georgian, Bulgarian, Romanian and other Orthodox Churches.

But, although practically all theologians and church hierarchs recognise the need for a renovation of the socio-political, moral and practical orientations to bring them in accord with the changing mentality of believers today, by no means all agree to just as decisive a modernisation of dogma and cult. Some of them believe, with reason, that a revision of the long-established dogmatic and canonical notions will only shake the already weakened positions of the Church and sow doubts as to the correctness of the Church's assertion of absolute truth and infallibility of church dogma presented as the highest achievement of man's spiritual life. In their view, strict observance of the traditional forms of church life and activity will play a stabilising role in preserving faith. Still, adherents of renovation of the entire religious complex are fairly numerous, and their positions are supported by a considerable number of believers.

Among priests and circles close to the Church, there is a tiny yet noisy group of extremists mostly engaged in anti-social activities, inciting hostility and hatred between believers and non-believers and compromising churchmen who respect Soviet laws on religious cults and the Constitution of the USSR. Using religious slogans as a cover, these extremists pursue their purely self-seeking interests. They distort the essence of socialist democracy, present in a false light the policy of the Communist Party and the Soviet state in the solution of religious issues, and gather "dossiers" for the lying bourgeois-clerical propaganda abroad. The activities of the extremists, who represent nobody but themselves, are condemned by religious leaders, priests, and the overwhelming majority of believers.

The leading hierarchs of the Russian Orthodox Church call for putting an end to the system of exploitation and enslavement of peoples, expose the inhuman nature of predatory wars and colonial plunder, and condemn various dictatorial regimes and their support by the international imperialism. At the same time Orthodoxy's modern social propositions, oriented towards perception by direct participants in the socialist transformations in the USSR, in the spirit of "Communist Christianity", take a positive attitude to the practical programme of socialist construction. They stress the fact that the economic and political foundations of socialist society fully accord with the spirit of the Gospel, and point to its viability, justice, and truly humane character. The desire of the Orthodox ideologists to give a positive interpretation of the socio-political, socio-economic, ecological, moral, scientific and other views popular in socialist society fully accords with the views of most believers and is approved by them.

The Church leaders' calls for ensuring progressive social reforms on the basis of true justice, equality and humanism are directly linked with the formation of religious worldview principles directed above all towards consolidating the positions of Christianity.

Renovation of Christianity is not restricted to a revision of the socio-political and socio-historical problems. One of the specific features of the renovation of the Orthodox Church today is an attempt by many theologians and churchmen to give a new interpretation of the Orthodox dogmatic principles without going beyond the framework of these principles, to emphasise some aspects of the religious dogma, leaving others in the background. Thus the idea of salvation—one of the central ideas of Christianity—is interpreted precisely in accordance with the system of ideas prevalent among believers today. Not so long ago, man's salvation, happiness and well-being were believed to be ensured, according to the Church, by the feat of prayer, ascetic life and rejection of the temptations of the sinful world, whereas now, in the view of Christian leaders, "Christians' retiring into themselves, and self-isolation from the people living in the world fall into the category of actions condemned by the founder and enlightener of all created things".[1] A refusal to actively participate in social affairs is now viewed as a consequence of an erroneous conception and even distortion of the essence of Christianity. In the words of Orthodox ideologists, a true Christian is not he who sets at naught his earthly life but he who is resolved to make it more beautiful through his labour and active participation in improving the conditions of man's life.

Contemporary Orthodox apologists are not content with revising socio-political theories only. Renovation is to cover the whole of the religious complex, including the entire system of notions of man and the world. Questions of the correlation between faith and knowl-

---

[1] *Bogoslovskiye trudy*, Moscow, 1973, X, p. 158.

edge, science and religion are given more and more attention in Orthodox theology. The Orthodox reorientation in relation to science consists not in counterposing to religion as was formerly the case. Orthodox ideologists now propose other variants of an individual's value orientation, they take a new approach to defining the ideal way of life for man, and revise the existing conceptions of family and marriage relations, the role of woman in society, etc.

The purpose of all this is, first, to work out new arguments for the apology of the Orthodox Church today; second, to stabilise religiosity at a time of devaluation of the system of religious concepts; third, to overcome the crisis of religious ideology; and fourth, to enhance the social prestige of religion in socialist society where the scientific materialist view prevails. Theologians sometimes say that intellectuals, especially young ones, are not interested nowadays in problems of the existence of God or the immortality of the soul, but in the role of religion in cultural and social life.[1] According to them, educated people are not to be carried away by liturgical actions and the message of prayers, but those same people willingly discuss Christianity as a part of the history of culture. It is here that the perspective of "spiritually directing" their consciousness along the channel of recognition of Christian values for "the great heritage of Christian civilisation" opens up.

Not restricting themselves to mere statement of the positive influence of religion on society's spiritual life, theologians and priests posit the following basic conceptions of its influence on culture.

First, the very emergence of Christianity changed, in their view, the moral content of the whole culture preceding it. The alleged perversion inherent in ancient art, its indecency combined with the spirit of corruption, posed a threat to the civilisation that followed it. Thus the theory of the role of Christianity in asserting the high moral principles of spiritual culture is used as justification for the existence of Christianity itself. Fully aware of the attractive-

---

[1] *Zhurnal Moskovskoy patriarkhii*, 1969, No. 5, pp. 54, 55.

ness of such a position, theologians persistently spread various proofs of their general premises on this count.

Second, the entire civilisation of the last two millennia, including national cultures, is declared to be Christian. Its basis is presented as entirely devoid of imperfect ideals; it rests on absolute values, the highest attainable under earthly conditions and satisfying the noblest aspirations of the human quest. The cementing principle of this highest stage of spiritual life is, in this view, the Church and its best representatives who produced the most remarkable artistic and intellectual masterpieces. It is precisely for this reason, according to the theologians, that modern man is not indifferent to the mosaic of Byzantine churches, the monuments of Christian culture, and the work of the Russian painters and craftsmen from whom the descendants have inherited unsurpassed spiritual values.

Third, theologists and priests insist that culture and religion have many features in common which raise the individual to a level where he can correctly appraise the ideal. Being the determinant component of culture, religion does not merely make a favourable impact on it but is also the principal premise for cultivating the sense of the beautiful and noble in man.

These are the principal premises of Orthodox theology on the question of the relationship between religion and spiritual culture. These propositions are traditional, but they are now being pushed to the foreground of theological culturology.

The canonical norms of church life, the traditional Orthodox cult, have also gone through considerable changes. A number of canons formulated in *Pravila svyatykh apostolov* (The Rules of the Holy Apostles) have never been revised, yet many of them are not only ever complied with but even never remembered. The reason is that of the 85 rules, many have become hopeless anachronisms. Thus Rule 5 obliges the priest to divorce his wife immediately if she attended horse races or feasted without his consent. Rule 9 demands immediate excommunication of all parishioners who leave the church "before the end of a prayer or communion". Rule 11 forbids a Christian to be treated by a Judaist, and Rule 81, "to ordain slaves without their masters' knowledge".[1]

We can cite dozens of canonical requirements that have been made null and void by the new conditions of life and changes in mentality. Nevertheless the Rules of the Holy Apostles themselves retain their aura of sacredness, immutability, and absolute truth. As for the Rules we mentioned, they are simply omitted from the list. The reason for this is clear. All apostolic Rules were brought to Russia from a slave-owning society, the one in which they had been formulated, and they continue to exist today, by force of the general Christian demand for the immutability of traditions, as anachronisms that are never mentioned.

Many deviations have been permitted that, far from being envisaged by ancient canons, directly contradict the Russian Orthodox Church's earlier practice. Thus certain limitations on the participation of women in church services have been lifted; they are now given communion from the Holy Gates rather than the side gates, permitted to serve as readers in the church and to sing in the church choir; bans have been lifted on the election of women as churchwardens and members of parish councils, etc.

The leaders of the Moscow Patriarchate have also sanctioned certain new norms of church life, including those that were previously categorically forbidden by the canons. One of these is the general confession, which has been introduced in the church order and even become an everyday occurrence, although the *Trebnik* (The Book of Needs), instructs priests to hear parishioners' confessions individually. Earlier, permission to general confession was only given in exceptional cases to individual priests (thus the Synod once granted permission to hear general confessions to Ioann of Kronstadt).

A new and more lenient attitude of the Church to the requirements of the canons on the observance of fasts by believers has been adopted and become universal. Previously, fasts were interpreted by the

---

[1] *Pravila svyatykh apostolov*, Moscow, 1912, pp. 7, 13, 108, 119, 120.

Orthodox Church above all as restrictions on food (no meat, butter or milk), while nowadays the Church stresses forbearance from sinful thoughts and deeds.

The Moscow Patriarchate is taking steps to replace the Old Style by the New one, now adopted by the absolute majority of the Christian Churches, including Orthodox ones (of the 15 autocephalous Orthodox Churches, only the Russian, Georgian, Serbian and the Church of Jerusalem still use the Old Style). At present, all the parishes of the Moscow Patriarchate abroad, as well as the Hungarian parishes of the Mukachevo diocese and the Estonian parishes of the Tallinn diocese are already using the New Style. The adoption of the New Style by the entire Russian Orthodox Church is put off for psychological rather than canonical reasons ("there are no canonical rules on calendar", states the author of the article "The Problem of the Church Calendar")[1]: most parishioners are accustomed to the Old Style and reject any innovations in this sphere of church life.

Quite a few changes, mostly unannounced, have been made by the Moscow Patriarchate in the cultic practices.

The fall of autocracy resulted in the withdrawal from the liturgical order of glorification of the czars and the exclusion from the church feasts of the so-called "czar's days" (the days of the ruling monarch's accession to the throne, the name-days of the czar and members of his family, etc.). When the Russian Orthodox Church declared itself loyal to the socialist social and state structure, prayers for Soviet power were included in the services. Anathematising was discontinued of opponents of the autocratic system as enemies of the Church, previously read out during the services for the Triumph of Orthodoxy on the first Sunday in Lent.

In contravention of the age-long tradition, services are held in many churches of the Moscow Patriarchate only on Saturdays, Sundays and feast days, not every day. Priests often omit certain parts of the services at their own discretion, which made the heads of the Russian Orthodox Church consider the question of introducing greater order in this spontaneous process,

---

[1] *Bogoslovskiye trudy*, Moscow, 1968, IV, p. 111.

ultimately caused by the fall in most parishioners' religious zeal.

The Moscow Patriarchate has modernised the canonical order of church life and cultic practices in the purely Renovationist spirit; however, this was achieved by degrees and rather unobtrusively, to avoid accusations of flouting ancient Orthodox traditions.

But the adaptation of the Russian Orthodox Church to the new conditions of its existence was not limited to revision of its socio-political views and modernisation of the liturgical order. The new trends necessitated by this adaptation have gone deep into the holy of holies of the Church—its religious dogmas, the sphere of the Orthodox dogmatics.

Traditional Russian Orthodoxy has always adhered to dogmatic conservatism, regarding the Byzantian interpretation of Christian dogmata as the only correct one and suitable to all times and peoples. Its ideologists therefore categorically objected to any changes in Orthodox religious dogma. To justify this position of the Church, its hierarchs and theologians usually cited the epistle of the Eastern patriarchs of 1723, which read in part: "Our dogmata and the precepts of our Eastern Church are inherited from ancient times, correctly and piously defined and confirmed by the holy ecumenical councils: it is not permissible to add to or detract from them anything at all."[1]

Theological thinkers of traditional Russian Orthodoxy, by their own admission, did not permit the least digression from accepted dogmatic formulas, definitions and even terms. Even the slightest renovations of theological arguments in Orthodox dogmata were regarded by the Church leaders of pre-revolutionary Russia as attempts on Russian Orthodoxy's integrity.

For this reason, the Church's top hierarchy did not support the proposal to modernise some of the most archaic dogmatic formulas, put forward in the years of the first Russian revolution by the liberal Renovationist movement in Russian Orthodoxy. The programme of

---

[1] Makariy. *Pravoslavnoye dogmaticheskoye bogosloviye* (Orthodox Dogmatic Theology), St. Petersburg, 1868, Vol. 2, p. 18.

modernisation of Orthodox dogmata worked out in the 1920s by the ideologists of Renovationist groups found no support among the main body of churchmen: it was not sanctioned even by the 1923 Council, not to mention the Old-Church supporters, the Tikhonians. Sergiy expressed his opposition to the renovation of the Orthodox dogmata on numerous occasions, and Patriarch Aleksiy continued this policy of his predecessor.

But real life ultimately proved stronger than the Moscow Patriarchate's protest against modernisation of Orthodox religious dogmata. An urgent need arose for renovating certain traditional dogmatic definitions to make them more consonant with the spiritual requirements of believers today and more flexible (the representatives of Russian Orthodoxy needed that flexibility in their theological dialogues with Catholic and Protestant theologians). To satisfy that requirement, the theological ecclesiastical circles of the Moscow Patriarchate, while continuing to profess their insistence on the immutability of the dogmatic foundations of Orthodoxy, began to look for arguments in favour of renovation of the most obsolete elements of Orthodox dogmata.

The idea of "theological development" offered a way out of the difficulty; according to that idea, the content of Christian dogmata could not be changed, but changes could and should be introduced in dogmatic formulations in order to make them consonant with the times and more convincing to the new generations of believers. The leaders of the Moscow Patriarchate set before the ideologists of Russian Orthodoxy the task of "explaining the truths of Christian faith in modern language and of perfecting theological knowledge".[1]

An indication of the adoption of the principle of "theological development" by the Russian Orthodox Church can be found in the statement made by Metropolitan Nikodim (Rotov) during his conversation with theologians of the FRG Evangelical Church: "With all our unshakeable loyalty to divine revelation and the Church's immutable doctrines, we are convinced that theology as an attempt to express, in the best possible

---

[1] *Zhurnal Moskovskoy patriarkhii*, 1967, No. 1, p. 25.

way, the Church's doctrine in the face of changing reality and changing human thinking, must truly undergo continuous change."[1] The same idea was even more definitely expressed in his report on "Tradition and Contemporaneity".[2]

Not confining themselves to mere statement of their readiness for renovating the obviously obsolete formulations of "dogmatic truths", the theological and ecclesiastical circles of the Moscow Patriarchate revised, cautiously but thoroughly, a number of orthodox interpretations both of certain dogmata and of conclusions drawn from them.

First of all, the orthodox interpretation of the Christian doctrine on suffering as a source of salvation was revised in a fairly radical manner. The essence of this interpretation, which the Russian Orthodox Church has adhered to for centuries, is as follows. The faithful were persuaded to believe that physical suffering, whatever its source (illness, harsh conditions of life and labour, self-torture, etc.), is the shortest and truest path to "heavenly bliss in the next world". Believers were told to follow the model of those righteous men and women, martyrs and great martyrs whom the church canonised only because they consciously inflicted suffering upon themselves "for the glory of God".

Since the sources of mass misfortunes of the people have been eliminated everywhere in socialist society, and singing praises of suffering as a means of salvation contradicts the believers' whole way of life, the ideologists of Russian Orthodoxy now insist that senseless suffering was never advocated by the entire Church, only by some of its members—"narrow-minded fanatics with distorted notions of Christianity"; their views must therefore be described as "a subtle and sophisticated falsification of the Christian doctrine". The "true Christian viewpoint" is not a defence of "meaningless apotheosis of suffering in general" but a call for "co-suffering with Christ, co-crucifixion with Him", i.e., for actions interpreted as "fruitful and selfless

---

[1] Ibid., No. 4, p. 40.
[2] *The Journal of the Moscow Patriarchate*, 1972, No. 12, p. 64.

activity ... for the benefit and happiness of all men on earth".[1]

True, the new interpretation of the Christian doctrine of suffering goes hand in hand with preachers' singing praises from the ambo to "the redeeming force of suffering", with invoking the well-known principle of Christianity; "Christ suffered, and He commanded us to suffer!" There has been no actual change therefore in the attitude of the adherents of Russian Orthodoxy to suffering, neither could there have been any such change, for suffering is the ideal soil for the emergence and reinforcement of religiosity. Formally, however, churchmen have given up the traditional standpoint on this issue and formulated a new approach to this dogmatic problem.

The conclusions from the dogmata of the resurrection of Christ and His ascension to heaven have also been substantively revised. In the past, Russian Orthodox theologians interpreted these dogmata as a Christian appeal to the believers to ignore real earthly life ("the city on earth") for the sake of "eternal bliss in the next world" ("the city of God").

Realising that these positions will not find a desired response in the minds of believers in socialist society to whom their earthly Homeland is so precious, the ideologists of modern Russian Orthodoxy declared earlier views to be erroneous and "deplorable extremes".[2] It now asserted that Christ's resurrection and ascension are not a sign to the Christians to ignore their earthly interests—on the contrary, they lend man's earthly life "a new sense and profound meaning".[3] Moreover, Christianity is now said to take a decidedly favourable view of men's earthly cares.[4]

The Christian dogma of salvation, i.e., of the attainment by believers of "eternal bliss in the next world" has also been revised in Russian Orthodox Christianity today. Earlier, the purpose of Christian life was, according to the Orthodox clergy, "personal

---

[1] *Zhurnal Moskovskoy patriarkhii*, 1963, No. 1, pp. 40, 41.
[2] Ibid., No. 10, p. 76.
[3] Ibid., 1964, No. 7, p. 34.
[4] Ibid., 1972, No. 1, p. 41.

salvation", on the basis of the principle of sinning together and seeking salvation separately. That was a religious sanctioning of individualism spawned by the conditions of an exploitative society.

In socialist society, the principle of collectivism has asserted itself. Taking this into consideration, the ideologists of modern Russian Orthodoxy now interpret "salvation" as a result of believers' joint efforts, as a kind of collective endeavour, rather than as a consequence of each individual's personal initiative. Then again, "salvation" itself is now seen as effectively serving one's neighbour on the social and moral planes rather than as an egoistic worry about one's own soul. "The Christian who engrosses himself in the narrow circle of his own, however lofty, spiritual and moral interests, thinking only of his own salvation," stated Metropolitan Nikodim (Rotov), "cannot be considered in harmony with the ideal of Christian Brotherly love and self-sacrifice, declared by the New Testament."[1]

In contravention of the view, traditional for the Russian Orthodox Church, that only Church members can hope to be "saved", salvation of those outside the Church is now regarded as possible—on condition that they perform good deeds. "... It is very important," said Patriarch Pimen, "to see good deeds performed outside the faith as the embryo, so to speak, of salvation..."[2]

Substantive corrections are also introduced in those Orthodox dogmas whose traditional interpretation stands in the way of achieving a mutual understanding with Catholics and Protestants.

It is precisely due to these considerations that the Russian Orthodox Church has revised the orthodox interpretation of the dogma on the Church. According to that interpretation, previously accepted as an indisputable truth, of the three Christian confessions only Orthodoxy was regarded as the "true Church", while Catholicism and Protestantism were included among nonecclesiastical organisations[3]. This view was rejected

---

[1] *The Journal of the Moscow Patriarchate*, 1972, No. 10, p. 52.
[2] Ibid., 1975, No. 2, p. 13.
[3] *Zhurnal Moskovskoy patriarkhii*, 1948, No. 12, p. 16.

by Catholic and Protestant theologists who saw it as discriminatory as far as their own confessions were concerned.

To eliminate this controversy, which ruled out the possibility of a Pan-Christian dialogue on the restoration of ecumenical unity, the ideologists of contemporary Russian Orthodoxy were obliged to seek new formulations. The idea was developed in their articles and reports that none of the now existing Christian Churches must be placed in a privileged position, for "all of them have a definite value in the eyes of God", and therefore the Most High shows no visible preferency for any of them.[1]

Considerable changes have also occurred in the interpretation by the official circles of the Moscow Patriarchate of the modes of achieving Pan-Christian unity. Traditionally minded Orthodox theologians insisted earlier that the blame for the splitting of Christianity into three confessional systems lay squarely with Catholics and Protestants, who "left the Church", destroying by their departure its unity.[2]

This narrow confessional interpretation of the causes and circumstances of the split within Christianity was rejected by non-Orthodox participants of inter-Christian conversations. There was no choice for the modern ideologists of Orthodoxy but to revise the orthodox position on this issue. They are now ready to acknowledge that, to some extent or other, all Churches, including the Orthodox one, were to blame for the schism in Christianity.[3]

The adherents of the Tikhonian-Sergian orientation thought of restoration of Christian unity only in terms of the "return" of Catholics and Protestants in the bosom of the "true Church". "Reconciliation between the Orthodox Church and those who have broken away from it," wrote Patriarchal Locum Tenens Sergiy, "can only consist in the Church's receiving them in its bosom,"[4] Contemporary Orthodox theologians express-

---

[1] *Zhurnal Moskovskoy patriarkhii*, 1968, No. 8, p. 67.
[2] *Patriarkh Sergiy i yego dukhovnoye nasledstvo*, p. 126.
[3] *Zhurnal Moskovskoy patriarkhii*, 1966, No. 4, p. 46.
[4] Ibid., 1931, No. 2, p. 6.

ing the official position of the Moscow Patriarchate, have displayed readiness to seek for approaches to Pan-Christian unity on the path of mutual rapprochement of all the Churches in the course of which not one of them could suffer any damage or gain any privileges.[1]

In the course of their conversations with Catholics, contemporary Orthodox theologians have given up their former negative attitude to *filioque,* which was always regarded as a purely Catholic innovation which entailed the dissent in Christianity in the 11th century. Today, official representatives of the Moscow Patriarchate agree to regard the Catholic doctrine of the procession of the Holy Spirit not only from God the Father but also from God the Son to be a quite permissible theological opinion (theologoumenon) the rejection of which will not be put forward as a preliminary condition to the solution of the problem of restoration of Pan-Christian unity.[2]

The same pliancy was also displayed in the appraisal of the Catholic dogma of bodily ascension of the Virgin Mary to heaven, previously rejected by Orthodox theologians. Quoting in his article "The Orthodox View of the Dogma of the Roman Catholic Church on the Ascension of the Virgin Mary to Heavenly Glory" some sharply negative statements on this dogma by Russian, Greek, Bulgarian and Romanian Orthodox theologians, Archpriest Vladimir Sorokin declared, on behalf of the Moscow Patriarchate, that "it appears necessary to introduce certain revisions in the Orthodox standpoint" previously expressed.[3]

Thus the 1960s were a period of a very intensive modernisation of both the ideology of Russian Orthodoxy and of its cultic-ritual practice. The modernisation was not given much publicity; it was very gradual and only involved those areas of Orthodox rite and dogma which had become obvious anachronisms, so that their renovation did not shock believers.

Having gone through the process of renovation,

---

[1] *The Journal of the Moscow Patriarchate,* 1972, No. 12, p. 65.
[2] Ibid., No. 1, pp. 53-73.
[3] *Bogoslovskiye trudy,* Moscow, 1973, X, p. 88.

Russian Orthodoxy became a more dynamic religion better adapted to the changing conditions of the Church's existence. Drawing the attention of Western church circles to the new state of Russian Orthodoxy, one of the leading figures in the Moscow Patriarchate stated during a meeting with foreign religious workers: "Despite the erroneous view of the Russian Orthodox Church as a Church of dead traditions, the present-day Russian Orthodox Church, living under new conditions entirely without precedent, is obviously a Church in eternal renewal."[1]

An important element of the process of adaptation of Russian Orthodoxy to existence under a socialist society was the 1971 Local Council.

## The Church After the 1971 Local Council

Patriarch Aleksiy (Simansky), who had headed the Russian Orthodox Church more than a quarter of a century, died in April 1970. Metropolitan Pimen (Izvekov), the oldest member of the Synod in the order of consecration and an old associate of the demised primate, became the Patriarchal Locum Tenens. He directed the preparations for the Third Local Council of the Russian Orthodox Church (the Moscow Patriarchate does not recognise the Local Councils of 1923 and 1925, convened by the Renovationists), which was held in May and June 1971 at the Trinity-St. Sergiy Lavra.

The Council discussed the main report by Metropolitan Pimen (Izvekov) "The Life and Work of the Russian Orthodox Church", and two co-reports: "The Ecumenical Activities of the Russian Orthodox Church" and "On Cancelling Anathemas on the Old Russian Rites" by Metropolitan Nikodim and "On the Peace-Making Activity of the Russian Orthodox Church" by Metropolitan Aleksiy. The Council approved the administration of the Church by the Synod and the patriarch in the period between the Councils,

---

[1] *Zhurnal Moskovskoy Patriarkhii*, 1964, No. 3, p. 48.

condemned the leadership of the Russian church emigration, and cancelled the anathemas imposed by the 1656 and 1667 Moscow Councils on the old Russian rites and the Old Believers adhering to them, referring to the latter as "Christians of the Orthodox faith". Metropolitan Pimen, Patriarchal Locum Tenens, was elected Patriarch of Moscow and All Russia.

The 1971 Council sanctioned the Church's support for the socialist social and state system and expressed complete satisfaction with the existing Soviet legislation on religious cults and the relationship between Church and state. It instructed the leadership of the Moscow Patriarchate to see to it in the future, too, "that our Church life should proceed within the framework of this legislation". Firm intention was expressed to develop further "good relations with our state" and allow no one to harm those relations[1]. "The Local Council of the Russian Orthodox Church," read the decisions of the Council, "in the name of its members—bishops, clergymen and laymen—citizens of the Soviet Union, expressed their unanimous approval and that of all those Russian believers whom they represent at the Council, of the efforts the Government of the USSR is making to ensure the all-round development of the life of the Soviet people and the establishment of a lasting and just international peace..."[2]

The 1971 Local Council approved the switch-over of the Russian Orthodox Church from the idea of "social neutrality" to active perception of the problems of social development and interpretation of these problems from the positions of "Communist Christianity". The Council documents stresssed once again that the Church regarded all the social undertakings initiated by the 1917 October Revolution as being in "accord with the ideals of the Gospel".[3] The Local Council instructed the theological and ecclesiastical leaders of the

---

[1] *The Local Council of the Russian Orthodox Church,* Published by the Moscow Patriarchate, Moscow, 1972, pp. 40, 41.

[2] Ibid., p. 141.

[3] Ibid., p. 41.

Moscow Patriarchate to further intensify their "service to society".

The Council paid much attention to the problem of further renovation of Russian Orthodoxy in accordance with the changing conditions of the Church's existence. It resolutely dissociated itself from religious conservatives—the traditionalists, stating that the "Church is a living organism",[1] and that the task of the hierarchs is "correlating the rules and traditions of the Church with its needs and the requirements of the times", and that the proximate goal of theology was "profound study of those questions whose fully scientific formulation was apparently entirely absent in dogmatic theology".[2]

After the Council, Patriarch Pimen championed that goal on many occasions. Thus in his address to the faculty and students of the Leningrad Theological Academy and Seminary he urged them "to spare no efforts in elaborating contemporary theological problems and in correlating them to pressing problems of our daily life".[3] In one of his speeches during his visit to Egypt, the head of the Russian Orthodox Church pointed to the desirability of "theological constructions" that are "in keeping with the 'renewal of life'...",[4] and in his speech on receiving the diploma of a Doctor of Theology from the Sofia Theological Academy he stressed that the Church "is not something that is historically immobile and frozen in her traditional mould"[5].

Other leading workers of the Moscow Patriarchate have also expressed themselves in the same spirit.

However, the Local Council did not support the modernists of the radical variety insisting on acceleration of the rate and expanding the scope of renovation of Russian Orthodoxy (immediate and universal adoption of the New Style, translation of the liturgy into Russian, etc.). The "Council fathers" also roundly

---

[1] *Zhurnal Moskovskoy patriarkhii*, 1971, No. 6, p. 8.
[2] Ibid., No. 7, pp. 26, 35.
[3] *The Journal of the Moscow Patriarchate*, 1972, No. 2, p. 27.
[4] Ibid., No. 8, p. 13.
[5] Ibid., 1975, No. 2, p. 13.

condemned the idea, long cherished by some of the clergy, of the possibility and desirability of further attenuation of the rigour of the liturgical order in the Russian Orthodox Church. "The Council reminds pastors lacking in diligence and zeal," said the Council's message to the clergy and laity, "of the need to perform, zealously and worshipfully, the liturgy and all-night vigil, baptism and confession, communion and extreme unction, as well as molebens, panikhidas, burial and other church services."[1]

After the Council, the Moscow Patriarchate's theologians and church leaders condemned, resolutely and categorically, both the inveterate conservatives—traditionalists fearful of any manifestation of the new, and radical-modernists proposing a drastic revision of the traditions. On behalf of the Moscow Patriarchate, Metropolitan Yuvenaly stated during a conversation with Catholics that both the conservative and extremist positions were dangerous to the Church.[2]

A balanced approach to the dogmata, canons and rites of the Russian Orthodox Church has been declared to be the standard of a truly ecclesiastical conduct and the norm of Orthodox theologising, envisaging a reasonable combination of traditionalism and innovation, of stability and renewal. The Council formulated the position of moderate renovation and expressed itself in favour of a more careful regulation of the process of renovation of Russian Orthodoxy by the Church, of firmer control over this process by the top hierarchs.

Implementing that kind of regulation, the leaders of the Moscow Patriarchate try, above all, to rid theologians and churchmen (and then rank-and-file Orthodox parishioners) of the customary contraposition of reform to tradition.

After the 1971 Council, the church press began to drive home the idea that traditionalism and reformism in no way exclude one another, that they are interconnected and mutually conditioned, if different, aspects of the internally contradictory process of renovation of

---

[1] *Zhurnal Moskovskoy patriarkhii*, 1971, No. 6, p. 9.
[2] *The Journal of the Moscow Patriarchate*, 1973, No. 8, p. 66.

religion and Church—a process which combines, in the words of Metropolitan Yuvenaliy (Poyarkov), "constancy and renewal, discipline and freedom..."[1]. Professor Zabolotsky of the Leningrad Theological Academy declared that "the life of Christ's Church is a dialectical process which cannot do without certain antinomies. Loyalty to Christ and falling away from Him, saintliness and sin, extremes in the interpretation of the truth leading to heresies contradicting one another..., traditionalism and renewal—... all this is natural in the living body of the militant church"[2].

Judging by the numerous statements of theologians and hierarchs of the Moscow Patriarchate, the leading circles of the Russian Orthodox Church prefer an interpretation of church renewal which does not oppose innovations, reforms and transformations to traditions as their antipode but, on the contrary, brings them in accord with the latter, enriching and developing rather than cancelling them. Metropolitan Nikodim said that "the Russian Orthodox Church, in obedience to the call of the times, saw the purport of her existence to be in the linking of religious principles with the needs of time..."[3]

Today, the Church regards traditions as accumulated religious experiences, as an expression of the fullness of supernatural revelation[4]. If these experiences are ignored, the ideologists of modern Russian Orthodoxy warned the clergy and parishioners, the Church "forfeits the basis for its existence in the future ... a state of unrest sets in, leading to departures from the Truth, such as the 'death of God' school, the so-called 'theology of secularity' and other subjectivist deviations..."[5].

Inasmuch as the concept of "tradition" acquired an obviously negative nuance in the eyes of the modernist theologians during the decade before the Council, strenuous attempts are made after the Council to

---

[1] *The Journal of the Moscow Patriarchate*, 1973, No. 8, p. 66.
[2] *Zhurnal Moskovskoy patriarkhii*, 1975, No. 6, p. 54.
[3] *The Journal of the Moscow Patriarchate*, 1973, No. 3, p. 47.
[4] Ibid., 1977, No. 1, p. 63.
[5] Ibid., pp. 65, 66.

rehabilitate that concept in the eyes of the clergy and the believers. The rule now is to stress the immutability of dogmatic definitions, although it is pointed out at the same time that tradition must not be regarded as a static and immutable institution. "Whereas Tradition has immutable elements, this immutability is not dead and static, but living, conscious and dynamic."[1] Hieromonk Iannuariy, instructor at the Leningrad Theological Academy, points to the danger of both conservatism and excessive renewal in dogmatic questions. In pursuing the task of preserving the immutability of dogmata, consistent traditionalism does not take into account the mutability of the world, while "excessive renewal ... can become a challenge to the social consciousness of the Church"[2].

Any other conception of the essence of religion and Church, one that ignores or belittles the role of traditions in church life, is now seen by the leadership of the Moscow Patriarchate as unprincipled "timeserving", pernicious to contemporary Russian Orthodoxy, as it is to any other creed[3].

The hierarchs of the Moscow Patriarchate endeavour to limit the sphere of church reforms and to slow down the general rate of renovation of present-day Russian Orthodoxy in order to make the whole process of renovation more amenable to control.

The church press and preachers condemn those theologians and churchmen who insist on a radical renewal of all the aspects of religion and church life in the shortest time possible. They are reproached for their attempts to modernise Russian Orthodoxy without proper consultation with the leaders of the Church or a sanctioning of the main body of parishioners. "A pastor's task," wrote the *Journal of the Moscow Patriarchate,* "is not to neglect or reject everything acquired by the Church in the course of centuries—that is the path of destruction, but to replenish everything that is saintly in it and to enrich it by profound piety,

---

[1] *The Journal of the Moscow Patriarchate,* 1982, No. 4, p. 42.
[2] Ibidem.
[3] Ibid., 1975, No. 10, p. 53.

solicitously guarding the spiritual legacy of the Church of Christ."[1]

Advocates of further church reforms are persistently told to bring their thoughts and actions in accord with a number of conditions without which their aspirations will harm modern Russian Orthodoxy irreparably. These conditions are as follows.

The renewal of Orthodoxy must not be understood as "a radical reconstruction of the Church" but only "as a new approach to the changing world, a readiness on the part of the Church to meet the new requirements of society, her constant 'openness' to mankind".[2] The renewal of Russian Orthodoxy is regarded as a continuation, under new historical conditions, of a long and stable church tradition.

Only those innovations are regarded as justifiable which do not imperil a single vitally important element of the church structure or reject any of the determinant religious ideas. Modernisation can only involve "ecclesiastical decisions and recommendations on questions that do not bear significance in eternity and often are not even within the immediate purview of the Church".[3] However, the question of which of these decisions and recommendations can and must be revised is not yet quite clear to the ideologists of Russian Orthodoxy themselves. Some theologians suggest that only those rites and rules of ecclesiastical life (the canons) should be revised, that have not been sanctioned by an Ecumenical or, at least, a Local Council.[4] Others believe that even the existence of such sanctions must not restrain the Church from revising obviously outdated canonical injunctions.

Special emphasis is placed on the need for an unhurried and gradual implementation of the reforms, and on obligatory sanctioning of these reforms by a Council representing the whole Church.[5] This standpoint has become, it must be assumed, the position of

---

[1] *The Journal of the Moscow Patriarchate*, 1974, No. 11, p. 23.
[2] Ibid., 1973, No. 9, p. 52.
[3] Ibid., 1975, No. 8, p. 56.
[4] Ibidem.
[5] Ibid., 1973, No. 11, p. 64.

the whole Church, because it was precisely this standpoint that Protopresbyter Prof. Borovoy expressed in his report "Church Life in Our Society" during conversations with the Evangelical Church of the GDR. "Our life in the new society," he said, "teaches us that the Church's true renewal is achieved only in a religious way, by collective reason and in observing religious unity and canonical law and order."[1]

Finally, before any church reforms are implemented, the minds not only of the whole episcopate and clergy must be prepared but also those of the bulk of the believers. This preparation is regarded by the church leadership as an additional guarantee that the innovations introduced will not be perceived by the believers as complete neglect for ecclesiastical traditions and a sharp breakaway from the "faith of our fathers".

In solving that complex problem of psychological preparation of the clergy and believers for a positive perception of the church reforms—a problem that had proved intractable to the renovationists of the 1920s—the ideologists of contemporary Russian Orthodoxy came to the conclusion that successful reformist activity required reliance on authorities that would be accepted absolutely without reservation by all Orthodox Christians. In Orthodoxy, the authorities of this kind are Ecumenical and Local Councils, as well as religious figures from the times of early Christianity and the epoch of the seven Ecumenical Councils—the so-called Fathers of the Church or Holy Fathers. It is the prestige of the ancient Councils and of the Holy Fathers that is used by the theological-ecclesiastical circles of the Moscow Patriarchate as the principal guarantee of the correctness of the programme for further renewal of Russian Orthodoxy implemented at present.

The logic of the reasoning and actions of contemporary religious ideologists is as follows. Inasmuch as the Fathers of the Church lived at a time of the formation of Christianity as a world religion, directly participating in the complex and contradictory process

---

[1] *The Journal of the Moscow Patriarchate*, 1974, No. 10, p. 72.

of the evolution and final elaboration of the foundations of Christian dogmatics and rites, they had to handle, theoretically and practically, the problem of adapting the religion to the new conditions of the Church's existence. Because of that they accumulated solid experiences in the struggle for the survival of Christianity, which can and must be used in handling the new problems of renovation of Russian Orthodoxy.

In substantiating the "authority of patristic theology" for contemporary theological thinking on the renovation of the religion and Church, Metropolitan Nikodim (Rotov) pointed out in his address on the occasion of the 30th anniversary of the Leningrad Theological Academy that the theology of the Holy Fathers was never abstract in character, that it was always marked by inherent vitality, promptly responding to topical issues and the spiritual requirements of contemporary Christians. Orientation towards patristic theology means to express ideas in modern language and to be true to the spirit of patristic heritage, revealing its vitality and an ability to provide answers in good time to religious, ethical and other problems on the basis of the doctrine of divine revelation.[1]

The leaders of the Moscow Patriarchate declared that one of the most important features of patristic theologising is a creative approach to religious and ecclesiastical problems, continual search for new arguments in defence of Christianity, and innovations in dogmata and liturgy, all of which justified, on a formal basis, the assertion that sanctioning of the renewal of Russian Orthodoxy is not a departure from orthodoxy, age-long Christian tradition or its replacement by something fundamentally new, something only recently introduced, but a mere reconstruction of the early Christian order in religious and ecclesiastical life, a return to the faith and cultic practice of the "Holy Fathers", a revival under new conditions of a purely Orthodox, patristic style in theology and church practice. In other words, the adherents of reforms are presented to the clergy not as experimenters attempt-

---

[1] See *The Journal of the Moscow Patriarchate*, 1977, No. 3, pp. 12, 13.

ing to introduce untested innovations in church life but merely as restorers returning to life the best traditions of Christianity from the first seven Ecumenical Councils.

By this approach, the official circles of the Russian Orthodox Church hope to present themselves to the believers not as religious reformers but as champions of ancient piety, of restorers of the Orthodoxy of the classical era, of true Orthodoxy freed from later historical additions, from the layers of subsequent epochs.

This far from subtle stratagem is having the desired effect on the rank-and-file believers brought up in the spirit of worshipful attitude towards the ecclesiastical authorities of the remote past, especially if one takes into account the fact that parishioners of Orthodox churches have never studied the works of the Holy Fathers and have but a vague idea of patristic views, mostly formed on the basis of what they hear in sermons. The reference to the Holy Fathers has a reassuring effect on them, helping them to overcome the psychological barrier of mistrust for proposed or initiated innovations in the sphere of dogmata, canonical order and liturgical practice.

Judging from statements of church leaders, everything is being done to restore the links between the present and the past of Russian Orthodoxy and to assert the Moscow Patriarchate's right to be heir to the entire millennial heritage of the Russian Orthodox Church, which they intend to use to meet the present-day needs of the faith.

How are these links established between the present and the past, and in what way are they used to regulate the process of renovation of contemporary Russian Orthodoxy?

The ecclesiastical authorities of pre-revolutionary Russia are described in the publications of the Moscow Patriarchate and in church sermons as persons having identical opinions with the ideologists of present-day Russian Orthodoxy; they are said to point the latter the principal directions of their theological, liturgical and practical ecclesiastical activity. The idea is vigorously cultivated that the principal propositions of the programme of church renewal now being implemented, a programme incorporating innovations in the field of dogma began to be worked out already before the Revolution, and not only by representatives of the liberal Renovationist movement that was in opposition to the established Church but also by the leading hierarchs and theologians who held purely traditional views and enjoyed the support of ecclesiastical authorities. "If we go back to the history of the Russian Orthodox Church," stated Patriarch Pimen, "her theological and religio-philosophical thought and her religio-social tendencies during the second half of the 19th and the 20th century, it becomes apparent that the problems of Church renewal ... were posed, discussed, passionately and ardently debated, and set down for solution in our theology, in our ecclesiastical and social circles in the very life of the Church long before they were brought up in the West or taken up by the ecumenical movement..."[1]. In more specific terms, Archbishop Pitirim asserts that "the formulation of the modern Russian theological thought" was begun by such theologians, hierarchs of the last century as Metropolitan Filaret (Drozdov), Archbishop Innokentiy (Borisov), Bishops Ioann (Sokolov) and Feofan (Govorov) the Recluse,[2] who, if the truth were to be told, were carriers of the most conservative principles in traditional Russian Orthodoxy, people who flatly rejected the need for reforms in the Church and in ecclesiastical ideology.

Such are the main trends in the theological activities of the ideologists of present-day Russian Orthodoxy in substantiating further modernisation of this religious ecclesiastical structure after the 1971 Council.

However, the theological-ecclesiastical circles of the Moscow Patriarchate do not restrict their post-Council activities to more theorising on the possibility and permissibility of a continuation (although under the Church's more stringent control) of the process of renewal of Russian Orthodoxy in keeping with the dynamics of social being. They continue the practice of

---

[1] *The Journal of the Moscow Patriarchate*, 1973, No. 11, p. 47.
[2] Ibid., 1975, No. 1, p. 64.

renewal of the principal aspects of Russian Orthodoxy begun in the late 1950s and early 1960s, although the process itself is now slower than in the pre-Council times.

Some idea of that process can be gleaned from Metropolitan Nikodim's report on "A Changing World (Information on and Analysis of Theological and Pastoral Trends in the Church after the 1973 Meeting in Zagorsk)" read at the Toronto conversations between theologians of the Moscow Patriarchate and of the Roman Catholic Church in June 1975. It lists certain concrete moves made by the Moscow Patriarchate after the 1971 Council (using clearly Renovationist terms, the speaker referred to them as "examples of our *aggiornamento* in the field of liturgical practice" and in some other spheres.[1]

According to Metropolitan Nikodim, one of the most important measures was the gradual introduction of Russian into divine service. There was some opposition to that move, he said, but increasing numbers of adherents of Orthodoxy approve of the idea of translating the entire liturgy from Church Slavonic into Russian.[2]

The liturgy of the presanctified gifts is now performed in the evening at all churches; previously, this was practiced only rarely because of a guarded attitude of a great many parishioners to that innovation. Nowadays the explanatory work done by the clergy is yielding fruit.

The speaker also said that general confession was now practiced much more often.

We can add that new prayers have been composed which reflect the situation in the world and the needs of Soviet believers. One of these prayers, invoking "God's blessing" on the African continent, was composed by Metropolitan Nikodim and introduced into ecclesiastical practice on Africa Day during divine service at the church of the Moscow Theological Academy on May 27, 1973.[3]

---

[1] *The Journal of the Moscow Patriarchate*, 1975, No. 10, p. 50.
[2] Ibid., p. 51.
[3] See *The Journal of the Moscow Patriarchate*, 1973, No, 8, p. 48.

In the post-Council period, there has been an upsurge of activity in the implementation of the principle of "theological development". In particular, the Orthodox attitude to the Catholic *"filioque"* principle is still under revision, as is the attitude to the Catholic dogma of the bodily ascension of the Virgin Mary.

Theologians of the Russian Orthodox Church are actively looking for formulations of Christian dogmata which would enable the Moscow Patriarchate to find a common language with members of the other modifications of Christianity. As stated by Patriarch Pimen, Orthodox and Western theologians have jointly worked out initial versions of theological formulas for All-Christian agreements ("ecumenical concensuses") on question of baptism and Eucharist (permissibility of two baptismal practices—of adults and infants); the question is studied of achieving an agreement on priesthood. The need has been recognised for preparing an "ecumenical agreement on the authority of the Bible, the Church as the repository of the Holy Scriptures and Holy Tradition, and the dogmatic power of the Church in the interpretation of the Holy Scriptures..."[1]

A considerable role in the formation of a general conception of renewal is expected to be played by the establishment of an optimum correspondence between the so-called "vertical" and "horizontal" theological problems. All Christian confessions without exception, including the Russian Orthodox Church, interpret "vertical" theology as the existing system of interpretation of dogmata, covering apologetics, dogmatics, exegetics, liturgics, etc. "Vertical" theology is a system of substantiation and defence of the doctrine of God, a set of proofs of the truth, usefulness and necessity of religion, and a set of rules determining the character and specific features of cultic practice.

"Horizontal" theology covers theological interpretation of various socio-political and cultural-historical problems which, under definite conditions, become especially topical for the Church. In this connection, the attention of Orthodox ideologists is focused on the

---

[1] *The Journal of the Moscow Patriarchate*, 1974, No. 8, p. 20.

interpretation of such problems as "measures to protect the environment from pollution and the other by-products of our technological civilization; the significance of social justice with regard to population growth, and food supply on a worldwide scale; city-planning in the light of the crisis brought on by the rate of technological development; the ethics of the progress being made in biochemical and genetic research", etc.[1] "Horizontal theology" covers questions of the present-day life of society seen in the light of corresponding dogma thus forming the religious-idealistic principles of the approach of believers to the phenomena and facts of reality.

After the 1971 Local Council and, presumably, in view of its general recommendations, many prominent ideologists of the Church not only support the earlier implemented programme of renewal of some aspects of dogma and cult intended to adapt them to new conditions of life—they also expand the range of socio-economic and socio-political problems drawn into the orbit of theological interpretation. Questions are now discussed in ecclesiastical literature that were thought irrelevant in the 1950s and 1960s. In particular, the early 1970s witnessed a rise in the interest for various acute problems of the ecological situation today, of protection of man's environment, responsibility of believers for ensuring social and moral progress, etc.

Extension of the range of new socio-political and socio-ethical questions dealt with by Orthodox theologians facilitates the development of notions of greater proximity of religion to believers' earthly interests, and its increased involvement in the solution of vital problems. These new problems are also the source of new difficulties for theology, as the need arose for linking up renewal conceptions with the entire totality of religious principles rather than with separate principles. In the view of theologians, there is nothing in the world today that would not be of interest to Christians, nothing in which they could not actively participate. At the same time that means that

---

[1] *The Journal of the Moscow Patriarchate*, 1974, No. 11, p. 45.

there is nothing in the world that could not be given a theological interpretation, with appropriate conclusions.

However, a revision of the existing traditions presumes theologians' loyalty to the foundations of Christian belief, to their religious views, their worldview, attitude to the world, and perception of the world. Revision of each of the orthodox notions cannot be carried out outside organic links with the entire totality of fundamental biblical-dogmatic principles, independently of the dogmata as a whole.

It should be stressed that at all the stages of the renewal of its conceptions the Russian Orthodox Church displayed caution and reserve. It always roundly condemned "elements of superficial fashion-consciousness, elements of hurried judgement and a tendency to draw arbitrary conclusions..."[1]

Its major hierarchs resolutely rejected Protestant theological innovations like the "death of God" school, the so-called "theology of secularity" and "other subjectivist delusions". These innovations were judged to be departures from the truth "contradicting the Church's age-long experience".

In the last decade, however, this moderation and reserve have apparently assumed the significance of a principle generally accepted by most hierarchs, theologians and priests. The Russian Orthodox Church has made repeated attempts within the framework of the World Council of Churches to curb the tendency observed among a number of Protestant Churches of the capitalist countries and some of their prominent representatives to push "horizontal" problems into the forefront of religious activity. Among these "horizontal" problems, American, British, Swiss and other theologians began to give prominence to political questions, suggesting solutions conforming to their class interests. These attempts assumed a particularly pronounced bias at the fifth assembly of the World Council of Churches held in Nairobi (Kenya) at the end of 1975.

In their speeches at the assembly, some theologians of the capitalist countries expressed their views, stem-

---

[1] *The Local Council...*, p. 89.

ming from their class positions, of the specific features of the present period in the development of society, views founded on arbitrary interpretation of Biblical texts; more than that, they slandered the foreign and home policies of the Soviet Union and other socialist countries, trying to distort the real position of the Church, clergy and believers in these countries, and to thrust their biased views and orientations on the Assembly.

These attempts were resolutely condemned by the representatives of the Russian Orthodox Church. They emphasised that this shifting of accents, with political problems replacing religious ones, leads to the transformation of the Church from a Christian institution into "a political or socio-economic force",[1] i.e. to the distortion of the fundamental notions of the role and purpose of the Church. Besides, this approach to the correlation of "vertical" and "horizontal" problems can, in the opinion of Orthodox ideologists, lead to secularisation of the Church and Christianity,[2] giving rise to doubts "whether we can call 'theology' what is preached from the ecumenical rostrum, especially pronouncements on horizontal actions"[3].

In the view of the ideologists of Orthodoxy, the absolutely necessary theological interpretation of the most important phenomena of the life of contemporary society, just as participation of believers in it, must not give rise to misconceptions about the life of society being the main subject matter of theology. In their view, conceptualisation of socio-economic and socio-political phenomena in the modern world does not at all justify attempts by various theologians to impose a bourgeois way of thinking on the Churches of the socialist countries to effect the "convergence of the socialist and capitalist systems; the division of the population of the world into rich and poor". In the view of Orthodox theologians, the existence in various countries of common problems—geographical, biological, anthropological, economic, political, and social—

---

[1] *The Journal of the Moscow Patriarchate*, 1976, No. 7, p. 68.
[2] Ibidem.
[3] Ibid., 1974, No. 11, p. 50.

"does not mean that they find identical solutions in different socio-economic systems".[1]

The Russian Orthodox Church thus resolutely opposes the use of the entire range of the so-called "horizontal" problems by some Protestant theologians for the defence and justification of the capitalist system alien to the working masses, and for distorting the essence of socialist society. At the same time, setting itself the general task of making a genuinely theological contribution to the understanding of problems that have a bearing on the theology of development, it does not only use the principle of division of theological problems into "vertical" and "horizontal", but also fills this principle with highly specific content.

In the Orthodox interpretation, the possibility of identification or equating of "vertical" and "horizontal" problems is rejected, and so is, more emphatically even, their independent consideration.

Fundamentally different and irreducible to each other in their content, these problems become inalienably united only insofar as different aspects of the life of society are correlated with their religious interpretation. In other words, "horizontal" problems involve an understanding and an evaluation of socio-political, cultural-historical and moral-aesthetic problems which fully rest on the dogmatic foundation of Christianity. In order to form a clear understanding of the question of justice as the basis of the life of society from the religious standpoint, one must, in the theologians' view, turn to the Bible. In order to determine the character of relations between men, one has to, as Professor Pariysky insists, realise that "the sermon establishes the relations to one's neighbour on the basis of love".[2] In defining their attitude to reality, believers are advised to understand clearly that they cannot at present stand aloof from the solution of the burning issues of today, that they cannot be indifferent to social evil and injustice, and that these issues cannot be resolved outside of Christian norms and demands.

Orthodox ideologists stress that excessive infatuation

---

[1] *The Journal of the Moscow Patriarchate*, 1974, No. 11, p. 52.
[2] *Zhurnal Moskovskoy Patriarkhii*, 1970, No. 3, p. 43.

with "horizontalism", mere use of socio-economic and socio-political problems as illustrations without any organic link with the fundamental aspects of the dogmata do little to consolidate the positions of religion. In their view, socio-political problems acquire their true religious-moral meaning and significance only when they appear to man in the light of basic Christian principles and become an inseparable part of his religious perception of the world. Moreover, Orthodox theologians are largely inclined to accept the view of the prominent Protestant theologian Dr. Visser't Hooft, Honorary President of the World Council of Churches, that "a Christianity that has lost its vertical dimension forfeits its salt and becomes not only lifeless in itself, but also useless to the world".[1] In the opinion of theologians, this means that not a single "horizontal" problem taken by itself makes sense for Christianity. Moreover, even such a phenomenon as humanism can turn, if unillumined by the idea of God-Man, into its opposite—into moral egoism and amoralism.

Finally, the unity of and differentiation between "vertical" and "horizontal" problems has this significance for Orthodox theologians that it permits the new interpretation of certain religious concepts to be brought to conformity with general doctrinal principles, with basic dogmatic formulations. The way in which this task, so important for the renewal of Orthodox ideology, is accomplished, can be illustrated by the new interpretation of asceticism.

In the not so distant past, asceticism was seen by the Orthodox Church as suppression and mortification of practically all sensual urges by such means as self-torture, self-exhaustion, self-flaggelation, etc. Hermits, recluses, men living in the wilderness or leading a life full of torment, deprivation and suffering were described as holy men performing feats for the glory of the faith. One such holy man was, in the view of the Church, Bishop Feofan the Recluse of Tambov, who cut himself completely from all contact with the world for thirty years. This conception of asceticism was fully

---

[1] *The Journal of the Moscow Patriarchate*, 1977, No. 1, p. 68.

in keeping with the general notion of the essence of sin-offering, with its strictly delineated conditions for attaining salvation and "life eternal".

In the view of Orthodox theologians today, asceticism must be regarded as believers' complete commitment to the cause of serving the common weal, and as correction of personal shortcomings and vices, immoral inclinations and evil designs. And another point: all this must be achieved through the individual's active participation in tackling the vital problems rather than through isolation from an active social life in the locked-in world of one's own individuality. This position appears quite consonant with the interests of believers. Indeed, if the Church calls for a fight against amoralism, describing this fight as an ascetic feat; if it calls for man's moral perfection, declaring this to be an ascetic service, then this evaluation of the essence of asceticism has none of the former negative meaning for believers. In this interpretation, the antithesis between Christian asceticism and true humanism does not appear self-obvious.

At the same time the "horizontal" evaluation of asceticism even in its new interpretation cannot, according to Orthodox theologians, have great value for the Church if it is not complemented by a "vertical" interpretation. Nowadays, as before, theologians insist that the goal and purpose of asceticism is godliness, involvement in the faith, and achievement of salvation, but this "vertical" interpretation is in its turn being revised to conform to the changing conceptions of the entire range of problems pertaining to "horizontal" theology. In other words, a new interpretation of socio-political and socio-historical problems inevitably necessitates a renovation of dogmata and cult, since both of these are regarded in contemporary Orthodox theology as two aspects of one task. On the other hand, the general conception of renewal of the fundamental principles of dogmata permits, in theologians' view, to achieve an identity of the Church and the world, to facilitate the mystical ascendance from the earthly to the heavenly, and to form the general view of man's need to consider the problems of the world in a system prompted by his religious worldview.

Thus by stressing the importance of practical combination of the horizontal and vertical vectors, Orthodox theologians focus on the direct links between religion and the entire diversity of contemporary socio-historical problems. For them, "the world is not something ... which does not concern the Christian individuality".[1] And that apparently means that the tendency in Orthodox theology of incorporating certain religious-theological generalisations and conclusions in any socially significant problem has become a generally accepted doctrine used to impart Providential meaning to the facts and phenomena of social life. The main purpose of this doctrine is therefore to incorporate Divine Providence in the texture of social history but in a different, non-orthodox formulation. It also strives to establish different proportions between ecclesiastical and non-ecclesiastical problems in the life of believers, taking into consideration, of course, the position of religion in the modern world. Finally, it serves the general tasks of modern religious renewal.

## Reorientation in the Evaluation of Scientific Knowledge

The Russian Orthodox Church also pays great attention to the correlation of faith and knowledge, science and religion.

In the second half of the 19th century, no longer able to fight science and assert a religious system of concepts by its old methods, Orthodoxy switched over to a different tactic. The essence of the reorientation was in drawing science in the orbit of religion and placing it in the service of theology rather than opposing science to religion, as before. This tendency, called "the law of spiritual diffusion"[2] by Archpriest Bogolyubsky, a prominent Orthodox theologian, essentially asserted alliance of knowledge and faith in which science was allotted an auxiliary role in the consolida-

---

[1] *The Journal of the Moscow Patriarchate*, 1978, No. 7, p. 63.

[2] N. I. Bogolyubsky. *Bogosloviye v apologeticheskikh chteniyakh* (Theology in Apologetic Readings), Moscow, 1915, p. 25.

tion of the foundations of a Christian worldview. This tactic was accurately assessed by Lenin, who stressed that "contemporary fideism does not at all reject science; all it rejects is the 'exaggerated claims' of science, to wit, its claim to objective truth".[1]

At present, the idea that natural science does not contradict but rather confirms the religious picture of the world is generally accepted in Orthodoxy. Some earlier evaluations of concrete scientific facts, including former attacks on Darwinism, are now rejected. Hardly any of the modern Orthodox theologians will support the view of Archpriest Potapyev that Michurin's experiments in evolving new varieties of plants "have a negative effect on the religious and moral ideas of Orthodox Christians".[2] None will agree with some pre-revolutionary churchmen who said that "God doesn't need our telephones, gramophones, or electric motors... He needs our good deeds, our living love, our loyalty to his will".[3] The basic assertion of the noncontradictory nature of the relation between faith and knowledge is a universal theological principle, it is concretely implemented in the following four most popular conceptions.

First, an inalienable link is postulated between religious belief and knowledge. "Scientific knowledge," says Professor Zabolotsky of the Leningrad Theological Academy, "is just as necessary for the Christian as his faith in Divine Providence."[4] This fact is, in his view, a practical realisation of the Biblical imperative that in the harmony of the Universe man is not master but also the custodian and reformer of nature. Such assertions cannot serve the interests of science, as the latter is declared to be compatible in man's consciousness with irrationalism and mysticism which are entirely alien to science in their essence, purpose and goals.

---

[1] V. I. Lenin, "Materialism and Empirio-Criticism", *Collected Works*, Vol. 14, Progress Publishers, Moscow, 1962, p. 125.

[2] I. V. Michurin. *Itogy shestidesyatiletnikh rabot* (Results of Sixty Years of Work), Moscow, 1949, p. 20.

[3] *Khristianin* (The Christian), 1912, Vol. 11, p. 69.

[4] *The Journal of the Moscow Patriarchate*, 1972, No. 4, p. 38.

Second, the theological proposition that scientific and religious knowledge are noncontradictory is gradually transformed into an unconditional recognition of their unity and the need for their synthesis. This viewpoint was most fully and comprehensively formulated by V. S. Solovyov.

Various aspects of Solovyov's "metaphysics of universal unity" were later developed by the theologians S. N. Bulgakov, P. A. Florensky, L. P. Karsavin, and others. At present, this position is recognised without reservation in the entire official Orthodox literature. Darwinism and Biblical creationism are regarded as noncontradictory principles of the entire diversity of the observable world. In all cases, however, the assertions of theologians about the unity of science and religion essentially assume subordination of reason to faith.

Third, one of the trends within the "metaphysics of universal unity", was headed by Priest Pavel Florensky, who attempted to resolve the objectively existing antithesis between science and religion on the basis of recognition of the antinomic character of truth. Florensky stressed that truth is real reasonableness and reasonable reality, finite infinity and infinite finitude, unity and multitude. For this reason, the multitude of divided truths contradict one another and manifest themselves in the incompatibility of such dogmatic conceptions as unitary essence and triunity, predestination and freedom of will.

To substantiate his basic proposition, Florensky resorted to mathematical apparatus, including his own studies in geometry, physics, technology, and topology. All this lent his theological work a solid and scientific aspect. It was no accident that he gradually became one of the most serious authorities in contemporary Orthodox theology.

Finally, the theological conception of the identity of faith and knowledge, borrowed without any substantive changes from early Christian theologians, has gained ascendancy in recent years.

Under the new historical conditions, this principle is used to draw religion in the orbit of real values. The principal goal in defining the relationships between science and religion is ultimately the consolidation of religious ideology and the raising of its authority and influence. It is precisely for this reason that Orthodox theologians stress that "opposition to progressive changes in society—in the field of science, technology, economy, and on the social plane—must be totally excluded today from the life of the Church and of Christians."[1]

It would be wrong to assume that the problem of relationship between science and religion in Orthodoxy is reduced to defence of the positions of religion against an onslaught of atheist criticism. While endeavouring to prove that science, just as faith, far from rejecting the religious picture of the world, confirms it, and that any conclusions of natural science ultimately do not contradict revelation, theologians insist on the priority of faith in any unity or identity of faith and knowledge. Their conclusions always boil down to the basic thesis: there would be no science without religion, modern culture and civilisation would be nonexistent without Christianity, and there is not true knowledge without true faith.

These basic propositions permit Orthodox theologians to draw far-reaching conclusions about the determinant role of Christianity in the humanisation of scientific progress, in the formation of its highly moral content. Religion is given pride of place, as it were, in preventing the use of science and knowledge for purposes hostile to man.

On the whole, this conception is called upon to create the impression that in the alliance of faith and knowledge the former plays the determinant role. In the words of V. Solovyov, knowledge based on experiment merely provides material for approaching the truth, and reason merely permits a clarification of some general forms of its developments. Truth "manifests itself only in the field of religious knowledge".[2] Compared to religion, science has a limited significance, for it cannot provide an answer to many

---

[1] *Zhurnal Moskovskoy patriarkhii*, 1967, No. 9, p. 34.

[2] V. S. Solovyov. *Sobraniye sochineniy* (Collected Works), St. Petersburg, Vol. 2, p. 331.

problems of life, still less can it define its own moral purpose. If that is so, no scientific achievements in the present or future can cancel the universal role of religion in the assertion of spiritual values.

This orientation has as its purpose not only the preservation of religion and consolidation of its positions but also the formation of a generalised system of views of the world and man's place in it, of a view of man's activity setting limits to the power of reason and raising obstacles in the way of men's cognitive and transformative activity.

Even more apparent is the tendency to assert the idea that faith has an advantage over knowledge in the assessment of the character and essence of the cognitive process, in the understanding of the meaning of truth and the paths of its comprehension. Of course, the position of modern Orthodoxy is quite different from the medieval contraposition of faith and knowledge. Today, theologians speak a great deal about the vast potential of science, revising their former views of its effect on the life of believers and society's intellectual development. But it is not such theological statements that determine the real position of Orthodoxy in interpreting the meaning of scientific cognition. This position is revealed in its full extent and in its essence in the consideration of its epistemological conception.

The latter has been most comprehensively elaborated in official Orthodox philosophy that is termed "academic philosophy", as it was taught at all the theological academies. The most prominent representatives of this philosophy—F. A. Golubinsky, V. D. Kudryavtsev, M. M. Tareyev, A. I. Brovkovich, V. I. Nesmelov, M. I. Karinsky, F. F. Sidonsky, V. N. Karpov, N. G. Debolsky and others—have formulated the fundamental principles of the understanding of the cognitive process. Let us consider them in the most general form.

The main subject matter studied by Orthodox theologians is an absolutely perfect being standing above the world and prescribing its laws to the world. Rejecting the materialist understanding of the unity of the world, they assert that the unity of the world does not lie in its material character but in an absolute, necessary and infinite being. The sources of this unity are in the act of creation. If that is so, the entire universe in all its diversity can only be understood and cognized if the idea of creation is recognised.

This fundamental premise of Orthodox theologians determined their attitude to various stages of cognition. Sensuous cognition was declared to be limited and rational one—inadequate. Only ideal cognition as a combination of the intuitive with the spiritual-mystical permits an understanding of the essence of being.

Thus the substantial basis of cognition in Orthodoxy is the idea of God. The purpose of cognition is reduced to explaining true life in accordance with the demands of faith, which enables man to clarify his position in the world and his attitude to the Creator. The Orthodox conception of the process of cognition thus obviously excludes the cognizing subject from the system of real relations, divorcing him from the concrete socio-historical conditions of his being. Besides, cognizing man is presented as an embodiment of the idea of God inherent in man as a living image of divinity. Cognition is thus directly correlated with faith and is declared to hold promise only if it incorporates the main dogmatic concepts.

The meaning of the Orthodox interpretation of the process of cognition is readily understood if illustrated by an interpretation of the life of society and the concrete forms of social structure. This is how Bishop Pitirim defines the essence of historical processes and specific features of their understanding: "Divine Providence and human freedom participate in the historical manifestation of each social formation. Each concrete form of social structure is subordinated to factors whose interaction is governed by law."[1] The task of theology, he continues, consists in clarification, through in-depth study of the revelation and the experience of Christianity's spiritual life, of the manifestations of that Providence in its interaction with the freedom of choice in the formation of contemporary social phenomena.

This is only one of the numerous examples of substitution of Divine Providence for historical necessity

---

[1] *Bogoslovskiye trudy*, Moscow, 1970, V, p. 225.

and freedom of choice for men's conscious activity. Dialectical materialism has long shown the complete untenability of any attempts to incorporate various transcendental forces in the historical process. The life of society and its changes and development are not determined by Divine Providence but by conditions of the material life of men, of classes and social groups. The existence and progressive development of society is based on the production of material wealth. But their immediate creators are men—the main productive force. That is precisely the reason why the working masses become creators of history, its motive force.

The task of science is to study the springs of historical development inherent in the conditions of material life. Cognition of these motive forces, which are often reflected in the minds of the masses in fantastic form, is the only path to the understanding of the laws governing history.[1]

The Orthodox theological interpretation of the unity of faith and knowledge is obviously an attempt to clear the path of religion with the aid of science. Scientifically oriented thinking is only recognised as consistent with reality when it agrees with Revelation and accepts the principal notions of dogma. Various constructs pertaining to man's cognitive ability are also reduced to the transformation of reasonable knowledge into the other-being of faith.

Having proclaimed the principle of noncontradiction of science and religion, Orthodox theology simultaneously stresses the imperfection and incompleteness of scientific knowledge. Besides, the basic mode of cognition of truth is believed to be "reasonable intuition". As for the results of the cognitive process, they are regarded as a moment of connection between the conditional and the unconditional (Nesmelov), or as perception of certain aspects of super-sensuous being (Kudryavtsev), or else as a mode of transition from the assertoric truth about the world containing merely an assertion of some fact to the apodictic truth of a

---

[1] See F. Engels. "Ludwig Feuerbach and the End of Classical German Philosophy", in: K. Marx, F. Engels, *Selected Works* in three volumes, Progress Publishers, Moscow, 1983, Vol. 3, p. 366.

dogma, irrefutable and unconditionally true (Florensky).

This interpretation of the cognitive process has nothing in common with science, as it merely defends religion, protects religion from scientific criticism, and shapes worldview orientations which oppose the dialectical materialist approach to cognition and transformation of reality. It creates an illusion of confirmation of the religious picture of the world by science and of completeness of the religious perception of the world as opposed to the imperfection and inadequacy of scientific cognition.

Such are some of the tendencies in the ideology and activity of Russian Orthodoxy today. They do not of course exhaust the entire range of problems that the Church is now endeavouring to make more up-to-date. At present, Orthodoxy revises its exegetics, liturgics, ecclesiology and other branches of theology, adapting itself to the new conditions of its existence, to the changed mentality of believers.

We can thus say that the new approach of the ideologists of Russian Orthodoxy today to the scientific and technological progress is undergoing certain changes, but the internal antithesis between science and religion remains unchanged, being an objective reality. It is from this reality that the Marxist-Leninist criticism proceeds in revealing the essence of any religious ideology.

*Chapter XI*

# THE PRESENT-DAY STRUCTURE AND ORGANISATION OF THE CHURCH

The functioning of the Russian Orthodox Church in a socialist society has left an imprint not only on its socio-political orientation, dogmata and rites but also on the church structure and organisational forms, which are also adapted to the new social reality.

## Parishes and Churches. Cloisters

The organisational structure and internal life of the Orthodox Church is regulated by the "Enactment on the Administration of the Russian Orthodox Church" adopted by the 1945 Local Council. The 1961 Council of Hierarchs introduced certain amendments in it pertaining to parishes.

The basic unit of the Russian Orthodox Church is a church *prikhod* (parish); hence the traditional name for the adherents of Orthodoxy, *prikhozhane* (parishioners). It is set up in the following manner.

Where the number of religious citizens who have attained the age of 18 is sufficient, they choose 20 or more persons (the so-called "church twenty") as constitutors; these request the executive committee of a district or city Soviet of People' Deputies to register the religious society. The Executive Committee of the Soviet in question passes on the believers' request, together with its own conclusion, to the Executive Committee of the territorial, regional or city (in the case of Moscow and Leningrad) Soviet of People's Deputies or the Council of Ministers of an autonomous republic, where it is considered within a month and passed on to the Council for Religious Affairs under the USSR Council of Ministers, which takes the final decision on registration (or refusal to registrate) and informs the religious society of that decision.

Upon registration, a religious society is given free use of a prayer building on terms stipulated by a contract between the religious society in question and a plenipotentiary of the executive committee of the district or city Soviet of People's Deputies. Besides, it can hold prayer meetings at other facilities rented from individuals or executive committees of district or city Soviets of People's Deputies.

Religious societies have the right to acquire church plate, religious cultic objects, and transport facilities; they can also rent, build and buy buildings for their needs, in accordance with the existing laws.

It is forbidden for religious societies to set up mutual aid funds, cooperatives, production associations and generally to use the property at their disposal for any purposes other than satisfying their religious needs; to render material assistance to their members; to organise special prayer assemblies for children, young people, women, etc., as well as Biblical, literary, handicrafts assemblies, groups, circles, departments, etc.; and also to arrange excursions, children's games, open libraries and reading-rooms, set up health homes or provide medical aid.

For the administration of the parish, the use of cultic property and external representation, a religious society elects, at a general meeting of believers who vote by show of hands, an executive body consisting of a chairman, his assistant and a treasurer, and also an auditing commission consisting of not more than three members. The meetings or sessions of the executive or auditory bodies of religious societies require no notification of or permission from the authorities.

The executive bodies of religious societies may use stamps, seals and forms bearing their name exclusively on occasions of religious nature.

The cultic property, placed at the disposal of believers by contract, acquired by them or donated to them is state property; it is held in usufruct by believers and registered at the executive committees of the district or city Soviets of People's Deputies. The users of cultic buildings as well as other property undertake to keep it in good repair as state property entrusted to them and to bear the whole of the expenses involved in its possession and employment (heating, insurance, protection, taxes etc.); to use that property exclusively for religious needs; to indemnify the state for damages in case of spoiling or loss of property; to have an inventory of the entire cultic property; and to put no obstacles in the way of regular inspection of the property by representatives of district and city Soviets of People's Deputies.

Prayer buildings of historical, artistic and architectural significance, that are on the Ministry of Culture's special lists, are handed over to religious societies on condition of obligatory compliance with the rules on registration and protection of monuments of art.

The executive body of a religious society hires, for the performance of cults, ecclesiastics (priests and deacons) and lower-ranking churchmen (readers, sextons, sacristans, candle-sellers, choristers, etc.), paying them salaries stipulated by contract. The executive body does not interfere in the liturgical activity of the clergy, neither do the latter interfere in the executive body's administrative and economic activity.

The sources of funds for the upkeep of the church and of the personnel are as follows. The sale of candles, prosphoras, pectoral crosses, paper bands placed on the foreheads of the dead, and other church paraphernalia provide the bulk of the church's income. The income from performing such rites as baptism, weddings and funeral services, as well as prayers for health and soul's repose, is also substantial. Another source is believers' voluntary donations (the so-called mug and plate collections).

All these incomes of religious societies are not taxed, but all priests and other ecclesiastical personnel pay income tax on their salary.

Part of their income is handed over by religious societies to the higher church bodies—for the maintenance of the entire apparatus of the Russian Orthodox Church, for financing undertakings by the Church, and for the payment of pensions to elderly clergymen. It has become a tradition in the parishes of the Russian Orthodox Church to contribute certain sums to the Peace Fund.

Apart from churches, religious activity in Russian Orthodoxy is centred at cloisters (monasteries and convents) of which there are now about two dozen. Most of them are in the Ukraine.

The income of Orthodox cloisters comes from the earnings of monks and nuns who paint icons, make church vestments etc., and work on a contractual basis in neighbouring state and collective farms.

There are two cloisters of the Russian Orthodox Church outside the USSR—the Gorneye Convent near Jerusalem and the St. Panteleimon Monastery on Mt. Athos (Greece). The number of the monks there is replenished by monastics from the cloisters on the territory of the Soviet Union.

## Dioceses and Exarchates

Church parishes within one or several districts of a city or region constitute deaneries. The ecclesiastics of the churches forming a deanery are subordinated to a *blagochinnyi*—a priest appointed to that post by a higher church authority. Just as rectors of parish churches, *blagochinnyis* do not interfere in the administrative and economic activities of their deaneries, confining themselves to questions of internal church life. Their functions include control over the liturgical activities of the clergy subordinated to them and the handling of conflicts among ecclesiastics.

Several deaneries form a diocese headed by a hierarch (a bishop, archbishop or metropolitan); these also run diocesan departments. Where there is a need for them, diocesan hierarchs set up, to aid them in their administrative work, diocesan councils consisting of the most experienced churchmen. The ruling hierarchs of the Moscow, Leningrad, Kiev and Minsk dioceses have vicar bishops. In keeping with a long-established tradition, some of the vicars of the Moscow diocese are appointed to various hierarchical posts at the foreign establishments of the Russian Orthodox Church.

At the beginning of 1986 the Russian Orthodox Church had 74 hierarchs, including 13 metropolitans, 37 archbishops, and 24 bishops [1].

The dioceses on the territory of the Ukraine form the Ukrainian Exarchate of the Moscow Patriarchate, headed by Metropolitan Filaret (Denisenko) of Kiev and Galich. In the Russian Orthodox Church an exarchate is a church district that has some autonomy but forms an integral part of the patriarchate.

The Russian Orthodox Church also has several exarchates abroad (see below).

### The Moscow Patriarchate. The Synodal Establishments

The dioceses and exarchates comprise the Moscow Patriarchate, as the Russian Orthodox Church is termed by analogy with the ancient Eastern patriarchates—those of Constantinople, Alexandria, Antioch and Jerusalem. Diocesan hierarchs and exarchs are directly subordinated to the Patriarch of Moscow and All Russia elected by a Local Council of the Russian Orthodox Church. The patriarch is accountable to the Local Council.

The Holy Synod helps the patriarch to run the practical affairs of the Church. The Synod consists of eight members—five permanent and three temporary ones. The permanent members of the Synod are the metropolitan of Krutitsy and Kolomna (the title of the hierarch heading the Moscow diocese), the metropolitans of Kiev, of Leningrad, of Odessa (Chancellor of the Moscow Patriarchate) and the metropolitan of Minsk (Chairman of the Department for External Church Relations). The temporary members of the Synod are all those hierarchs who are summoned, in rotation, to Moscow for the synodal sessions. On some occasions the Synod holds extended sessions—when the questions discussed are especially important or when the synodal session must be attended by hierarchs directly involved in the problems discussed.

---

[1] *Pravoslavnyi tserkovnyi kalendar na 1986 g. Vkladysh* (Orthodox Church Calendar for 1986. Insert).

The decisions of the patriarch and the Synod are implemented through the Chancellery of the Moscow Patriarchate, which was headed over many years by Metropolitan Aleksiy of Tallinn and Estonia, since 1986 it is headed by Metropolitan Sergiy (Petrov) of Odessa and Kherson.

The various branches of church activity are managed by synodal departments.

The largest and the most important of these is the Department for External Church Relations performing numerous external functions and headed by one of the most influential hierarchs of the Russian Orthodox Church. Between 1946 (the year when the department was set up) and 1960 it was headed by Metropolitan Nikolai, Patriarch Aleksiy's closest associate; in 1960-1972, by Metropolitan Nikodim; in 1972-1981, by Metropolitan Yuvenaliy; and since 1981, by Metropolitan Filaret (Vakhromeyev).

In the first place, the Department of External Church Relations of the Moscow Patriarchate runs the foreign establishments of the Russian Orthodox Church. Apart from the foreign exarchates and deaneries of the Moscow Patriarchate, it has the following establishments abroad: the Russian Orthodox Mission in Jerusalem; the representations of the Russian Orthodox Church at the Patriarch of Antioch and All the East in Damascus, at the World Council of Churches in Geneva, and at the Christian Peace Conference in Prague; *podvorya* in Beirut, Sofia, Tokyo, and Belgrade; and a number of parishes in different countries.

The Department keeps up the links between the Moscow Patriarchate and the other Orthodox Churches, participating in all undertakings of the Orthodox Churches. It maintains contacts with other Christian Churches as well as with non-Christian confessions, participating in international ecclesiastical undertakings, sending abroad and receiving church delegations and groups of pilgrims, organising theological meetings and discussions, etc.

The Department of External Church Relations is the vehicle by which the peace-making activity of the Russian Orthodox Church is directed and implemented: regional and international church actions in defence of peace are organised, and collaboration is established with such public organisations as the Soviet Peace Committee, the Soviet Committee for European Security and Cooperation, the Soviet Afro-Asian Solidarity Committee. The Union of Soviet Societies for Friendship and Cultural Relations with Foreign Countries, the Soviet Committee for Cultural Relations with Compatriots Abroad, the Soviet Peace Fund, etc.

The Department for External Church Relations of the Moscow Patriarchate has branches in Kiev and Leningrad.

Very active is the Publishing Department of the Synod of the Russian Orthodox Church. It has been headed since 1962 by Metropolitan Pitirim (Nechayev). Apart from publication of various literature, the department studies church MSS and liturgical texts compiled in the 15th-17th centuries, organises exhibitions of photographs in foreign countries illustrating the life and activity of the Russian Orthodox Church, and the shooting of documentaries (both by the Central Documentary Film Studios of this country and by foreign TV companies). It also keeps up contacts with foreign ecclesiastical journalists and international organisations of Christian journalists.

Attached to the Synod are two committees—one on education and another on pensions.

The system of synodal establishments includes the Economic Management Department, of which the principal function is to provide the parishes of the Russian Orthodox Church with everything necessary for the services. In 1980, several new workshops began to operate in the village of Sofrino near Moscow, where liturgical objects are produced at a modern technological level. They meet the needs not only of the Moscow Patriarchate but also of other Local Orthodox Churches. Some dioceses (e.g., those of Astrakhan, Irkutsk, Leningrad, and Perm) have diocesan candle workshops.

Work on repairing and restoring churches, monasteries and other cultic buildings also comes within the purview of the Economic Management Department.

All the work of this department is financed from the funds of the whole Church, made up of the contributions of diocesan departments and patriarchal *podvorya,* as well as the receipts from the sale of synodal workshops' products.

## Ecclesiastical Educational Establishments

Priests, deacons, theologians, church administrators and workers of synodal establishments are trained by the Moscow Patriarchate at seminaries and academies, i.e., secondary and higher educational establishments. Before the Revolution, similar educational establishments pursued two tasks: educating the children of the clergy and training clergymen, whereas now the seminaries and academies of the Moscow Patriarchate pursue only the second of these goals.

At present the Russian Orthodox Church has three theological seminaries (the Moscow one at Zagorsk, and those of Leningrad and Odessa) and two theological academies—in Moscow and Leningrad. Besides, the Leningrad seminary and academy have a precentors' class each.

A theological seminary is a specialised secondary educational establishment of the Moscow Patriarchate that trains clergymen. A theological academy is a specialised higher educational establishment of the Moscow Patriarchate.

Persons of both sexes can be enrolled at the precentors' classes of the Leningrad theological academy and seminary. They have to meet the same requirements at the entrance exams as those entering a theological seminary.

Apart from Soviet citizens, foreign students also study at the Leningrad theological seminary and academy—mostly members of Orthodox and Non-Chalcedonian Churches of India, Kenya, Tanzania, Uganda, Ethiopia and other countries.

The Moscow seminary and academy have correspondence departments whose purpose is to provide theological education for parish clerics of the Russian Orthodox Church. The correspondence courses are open to priests and deacons.

## Publishing Activities

The Publishing Department of the Moscow Patriarchate brings out extremely varied religious literature, including literature for liturgical purposes.

First of all the Moscow Patriarchate publishes nine periodicals in the USSR and abroad, including *The Journal of the Moscow Patriarchate*—the official organ of the Russian Orthodox Church. It was founded in 1931 by Deputy Patriarchal Locum Tenens Sergiy (Stragorodsky), and appeared until 1935; in 1943 the publication was resumed, and it has been coming out monthly ever since. *The Journal* carries official materials, theological articles, news items, etc. It has several permanent sections: *Church Life* (information on the life of the dioceses and theological schools, consecration of bishops, obituaries, etc.); *Sermons* (materials on the methods of preaching, as well as model sermons); *The Peace Movement* (materials on the peace-making activity of the Russian Orthodox Church); *Orthodox Sister Churches: Current Events* (information on the life of other Orthodox Churches); *Ecumena* (materials on inter-church contacts of the Moscow Patriarchate); *Theology* (articles and reports of theoretical nature); *Liturgical Practice* (materials on the basic elements of the Orthodox cult); *Books and Publications* (reviews of the Moscow Patriarchate's publications and of theological literature published abroad).

Since 1971 *The Journal of the Moscow Patriarchate* has been appearing in two languages—Russian and English.

The theoretical organ of the Russian Orthodox Church is the collection of papers *Bogoslovskiye trudy* (Theological Studies), which has been coming out since the late 1950s. Twenty-seven volumes had been produced by the end of 1986. They contain works by contemporary theologians of the Russian Orthodox Church, by foreign church authors and by the "Fathers of the Church", including those translated into Russian for the first time. In some of the volumes materials have appeared on theological conversations between theologians of the Moscow Patriarchate and those of other Christian confessions. Some of the volumes are devoted to one subject; thus Vol. VIII was entirely devoted to Vladimir Lossky (published here were his "The Mystical Theology of the Eastern Church", "Dogmatic Theology", "'The Vision of God' in Byzantine Theology", "La synthèse Palamite", "Domination et règne"); Vol. XIII, to Professor N. D. Uspensky of the Leningrad Theological Academy: "The Anaphora (An Essay in Historico-Liturgical Analysis)" and "The Conflict of Two Theologies in the 17th Century Correction of Russian Service Books", a number of articles on Uspensky and a list of his works; and Vol. XX, to Metropolitan Nikodim (Rotov); the work "The History of the Russian Orthodox Mission in Jerusalem" and his Master's thesis "Pope John XXIII", articles about the Metropolitan and a list of his works. Unlike *The Journal of the Moscow Patriarchate,* which is addressed not only to the clergy but also to the rank-and-file believers, *Bogoslovskiye trudy* is intended for priests and theologians.

The Ukrainian Exarchate of the Moscow Patriarchate has its own monthly *Pravoslavnyi visnik* (Orthodox Bulletin) published in Ukrainian since 1946 (first in Lvov and now in Kiev). It has the same sections as *The Journal of the Moscow Patriarchate,* but a considerable part of its materials is devoted to the church life of the Ukrainian Exarchate.

The other six journals of the Moscow Patriarchate are published abroad: *Vestnik russkogo zapadno-yevropeyskogo patriarshego ekzarkhata* (Bulletin of the Russian West-European Patriarchal Exarchate, *Messager de l'exarchat du Patriarche Russe en Europe Occidentale*) appears in France in Russian and French; *One Church* appears in the USA; *Stimme der Orthodoxie* (The Voice of Orthodoxy) in German in the GDR; *Kanadskiy pravoslavnyi visnik* (Canadian Orthodox Bulletin) in Ukrainian in Canada, *Egyhazi Kronika* (Church Chronicle) in Hungarian in Hungary, and *The Journal of the Russian Orthodox Church in Japan,* in Japanese.

Each year the Moscow Patriarchate publishes *The Orthodox Church Calendar* in several formats—table, wall and pocket or souvenir calendars. The table calendar has these sections: on church feasts, anniversaries and commemorative days, and fasts; the calendar proper; the order of apostolic and evangelical readings; paschal tables for the next 20 years; an alphabetic list of the saints mentioned in the calendar; an alphabetic list of the miracle-working icons of the Mother of God; Akathistos for Jesus Christ, the Mother of God and the most venerated of the saints. A supplementary sheet carries the pictures of all the bishops of the Russian Orthodox Church. The illustrations in the calendar include photographs of the most revered icons and of churches. The Ukrainian Exarchate of the Moscow Patriarchate publishes *The Orthodox Church Calendar* in Ukrainian.

The Bible has been published several times: in 1956, 1968, 1976, and 1983. The 1968 Bible was reprinted several times, one of these was the 1976 jubilee stereotype edition on the occasion of the centenary of the appearance of the Bible in Russian (1876). The appendices to all the editions include an index of New Testament church readings (paroemias); indices of the numbers of psalms and titles of books; lists of canonical and non-canonical books; a biblical calendar; maps of Palestine; the plan of Jerusalem. A set of photographs of the most revered icons is a supplement to the Bible.

The New Testament has been published many times, with the following appendices: Epistles of St. Paul (a table); On the Holy Scripture of the New Testament; On Monetary Units; The Sequence of Events according to the Four Evangelists; The Sequence of the Events According to the Acts of the Apostles; An Index of Evangelical and Apostolic Church Readings; Historical Maps.

In the 1950s, *Liturgical Instructions for Clergymen*, containing scenarios for church services for each day of the year, appeared regularly. A great many liturgical books have been published. They include: *Service Book, The Book of Needs, the Psalter, The Menaion, The Book of Hours, The Octoechos*, separate services on feast days and prayer-books in Russian and Ukrainian. A four-volume *Manual for the Clergy* has been published, and a multi-volume *Menaion* is soon to come off the press.

The works of major church leaders of the Moscow Patriarchate have been published many times. The first such publication was the book *Patriarkh Sergiy i yego dukhovnoye nasledstvo* (Patriarch Sergiy and His Spiritual Heritage, 1947). In the 1940s and 1950s, selected speeches by Metropolitan Nikolai (Yarushevich) appeared in Russian and in several foreign languages, and also his *Exhortations and Speeches* in four volumes. Four volumes of the speeches and sermons of Patriarch Aleksiy (Simansky) have come out, and the fifth volume is to appear soon. A one-volume collection of the *Sermons, Speeches, Messages, Addresses, 1957-1977* of His Holiness Patriarch Pimen was brought out in 1977.

There are also numerous publications characterising the general state of the Russian Orthodox Church and the principal aspects of its activity: *The Truth about Religion in Russia* (1942), *The Russian Orthodox Church and the Great Patriotic War* (1943), *The Russian Orthodox Church. Order, Position, Activity* (1958), *The Russian Orthodox Church* (1980).

A number of books have been devoted to the most important events in the ecclesiastical life of the Moscow Patriarchate: *The 50th Anniversary of the Restoration of the Patriarchate, The Local Council of the Russian Orthodox Church. Documents, Materials, Chronicle, The Moscow Patriarchate, 1917-1977, The 60th Anniversary of the Restoration of the Patriarchate.*

The publications of the Moscow Patriarchate provide information on many peace-making moves of the Russian Orthodox Church: *The Conference of All Churches and Religious Associations in the USSR on Safeguarding Peace* (1953), *Contribution to Peacemaking by the USSR Religious Organisations* (1977), *Religious Workers for Lasting Peace, Disarmament and Just Relations among Nations* (1978).

The patriarch's Christmas and Easter messages and other official ecclesiastical materials regularly appear in separate pamphlets.

The Moscow Patriarchate bears the expenses involved in the production of all the books and journals at state printing-houses. It also distributes its publications through its own channels, including sales at churches.

*Chapter XII*

# THE RUSSIAN ORTHODOX CHURCH IN THE SYSTEM OF CONTEMPORARY CHRISTIANITY

The Russian Orthodox Church maintains close contacts with other Christian confessions and denominations—both at the regional and international levels. Its ideologists regard such contacts both as a factor in achieving a greater stability in present-day Christianity, which has now entered a period of acute universal crisis, and as a means of restoring pan-Christian unity—which never in fact existed.

Below, we shall outline the most significant of these contacts and their principal results.

## Relationships with the Other Orthodox Churches

Although the Local Orthodox Churches have common dogmata and fundamentally the same liturgical practice, their relationships were never smooth or stable. "The relationships of the Local Orthodox Churches between themselves," stated the Patriarchal Locum Tenens Metropolitan Pimen (Izvekov), at the 1971 Local Council, "are not invariably serene and unclouded... While preserving their unity of faith and full communion in the Sacraments, the Local Orthodox Churches may still have their differences, of which history can show us a great many examples".[1]

---

[1] *The Local Council of the Russian Orthodox Church (May 30-June 2, 1971).* Published by the Moscow Patriarchate, Moscow, 1972, p. 58.

In this case, the relations between the Russian Orthodox Church and the other branches of ecumenical Orthodoxy are not exceptions, either. The dominant trend in these relations, especially after World War II, has been the desire of the Moscow Patriarchate to consolidate its links with all the Orthodox Churches.

The Moscow Patriarchate normalised relations with the filial Churches. It granted autocephaly to the Polish Orthodox Church (1948), to the Czechoslovak Orthodox Church (1951), and to the American Orthodox Church (1970). In 1951, the Moscow Patriarchate recognised the autonomy of the Finnish Orthodox Church, and in 1970 granted autonomy to the Orthodox Church of Japan.

Relations with a number of Local Churches were also normalised. As the Transcarpathian region became part of the Ukraine, the Serbian Church handed over the Mukachevo diocese to the Moscow Patriarchate's jurisdiction. In their turn, the parishes and deaneries of the Russian Orthodox Church in Yugoslavia came under the jurisdiction of the Serbian Church. The Moscow Patriarchate handed over its parishes and the Convent of the Protecting Veil of the Mother of God, which are on Bulgarian territory, to the Bulgarian Orthodox Church; the Russian St. Nicholas's Church in Bucharest, to the Romanian Orthodox Church; all its churches and parishes in Czechoslovakia, to the Czechoslovak Orthodox Church; and the New Valaam Monastery and the Lentulla Convent, to the Orthodox Church of Finland.

The Moscow Patriarchate takes an active part in the search for forms of Pan-Orthodox cooperation. This cooperation was initiated in 1948 at the meeting of the heads and representatives of the Local Orthodox Churches by the Moscow Patriarchate during the celebrations of the quincentenary of the autocephaly of the Russian Orthodox Church. Somewhat later such meetings became regular and have gone down in history as the Rhodes Pan-Orthodox Conferences.

The first conference in Rhodes was held in 1961. Here, representatives of the Local Orthodox Churches considered the question of a future Pan-Orthodox

Council. In this way the attempts frequently undertaken in the past were renewed.

The First Pan-Orthodox Conference in Rhodes also worked out a long catalogue of topics (more than 100) to be considered at the Council. They were grouped under eight headings: Faith and Dogma; Divine Service Administration and The Church System; The Relations of the Orthodox Church with the Rest of the Christian World; Orthodoxy in the World; General Theological Subjects; Social Problems. All Orthodox Churches were requested to express their views on the list of topics to be considered at the Pre-Council.

In the course of the debate on the catalogue, the Moscow Patriarchate's delegation suggested the removal of some of the subjects (The Development of Internal and External Missionary Work, The Methods of Fighting Atheism and False Doctrines Like Theosophy, Spiritism, Freemasonry, etc.) and addition of some others (Cooperation between the Local Orthodox Churches in the Realisation of the Christian Ideas of Peace, Fraternity and Love among Peoples, Orthodoxy and Racial Discrimination, Orthodoxy and the Tasks of Christians in Regions of Rapid Social Change).[1]

The Synod of the Russian Orthodox Church approved the list of topics for the future Pre-Council worked out by the Rhodes Pan-Orthodox Conference and resolved to set up a special theological commission for dealing with questions on that list. By 1968, the commission had carried out its task, preparing for the Synod draft statements on all the topics indicated in the catalogue.

Besides working out the topics for the future Pre-Council, the First Conference passed the decision "On the Study of Ways for Achieving Closer Contacts and Unity of Churches in a Pan-Orthodox Perspective", envisaging the search for contacts with Ancient Eastern (non-Chalcedonian) Churches (Monophysites), the Old Catholic, Anglican, Catholic, and Protestant Churches, as well as with the World Council of Churches.

This decision was further developed in the docu-

---

[1] *Zhurnal Moskovskoy patriarkhii*, 1961, No. 11, pp. 18-21.

ments of the Second Rhodes Pan-Orthodox Conference of 1963. Its participants favoured a dialogue with the Roman Catholic Church on an equal basis. It was resolved that each of the Local Orthodox Churches would decide for itself whether to send observers to the Second Vatican Council of the Catholic Church then in session or not (the Russian Orthodox Church did).

The Third Rhodes Pan-Orthodox Conference (in 1964) decided to set up inter-Orthodox theological commissions on dialogue with Anglicans and Old Catholics. The first session of these commissions was held in Belgrade in 1966. The Russian Orthodox Church was represented on both of these commissions.

The Fourth Pan-Orthodox Conference held at Geneva in 1968 confirmed the decisions of previous conferences on the need for a dialogue with Anglicans and Old Catholics. It set up an inter-Orthodox theological commission on dialogue with Ancient Oriental (Monophysite) Churches and decided to continue Orthodox-Catholic contacts. It also favoured the establishment of contacts with Lutherans and passed recommendations on increasing the contribution of Orthodoxy to the activity of the World Council of Churches.

The principal item on the agenda of the Fourth Conference was the preparations for the future Pan-Orthodox Council that was termed the Holy and Great Council, not just the Ecumenical Council. Instead of preparing a Pre-Council, it was decided to hold a series of Pre-Council conferences for drafting the agenda of the future Council.

Six themes were chosen from the extensive Rhodes catalogue: The Sources of Divine Revelation; Greater Participation of Laymen in Divine Service and Church Life as a Whole; Coordinating Ecclesiastical Rules Concerning Fasting in Accordance with Present-day Requirements; Impediments to Marriage; The Calendar Problem; Oikonomia in the Orthodox Church. The elaboration of these topics was entrusted to the individual Local Churches. The Russian Orthodox Church took upon itself the task of elaborating the topic of impediments to marriage and the calendar problem.

To study the elaborated topics, an Inter-Orthodox Preparatory Commission of the Holy and Great Council of the Eastern Orthodox Church was instituted. At its 1971 session in Geneva the commission analysed the reports of the Local Churches on these topics, drew up its conclusion on them and passed the decision to convene the First Pre-Council Pan-Orthodox Conference in 1972.

But the Conference in Geneva was only held in 1976. The Russian Orthodox Church was represented there by a large delegation which made a constructive contribution to all aspects of the Conference's work.

The Conference was preceded by two meetings of heads of the Local Churches' delegations. The first of these discussed the proposed agenda of the conference: (1) Review of the list of themes of the Holy and Great Pan-Orthodox Council; (2) General review and appraisal of the progress of the Orthodox Church's relations and dialogues with the World Council of Churches; (3) Examination of the problem of joint celebration of Easter by all Christians on the same Sunday, and other items.

The second meeting worked out the following principles of the Conference's work: (1) The Holy and Great Council of the Orthodox Church should meet as soon as possible. (2) It should be of short duration. (3) It should not touch on the holy dogmas of the Church and the Holy Canons as such, although it was not to exclude the possibility that the Council might, in the course of its examination of the various problems confronting it, elucidate theological, ecclesiastical and canonical thoughts that would interpret and assert Orthodox dogma and canonical order. (4) The Holy and Great Council of the Orthodox Church that was being prepared should not be regarded as unique and automatically ruling out the subsequent convocation of other Holy and Great Councils.

The Conference revised the Rhodes catalogue of topics for the future Council and drew up a shorter one on its basis, including 10 sections: (1) The Orthodox Diaspora; (2) Autocephaly and How It Is to Be Proclaimed; (3) Autonomy and How It Is to Be Proclaimed; (4) The Dyptichs; (4) The Question of a

Common Calendar; (5) Impediments to Marriage; (6) Adaptation of Ecclesiastical Rules on Fasting; (7) the Orthodox Churches Relations with the Rest of Christendom; (8) Orthodoxy and the Ecumenical Movement; (9) The Contribution of the Local Orthodox Churches to the Triumph of the Christian Ideas of Peace, Freedom and Fraternity among Peoples, elimination of racial discrimination. It was decided to include these topics in the agenda of the Pan-Orthodox Council.

The Conference stated its recommendation to hand over a number of other topics (The Sources of Divine Revelation; The Meaning of the Church; Codification of the Holy Canons and the Canonical Decisions; Akribeia and Oikonomia; Monasticism) to Local Orthodox Churches for special study, that they might later be considered at an Inter-Orthodox forum.

The other topics of the First Rhodes Pan-Orthodox Conference that were removed from the revised catalogue were forwarded by the Pre-Conference to the individual Local Churches for special study.

The Conference went on record for continuing dialogue between the Orthodox Church and the Ancient Oriental Churches, as well as Anglicans and Old Catholics, and a dialogue with Roman Catholics. It also proposed the setting up of an Inter-Orthodox theological commission on dialogue with Lutherans.

After discussing the question of the Orthodox Church's participation in the World Council of Churches, the Conference decided that the contribution could only be increased through election of Orthodox theologians to the leadership of the WCC, for only then would texts compiled there satisfactorily reflect Orthodox theological and ecclesiastical opinion.

Representatives of the Russian Orthodox Church take an active part in all the Pre-Council moves. However, the leaders of the Moscow Patriarchate do not share the optimism of those participants of Inter-Orthodox meetings who believe the convocation of an Ecumenical Council to be an easy task to be soon carried out. In his address to the 1971 Local Council, Patriarchal Locum Tenens, Metropolitan Pimen (Izvekov), declared that a Pan-Orthodox Council could only be convened and successfully held after the contradictions between the individual Local Orthodox Churches were resolved in the course of preparations for that momentous event. In his report at the celebration of the 60th anniversary of the restoration of the Patriarchate in the Russian Orthodox Church he was just as reserved in appraising the prospects for the convocation of the Pan-Orthodox Council.

One of the disputed issues is the number of autocephalous and autonomous Churches. For instance, the Constantinople Patriarchate, and several other Local Orthodox Churches following in its wake, do not recognise the autocephaly of the Orthodox Church in America and the autonomy of the Japanese Church; they also regard the Autocephalous Churches of Georgia and Czechoslovakia as autonomous. For this reason, the American and Japanese Orthodox Churches were not invited to the First Pre-Council Pan-Orthodox Conference: on the recommendation of the 1971 Inter-Orthodox Preparatory Commission, invitations to such conferences are sent out by the Constantinople Patriarchate.

There are differences, and extremely serious ones, on practically each of the ten sections of the catalogue of topics for consideration at the Pan-Orthodox Council. The elimination of these differences may well take a great deal of time, which makes the prospects for a successful holding of the Holy and Great Council of the Oriental Orthodox Church very remote.

In the meantime, theological discussions are taking place at various levels with the participation of Moscow Patriarchate's representatives. The discussions reveal the polarity of the social positions of the Local Orthodox Churches functioning in fundamentally different social structures. This also leaves its imprint on the solution of ecclesiastical problems proper, like the issues of internal and external missions, the attitude to non-believers, etc. The Russian Orthodox Church and the other Local Orthodox Churches functioning in socialist society propose more radical solutions of social problems than the Orthodox Churches of the capitalist countries. There is little hope of achieving unity on these issues.

Differences of a religious-ecclesiastical nature also make themselves felt in confessional and liturgical traditions, in approaches to the interpretation of canons and dogmata. The Moscow Patriarchate mostly adheres to very moderate positions on problems of doctrine and rites discussed at inter-Orthodox conferences, reluctantly responding to the initiatives of other Local Orthodox Churches, such as the suggestion for a universal adoption of the New Style. Some of these initiatives such as the permission for the clergy to marry for the second time or for women to serve in churches as priests, are rejected out of hand.

## Theological Dialogues with Representatives of Foreign Churches

Apart from participation in various Pan-Orthodox moves the Moscow Patriarchate maintains wide contacts with representatives of other Christian confessions and denominations.

True, the ideologists of contemporary Russian Orthodoxy assert that the champions of this religion were never hostile to other faiths. "Our ancestors," declared Metropolitan Nikodim (Rotov) of Leningrad and Novgorod at the 1971 Local Council, "were never prone to religious intolerance towards Western Christianity, in spite of the fact that, naturally, they could not help but hear rumours of disagreements and struggle between Rome and Byzantium. This calm and peaceable attitude to the ecclesiastical West was long preserved in ancient Rus, although this did not mean that our Christian people were entirely indifferent to the discord and divisions of the Church..."[1] That same hierarch was compelled to admit, though, that as early as the 11th century, "in the West as in the land of Russia, signs of growing estrangement between various confessions gradually became more and more evident. Time increased mutual distrust and estrangement, while isolated attempts to restore unity led nowhere"[2].

Indeed, the pre-revolutionary Church identified only

---
[1] *The Local Council of the Russian Orthodox Church*, p. 68.
[2] Ibid., p. 69.

Orthodoxy with "the True and Apostolic Church" (meaning the Niceno-Constantinopolitan creed), many other confessions were regarded as non-church associations. Adapting itself to the new conditions of being, the Russian Orthodox Church revised these traditional concepts, too. All heterodox confessions are now termed Churches, and present-day followers of Russian Orthodoxy find something in them that can be learnt and borrowed.

The closest and most stable relations exist between the Moscow Patriarchate and the Non-Chalcedonian (Monophysite) Churches which, since 1971, are usually called the Ancient Oriental Churches: Armenian, Ethiopian, Syrian, Coptic and Malabar (India). "The Russian Orthodox Church," stated the 1971 Local Council, "considers the Ancient Eastern Churches as autocephalous on the grounds of their historical position and canonical structure. It respects their independence, reverences their piety, has no intention of interfering in their traditional rite of worship. In future consultations the Russian Orthodox Church will hold firmly to the conviction that the conciliar structure of the Church is of permanent validity and that Church Councils, particularly the Ecumenical Councils, have preserved and will in the future continue to preserve the truth according to the prompting and enlightenment of the Holy Spirit"[1].

In 1971, the Synod of the Russian Orthodox Church resolved that the Moscow Patriarchate must take a more active part in the preparation and conduct of an official dialogue between the Local Orthodox and Ancient Oriental Churches.

Visits by the heads and hierarchs of the Ancient Oriental Churches to the Moscow Patriarchate and the visits of the head of the Russian Orthodox Church to the Armenian, Ethiopian, Coptic, Syrian and Malabar Churches, have become regular occasions. During these visits, agreement on many issues, including those of doctrine and rites, is invariably stressed.

The Moscow Patriarchate's periodicals now devote more space to closer unity between the Local Orthodox

---

[1] Ibid., p. 74.

and Ancient Oriental Churches. Articles and shorter items are regularly published on the life of the Armenian, Ethiopian, and other Churches of the same confession, as are statements of their theologians and church leaders.

Beginning with the 1972/1973 academic year, the curriculum of the theological schools of the Moscow Patriarchate includes a new subject—History of the Ancient Oriental Churches. More students from the Ancient Oriental Churches now attend the educational establishments of the Moscow Patriarchate; some of them have not only graduated from theological academies but also defended their Master's and Doctoral theses.

The Department of the Ancient Oriental Churches has been set up at the Moscow Theological Academy; late in 1974 B. A. Nelyubov, Assistant Professor of that Department, defended a Master's Thesis on "Ancient Oriental Churches", in which "he strove to emphasize not so much the differences which have often given rise to mutual alienation and prejudicial attitudes, but rather the idea of internal kinship and unity with these Churches—a unity which has been severed for various reasons often having nothing to do with the Churches themselves..."[1]

Representatives of the Moscow Patriarchate work actively in the Inter-Orthodox Theological Commission on Dialogue with the Ancient Oriental Churches.

The contacts of the Moscow Patriarchate with the Anglican Church are also rather extensive and fruitful. In the materials of the 1971 Local Council, the relations between the Russian Orthodox Church and the Anglican confession were referred to as "traditionally friendly and full of good will".[2] Although, in the words of Patriarch Pimen (Izvekov), "the seed of dialogue" between theologians of the Russian Orthodox and Anglican Churches was "sown" as early as the beginning of the 18th century (the reference was to the support by the Synod of the Russian Orthodox Church in 1723 for the idea of conversations with

---

[1] *The Journal of the Moscow Patriarchate*, 1975, No. 2, p. 22.
[2] *The Local Council of the Russian Orthodox Church*, p. 76.

Anglicans, which was not realised because of the opposition of the Eastern patriarchs and the death of Peter I [1]), contacts between the leaders and hierarchs of the Moscow Patriarchate and the Anglican Church only became regular early in the 1940s, when Archbishop Cyril Garbet of York visited Moscow in September 1943.

Later the Moscow Patriarchate received the heads of the Anglican Church, the Archbishops of Canterbury Dr. Arthur Michael Ramsey (1962) and Dr. Frederick Donald Coggan (1977). In 1964, Patriarch Aleksiy paid a return visit to Great Britain. A delegation of the Russian Orthodox Church was present at the enthronisation, in 1980, of the present head of the Anglican Church, Dr. Robert Runcie. There have been numerous exchanges of official delegations and groups of theologians, clerics and laymen between the Moscow Patriarchate and the Anglican Churches of Great Britain, the USA, and Australia.

Along with maintaining bilateral contacts with Anglican representatives, the hierarchs and theologians of the Moscow Patriarchate take an active part in the Pan-Orthodox dialogue with the Anglican Church. In particular, they work on the Anglican-Orthodox Joint Doctrinal Commission of which the first plenary session was held at Oxford in 1973, and the second, in Moscow in 1976. Subsequently, the Commission held its sessions annually.

The only real and quite tangible result of these Orthodox-Anglican contacts was the establishment of easy and business-like relations between the theologians of the Orthodox and Anglican Churches, the readiness of each side to discuss controversial issues in a constructive spirit. As for the principal goal of the Orthodox-Anglican meetings—the achievement of confessional unity, there has been little or no progress at all in that direction, despite numerous dialogues.

The reason is not only the existence of serious doctrinal, dogmatic, canonical and liturgical differences of a fundamental nature between the Orthodox Church and Anglicans that are practically ineliminable

---

[1] *The Journal of the Moscow Patriarchate*, 1976, No. 11, p. 49.

(at least in the foreseeable future), which makes the hierarchs of the Moscow Patriarchate refer the possibility of attaining a unity of faith with Anglicans to a distant future.[1] Neither side has so far worked out a unified approach to understanding the essence of those problems that have to be discussed in the course of the Orthodox-Anglican dialogue, or a clear realisation of the nearest and ultimate goals of such a dialogue. That was precisely what Patriarch Pimen (Izvekov) said in his address to participants in Moscow sessions of the Anglican-Orthodox Joint Doctrinal Commission. "As I see it," he said, "we Orthodox must clarify and agree among ourselves upon exact definitions of certain things on the agenda before the start of the theological conversations with our Anglican brothers: (1) How do we define the signs of a true Church, that is to say, by what criteria do we determine a grace-endowed Christian community as a member of the One, Holy, Catholic and Apostolic Church? (2) the Church of the Seven Ecumenical Councils has undergone an extensive inner evolution. She has been developing dynamically on the foundation of her eternally vital Tradition. When we call upon the Anglicans to show their faith in the teaching and practice of the Undivided Church of the Seven Ecumenical Councils, we must be prepared to show our brothers what throughout these centuries in the teaching of the Holy Fathers was an unchanging, albeit organically developing, continuation of the Apostolic Tradition, and what was part of the historically conditioned and changing side of the Church, determined and circumscribed by the cultural and historical context; and finally, (3) what is our attitude to Anglicanism of today in all its varied and rich complexity?"[2]

In the view of the head of the Russian Orthodox Church, the Anglican participants of the dialogue face just as many unsolved problems. "Before our Anglican brothers," he stressed, "stands no less difficult and complex task of preparing themselves in agreement and unanimity: (1) To pass their dogmatic resolutions

---

[1] *The Local Council of the Russian Orthodox Church*, p. 68.

[2] *The Journal of the Moscow Patriarchate*, 1976, No. 11, p. 49.

officially, in a council of all their bishops, making them obligatory for the whole Church and for all Anglican communities, so that we should be able to see clearly what constitutes and what does not constitute the teaching of their Church; (2) the whole of the Anglican Church must be prepared to confirm as dogma the pronouncement by the Anglican members of the Anglican-Orthodox Commission of the Lambeth Conference that priesthood is a sacrament ("mysterion") (1930); (3) they must be prepared to make a solemn announcement on behalf of the whole Anglican Church, interpreting the '39 Articles' in the spirit of the Undivided Church of the Seven Ecumenical Councils... (4) they must be prepared to repeat and confirm on behalf of the whole Anglican Church the teaching on the Eucharist laid out in the 1930 statement by the Lambeth Conference; (5) they must be prepared to consider the *filioque* not a dogma, but a theologoumenon; (6) they must be ready to hold dialogues with representatives of the Free Churches, including the Methodists, in the spirit of the points put forward above; and in the same spirit, to resolve the question of the service and role of women in the Church..."[1]

It is clear from these statements that the participants in the Orthodox-Anglican dialogue on questions of unity remind one of builders who have begun to construct a bridge without reaching an agreement on how it should be built.

The Russian Orthodox Church established contacts with Old Catholics already at the time of the emergence of that denomination: its representatives attended the first Old Catholic congress in Munich in 1871, and also subsequent forums of Old Catholics. It took due account of what the programme worked out by the Munich Congress said: "We express our hope for a re-union with the Greek Church and reconciliation with other denominations".[2]

In response to the interest shown by Old Catholics in

---

[1] Ibid., pp. 49-50.
[2] *The Moscow Patriarchate, 1917-1977*, published by the Moscow Patriarchate, Moscow, 1978, p. 49.

a rapprochement with Orthodoxy, the Synod of the Russian Orthodox Church set up in 1892 a commission in St. Petersburg to consider the question of a possible union of Old Catholics and the Orthodox. A similar commission was established by Old Catholics in Rotterdam. The St. Petersburg-Rotterdam Commission existed until 1914, studying the theological aspects of the doctrinal differences between the Orthodox and Old Catholics. No results were achieved, the primary course being the fact that the Orthodox side did not recognise Old Catholicism as a Church, seeing it as something on the other side of the Church fence and interpreting the restoration of unity as Old Catholicism's "return" to the positions of Orthodoxy.

The Russian Orthodox Church resumed the contacts with the Old Catholics in 1948 through an exchange visits by delegations. Since that time, representatives of the Old Catholic Church have attended the Moscow Patriarchate's official celebrations, while the latter sends its representatives to the Old Catholics' international congresses.

In 1961, The Inter-Orthodox Theological Commission on Dialogue with Old Catholics, which included representatives of the Russian Orthodox Church, was set up by decision of the First Rhodes Pan-Orthodox Conference. At its four sessions in 1966, 1970, 1971 and 1973 the commission determined the range of questions to be considered in the course of the dialogue, and also the goals and method of their study and discussion.

The dialogue itself began in 1975. Several sessions were held, one of them in 1981 in Moscow. They considered the most important dogmatic differences between the Orthodox and Old Catholics. These differences are numerous, while decisions on which agreement has been reached are still very few. Hence the reserved tone of the Moscow Patriarchate's official statements on the nearest prospects for the dialogue. Noting the "undoubted progress" in the relations between Old Catholicism and Orthodoxy, one of the leading hierarchs of the Russian Orthodox Church pointed out at the same time "the very considerable difficulties" in this path, stressing that "these difficulties are of a dogmatic and hagiological nature, canonic and liturgic".[1]

The relations between the Moscow Patriarchate and the Roman Catholic Church became established and acquired stability only during the pontificate of Pope John XXIII (1958-1963). Observers from the Russian Orthodox Church were present at all the sessions of the Second Vatican Council (1963-1965), while an official representative of the Vatican was among the guests of honour of the 1971 Local Council of the Russian Orthodox Church and the celebrations on the occasion of the 60th anniversary of the restoration of the Patriarchate in the Russian Orthodox Church (1978).

The first meeting of theologians from the two Churches took place at the Leningrad Theological Academy late in 1967. Subsequently, these meetings became regular, they are held alternately in Italy and the Soviet Union. At the beginning, these meetings discussed primarily social problems. The second conversations (in Bari in 1970) were devoted to "The Christian's Role in a Developing Society". The participants of the third conversations (the town of Zagorsk, 1973), discussed the position of the Church in a changing world. The subsequent meetings considered problems of confessional and doctrinal character: "Proclaiming the Good News of Salvation in a Changing World" (Trento, 1975), and "Local Churches and the Ecumenical Church" (Odessa, 1980).

Since 1972, the Moscow Patriarchate has been cooperating with the Catholic peace-making organisation Pax Christi International. Bilateral contacts have been established between the Russian Orthodox Church and the Catholic Churches of France, the USA and other countries.

To study the Western church tradition, the theological academies of the Russian Orthodox Church sent several groups of their graduates to higher educational establishments of the Catholic Church in Rome, Paris and Freiburg (the FRG). In 1975, the Jesuit Father Miguel Arranz, Professor of the Pontificat Oriental

---

[1] *The Local Council of the Russian Orthodox Church*, p. 78.

Institute in Rome, Inspector of Russicum over a period of five years, defended his Master's thesis at the Leningrad Theological Academy.

Ecclesiastics and laymen of the Russian Orthodox and Roman Catholic Churches have gone on pilgrimages to each other's countries.

Representatives of the Russian Orthodox Church participate in the work of the Joint Inter-Orthodox-Roman Catholic Commission on Dialogue set up on the decision of the First Pre-Council Pan-Orthodox Conference.

Although the general tone of the communiques and final documents issued after each meeting between theologians of the Russian Orthodox and Roman Catholic Churches is invariably correct (exchanges of views are described in them as "frank and lively"[1]), agreement between the participants is rare and extremely limited.

The documents mostly state the existence of fundamental differences on a wide range of doctrinal issues. Here is a description, for instance, of the attitude of each of the Churches to the dogma of the Pope's infallibility: "While recognizing certain difficulties in the understanding of the meaning of this dogma, the Catholic side emphasized its perpetual significance for its Church, viewing the Pope's infallibility as a doctrinal infallibility which the Church as such possesses. The Orthodox side in turn emphasized the unacceptability by it of the dogmatized forms of Church government and the Pope's infallibility. At the same time, communion between the Local Churches should not lead to the recognition of the exclusive authority of one Church over the others".[2] These differences in the approaches to identical confessional problems clearly rule out any unity in matters of faith (and it is this unity that is the ultimate aim of inter-Church theological dialogues)— not only in the near future but also in the remotest perspective.

Finally, the last three decades have seen an extremely significant extension and consolidation of the Moscow

---

[1] *The Journal of the Moscow Patriarchate*, 1980, No. 10, p. 45.
[2] Ibid.

Patriarchate's contacts with Protestant confessions and denominations, in the first place with Lutheran and Reformed Churches. Formally, the goal of these contacts is the same as ever: the search for ways and forms of achieving confessional unity; in actual fact, though, they are directed towards reaching mutual understanding and coordinating their activities in consolidating the positions of Christianity in the modern world, towards attenuating the general crisis of religion and the church.

Since the end of the 1940s, stable links have existed between the Russian Orthodox Church and the Evangelical Churches of the GDR. In 1974, the first theological conversations were held in Zagorsk between official representatives of the Moscow Patriarchate and a delegation of the Evangelical Union of the GDR, which began a series of such meetings convened alternately in the USSR and the GDR. These meetings repeatedly pointed to fundamentally different approaches to the solution of the same theological problems by the Orthodox and Lutherans, which rules out at present the identity of opinions. "Orthodox and Lutheran theologians participating in the dialogue," said Bishop Dr. Werner Krusche, head of the German delegation, at the opening of the fourth theological conversation ("Zagorsk-4"), "have their own definite forms of thinking, they operate with different categories and sometimes use different terms. All this creates certain difficulties, as it is sometimes hard to bring out the community of viewpoints on a given issue".[1]

The contacts between the Moscow Patriarchate and the Evangelical Church in the FRG were established in 1959; the communication between them assumes different forms. One of these is regular theological conversations on a wide range of social and confessional problems. These conversations came to be known as Arnoldshains—after the Evangelical Academy in Arnoldshain, FRG, where the first of these conversations were held. In 1981, the ninth conversations of this kind (Arnoldshain-9) were held.

---

[1] *Zhurnal Moskovskoy patriarkhii*, 1981, No. 7, p. 60.

Like the other Orthodox-Protestant dialogues, the Arnoldshain I-IX conversations have consolidated relations between the Russian Orthodox and Evangelical Churches of the FRG, but made no headway at all in respect to greater confessional community as both sides often admitted.

In 1970, regular theological conversations began between delegations of the Russian Orthodox Church and the Evangelical Lutheran Church of Finland. They are held alternately in Finland and the Soviet Union, and cover a wide range of both specifically religious and social problems. Participants of the conversations point out that they reach agreement on social problems more readily than on confessional ones.

In fulfilment of the decisions of the Fourth Pan-Orthodox Conference, a commission on Pan-Orthodox-Lutheran dialogue was set up. A similar commission was formed by the Lutheran World Federation. The first session of the mixed Orthodox-Lutheran Theological Commission on Dialogue was held in Finland in 1981. It was attended by a delegation from the Russian Orthodox Church. Participants in the conversations confirmed the need for further bilateral theological meetings of the Arnoldshain and Zagorsk type, regarding them as a necessary premise for further development of a Panorthodox-Lutheran dialogue.

Representatives of the Russian Orthodox Church take an active part in the Orthodox-Reformed conversations, the first of which was held in 1972 in Debrecen, Hungary; all the subsequent meetings of theologians of these confessions were called "Debrecens".

Summing up their views on the Orthodox-Heterodox dialogues, their participants unanimously point to their purely theoretical character and to the fact that they make no palpable impact on the practical aspects of the historically established relationships between the various modifications of Christianity, relationships that reflect the confessional isolation of each of them.

## Participation in the Ecumenical Movement

The Moscow Patriarchate's participation in dialogues with representatives of the various Christian Churches was the initial stage of its involvement in the ecumenical movement—an association of confessions and denominations purporting to achieve a Pan-Christian unity. This movement is coordinated by the World Council of Churches. However, the Moscow Patriarchate's joining the WCC was preceded by its activities within the framework of another interconfessional Christian association—the Conference of European Churches (CEC) founded in 1958.

The first general assembly of the CEC was held in early 1959 in Nyborg, Denmark. Its topic was "The European Christianity in the Secularised World Today". The assembly came to the conclusion that "the common task of the European Churches is an allout development of contacts between them and in the first place, consolidation of the efforts aimed at freeing peoples of Europe and of the whole world from the threat of an atomic war".[1]

Subsequent assemblies, meetings and conversations were devoted to questions of church unity, as well as to peacemaking issues. Thus the Eighth CEC General Assembly held in October 1979 on Crete discussed the subject "For the Strength of the Holy Ghost: In the Service of Peace"; the discussions were held in four sections: (1) Separated Churches in Europe. Ways of achieving cooperation and unity; (2) Theology in Europe—between spirituality and world experience; (3) Sermons and services—the tasks of the Churches of Europe; (4) The preservers of creation and peacemakers in a troubled world.

This ecumenical organisation comprises 116 Churches of 26 states of Europe. The Russian Orthodox Church takes an active part in all the undertakings of the CEC, sending representative delegations to each of its general assemblies. Metropolitan Aleksiy was elected CEC President. The Moscow

---

[1] Zhurnal Moskovskoy patriarkhii, 1959, No. 4, p. 37.

Patriarchate joined the CEC-directed movement when it already had some experience of participation in bilateral contacts with representatives of other confessions and interconfessional associations. This happened in the beginning of the 1960s, but the preparatory work had been done in the 1950s.

By that time, the CEC leadership, worried by the non-participation in the ecumenical movement of the Churches and church associations from the socialist and developing countries, had given up the obviously pro-imperialist orientation and open Pan-Protestantism characteristic of the initial stage of ecumenism. That was reason for the Moscow Patriarchate's revision of its negative attitude to the ecumenical movement expressed in the resolution of the conference of heads and representatives of the Local Orthodox Churches held in Moscow in 1948 on the occasion of the quincentenary of the autocephaly of the Russian Orthodox Church.[1]

In August 1958, the first official meeting of representatives of the Russian Orthodox Church and the WCC leadership was held in Utrecht, the Netherlands. The purpose of the Utrecht meeting was to sum up the results of the written exchange of opinions between the Moscow Patriarchate and the WCC. The agenda included the following questions: (1) The Russian Orthodox Church and the World Council of Churches; (2) Christian Unity in the Defence of Peace; (3) The Russian Orthodox Church and the Socio-Political Problems of Our Times; (4) The World Council of Churches and Church Unity; (5) Common Concern of the Churches for Religious Freedom. The first three agenda items were suggested by the Moscow Patriarchate, the last two, by the WCC.

During the conference, several "most persistent tendencies" of the WCC were pointed out which were completely unacceptable to the Russian Orthodox Church; these included neglect for the unity of creed; a levelling idea of a dogmatic minimum as the basis of Christian unity; the conviction of a number of leaders of the ecumenical movement that not one of the

---

[1] *Zhurnal Moskovskoy patriarkhii*, 1948, Special Issue, p. 26.

existing Christian confessions possesses the whole truth or is Christ's Church; the orientation towards a purely external unification of Christian Churches and groups as a result of which they become political instruments— and this distorts the path of the ecumenical movement and increases the gap between it and Orthodoxy. On the other hand, the Moscow Patriarchate's delegation emphasised that the ecumenical movement held an attraction for the Orthodox Church in that it offered a prospect for overcoming age-old divisions and a hope for a common confession shared by all Christians in the fullness of church life. The Orthodox delegation also stressed such actions of the WCC movement as the statement on the existence in the world of "social, political, ecumenical and moral conditions which make it the duty of all Christians to fight for justice, freedom and peace"; also the WCC's condemnation of nuclear weapons, and various manifestations of interchurch assistance.

After the discussion, the participants of the Utrecht conference published a communique summing up the results of their work: exchange of information, setting forth their respective viewpoints, and attainment of a more complete mutual understanding.[1]

The WCC invited the Moscow Patriarchate to send observers to the coming session of the Central Committee, and representatives of the Russian Orthodox Church promised that they would report the results of the meeting to the patriarch and the Synod, and also to the Local Orthodox Churches which had jointly formulated their attitude to the ecumenical movement at the 1948 Conference in Moscow (a resolution on the refusal of the Orthodox Churches to cooperate with the ecumenical movement "in its present-day form" was then signed by the heads of the Russian, Georgian, Serbian, Romanian and Bulgarian Churches, as well as representatives of the Alexandrian, Antiochene, Polish, Albanian and Czechoslovak Churches).[2]

In December 1958 the Synod discussed the results of the meeting of its representatives with the WCC

---

[1] *Zhurnal Moskovskoy patriarkhii*, 1958, No. 9, pp. 35, 36.
[2] Ibid., pp. 22-29.

leadership and passed a resolution "to approve the concrete steps towards the development of relationships between the Russian Orthodox Church and the World Council of Churches, to adopt a sympathetic attitude to the invitation extended to representatives of the Russian Church to attend a regular session of the WCC Central Committee as observers, and to invite a delegation of the World Council of Churches headed by Dr. Willem A. Visser't Hooft, General Secretary, WCC, to visit the Russian Orthodox Church".[1]

In fulfilment of these decisions, two delegates from the Moscow Patriarchate spent a month in the summer of 1959 at the WCC headquarters in Geneva studying the work of its General Secretariat and departments.

In August 1959, a regular session of the WCC Central Committee was held on Rhodes. For the first time in the history of the ecumenical movement the Russian Church was represented at it by two observers. Among other questions, the session discussed the report on "Relations with the Orthodox Church of Russia". A unanimously adopted resolution on that report read: "The Central Committee welcomes the development of relations between the World Council of Churches and the Moscow Patriarchate... It is suggested that exchange of theological students as well as literature and documents should be discussed at a suitable time".[2]

In 1960, the World Christian Youth Commission convened in Lausanne a European Christian Youth Assembly which was attended by observers from the Russian Church.

In August of that year, a regular session of the WCC Central Committee was held in St. Andrews, Scotland. Before that, the same city hosted plenary sessions of WCC commissions on "Faith and Order" and international affairs. The Russian Church was represented at these ecumenical forums by its observers.

The rapprochement between the Moscow Patriarchate and the WCC was nearing a moment when the Russian Orthodox Church would join the ecumenical

---

[1] *Zhurnal Moskovskoy patriarkhii*, 1961, No. 8, p. 20.
[2] Ibid., 1959, No. 10, p. 49.

movement, assuming all the rights and obligations that would follow from that act.

The Moscow Patriarchate's joining the WCC was formalised at the WCC Third General Assembly held in New Delhi, India in November and December 1961. At that Assembly, 23 Churches became members of the WCC, including four Orthodox ones: Russian, Romanian, Bulgarian and Polish. The number of autocephalous Local Orthodox member-Churches of the WCC grew to ten. Subsequently, the other Local Orthodox Churches (both autocephalous and autonomous), with the exception of the Albanian Church, joined the WCC.

The Third WCC General Assembly included five representatives of the Russian Orthodox Church in the Central Committee: three hierarchs, one priest and one layman. Archbishop Nikodim (Rotov), head of the Moscow Patriarchate's delegation, was elected a member of the WCC Executive Committee.

The Moscow Patriarchate's joining the WCC significantly strengthened Orthodox presence in the coordinating body of the ecumenical movement. At the Third WCC General Assembly, only 75 of the 625 official delegates represented Orthodox Churches, while at the Fourth Assembly, held in 1968 in Uppsala, Sweden, the Orthodox delegation accounted for 140 of the 704 delegates; 35 of them represented the Moscow Patriarchate.

The most important thing, however, was not mere growth of Orthodox presence, Russian Orthodox presence in particular, at the main forum of the ecumenical movement. Members of the Local Orthodox Churches, the Russian Church included, began to take a more active part in the WCC's varied activities.

Thus the delegates of the Moscow Patriarchate took an active part in the work of all the six sections of the Uppsala General Assembly and of all its committees. Not content with the mere discussion of the problems raised in the official reports at the Fourth Assembly, the theologians of the Russian Orthodox Church strove to influence the agenda of this and subsequent meetings.

In particular, they proposed that the WCC Commission on the Church and Society should elaborate the following topics: The Scientific and Technological Progress and Humanism; Social Development towards the Harmony of the Social and the Personal; Property as an Indicator of Social Progress; The Role of Socio-Economic Factors in Raising Developing Countries to the Level of Developed Ones; The Paths of Peaceful Coexistence and Cooperation; The policy of Peace as a Factor of International Development towards the Common Weal; Cultural and Scientific-Technological Links for the Benefit of the World; The Overcoming of Alienation; The Service of Mankind as a Means of Consolidation of the Catholic Self-consciousness of Churches, etc.

Other Local Orthodox Churches were also much more active at Uppsala than at previous WCC General Assemblies. That was apparently a consequence of the fulfilment by the Uppsala Assembly's Orthodox delegates of the decisions of the Fourth Pan-Orthodox Conference which insisted on "a more systematic and full participation of the Orthodox in the work of the World Council of Churches".[1]

The participants of that conference pointed to Protestant domination in both the administrative bodies of the WCC, where they make up 99 per cent of the total number of their employees and at all the ecumenical forums, which explained, in the speakers' view, the purely Protestant character of the principal WCC documents. It was proposed to work out and implement concrete measures for a significant increase of the influence of Orthodoxy on the ideology and practice of the present-day ecumenical movement. Representatives of the Moscow Patriarchate recommended to the Conference to raise at the WCC the issue of setting up a special body within the framework of the Faith and Order Commission for the attainment of a fuller theological cooperation (including cooperation in preparing documents) between the Orthodox Churches and the WCC.[2] The head of the delegation

---

[1] See *The Journal of the Moscow Patriarchate*, 1969, No. 1, pp. 45-53.

[2] Ibid., 1968, No. 7, p. 54.

of the Constantinople Patriarchate expressed the desire at the Conference that ecumenical conferences, congresses and assemblies organised by the WCC be held more often in countries with predominantly Orthodox populations, and that more Orthodox theologians be invited to participate in them.[1]

A report compiled on the basis of recommendations of the participants in the Fourth Pan-Orthodox Conference and adopted as a Pan-Orthodox document, suggested the following measures to step up the activity of Orthodox churchmen in the work of the WCC: increasing the number of Orthodox employees in the administration; greater coordination of the activity of Orthodox representatives in the WCC; instituting the office of an Orthodox secretary, (or a secretary for the Orthodox) in the Faith and Order Commission; careful preparation for Orthodox divine services held within the framework of WCC activities; increasing Orthodox participation in the periodical and other WCC publications; organisation of systematic training of theological Orthodox personnel capable of working fruitfully in the ecumenical movement, etc.[2]

The Moscow Patriarchate took an active part in the realisation of all these proposals. Problems of the ecumenical movement are regularly discussed at the sessions of the Synod of the Russian Orthodox Church. The Commission for Inter-Christian Relations was set up and later in August 1963, transformed into the Commission on Problems of Christian Unity; later it came to be known as the Synod Commission on Problems of Christian Unity and Inter-Church Relations.

To achieve a more active participation of its representatives in WCC actions and to ensure their more competent approach to interconfessional problems, the leaders of the Moscow Patriarchate began to pay more attention to the ecumenical training of its theological personnel and to teaching them to conduct ecumenical discussions. Theological school graduates, stated the Rector of the Moscow Theological Academy, must be "not only learned theologians and men of high

---

[1] Ibid., 1969, No. 2, p. 51.
[2] Ibid., 1969, No. 2, p. 50.

Christian motivation—they must also be prepared for wide-ranging ecumenical activity".[1]

Ecumenical problems have been included among the subjects for course papers and Candidate's theses of students of the theological academies of the Moscow Patriarchate. Theological dissertations are also devoted to these subjects.

Some undergraduates and postgraduate students of the Moscow Patriarchate's theological schools directly participate in the ecumenical movement. Some academy graduates are sent to continue their theological studies and to lend these studies an ecumenical slant to the WCC Institute of Bossey near Geneva (in winter, the Bossey Institute becomes a kind of ecumenical postgraduate course, and in summer, the venue of various ecumenical undertakings).

The efforts of the Local Orthodox Churches (including the Russian one) to increase their influence on the ecumenical movement have borne fruit. Thus, of the six presidential posts of the WCC one has been filled by an Orthodox representative. The Fifth WCC General Assembly, held in 1975 in Nairobi, Kenia, elected to that post a hierarch of the Russian Orthodox Church—Metropolitan Nikodim, and after his death the presidential vacancy was filled by Catholicos-Patriarch Iliya II of All Georgia. The representation of Orthodox Churches in the Central and Executive Committees of the WCC was also extended. Five representatives of the Moscow Patriarchate were elected to the WCC Central Committee, and one of them is a member of the WCC Executive Committee.

During the 1977 Thirtieth Session of the WCC Central Committee, Archbishop Edward Scott, WCC Moderator, and Dr. Philip Potter, then WCC General Secretary, met the members of the WCC Central Committee from the Local Orthodox Churches and the Orthodox members of the WCC staff. The need for increasing Orthodox contribution to WCC activities was discussed and measures were outlined "whereby the Local Orthodox Churches could participate in the

---

[1] *The Journal of the Moscow Patriarchate*, 1965, No. 4, p. 26.

ecumenical movement more fully..."[1] Later these discussions became regular. In 1978, the WCC Executive Committee meeting in Helsinki decided "to conduct a special consultation devoted to the solution of the problems which still prevent adequate participation on the part of the Orthodox in the life of the World Council of Churches".[2]

Such a consultation was held in 1981 in Sofia. It was attended by representatives of 13 autocephalous Local Orthodox Churches and leading WCC figures headed by Phillip Potter. The following four themes were on the Consultation agenda:

(1) The Orthodox Understanding of Ecumenism and the Orthodox Participation in the World Council of Churches. In discussing that theme the participants in the Consultation "emphasized that the WCC was a very important ecumenical fellowship which provided the Orthodox Churches a platform for continuing theological dialogue on Christian unity, an instrument for inter-Church aid and for cooperation in the work for peace and justice."

(2) The Orthodox Experience and the Problems in the World Council of Churches. The Communique of the Consultation stated that the Orthodox "Churches believe that ... they should be able to do their work in the Council on the basis of their ecclesiology and according to their own rationale".

(3) The Perspectives of the Orthodox Contribution to the Activities of the World Council of Churches. The proposals made on this score included (a) "the recognition of the special ecclesiological prerequisites for the participation of the Local Orthodox Churches in the World Council of Churches; (b) extending "the participation of representatives of the Local Churches in the activities of all agencies of the World Council and its staff"; (c) ensuring "participation of the Orthodox representatives in the preparation of documents pertaining to the questions of Faith and Order and other programmatic issues essential for the WCC at all the stages of their elaboration"; (d) "broader involvement

---

[1] Ibid., 1977, No. 10, p. 58.
[2] Ibid., 1979, No. 3, p. 58.

of the representatives of the Local Orthodox Churches as speakers, advisers, experts, moderators, vice-moderators and reporters in various undertakings of the World Council of Churches".

(4) Jesus Christ—the Life of the World. That was the main theme of the Sixth General Assembly of the WCC (1983, Vancouver, Canada). The Consultation marked the beginning of inter-Orthodox study of this subject.[1]

Representatives of the Russian Orthodox Church took an active part in the discussion of all the themes. At the Consultation, the Russian language was recognised as one of the working languages of the WCC.

Along with various actions intended to expand the sphere of Orthodox Churches' activity in the WCC, the Moscow Patriarchate has done much to strengthen the influence of the Churches and associations from the socialist countries on the ecumenical movement. The need for such efforts is clear from the fact that the WCC governing bodies displayed a tendency to infringe on the rights of religious organisations of the socialist countries. There were very few religious figures from the socialist countries in the governing bodies and among the staff of the WCC; they were rarely and reluctantly invited to take a direct part in the work of ecumenical organisations, and their views were mostly disregarded in the working out of the WCC fundamental documents on socio-political problems.

In this respect, the Fifth General Assembly of the WCC was probably the most characteristic. Ninety-seven of its delegates were citizens from the socialist countries, including 27 from the Soviet Union. They took part in the work of all the six sections of the Assembly, but not one of them was the reporter or co-reporter. At the assembly, attempts were made (and they were not stopped by the WCC leadership) to create provocative situations, to discredit the religious organisations of the socialist countries, and to push the ecumenical movement along the path of open anti-Sovietism and anti-communism.

---

[1] *The Journal of the Moscow Patriarchate*, 1981, No. 8, pp. 73-75.

Metropolitan Yuvenaliy, then head of the Department for External Church Relations, thus described his impressions of the Nairobi Assembly in an interview with a TASS correspondent: "I would like to note (and I am convinced of it) that Orthodoxy could have made a greater contribution to the assembly and so could the Churches from the socialist countries had an adequate possibility been provided for them to share their experience of witness and service. Unfortunately, the representatives of the Churches from the socialist countries were not included in the number of the numerous speakers who reported on the basic themes of the assembly. There were moments when we clearly perceived—with certain encouragement on the part of some WCC leaders—a tendentious attitude to our country which we, as well as other delegates, felt as a discordant note in the general tone of the assembly..."[1] The situation created by the proimperialist circles of the WCC was described in similar terms in "The Holy Synod Message of the 5th WCC Assembly and Its Results".[2]

What "moments" did Metropolitan Yuvenaliy refer to?

First, there was the desire by some ecumenical leaders to force through, as an official document of the WCC General Assembly, the slanderous letter of two rabid extremists, Yakunin and Regelson, crudely distorting the position of religion and the Church in the USSR and containing groundless attacks against the leadership of the Russian Orthodox Church. That episode was described in the message of the Synod of the Russian Orthodox Church as an attempt, "not without the encouragement of certain WCC officials—to substitute the voice of Russian Orthodox Church delegates with that of ecclesiastical dissidents whose relations with ecclesiastical authorities are strained and who do not share the mood of the great majority of Church members".[3]

Only vigorous moves by religious figures not only

---

[1] Ibid., 1976, No. 2, p. 56.
[2] Ibid., 1976, No. 4, pp. 4-8.
[3] Ibid., p. 16.

from the socialist and developing but also from some capitalist countries, who exposed in their speeches the slanderous character of the quasi-ecclesiastical dissidents' letter and the provocative goals of the fuss raised by certain WCC leaders about that letter, prevented the inclusion of that crude, malicious anti-Soviet fraud among the official documents of the WCC and its General Assembly.

Second, during the discussion of the resolution on disarmament and the Helsinki Conference an amendment was introduced on the alleged violations of religious freedom in the USSR—in contravention of the seventh principle of the Final Act of the Conference in Helsinki. The amendment was introduced in a situation when the accepted Assembly procedure was violated and the representatives of the Churches from the Soviet Union were not given an opportunity to present an objective picture of the real state of affairs.

Although the original wording of the amendment was attenuated, it still retained its anti-Soviet slant and was "used by certain participants in the assembly to compromise the Soviet Union".[1] The adoption of the amendment under pressure from the governing bodies of the WCC was described by religious organisations of the socialist countries, including the Russian Orthodox Church, as a political provocation.

Third, the leading circles of the WCC tried to prevent the election to the office of WCC President of a representative from the Moscow Patriarchate, although there were neither formal nor factual grounds for doing that. Despite all attempts, Metropolitan Nikodim (Rotov) was elected President of the WCC from the Orthodox Churches.

The Moscow Patriarchate criticised the WCC governing bodies, insisting on greater possibilities for the Churches from the socialist countries to participate in the ecumenical movement. The criticism was effective, and in 1977 the first consultation of WCC leaders and representatives of the member-Churches from the socialist countries was held in Budapest, which was also the venue of the second such consultation in 1980. At

---

[1] *The Journal of the Moscow Patriarchate,* p. 13.

the latter, a certain growth in the number of religious workers from the socialist countries among the WCC staff was noted. It was also pointed out that after the 1977 consultation more than half of the commission and working group sessions were held in Eastern Europe. The programmatic priorities of the WCC and the participation of the East European Churches in them were discussed during the consultation. Special attention was paid to the WCC programme for fighting racism. The participants in the consultation expressed the hope that their Churches would be adequately represented among the delegates, speakers and leadership of the forthcoming Sixth WCC General Assembly.

The forms of the Moscow Patriarchate's participation in the ecumenical movement are extremely varied. Its representatives are directly involved in the discussion at ecumenical forums of a wide range of socio-political and confessional-doctrinal problems.

During discussion of social problems, which figure prominently at ecumenical forums, the theologians of the Russian Orthodox Church adhere to the positions of religious citizens of socialist society. This leads them to conflicts with Western pro-imperialist interpretation of facts of social life, the characteristic feature of which is substitution of artificial schemata borrowed from bourgeois ideologists for the real social relations existing in the modern world.

Instead of noting the existence of the capitalist and the socialist systems in the world Western ecumenical leaders prefer to divide the world on a different principle—into the "rich North" and the "poor South", insisting that the former must find the means for aiding the latter. This is an obvious attempt to camouflage the true social meaning of the present division of the world and to equate the socialist countries with the capitalist ones. In this connection, the idea of "equal responsibility" of the developed countries before the Third World nations is widely cultivated. According to that idea, the USSR and the USA, Great Britain and Czechoslovakia are all equally responsible for the present sorry plight of the developing countries. That is an attempt to shift part of the blame of the imperialist powers, which grew rich through exploitation of their colonies, to the socialist states which have had nothing to do with colonialist expansionism.

Western ecumenical leaders endeavour to use this blameshifting as a means of compromising the Soviet Union and other socialist states in the eyes of the peoples of the developing countries, which have had a full taste of the horrors of colonialism and are trying to evade the neocolonialist traps set by the imperialist powers. The proimperialistically minded ecumenists of the West are trying to channel the just social hatred of the people's masses in the former colonies for the imperialists and colonialists against the countries of the socialist community, slanderously portraying them as accomplices in the colonial plunder of the past bearing the common burden of responsibility for its present consequences.

This division of the world is sharply criticised by the ecumenical leaders of socialist countries, including theologians of the Russian Orthodox Church. In his report on the "Responsibility of the Church in the World Today" delivered at one of the ecumenical gatherings, Professor Nikolay Zabolotsky of the Leningrad Theological Academy said: "It is an oversimplification to bandy about the terms 'rich' and 'poor' nations, since such qualities are relative. The time has come to look the truth in the eye and to assess the capitalist and socialist paths of development, with their possibilities and prospects for the solution of problems facing the world, bearing in mind the one and only Earth, upon which we stand, our common habitation".[1]

Wide support has also been given in the Western ecumenical circles for the profoundly reactionary idea of "ideological convergence", also borrowed from contemporary anticommunists.

The gist of the theological modification of this idea consists in the search for such a social form which would eliminate the shortcomings of both capitalism and socialism while synthesising their advantages. This obviously provocative approach pursues two goals. On the one hand, an attempt is made to convince the

---

[1] *The Journal of the Moscow Patriarchate*, 1978, No. 7, p. 63.

working masses preferring the socialist way of life that socialism shares certain grave defects with capitalism. In other words, it is intended to compromise socialist society, by ascribing to it the sores of the capitalist system, simultaneously whitewashing and "ennobling" capitalism by ascribing to it the advantages of socialism.

Western ecumenists of the anticommunist variety see convergence as a one-way street. In their view, socialism must completely absorb elements of capitalism, transforming its very essence, while capitalism may retain its identity, remaining free from external influences and fully protected from the penetration of socialist elements. In other words, mutual convergence of capitalism and socialism is in the final analysis interpreted as the spreading of bourgeois influence on the socialist countries.

The propaganda of these social conceptions by Western ecumenical leaders during inter-Christian discussions is evaluated by the Moscow Patriarchate's theologians as an attempt to lend the limited class bourgeois views the appearance of a supraclass standpoint common to all mankind and allegedly equally acceptable to all the participants of the ecumenical movement. In speaking on the problems of contemporary ecumenism, Professor Zabolotsky especially emphasised the hopelessness of working out a unified ecumenical approach to social phenomena, to the social structures of our times, since the ecumenical movement comprises adherents of both capitalism and socialism. "...No united ideology is possible," he stated, "with Christianity fragmented and the divergences that are present in the socio-political reasoning of Christians, some of whom belong to the capitalist world and some to the socialist...".[1]

In their controversy with religious workers from the socialist countries Western theologians allege that the advocacy of progressive socio-political ideas by the former results from their lack of objectivity caused by pressure from the authorities. Rejecting this allegation out of hand, Patriarch Pimen, head of the Russian Orthodox Church, pointed out in his speech at a public

---

[1] Ibid., 1974, No. 11, p. 51.

meeting in the conference hall of the WCC headquarters in Geneva in September 1973 that such an approach to the position of the Christian Churches of the socialist countries (including the Russian Orthodox Church) was basically incorrect. "In the course of our ecumenical discussions," he said, "we from the Soviet Union, like our brothers from the other socialist countries, have frequently encountered a certain failure to understand our position on the part of our Western brothers, and sometimes even experienced their direct distrust of us. This does not surprise us. These difficulties arise mainly when we are considering social problems, mutual relations between the individual and society, the Church and the State. Our opponents are, we are convinced, more often than not, under the influence of propaganda hostile to our society which is widely spread in the West. This prevents them from seeing the indisputable merits of the socialist way of life, one which is, in our view, largely in keeping with the ideals of Christianity. Our opponents lose sight of the fact that the yardsticks of capitalist society are inapplicable to our society, which is qualitatively different... Thus to the question of our Western brothers: 'Surely you must have some shortcomings which ought to be condemned the way we do in our own countries?' we reply: 'Yes, we have our shortcomings, but they are not antagonistic. Our citizens are not alienated from society and society is not alienated from them. We have no one and no reason to engage in condemnation. We ourselves must work to correct our shortcomings, to perfect our society."[1]

This statement expresses the viewpoint of the religious citizens of socialist society who see the world in the light of their social interests, and it shows convincingly that it is difficult to achieve unanimity on socio-political questions with the adherents of the bourgeois way of life; and to create a unified, universal ecumenical social ideology equally acceptable to all.

In practice, these attempts lead to putting forward, under the guise of ecumenical social doctrines, pro-

---

[1] *The Journal of the Moscow Patriarchate*, 1973, No. 11, pp. 51, 52.

Western doctrines expressing the bourgeois view of the problems in question, to which the religious figures of the capitalist countries still predominant in the WCC adhere. True, the leading circles of the WCC cannot entirely ignore the social heterogeneity of the ecumenical movement, especially after the joining of the latter by the Christian Churches and associations of the socialist and developing countries; neither can they ignore the mood of the religious masses. For this reason the WCC is compelled to pass decisions on certain socio-political issues that are unpalatable to the imperialist forces.

Among other things, the Western imperialist circles resent the criticism of colonialism and neocolonialism in the ecumenical documents, the condemnation of imperialist intrigues in Angola and the African continent as a whole, the realistic assessment of the situation in the Middle East, actions against racism, etc. Although ecumenical evaluations of these facts are given from abstract Christian positions and are not taken to their logical conclusion, the very existence of these evaluations in the documents of the WCC and its sections is thoroughly distasteful to the reactionary ecclesiastical circles of the West that use religious arguments to defend the social positions of imperialism. Each time such an evaluation is expressed, these reactionary circles raise an uproar about the existence of "communist influences" in contemporary ecumenism, looking for the "hand of Moscow" in the actions of the WCC, doing their best, in short, to push the ecumenical movement over to anticommunist positions and to provoke the WCC into taking anti-Soviet action.

The prevalence of socio-political problems, in the ideology and practice of contemporary ecumenism, which has especially increased in recent times, has long been regarded by many theologians as an alarming symptom. They see this prevalence as evidence of the realisation by the participants in the ecumenical movement of the hopelessness of the attempts to achieve a joint solution of debatable confessional problems—a solution intended to create the premises for a future restoration of Pan-Christian unity which is the primary goal of the WCC activity. That goal, as Archbishop Mikhail (Mudyugin), one of the most active participants in the ecumenical discussions, declared in his analysis of the WCC Fifth General Assembly, "has been relegated to the background in the consciousness of many of our Protestant brethren, who constituted the majority at the assembly and the ecumenical movement as a whole".[1]

There is nothing unexpected about this state of affairs. In the decades of their ecumenical activity the ideologists of the WCC member-Churches had enough opportunity to see for themselves that even the first steps of disunited Christianity towards a confessional unity are extremely difficult and quite uneffective. The contemporary ecumenical movement, which includes Protestants, the Orthodox and Monophysites, is extremely heterogeneous confessionally. Protestants themselves, who still dominate the WCC and its departments, cannot yet come to an agreement on many important dogmatic questions. They find it even more difficult to find a common language with the Orthodox and the Monophysites as there is too much to divide them on the confessional plane. Theological discussions on doctrinal questions have therefore long lost their perspective and are at present more reminiscent of exercise in rhetoric than of search for mutually acceptable solutions.

Even the principal goal of the ecumenical movement is still differently understood by its participants. In the view of Orthodox ecumenists, "the basic goal of the ecumenical movement [is] overcoming the confessional differences between Christians and striving for unity"[2]. But the meaning of this unity is not yet clear to them, and they describe it in very vague terms.

Here is one such characteristic description. "It is not at all a question of one Church joining another," said Protopresbyter Professor Vitaly Borovoy, who has worked a long time on the staff of the WCC, in a sermon during an ecumenical divine service at the Church of the Protecting Veil of the Mother of God at the Trinity-St. Sergiy Lavra, "(we reject this path out of

---

[1] *The Journal of the Moscow Patriarchate*, 1976, No. 7, p. 61.
[2] Ibid., 1976, No. 7, p. 60.

hand), and not of levelling off ritual, cultural and historical differences among Christians—Christianity is extremely rich, varied and comprehensive, and it would be a tragedy if we attempted to reduce the whole of varied Christianity to one historical type or form. It is a question of jointly and fraternally coming along a slow and difficult path to a common understanding of a unified basis of Christianity, of the basis of faith and of all that which we call canonical order".[1]

Thus the theologians of the Moscow Patriarchate interpret the ecumenical unity of the member-Churches of the WCC as establishment of unity in questions of faith and the most important forms of church life.

Protestant church leaders have a different view of the goal of the ecumenical movement. At an ecumenical service in the Leningrad prayerhouse of Evangelical Baptist Christians, Presbyter S. Fadyukhin said this: "The movement for closer links between and unification of all the Christians is called 'ecumenism'. It should be noted that some persons have an erroneous idea of ecumenism, believing that all Protestants must become Orthodox or that all the Orthodox must become Protestants. In reality, however, it means that Christians must jointly proclaim the Gospel of Christ and serve the people around us with love".[2] If we follow the logic of the Baptist Presbyter, the goal of the ecumenical movement is not at all the unity of faith but merely a unity of action, the present plurality of confessional doctrines and canonical orders remaining intact.

The level of the present state of Christian unity is also differently understood in the ecumenical circles. Protestants believe that Christians have always been and still are united, only this unity is not realised by them owing to confessional differences. The task of the ecumenical movement is to help its participants to become aware of this unity and to demonstrate this realisation through joint action. As to the Orthodox they believe that real Christianity is disunited, divided

---

[1] *Zhurnal Moskovskoy Patriarkhii*, 1978, No. 5, p. 58.
[2] *Bratskiy vestnik*, 1976, No. 2, p. 22.

into numerous confessions and denominations; this disunity must be overcome, and the ways and means of establishing real unity must be found.

Different theological traditions of the Protestant and Orthodox participants in the ecumenical movement stand in the way of finding common and mutually acceptable approaches to the solution of many confessional problems.

Take the problem of baptism, for instance. The participants in the ecumenical movement practice several distinctly different modes of baptism. Contemporary ecumenists have so far failed to answer the question of what suits best the prospects of achieving Pan-Christian unity—recognition of these modes as equal or giving preference to one of them.

No solution has been found for the problem of the Eucharist: can Christians of different confessions and denominations with serious confessional differences (including fundamentally different conceptions of the essence of the Eucharist) receive the Eucharist together or not. Protestants believe that they can, and they therefore widely practice the so-called intercommunion—Christians of different confessional orientations jointly receiving the Eucharist. The Orthodox, on the other hand, categorically reject this, stating that only Christians who share the view of the Eucharist as the sacrament of mystical partaking of the "body and blood of the Lord" under the guise of bread and wine can jointly receive the Eucharist.

The problem of priesthood is also given different solutions by the participants in the ecumenical movement. The Orthodox view the ordination of priests as a sacrament. They ascribe priests a special gift of the Holy Spirit's grace, concentrate ecclesiastical power in the hands of the episcopate elected from among the "black clergy" (the monks), do not allow women to become priests, referring to the absence of women priests in the Evangelical times, etc. Protestants, on the other hand, do not recognise priesthood as a sacrament and reject the grace of clerics. Many of Protestant confessions know not episcopal power, and widely practice priesthood of women. In some Protestant Churches women occupy not only priestly but also episcopal offices. Of the six Presidents of the World Council of Churches two are Protestant women.

Believing it necessary to bring closer together the positions of the Orthodox and Protestant members of the ecumenical movement on the three problems mentioned here, the WCC commission on Faith and Order prepared the drafts of consensuses on baptism, the Eucharist and priesthood and sent them to the WCC member-Churches for consideration and subsequent adoption. The Moscow Patriarchate also received these drafts, entrusting the Synod Commission on Christian Unity and Inter-Church Relations to consider them and to pass judgement on them. That judgement was later approved by the Synod of the Russian Orthodox Church and sent to the WCC as an official document.

All three consensuses were welcomed by the Synod as "the first real though modest and purely theoretico-theological step on the long and difficult path leading to unity". At the same time the synodal commission made a number of critical remarks on each of the consensuses, stressing in particular that "in their present form these consensuses are by no means full enough to satisfy the requirements of a genuine agreement of the Churches from the point of view of doctrinal norms and the fundamentals of the canonical order of the Early Undivided Church".[1]

In its analysis of the consensus on the Eucharist the Synod commission stated that "the final aim of the ecumenical movement towards Christian unity is not intercommunion, which is wholly unacceptable to the Orthodox consciousness, but the restoration of full Eucharistic communion after the achievement of unity in faith and in the fundamentals of canonical order".[2] The consensus on mutually recognised priesthood was especially sharply criticised by the synodal commission: "The document continues to reflect the one-sided opinion of Protestant and Free Churches. It still does not reflect the early catholic tradition sufficiently".[3]

---

[1] *The Journal of the Moscow Patriarchate*, 1977, No. 7, p. 58.
[2] Ibid., p. 61.
[3] Ibid.

Thus all three drafts of ecumenical agreements on confessional problems proved to be unacceptable to Russian Orthodoxy.

The lack of progress in the ecumenical theological discussions on confessional problems, the absence of real proofs of a fundamental possibility of overcoming the existing dogmatic differences between the WCC member-Churches, the inability of the theologians of different confessions to find a common language in discussing the doctrinal aspects of Pan-Christian unity—these are the causes that bar the way of contemporary ecumenical theological thought out of its impasses, and that make the members of the ecumenical movement (especially its Protestant majority) increasingly prefer socio-political problems to confessional ones. This tendency has recently become so strong that the Moscow Patriarchate openly expressed its criticism of the existing situation.

The leadership of the Russian Orthodox Church accused the WCC of the so-called horizontalism—the preponderance of concern for the purely earthly, social questions (the horizontal cross-section of WCC activity) over the purely religious, confessional concerns (the vertical or longitudinal section). "The almost exclusive stressing of 'horizontalism' in reference to salvation," said the message of Patriarch Pimen of Moscow and All Russia and of the Holy Synod of the Russian Orthodox Church to the Central Committee of the World Council of Churches, "may create the impression in many Christians for whom the sacred traditions of the Early Church are precious that in modern ecumenism there is a new temptation to be ashamed of the Gospel of Christ Crucified and Resurrected..., which results in keeping silent about the very essence of His Gospel from a false fear of being considered old-fashioned and losing popularity".[1] On another occasion, Patriarch Pimen expressed himself just as definitely: "We maintain that it is necessary for the WCC to achieve a harmonic combination between the vertical and horizontal directions of its activities".[2]

---

[1] *The Journal of the Moscow Patriarchate*, 1973, No. 9, p. 8.
[2] Ibid., 1973, No. 11, p. 49.

The article on "The Thirtieth Anniversary of the World Council of Churches", noted that "one of the most important points determining the WCC's activities in recent years has been the struggle to balance the so-called horizontal and vertical planes in these activities".[1] The absence of such a balance is one of the external manifestations of the crisis in modern ecumenism, or its inability to solve the primary task for which the WCC was founded and is functioning.

Such are the principal aspects of the Russian Orthodox Church's participation in the ecumenical movement.

---

[1] Ibid., 1979, No. 2, p. 68.

## Chapter XIII
# THE RUSSIAN ORTHODOX CHURCH ABROAD

Church parishes consisting of adherents of Russian Orthodoxy exist not only in the Soviet Union but also abroad, practically on all the continents. Members of these parishes have become citizens of other states; they have assimilated the socio-political ideas of the Western world, retaining just their religious views in a Russian Orthodox interpretation.

### The Emergence of Russian Orthodoxy Abroad

The first seats of Russian Orthodoxy abroad appeared as early as the 18th century.

Some of these parishes were established by Russians, Ukrainians and Byelorussians who found themselves outside Russia for some reason or other, mostly in search of jobs, land, a happy lot—all those things that they could not find at home. In the 19th and early 20th century thousands upon thousands of indigent people left the confines of the Russian Empire and headed for Western Europe, Asia, the North-American continent, Latin America and even far-off Australia.

Reared and educated in an Orthodox environment, they retained their loyalty to the old religion in their new places of settlement. Church parishes were set up, churches were built, and spiritual life continued in customary religious-ecclesiastical forms—a constant reminder of Homeland.

Other parishes of the Russian Orthodox Church

appeared as a result of missionary activity of the priests and hierarchs of the Russian Orthodox Church.

At the very end of the 18th century, the Kadiak Orthodox Mission was set up, which started the spreading of Russian Orthodoxy on the Aleutian Islands and on the North-American continent. Monk Gherman, who died in 1837, worked within the framework of that mission; he was canonised by the Orthodox Church in America as its first saint and is worshipped as St. Gherman of Alaska.

Later the North American parishes of the Russian Orthodox Church were united in the diocese of Kamchatka, the Kurils and Aleutians, of which the first ruling bishop was Innokentiy (Popov-Veniaminov), canonised in 1977 by both the Russian and the American Orthodox Churches and glorified as the "apostle of America and Siberia". Later that diocese was transformed into the diocese of the Aleutians and Alaska, whose see was moved to San Francisco in 1872; and in 1900, it was renamed the Aleutian and North-American diocese (with the see in New York—since 1905). Several suffragan dioceses were set up. In 1907, the diocese was named the Russian Orthodox Greek Catholic Church in North America within the purview of the hierarchy from the Russian Church, and later the Russian Orthodox Greek-Catholic Church of North America (Metropolitanate), which in 1970 was granted autocephaly issuing from the Moscow Patriarchate.

In 1870, the Japanese Orthodox Mission was set up, which began spreading Russian Orthodoxy among the local population. The Russian Orthodox Church set up its missions in Iran, China and Korea.

The number of parishes of the Russian Orthodox orientation abroad grew after the October Revolution (1917) and the Civil War in Russia after a wave of emigration, most emigrants belonging to the Russian Orthodox Church.

A second influx of parishioners in Russian Orthodox churches abroad took place after the Second World War, when many former Soviet citizens found themselves abroad as "displaced persons". These included both traitors to their Motherland who collaborated with the Hitlerites during the war and now tried to escape from the people's just trial by running away to the West, and people brought to Nazi Germany as forced labourers or prisoners of war and intimidated, misinformed and blackmailed by Western intelligence services into staying abroad.

In the 1950s-1970s, the fates of Russian Orthodox parishes abroad varied.

Some of the parishes (both those that emerged due to missionary activities and those that were founded by emigrants) became part of the Local Orthodox Churches. They therefore changed their jurisdiction and ceased to be Russian Orthodox parishes (even where they consisted of Russian parishioners).

In two cases, Russian Orthodox parishes became the nuclei of newly formed Local Orthodox Churches. That was precisely what happened in the USA, where most of the parishes of the Autocephalous Orthodox Church in America are former parishes of the American Metropolitan District of the Russian Orthodox Church. The Japanese Autonomous Orthodox Church also formed on the basis of parishes established through the activities of the Russian Orthodox missionaries.

A fairly large number of Russian Orthodox parishes abroad did not join other Orthodox Churches or gain ecclesiastical independence. They still claim to be members of the Russian Orthodox Church, although the concrete forms of that membership vary. We refer here to two groups that are not in contact with each other: the foreign parishes of the Moscow Patriarchate and the parishes of the "Russian Orthodox Church Outside Russia" or the "Russian Foreign Church".

Let us consider each of these two structures, which are continually in a state of confrontation.

### The Foreign Parishes of the Moscow Patriarchate

In many countries of the world there are Orthodox parishes that regard themselves as an integral part of the Russian Orthodox Church and retain canonical links with the Moscow Patriarchate. The members of those parishes have long become citizens of the states in which they live, and many of them were born in those countries.

There are more than 40 such parishes in the USA (after the formation of the American Local Orthodox Church they were invited to transfer to the latter's jurisdiction, but they expressed a desire to remain in the Russian Orthodox Church[1]); such parishes are numerous in Canada (they were previously united in the Edmonton-Canadian diocese of the Moscow Patriarchate, abolished after the granting of autocephaly to the American Orthodox Church); there are also such parishes in Latin America, in Western Europe and on other continents. At the time of the 1971 Local Council of the Russian Orthodox Church, the Moscow Patriarchate had 124 parishes abroad, which sent 25 delegates to the Council.[2]

In those countries where the number of foreign parishes of the Russian Orthodox Church is insignificant, they are united in deaneries. The Moscow Patriarchate has deaneries in Hungary, Finland, Mexico and Japan.

Where there are many parishes, they form dioceses, such as those of Berlin, Brussells, Vienna, the Hague, Düsseldorf, Zürich, etc. The dioceses form part of the foreign exarchates of the Moscow Patriarchate: West European, Central European, of Central and Southern America. The foreign parishes of the Russian Orthodox Church in Canada and the USA have a special status; they are administered by one of the suffragans of the Moscow diocese who bears the title of Administrator of the Patriarchal Parishes in Canada and a.i. in the USA.

The hierarchs, clerics and laity of the foreign parishes of the Russian Orthodox Church abroad take an active part in the interconfessional contacts of the Moscow Patriarchate, especially in establishing links with other Orthodox Churches whose parishes are also scattered throughout the world.

---

[1] *Zhurnal Moskovskoy patriarkhii*, 1970, No. 5, pp. 21, 22.

[2] V. A. Kuroyedov, *Religiya i tserkov v Sovetskom gosudarstve* (Religion and the Church in the Soviet State), Moscow, 1981, p. 110.

The process of renewal of Russian Orthodoxy, especially of its doctrine and rites, did not bypass the foreign parishes of the Moscow Patriarchate. Moreover, it is even more intense there, which reflects the desire of the members of these parishes to adapt their confession more fully to existence under conditions of confessional pluralism.

Contrary to the age-long tradition and to the practice of the domestic parishes of the Moscow Patriarchate, divine services in the foreign parishes of the Russian Orthodox Church are conducted not only in Church Slavonic but also in the local languages (English, French, Spanish, German, etc.). The reason for that is that the new generations of emigrants have a poor command even of Russian, to say nothing of Old Church Slavonic.

All the foreign parishes of the Russian Orthodox Church have long switched, with the permission of the Moscow Patriarchate, to the New Style, and thus celebrate Easter simultaneously with Western Christians.

The parishes being scattered, with many parishioners living dozens and even hundreds of miles from the nearest Orthodox church of their jurisdiction, services are irregular and are mostly held on feast days. Liturgy is often held in the evening; the liturgy of presanctified gifts is intended to give a chance to receive the Eucharist to those parishioners who live far from their church and cannot get to it in time for the morning service, which cannot end later than noon.

All the foreign exarchates of the Russian Orthodox Church and even some deaneries have their own publications. Besides, the parishioners of the Russian Orthodox churches abroad receive *The Journal of the Moscow Patriarchate* in English, especially intended for them.

## The Russian Orthodox Church Outside Russia

A considerable part of the foreign Russian Orthodox parishes have found themselves under the influence of emigrant clergymen who endeavour to exploit Russian

Orthodoxy as an ideological banner of the counter-revolution and intervention. These political intriguers and the parishes supporting them, which pretentiously call themselves the Russian Orthodox Church Outside Russia or the Russian Foreign Church, are also known as the Karlowitz group or the Karlowitz schism.

This association has its origin in the Higher Russian Church Administration Abroad (the "foreign HRCA") headed by Metropolitan Antoniy (Khrapovitsky). Having moved from Turkey to Yugoslavia, it convened in November 1921, in the Serbian town of Sremski Karlovci (Karlowitz), a General Assembly of Representatives of the Russian Foreign Church later termed the Russian Church Council Abroad. The Assembly was attended by anti-Soviet minded bishops and priests, as well as by former czarist officials, members of the former Russian aristocracy and generals of the routed White Guards; many of them had attended the 1917/1918 Local Council and the 1919 Stavropol Council.

The Karlowitz Council demonstrated from the outset its purely political character. It called for a consolidation of emigrant forces on an anti-Soviet basis and for organising a new intervention of the Entente against Soviet Russia to force the monarchist form of government on the country. It elected the governing body of the Russian ecclesiastical emigration—the Higher Russian Church Administration Abroad consisting of a Synod and a church board. The Karlowitz Administration was headed by Metropolitan Antoniy (Khrapovitsky); later it was reorganised to become a Hierarchical Synod, also headed by Antoniy.

The Karlowitz group declared itself to be the only true part of Russian Orthodoxy and broke off all links with the Moscow Patriarchate. As a church organisation, it has not been recognised by a single Christian confession and is completely isolated not only from the Orthodox Churches but also from Christianity as a whole.

After the death of Metropolitan Antoniy in 1936, the Hierarchical Synod came to be headed by Metropolitan Anastasiy (Gribanovsky). In 1938, he held a second council, also in Sremski Karlovci, which again confirmed the anti-Soviet and anti-communist bias of the entire political and ideological activity of the reactionary sections of the Russian emigration.

At first, the leaders of the Karlowitz group mostly placed their hopes on the imperialist circles of the Entente, endeavouring to incline its member countries to a new round of armed struggle against the Soviet Republic. This was clearly seen from the appeal of the Hierarchical Synod to the Genoa Conference issued by Metropolitan Antoniy on behalf of the Karlowitz Council in February 1922. It called on the governments of the European countries and the USA not to recognise the Soviet state, to exert pressure on it (even organising a new intervention if necessary), to crush it, and to restore the pre-revolutionary state and social system.

However, the capitalist countries, then in the grip of a most acute socio-economic and political crisis, were not in a position to mount a new interventionist venture, and these appeals found no support, which is still regarded by the Karlowitz schemers as a grave political miscalculation of the West.

At the end of the 1930s, the leaders of the Karlowitz group counted on German fascism, which they saw as their natural ally in the struggle against "Godless Bolshevism". In a "message of gratitude" presented by Metropolitan Anastasiy to Hitler in 1938, the *Führer* was raised to the rank of a "leader in the world struggle for peace and the truth"; an appeal was made to him to start an aggression against the Soviet Union at the earliest possible date. The Nazi Germany's attack on the USSR was received by the Karlowitz episcopate and clergy with unconcealed delight. In their sermons and articles they blessed the Hitlerites' cruel reprisals against the Soviet people. In the first issue for 1942, *Tserkovnaya zhizn,* (Church Life), the official organ of the Karlowitz Hierarchical Synod, stated in its editorial "The Orthodox Church against Communism": "All over the globe, the Russian Church Outside Russia closely follows the course of the war in the East, supporting with its prayers the selfless fighters against the Godless and always ready to help them in their struggle to the best of its abilities."

To organise religious-political propaganda in favour of the Nazi invaders, the Karlowitzers set up special missionary courses in Belgrade. The leaders of the Karlowitz group actively aided Hitlerites and the traitors of the Soviet country who collaborated with them in recruiting all sorts of renegades, and simply disoriented and intimidated people, to army units for active service on the side of the Nazi Reich. In particular, Metropolitan Anastasiy and the clergy within his jurisdiction directly participated in the formation on Yugoslav territory of the so-called Russian protective group, which was used by the Nazi command in the fight against the national-liberation movement of the Yugoslav people. The Karlowitz hierarchs sent regimental chaplains to the corps of the Nazi General Panwitz. Metropolitan Anastasiy rendered all possible assistance to the traitor Vlasov, providing "spiritual nourishment" to his followers and sowing in their hearts the poisonous seeds of hatred for the socialist system, for the Motherland they betrayed.

At the end of World War II, Metropolitan Anastasiy, after an unsuccessful attempt to get into neutral Switzerland, settled with the remnants of the Hierarchical Synod in Munich, where they were given shelter by the Western occupation authorities which intended to use the episcopate and clergy of the Karlowitz group for their own purposes.

Sucking up to their new masters, the associates of Metropolitan Anastasiy began to work on "displaced persons"; among these were not only traitors who voluntarily collaborated with the German invaders but also POWs and driven to Germany as forced labourers. The Karlowitzers concealed the former, obstructing their being handed over to the Soviet courts, and tried to persuade the latter to stay in the Western countries.

The efforts of the Karlowitz episcopate and clergy in cooperating with the "cold war" champions and militant anti-communists were highly appreciated by the American secret services. In 1950, Metropolitan Anastasiy and other leaders of the Russian Orthodox Church Outside Russia were permitted to enter the USA, which they did immediately, transferring their headquarters across the Atlantic.

Not long before his death, Metropolitan Anastasiy gave up the leadership of the Karlowitz group, unable to cope with the strife within the Hierarchical Synod. In 1965, Metropolitan Filaret (Voznesensky) became the head of the group. He continued the anti-Soviet and anti-communist traditions of his predecessors. Under his direction, the third Council of the Russian Orthodox Church Outside Russia was held in 1974; it did not introduce any fundamentally new elements in the ideology or activities of this religious-political group of anti-Soviet ecclesiastics. After the death of Filaret in November 1985, a council of Karlowitz bishops elected the fourth head of the Karlowitzers—Archbishop Vitaliy (Ustinov), distinguished for his active anti-Soviet stance, especially during the Nazi aggression, when he was in the capital of the Third Reich. During the elections he did not get the necessary number of votes and took up the post of head of the Russian Church Outside Russia only after lots were drawn.

The headquarters of the Karlowitz religious-political organisation is in New York. The actual centre of the Russian Church Outside Russia is at the Holy Trinity Monastery near Jordanville, NY, USA. Situated in the monastery is a theological seminary producing several graduates each year. It also houses the press, where religious and political literature is published, including calendars, leaflets, pamphlets, books, the fortnightly *Pravoslavnaya Rus* (Orthodox Russia) (the official organ of the Karlowitz group) and its monthly supplement, *Pravoslavnaya zhizn* (Orthodox Life).

The Karlowitz Hierarchical Synod has within its jurisdiction some 350 church parishes united in 18 dioceses—eight in North America, five in Western Europe, three in South America and two in Australia and New Zealand. In some dioceses churches are very few in number. Many of them are housed in former garages, warehouses, barracks, summer houses and city flats. Some of the parishes have no churches at all, so that services are held at parishioners' flats.

There is an acute shortage of priests in the Karlowitz pseudo-Church. In all the dioceses taken together there are less than three hundred priests, and most of them are of an advanced age.

The ideological and political principles of the Russian Church Outside Russia worked out by its leaders in the early 1920s have not changed much since then. They are formulated in the materials of all the four Councils, in the speeches and publications of Karlowitz hierarchs, priests and theologians.

The main focus is an anti-Sovietism and anti-communism, which are elevated to the rank of a religious dogma and form the cornerstone of the ideology of the Russian Church Outside Russia. The starting-point of this doctrine is distortion of the social essence of the October Revolution in Russia (1917) and of the influence of the revolutionary process on the country's destiny and on the course of world history.

The radical social change in the destiny of Russia, which came about due to the October Revolution, is presented by the Karlowitzers as an accident in Russian history without any objective premises for fruitful development. The revolution is slandered as a "plot", a "narrow coup" without support among the popular masses, and as "social mutiny". In reality, however, the October Revolution, proletarian in its content, was a profoundly popular revolution, as indicated by the alliance of the working class and the peasantry and the joint struggle of all the working people against the forces of the counter-revolution and foreign intervention.

An important element of the ideological weaponry of the Karlowitz group is distortion of the essence of the socialist state and social system and cultivation of a hostile attitude to Soviet power among the Church's adherents. In particular, Karlowitz leaders widely spread the tales about "incongruity" between the socialist system and the social conditions in Russia, about "unpreparedness" of its peoples for this system, etc. The seventy-year-long history of the first socialist country in the world, which strides along the path of socialist development, has convincingly shown the strength of the Soviet system, the Soviet people's complete support for Soviet power and readiness to improve socialist society. But Karlowitz hierarchs and priests close their eyes to the actual state of affairs, using slander to keep alive the spirit of anti-Sovietism among emigrants. Open calls for the "overthrow" of Soviet power continue to flow from the publications of the Russian Church Outside Russia and from the ambos of Karlowitz churches.

The prime target of Karlowitz criticism is the ideology of Marxism-Leninism. Karlowitz ideologists clearly revealed their openly anticommunist bias as early as 1921, when their Council decided to "condemn the false doctrine of socialism and its most consistent form—Bolshevism or Communism—as a basically anti-Christian doctrine". Karlowitz leaders have remained loyal to that position to the present. Thus the 1974 Council called on the Soviet people "to reject Marxism-Leninism in their life".

The ideologists of the Karlowitz group are doing everything to smear scientific socialism, to discredit it in the eyes of the world public by ascribing to it goals and tasks which it never set itself. *Pravoslavnaya Rus* and other publications of the Russian Church Outside Russia assert year in, year out that the "principal goal of communism is the destruction of religion".

The ideological struggle against these assertions is presented by the Karlowitzers as a purely administrative persecution of the clergy and believers, as repressions against and even physical destruction of religious people by "atheists-iconoclasts". This kind of slanderous assertions were made, e.g., at the 1974 Council both by the author of the main report and by the speakers. Karlowitz publications are also full of this sort of calumny.

Although the main element of the ideological activity of the reactionary circles of the Russian ecclesiastical emigration are attacks against the Soviet social and state system and slandering socialism, they are aware that this is not sufficient to attract the masses of emigrants. A positive programme capable of winning the emigration is needed. The need for such a programme was voiced already at the first Karlowitz Council, and it was also widely debated by the participants in the 1938 Council. The organisers of the subsequent Councils also turned to this issue, defending the programmatic principles of the Russian Church Outside Russia at great length.

What have the leaders of the Karlowitz group to offer their adherents as a social ideal?

They are looking for such an ideal and find it, neither in the present nor the future but in the remote past. There is nothing strange or unexpected about it. The present of the capitalist world in which the emigrants have to live is so dismal that even these political-religious schemers do not dare to hold it up as a socio-political model. The cheerlessness of the present gives rise to uncertainty about the future and even fear of it. There is but one way out—to look for the ideal in the past, and very remote past at that; it is this way out that is offered to the Russian emigration adhering to the Karlowitz orientation.

Playing on the dissatisfaction of the greater part of the Russian emigration with the present and its uncertainty about the future and exploiting the nationalist feelings of the emigrants, the top leaders of the Russian Church Outside Russia have suggested a return to the holy Orthodox Russia of the pre-Petrine times as the programme of the future social order in Russia. Formulated by the Second Karlowitz Council, this demand runs all through the decisions and other materials of the Third Council as well, which called for a loyalty to the ideal of the past and future Orthodox Russia. Pre-Petrine "holy Rus" is shown by Karlowitz ideologists through rose-coloured spectacles. It is presented to the emigrant believers as a kind of "Golden Age" in the history of Russia and an ideal embodiment of the Christian principles of ecclesiastical, social and state structure.

Propaganda of monarchism is one of the mainstays of the ideological and ecclesiastical-practical activity of the episcopate and clergy of the Karlowitz orientation. It is drummed into the minds of the rank-and-file parishioners of Karlowitz churches, as well as of the rest of the Russian emigration, that autocracy is a Christian ideal of state power, and that the demand to revere the czar as the "Lord's anointed sovereign" is a dogma of the Orthodox faith, violation of which entails excommunication. The existence of autocracy is declared to be a necessary premise of the flourishing of Orthodoxy.

The leaders of the Karlowitz group have created a cult of the last Russian czar, which they do their best to foster among emigrant circles. The emigrant religious-political schemers have declared this killer of the revolution, nicknamed by the people Nicholas the Bloody and executed after a trial by a revolutionary court, to be an "innocent sufferer for the faith". The czar and his whole family were included among the so-called "Russian new martyrs" and canonised (the official canonisation of the royal family took place on November 1, 1981, at a hierarchical council of the Russian Church Outside Russia), although a great number of Russian emigrants opposed that political action.

Karlowitz leaders maintain close contacts with various monarchist organisations and associations of the Russian emigration, readily offering them space in their publications, including the official organ of the Russian Church Outside Russia.

The Karlowitz religious-political group is part of the international reaction, as is clear not only from its ideology but also from its activity, which is openly anti-socialist and aimed at active opposition to progressive tendencies in social development.

The episcopate and priests of the Russian Church Outside Russia have joined hands with those who are hostile to detente and to peaceful coexistence of states with opposite socio-political systems. Every instance of aggravation of international tension by the imperialist circles of the West is openly welcomed by Karlowitz politicians, while progress in the policy of peaceful coexistence plunges them in gloom.

From the first days of its existence, the Soviet Union has championed peace, universal disarmament and non-use of force in international relations. But the international reaction headed by US militarists still hopes to drive mankind back to the trenches of the cold war and to hold people of the world in fear of a nuclear catastrophe. The leaders of the Russian church emigration also dream of this, taking various moves to wreck detente.

First of all, Karlowitz leaders endeavour to persuade the West that only the Soviet Union and the other socialist countries gain from detente, which has nothing positive to offer to the capitalist countries. Peaceful coexistence of states with differing social systems is described to the Western public as a kind of trap to which the "Satanic force of communism" is trying to lure the "free world". The fact that stable peace is in the interest of the whole humanity, which rightly sees such peace as a guarantee of its further existence, is deliberately kept silent about.

The Karlowitz leaders were particularly displeased at the signing in 1975 of the Helsinki agreements which opened the way to the establishment of lasting peace in Europe. In one of its issues, the official organ of the Russian Church Outside Russia cast a slur on both the Helsinki conference of heads of 35 states and the final document they signed, calling the conference an "act of great deception", and the document, a "scrap of paper".

Opposing the improvement of relations between the USSR and the USA, Karlowitz clerics make common cause with extreme reactionaries in the USA endeavouring to persuade the administration to adhere to the positions of cold war. Attempts are made to intimidate the American public by talk of all kinds of "horrors" that would inevitably come in the wake of any relaxation in the confrontation between the USA and the USSR—such as an "infiltration of communism" on the American continent that is said to be an inescapable concomitant of extended contacts between governmental, business, public, cultural and educational bodies of both countries.

The leaders of the Karlowitz group ally themselves with various anti-Soviet organisations, associations, groups and individuals hostile to the USSR. In particular, they have extensive links with the People's Labour Union—a White emigrant organisation actively collaborating with the secret services of the imperialist states.

During the Second World War, the People's Labour Union placed itself at the disposal of the Nazi authorities, becoming their accomplice in the crimes they perpetrated on the temporarily occupied territory of the Soviet Union and other countries. After the defeat of Nazi Germany, the Union's activists conducted anti-Soviet agitation among "displaced persons", recruiting agents for subversive activities and building up their own organisation. Relying on the support of the international reaction, the Union now steps up its anti-Soviet activity. Its programme has a great deal in common with the activity of the Russian Church Outside Russia, which unites these two organisations in their struggle against the USSR and the Marxist-Leninist worldview dominant in it. The forms of this collaboration are extremely varied, and the collaboration itself is facilitated by the fact that some of the Union's activists (like G. A. Rar and others) simultaneously occupy important positions in the Karlowitz group. The ideologists of the Russian Church Outside Russia use in their propaganda the slanderous materials on the alleged "persecution of faith and the Church in the USSR" fabricated by the People's Labour Union. It was this sort of material that formed the basis of Rar's report at the Third Karlowitz Council "The Suffering Church at Home, Its Zealots and Detractors", in which there was not a trace of truth. In their turn, the Union's publications feature prominently the ideological and political activities of the Karlowitz group.

The main efforts of the Karlowitz group are aimed at misinforming the Russian emigration and the Western public as regards the position of religion and the Church in the Soviet Union, and at distorting the essence of the scientific-atheistic education of the Soviet people.

The Karlowitz press keeps silent about the fact that there are numerous religious associations in the USSR, including those that before the Revolution, in the times of the "Holy Orthodox Russia" glorified by the Karlowitzers, were either persecuted by czarism and church authorities (such as Old Believers) or subjected to all kinds of discrimination that made their normal functioning difficult (e.g., Baptists and Moslems). There is no mention in it of the fact that more than 20,000 churches, synagogues, mosques, kirks, and prayer-houses of nearly 40 confessions and denominations function in the cities and villages of the Soviet

Union, where members of all the nationalities of the country satisfy their religious needs. Nothing is said of the existence in the USSR of cloisters, secondary and higher theological schools, of the publication of religious literature: the Bible, the Koran, prayerbooks, calendars, collections of sermons, journals, etc.

The most improbable fabrications about "persecutions of faith and the Church in the USSR" appear practically in every issue of *Pravoslavnaya Rus, Pravoslavnaya zhizn* and other Karlowitz publications. The schemers in cassocks are not at all embarrassed by the fact that not only official representatives of religious associations in the USSR but also foreign religious figures visiting this country repeatedly pointed to normal conditions in the Soviet Union for professing religion. "The view is current in our country," said Father Julio Garcia, a Mexican priest who visited the Soviet Union, "that a representative of the authorities stands here behind the bishop with a rifle, that the clergy is controlled. People think that believers need a pass from the civil authorities to enter the church. But I have seen with my own eyes that people are free here. All those who want to go to church do so, and those who do not, stay away. During my stay here I did not witness a single negative act towards believers by non-believers...".[1]

Indulging in wishful thinking, Karlowitz falsifiers assure their adherents that the bulk of Soviet believers reject socialism, that they are in opposition to their government, constituting a kind of "internal emigration". But the real picture is quite different. Religious Soviet people are profoundly loyal to the socialist social and state system, they actively support the Soviet government's domestic and foreign policies, they love their Homeland and hate its enemies. "The Church members," wrote Professor Nikolay Zabolotsky, a prominent theologian of the Russian Orthodox Church, "do not consider themselves as anything but citizens of their own Motherland, and act under all circumstances just as members of the Soviet society should. Bishops, priests, deacons, parishioners and

---

[1] *The Journal of the Moscow Patriarchate,* 1976, No. 11, p. 20.

monks regard the Soviet system as a natural and providential norm of political and social build-up voluntarily chosen by the people, and they live under, take part in and support this system...".[1]

To expand the sphere of its ideological subversive activity and to step up religious-political propaganda in the traditional anti-Soviet spirit, the Russian Church Outside Russia has set up a number of associations— committees, funds, centres, brotherhoods, sisterhoods, etc. These associations have two main purposes.

Some of them aim at religious-political indoctrination of various strata and groups of the Russian emigration intended to keep up their nationalist and monarchist feelings and anti-Soviet spirit. Here belong, in particular, the Russian Church and Cultural Centre Vladimirovo attached to the Cathedral Church of the Intercession in Chicago, the Cultural and Educational Society in the Canadian diocese, two brotherhoods and seven sisterhoods in the German diocese (the FRG), etc. There are also several youth and children's organisations: the Circle of Vladimir Youth, the Patriotic Organisation of Russian Scouts, the National Organisation of Russian Scouts, the Organisation of Knights, etc. Nearly in all these associations, religious and political education is combined with military training— in order to train organisers and participants in the "liberation of Russia from atheist Bolsheviks".

Other organisations are intended to find ways of exerting a direct influence on the Soviet people. One such organisation is the Pravoslavnoye delo (Othodox Cause) brotherhood which has existed since 1959 and is headed by Archbishop Antoniy (Bartoshevich) of Geneva and West Europe, an inveterate monarchist and arch-enemy of Soviet power.

From its very inception, Pravoslavnoye delo has been sending anti-communist religious-political literature to this country. In recent years, it began to send its materials by mail, addressing them to Soviet offices and individual citizens. The letters and parcels contain leaflets and pamphlets of political rather than religious nature intended to rouse the addressees' interest for religion,

---

[1] *The Journal of the Moscow Patriarchate*, 1972, No. 12, p. 41.

to sow doubts about the correctness of the scientific materialist worldview, and, most importantly, to stir up hostility towards the ideology of the socialist social and state system, towards the Soviet way of life. They sow the poisonous seeds of strife between believers and atheists, the latter being presented as enemies of believers who humiliate and insult their religious feelings.

The 1974 Council resolved to expand and step up the activities of Pravoslavnoye delo. It was suggested to set up divisions of the brotherhood in the United States, Canada and Australia (previously, they only existed in Western Europe). It was recommended to involve the youth organisations of the Russian Church Outside Russia in the work of the brotherhood, and so on. In fulfilment of that decision, the leaders and activists of Pravoslavnoye delo are doing their best to stir the Russian emigration to a more active participation in the religious and political indoctrination of Soviet citizens. But they have to admit that theirs is an uphill job. Indeed, the Soviet people educated in the spirit of selfless loyalty to the socialist system and communist ideals, rebuff the moves by the ideological saboteurs in cassocks, expose their designs, and oppose their civic and worldview maturity to the Karlowitz schemes.

Busy with their intrigues of the lowest description, the leaders of the Karlowitz group pay less attention to religious and ecclesiastical problems than to political and ideological ones. The rank-and-file members of Karlowitz parishes reproach, with good reason, their pastors and archpastors for their excessive infatuation with politics—to the detriment of their ecclesiastical duties. Although Pravoslavnaya Rus refers to these reproaches as "slanderous accusations", the facts cited here prove that they are justified.

Despite all-out support from the forces of the international reaction, the Karlowitz religious-political group is in a state of acute crisis that grows worse with every passing year. The isolation of the Russian Church Outside Russia increases. Suffice it to say that not a single Christian confession or denomination was represented at the 1986 Council. The criticism of the ideology and practices of the Karlowitz group by official representatives of Christian Churches becomes increasingly sharp. The conflict between the Karlowitz hierarchy and clergy, on the one hand, and the laity, on the other, assumes sharper forms, splitting that organisation into hostile groups. The publications of the Russian Church Outside Russia are full of complaints about disrespect shown by many parishioners towards their pastors and archpastors. One of the causes for the conflict between the laity and the Karlowitz clergy is the latter's refusal to allow parishioners to take a more active part in the organisation of parish life, in the running of the parish. Such a refusal is usually explained by the "noncanonical" nature of the democratic principles of church life. But its true cause is different. Bearing in mind the laity's dissatisfaction with the clergy's political scheming, the Karlowitz top leaders fear that expansion of parishioners' rights will lead to the strengthening of ecclesiastical tendencies in parish life at the expense of political ones. They therefore revile those parishioners who demand a restructuring of parish life on democratic principles, stubbornly insisting in their publications that "there can be no room for democracy in Church".

The level of religiosity and ecclesiastical-political activity of many believers of the Karlowitz orientation is steadily going down. The Karlowitz hierarchs admit that for most Russian emigrants formally counted among parishioners of the Russian Church Outside Russia, membership in Orthodoxy "is of purely formal significance". Describing the mentality and state of religiosity of these persons, one of the leaders of the Russian Church Outside Russia wrote that as a rule they did not know the doctrine of the Orthodox Church, and neither did they have any interest for it, wholly engrossed in their mundane concerns.

Many visitors to Karlowitz churches display an absence of proper religiosity and a negligence in the observance of elementary cultic injunctions. The Karlowitz press brands them as people whose communion with religion is nothing more than dropping at a church after a heavy breakfast, listening to beautiful singing, making several careless signs of the cross without any meaning or sense, lighting two or three candles, pushing in the crowd while completely ignoring the solemnity of the service, bowing to acquaintances and promptly withdrawing, preferring to smoke within the church's grounds and chatting with acquaintances of the same spiritual calibre.

There has been a marked fall in the influence of the Karlowitz hierarchy on the younger generations of Russian emigrants. This fact was plainly admitted by Archpriest Lukyanov, who stated at the 1974 Council that only about a fourth of third-generation emigrants attended church. Similar admissions have been made by the Karlowitz leaders after the Council. In particular, *Pravoslavnaya Rus* wrote that a relatively small proportion of Russian children attended church schools supervised by the Karlowitz group.

What worries Karlowitz leaders even more than the growth of religious indifference among parishioners or the falling influence on the young people is the withdrawal of increasing numbers of Russian emigrants from the positions of militant anti-Sovietism, the growth of the emigrants' sympathies for their former Homeland, and a soberer approach to the revolutionary reforms in the Soviet Union. In open alarm, *Pravoslavnaya Rus* writes of the existence among the Russian emigrants, within the sphere of the Karlowitzers' influence, of those who justify the revolution and extol the name of Lenin.

Recently, the leaders of the Russian Church Outside Russia has made yet another attempt to alleviate the crisis of their organisation and to step up their anti-communist activity. For that purpose, they decided to exploit the approaching millennium (in 1988) of the adoption of Christianity in Rus ("the baptism of Rus").

The Hierarchical Synod of the Russian Church Outside Russia sanctioned the setting up in 1977, under its auspices, of a Preparatory Commission for the Celebration of the Millennium of the Baptism in Russia, whose members include anti-Soviet religious politicians of all ranks headed by Archpriest Kiselyov, former confessor of General Vlasov, the traitor of the Soviet people. Since 1978, the Commission has been publishing the quarterly *Russkoye vozrozhdeniye* (Russian

Revival), which calls itself an "independent Russian Orthodox national organ".

Judging by the activity of the Commission and the contents of the quarterly, the focus is not so much on the coming jubilee of Russian Orthodoxy as on a further whipping up of anti-communist hysteria among emigrants. The Commission and the quarterly are looking for ways of stepping up the slanderous campaign against the Soviet Union and the other countries of the socialist community, falsifying the position of religion and the Church in the USSR, etc.

All these actions are yet another proof that the Karlowitz group remains a political rather than religious organisation concerned with affairs that have nothing to do with ecclesiastical functions.

# AFTERWORD

Today, Orthodoxy as a variety of the Christian confession is one of the most widespread religions. Over the centuries it has gone through several stages of development, reflecting to some extent historical changes in the life of society. After a period of struggle against paganism, Christianity became a dominant religion in the Middle Ages, and has now reached a stage when the extent and depth of its influence on the historical process are limited. Progress in production and culture has made these changes objectively inevitable. Social practice has put to a severe test all the dogmata of the Orthodox religion, just as of the other religions of the world. The assimilation of certain principles and truths common to all humanity and connected with the consolidation of moral-ethical values evolved over centuries have ensured a degree of stability of Orthodoxy, determining its place in the complex evolution of society. The Russian Orthodox Church which has followers on all continents, still retains its principal positions, in the area of settlement of East Slavonic peoples, in the first place on the territory of the USSR.

The adoption of Christianity by Rus was an important historical event with varied and ambivalent consequences. The new religion was first of all adopted by the feudalised aristocracy of Kievan Rus. It served the interest of the upper strata of society better than pagan polytheism, sanctifying and ideologically consolidating the emergent relations of feudal domination and subordination. Orthodoxy became a state religion. But its spreading among the people's masses was a long and arduous process involving direct pressure from secular authorities and the princes of the Church. Former pagan beliefs proved so tenacious that the Church in Rus had to include elements of former cults in its everyday practice, reconcile itself with others and close its eyes to others still. That was the only way for Christianity to become a generally accepted confession throughout Russia. This syncretism made itself felt over centuries to come.

The Orthodox Church became a striking embodiment of the feudal system with its hierarchical social structure, domination of big land ownership, and caste seclusion. Having become to some extent independent of the Constantinople patriarchs, the Russian church organisation began to acquire land property and developed into a major force in the country's political and ideological life. Cloisters sprang up in the major centres of the states, the church hierarchs set up a system of dioceses and an extensive network of parish churches. The introduction of Christianity made a definite impact on the development of culture. Liturgical books and canonical literature facilitated the spreading of literacy—though the extent of this process was limited. The construction of cultic buildings brought with it the development of architectural and painting styles, mostly based on local artistic and cultural traditions embodied in the work of medieval masters. The achievements of Byzantine culture were also absorbed, and with it some elements of antiquity.

At the time of feudal fragmentation, the Russian Orthodox Church retained external unity, although practically it did almost nothing to prevent the fragmentation of Russian principalities, itself sinking in the mire of strife among the princes and boyars. Just as the rest of Russia, the Orthodox Church suffered greatly in the devastation wrought by Batu Khan. The wholesale ruin of the country, the extermination and captivity of the population affected the churches and monasteries, too. And yet the cruel Horde's yoke was not so harsh for the clergy as it was for the rest of the population.

Part of the Golden Horde's policy of subjugating Rus was advances to the Orthodox Church, whose privileges were preserved and confirmed. That inevitably led to the contradictory role of the Church in the people's liberation struggle against the foreign invaders. Only when this struggle intensified in the course of time did some Orthodox hierarchs support it, as happened on the eve of the Battle of Kulikovo Field or at the time of the overthrow of the Horde's yoke. In this situation, the Church's position was dual. On the one hand, the foreign invasion and a long subjugation of the people were regarded, in accordance with the dogmata of the Christian religion, as "God's punishment" of people for their sinful life, and they had to be accepted with humility and meekness. However, real life and the people's determination to liberate their country came in conflict with these ideological principles, engendering quite a different mood in the ecclesiastical circles. To preserve their power over the minds of parishioners, the clergy had to support the patriotic feelings and actions of the masses.

The establishment of the Russian centralised state and the overcoming of the disunity among the lands and principalities were at the same time a significant stage in the development of the Orthodox Church. The ecclesiastical organisation of North-Eastern Rus came into the forefront, especially after the transfer of the metropolitan see from Vladimir to Moscow. A strong grand-ducal power was in the interest of the Church, especially after the fall of the Horde's yoke. Supporting the grand dukes of Moscow, the clergy contributed to the unification of the Russian lands. The supreme authority displayed its gratitude for the support, and the possessions of church hierarchs and major monasteries grew, as did the number of peasant serfs on the spiritual lords' estates. In 1589, the Russian Patriarchate was established. Simultaneously, however, tendencies became apparent which pointed to the development of a conflict between secular authority and the Church in the economic and political spheres. Although the government supported the struggle of the champions of Orthodoxy against heretical trends, the elements of secularisation in the policy of grand dukes and czars were becoming increasingly pronounced, and these were in the interests of the broad circles of secular feudals. In the late 16th century restrictions were imposed on the immunity of church estates from taxes. In the next century, despite all fluctuations in the rulers' policy this line was continued. The hard trials of the Time of Troubles to some extent enhanced the prestige of the Russian Orthodox Church in the state, since the more far-sighted hierarchs supported the people's struggle against the foreign invaders. But this situation was short-lived.

Russia's entry in a new stage of historical development, when the feudal system became deformed and elements of bourgeois relations developed inside it, had a direct effect on the position of the Orthodox Church. Increasingly acute social conflicts, peasant wars and urban uprisings against the background of growing oppression by serf-owners shook the whole ecclesiastical organisation of Russia to the very foundations. The middle of the 17th century saw the rise and expansion of the movement of Old Believers—schismatics opposed to the official Church—which eventually assumed a great scope. Patriarch Nikon's church reform met with strong resistance, which assumed a social colouring while remaining externally within the framework of dogmatic controversy and within a religious worldview. Since this movement involved broad masses of peasants and town dwellers, it signified a profound crisis of the official Russian Orthodox Church. The Old Believers' dissent, going through ups and downs, became an inalienable part of the subsequent history of the Church. In the 17th century, the Church's claims to supremacy in the political system of Russia were also defeated. The deposition of Patriarch Nikon, and actual abolition of the Patriarchate in the early 18th century, indicated a strengthening of supreme secular authority and its evolution towards absolute monarchy. Peter the Great's reforms imposed considerable restrictions on the clergy's rights to dispose of the profits from the estates and the peasants' forced labour. The establishment of the Synod, a government body for the administration of ecclesiastical affairs, made the Church part of the state apparatus of

Russia. Subsequent development went along this path, though not without deviations. Secularisation of church property and exemption of nearly a million peasants from the power of the clergy in 1764 consolidated the "etatisation" of the Church. Clerics more and more became like state department officials. At the same time the supreme authority continued to use religious ideology for its own purposes, regarding it as an important element of policy and of the practice of government. During popular antifeudal movements, especially in the times of Yemelyan Pugachov, the government resorted to the services of the clergy to "pacify" all dissatisfied elements. However, complex processes of erosion went on within the clerical estate as well, so that some parish clergymen joined the rebels. In the 19th century, this estate produced men for whom the struggle for social justice on the side of revolutionary democrats and Narodniks became the meaning of their life.

Throughout the 18th century, the process of secularisation of culture and of its emancipation from the fetters of religious ideology, begun in the previous century, continued and became deeper. A new step in that direction was made in the 19th century, the age of the efflorescence of Russian national culture. However, the ruling classes and the autocratic government did not give up their intentions to place ideological barriers in the path of society's progressive development with the aid of Orthodox dogmata. Theology increasingly merged with the apologetic monarchist ideas of the ruling circles; the notorious reactionary triad—autocracy, Orthodoxy, *narodnost*—was spread and officially supported. At the same time the sphere of the Church's activity on the state and political plane was narrowed, and measures were taken to turn priests into officials in the government's pay.

In capitalist Russia after the 1861 abolition of serfdom the Orthodox Church supported private ownership, reconciliation with the existing state of affairs, and autocracy. The revolutionary process spreading throughout the country made the Church look for ways of retaining its position. The 1905-1907 revolution gave an impetus to the growth of the renovationist movement in the Russian Orthodox Church, but its alliance with the forces of the old regime proved in many respects fatal for it. The restoration of the Patriarchate did not save the situation. The October Revolution in Russia revealed the sores of exploitative society, and the Russian Orthodox Church faced the dilemma of choosing its path into the future. During the Civil War the clerics were as a rule on the other side of the barricades. The masses of believers did not follow their pastors. They chose the path of constructing a new society in their native country under the leadership of the working class of Russia and its Leninist Party.

Russia's transition from an antagonistic class society to socialism, a radical change in the ideological and cultural make-up of the working masses, separation of the Church from the state and from schools, and the guaranteed freedom of conscience created a new situation. From confrontation and anti-Sovietism, the Russian Orthodox Church moved in the course of time to recognition of historical reality. This trend became especially pronounced in the years of the Soviet people's struggle against German fascism. The Church actively joined that struggle, which accorded with the vital tasks of the epoch. Those church circles outside the Soviet Union that stuck to the discredited anti-Soviet policies suffered a serious moral defeat in the eyes of society.

In the face of the threat from the aggressive forces of international imperialism which is ready to plunge the planet into nuclear disaster, the Orthodox Church had to adopt a clear-cut position. And so it did, declaring its adherence to the idea of peace and elimination of the threat of a new world war. These positive tendencies in the activities of the Russian Orthodox Church are in line with the mainstream of social development today.

One of the most burning problems of our times is that of ecology—of environmental protection. The Orthodox Church cannot keep aloof from its solution. It also bears a great responsibility for preserving the monuments of the past that are in the hands of ecclesiastical organisations. As often as not it is a question of preserving cultic monuments that are among the masterpieces of national culture.

The advances of the scientific and technological revolution and intensification of the country's economic development in accordance with the decisions of the 27th Congress of the CPSU leave less and less room for any forms of idealistic, let alone mystical, world outlook, consolidating the positions of atheism. But the fact that millions of people still believe in God cannot be underestimated. Only time, experience and painstaking effort can help overcome religiosity. All those elements in Orthodoxy that are in accord with society's progressive development are ultimately integrated, losing their specifically religious integument. The 20th century has played an outstanding role in this long and difficult process. The present book, containing an outline of the thousand-year-long history of the Russian Orthodox Church, should offer the reader a wealth of material for contemplation, assessment and conclusions. If this objective is achieved, its writers will regard their task as fulfilled.

# LIST OF ABBREVIATIONS

AI — *Akty istoricheskiye, sobrannye i izdannye Arkheograficheskoy komissiyei* (Historical Acts Collected and Published by the Archaeographical Commission)

ChOIDR — *Chteniya v Obshchestve istorii i drevnostey rossiyskikh pri Moskovskom universitete* (Readings at the Society for Russian History and Antiquities at Moscow University)

Deyaniya — *Svyashchennyi sobor pravoslavnoy Rossiyskoy tserkvi. Deyaniya.* (The Holy Council of the Orthodox Russian Church. Acts), Moscow, 1918, Book I, Issue 1-2, Petrograd, 1918

DDG — *Dukhovnye i dogovornye gramoty velikikh i udelnykh knyazei XIV-XVI vv.* (Wills and Agreements of Grand Dukes and Appanage Princes of the 14th-16th centuries), Moscow — Leningrad, 1950

DKU — *Drevnerusskiye knyazheskiye ustavy XI-XV vv* (Old Russian Princely Statutes of 11th-15th Centuries), Moscow, 1976

DRV — *Drevnyaya Rossiyskaya vivliofika, soderzhashchaya v sebe: sobraniye drevnostey Rossiyskikh, do istorii, geografii, genealogii Rossiyskiya kasayushchikhsya...* (An Ancient Russian Library Comprising a Collection of Russian Antiquities Pertaining to Russian History, Geography, and Genealogy)

GATO — *Gosudarstvennyi arkhiv Tulskoy oblasti* (The State Archives in Tula).

MIA — *Materialy i issledovaniya po arkheologii SSSR* (Materials and Studies on the Archaeology of the USSR)

Materialy — *Materialy dlya istorii raskola za pervoye vremya yego sushchestvovaniya* (Materials for the History of Dissent in the First Period of Its Existence)

NPL — *Novgorodskaya pervaya letopis starshego i mladshego izvodov* (The First Novgorod Chronicle of the Older and Younger Izvods). Moscow — Leningrad, 1950

PDP — *Pamyatniki drevney pismennosti i iskusstva* (Monuments of the Ancient Written Language and Art)

PRP—*Pamyatniki russkogo prava* (Old Russian Legal Manuscripts)

Pribavleniya—*Pribavleniya k "Tserkovnym vedomostyam"* (Additions to *Tserkovnye vedomosti*)

PSRL—*Polnoye sobraniye russkikh letopisey* (A Complete Collection of Russian Chronicles)

RIB—*Russkaya istoricheskaya biblioteka, izdavayemaya Arkheograficheskoy komissiey AN SSSR* (The Russian Historical Library Published by the Archaeographical Commission of the USSR Academy of Sciences)

RIO—*Sbornik russkogo istoricheskogo obshchestva* (Collection of the Materials of the Russian Historical Society).

RO GBL—Rukopisnyi otdel Gosudarstvennoy biblioteki SSSR im. V. I. Lenina (The Manuscripts Department of the V. I. Lenin State Library of the USSR) (Moscow)

SGGD—Sobraniye gosudarstvennykh gramot i dogovorov, khranyashchikhsya v Gosudarstvennoy kollegii inostrannykh del (Collection of State Charters and Treaties Preserved at the State Collegium of Foreign Affairs)

TODRL—*Trudy Otdela drevnerusskoy literatury Instituta russkoy literatury (Pushkinskogo Doma) Akademii nauk SSSR* (Papers of the Department of Old Russian Literature of the Institute of Russian Literature [The Pushkin House] of the USSR Academy of Sciences)

TsGADA—Tsentralnyi gosudarstvennyi arkhiv drevnikh aktov (The Central State Archives of Ancient Acts)

TsGAOR SSSR—Tsentralnyi gosudarstvennyi arkhiv Oktyabrskoy revolyutsii (The Central State Archives of the October Revolution)

TsGIA SSSR—Tsentralnyi gosudarstvennyi Istoricheskiy arkhiv (The Central State Historical Archives in Leningrad)

PSZ—*Polnoye sobraniye zakonov Rossiyskoy imperii* (Complete Code of Laws of the Russian Empire)

Yezhegodnik MIRA—*Yezhegodnik Muzeya istorii religii i ateizma* (Yearbook of the Museum of the History of Religion and Atheism)

# NAME INDEX

## A

Adam, Clement—68
Adrian, Patriarch of Moscow—81, 84, 85, 105
Afanasiy, Bishop of Kazan—147
Agafanghel, Metropolitan of Yaroslavl (formerly Archbishop of Riga and then of Yaroslavl)—259, 286, 296, 310
Aksakov, N. P.—181
Akvilonov, Ye.—203
Aleksey, Czarevich—109
Aleksey, Metropolitan—53, 103
Aleksey Mikhailovich—88, 91, 96, 100, 101
Aleksey, priest—72
Aleksey, Metropolitan of Tallinn and Estonia—378, 404
Aleksey (Ridiger), Metropolitan—232
Aleksey (Simansky), Patriarch—317, 319, 323, 340, 346, 347, 384, 395
Alexander I—136, 139-41, 143
Alexander II—153
Alexander III—161, 172
Alexander Nevskiy—46, 48, 316
Alexander, St., of the Svir—277
Alexandra Fyodorovna—254
Ambrose, Metropolitan of Byelaya Krinitsa—144
Amvrosiy, Metropolitan of Moscow—130
Amvrosiy (Podobedov), Metropolitan of St. Petersburg—139, 163
Anastasiy (Gribanovsky), Metropolitan (formerly Archbishop)—273, 431-34
Andrey Bogolyubsky—37, 39, 50
Andreyev, L. N.—221
Andrey (Ukhtomsky), Bishop of Ufa—260
Anichkov, D. S.—129
Anna Ioannovna—119, 120

Anna, sister of Emperor Basil—24
Anthony, St., the Great—9
Antonin (Granovsky), Bishop of Narva (later Archbishop)—196, 221, 286, 287, 298, 304
Antoniy (Khrapovitsky), Metropolitan of Volynia (earlier-Bishop)—201, 210, 214, 220, 253, 273, 431
Antoniy (Melnikov), Metropolitan—323
Antoniy (Rafalsky)—146, 148
Antoniy (Vadkovsky), Metropolitan—173, 174, 179, 180, 182, 185, 186, 189, 195, 197, 206, 208, 209, 224, 259, 281
Appolinaris, St., Bishop of Ravenna—47
Arakcheyev, A. A.—141
Arkadiy, Archbishop of Novgorod—40
Arkhipov, A. V.—205, 207
Arranz, Miguel—400
Arseniy, Archbishop of Pskov—216, 217, 256
Arseniy (Matseyevich), Metropolitan of Rostov—122
Arseniy the Greek—92
Avgustin (Nikitin), Hieromonk—322
Avksentyev, N. D.—262
Avraam, Archbishop—142
Avvakum, Archpriest—59, 89, 93, 100, 101

## B

Bardas Phocas—24, 25
Barsov, T.—138
Bashkin, Matvey—74
Basil II—24, 25
Basil, St., the Great—25, 27
Basilios, Metropolitan of Warsaw and All Poland—17

Batu—52, 448
Bazilevich, K. V.—72
Beck, H. G.—40
Begunov, Yu. K.—46, 51
Beletsky, S. P.—254
Belikov, D. N.—216
Belkov, Ye.—285-87
Belyakova, Ye. V.—61
Berdyaev, N. A.—324
Beskrovny, L. G.—83
Bobrinsky, V. A.—262
Bogolyubsky, N. I.—366
Bolotnikov, Ivan—79
Boris, Bishop—174
Boris, Prince—45, 46
Borovkova—Maikova, M. S.—67
Borovoy, V.—353, 421
Brikhnichev, I.—222
Brilliantov, A.—205, 207
Bronzov, A.—199
Brovkovich, A. I.—370
Bryanchaninov, A.—253
Budovnits, I. U.—63
Bulavin, Kondratiy—124
Bulgakov, S. N.—262, 324, 367
Bulygin, I. A.—84, 107, 111, 113, 117
Buyevsky, A. S.—322

**D**

Damian, Archbishop of All Albania—16, 17
Damianos, Archbishop of Sinai, Pharan and Raifa—20
Daniil, Archpriest of Kostroma—89
Daniil, Archpriest of Temnikov—89
Daniil, Metropolitan—68
Dashkov, Georgiy—119
Davydov, 8—115
Debolsky, N. G.—370
Dementyev, Ivan—101
Denikin, A. I.—272, 273
Denis, priest—72, 73
Dernov, A.—256
Diderot—131
Dimitrios I, Patriarch, Archbishop of Constantinople—9
Dmitriev, S. S.—136, 139, 140, 143

Dmitriy Aleksandrovich, Prince—46
Dmitriy Aleksandrovich, Prince—46
Dmitriy, Archbishop of Kherson—191
Dmitriy Donskoy—49, 50, 316
Dmitriy Shemyaka—66
Diodoros, Patriarch of the Holy City of Jerusalem and All Palestine—11
Dobromyslov, K. N,—218
Dobrynya—26
Dolgorukiys, the—120
Dorofej, Metropolitan of Prague and All Czechoslovakia—18
Dorotheus—56
Dosifey, Hegumen—101
Dyakonov, M.—66

**C**

Catherine II—121, 125, 126
Chayev, N. S.—65, 85
Cheltsov, M.—181
Cherepnin, L. V.—86, 100
Chevally, De—275
Chicherin, D. I.—126
Chrisostomos, Archbishop of Cyprus—16
Coggan, Frederick Donald—395
Constantine, Czar—67
Copernicus, Nicolaus—130
Cyprian, Metropolitan—51, 58, 62, 65, 66
Cyril (Garbet), Archbishop of York—395

**F**

Fadyukhin, S.—421
Feodor, Bishop—43
Feodor, Bishop of Tver—55
Feodosiy Kosoy—74, 75
Feodosiy of Pechery—46, 47, 55
Feofan (Govorov) the Recluse, Bishop—356, 364
Feognost, Metropolitan of Kiev—174
Filaret (Denisenko), Metropolitan—322, 323, 377
Filaret (Drozdov), Metropolitan—143, 146-56, 159, 162, 163, 356

Filaret, Patriarch of Moscow—81, 84
Filaret (Vakhromeyev), Metropolitan—321-23, 378
Filaret (Voznesensky), Metropolitan—434
Filipp, Metropolitan—69
Filonenko, F. D.—260
Flavian (Gorodetsky), Metropolitan of Kiev—180, 194, 255
Florensky, P. A.—367, 368, 372
Fonkich, B. L.—78
Fontenelle—130
Fyodor, Deacon—100, 101
Fyodor Ivanovich—69

E

El Ghazzali—72
Elizaveta Petrovna (Elizabeth)—120, 121
Engels, Frederick—70, 87, 100, 164, 327
Ephraem, Metropolitan in Kiev—29
Evfimiy, senior chorister of the Chudov Monastery—92
Evfrosiniya of Suzdal—277

G

Gapon, G. A.—178-80, 199
Garcia, Julio—441
Gavriil, Archpriest—72
Gennadiy, Archbishop of Novgorod—67, 71-73
Gennadiy, Bishop of Suzdal—128
Georgios, Metropolitan of Kiev—46
Gherman, Archbishop of Kazan—69
Gherman of Alaska—427
Gherman, Patriarch of Serbia—14
Ghermoghen, Bishop of Saratov—190, 201, 215, 253, 272
Ghermoghen, Patriarch of Moscow—79, 80
Gibbenet, N.—98
Gleb, Prince—45, 46

Godunov, Boris—77-79
Golenishchev-Kutuzov, I. N.—71, 72
Golitsyn, A. N.—139, 141, 143, 146
Golitsyns, the—120
Golubinsky, F. A.—324, 370
Golubinsky, Ye. Ye.—27, 31, 60-62, 72, 95
Golubtsov, A.—92
Golynets, V. F.—214
Gorchakov, M. I.—84, 85, 114
Gorky, Maxim—221
Gorsky, A. D.—59
Gregory VII—32
Gregory of Sinai—56
Gregory Palamas—55
Grekulov, Ye. F.—109, 153, 160, 257
Grenard—275
Grigoriy, Bishop of Kaluga—148
Grigoriy (Yatskovsky), Archbishop of Yekaterinburg—310
Grigoryev, Sila, editor—92
Grinevich, A. G.—205, 207
Gryaznov, Ivan—127
Guchkov, A. I.—262

H

Herzen, A. A.—139, 148
Hitler, Adolf—316, 432
Holbach—131

I

Iakov, Bishop of Kishinev—174
Iakov Mnich—25, 27
Iannuariy, Hieromonk—351
Ibn-Khordadbek—23
Ignatius, Patriarch of Antioch and All the Orient—10
Ignatiy (Bryanchaninov), Bishop of Stavropol—147
Ignatyeva, S. S.—224, 225
Igor, Grand Duke of Kiev—24
Igor Svyatoslavich—34
Ilarion, Metropolitan of Kiev—26, 29, 30, 43
Iliodor, Hieromonk—224, 255
Iliya II, Catholicos-Patriarch of All Georgia—13, 410
Innokentiy (Borisov), Archbishop—356

Innokentiy (Borisov), Archbishop—356
Innokentiy (Popov-Veniaminov), Bishop—427
Ioakim, Patriarch of Antioch—77
Ioakim of Korsun—26
Ioakim, Patriarch of Moscow—81, 84, 85
Iakov, Bishop of Nizhniy Novgorod—256
Ioann II, Metropolitan—33
Ioann, Archbishop of Novgorod—62
Ioann, Archimandrite—128
Ioann, Bishop of Suzdal—44
Ioann (John), Metropolitan of Helsinki—19
Ioann Sergiyev (of Kronshtadt)—175, 253, 338
Ioann (Sokolov), Archimandrite—148, 153, 154
Ioannikiy, Metropolitan of Kiev—162
Ioasaf I, Patriarch of Moscow—81
Ioasaf II, Patriarch of Moscow—81
Ioasaf (Gorlenko), Bishop of Belgorod—220
Iona, Metropolitan of Moscow and All Russia (formerly Bishop of Ryazan)—60, 66
Iona, Metropolitan of Rostov—101
Iosif (Ivan Nasedka)—92
Iosif, Metropolitan of Astrakhan—272
Iosif of Volotsk (Sanin)—64, 67, 71-73, 76
Iosif, Patriarch of Moscow—81, 84, 90, 91
Iosif (Petrovykh), Metropolitan of Leningrad—313
Iov, Patriarch of Moscow and All Russia—11, 78, 79
Irina Mikhailovna, Czarevna—92
Isaac Cyrus—56
Isidore, Metropolitan—60
Isidor, Metropolitan of St. Petersburg—147
Ivan III Vasilyevich—58, 64, 67, 72, 73
Ivan IV Vasilyevich the Terrible—63, 68, 69, 74, 76
Ivan Chorniy—(the Black)—73
Ivan Popyan—39
Ivan Volk (the Wolf) (Kuritsyn)—74
Ivanov, Ivan—126
Izvolsky, P. P.—212, 214
Izyaslav Yaroslavich, Prince—28

## J

Jahja of Antioch—24
Jeremiah II, Patriarch of Constantinople—77, 78
Jerome, Archbishop of Kholm and Warsaw—174
Jesus Christ—70, 72, 75, 95, 152, 153, 263, 274, 289, 292, 316, 325, 342, 343, 350, 352, 383, 405, 412, 421, 424
John XXIII—382, 399
John Climacus—56
John, St., the Divine—332
Justinian, Patriarch of All Romania—14

## K

Kalinovsky, S.—285, 286
Kapiton—102
Kapterev, N. F.—82, 95-98, 101
Karínsky, M. I.—370
Karpov, N. V.—324, 370
Karsabin, L. P.—367
Kartashev, A. V.—96, 262
Kashinskaya, Anna—220
Kazakova, N. A.—64, 71, 72
Kazansky, P.—63
Karensky, A. F.—262
Khoroshev, A. S.—45, 66
Khovansky, V. A.—139
Khvostov, D. I.—139
Kirill I, Bishop of Suzdal—44
Kirill, Metropolitan—310
Kirill, Metropolitan of Kiev—48, 55
Kirill, St., Novo-Ozersky—277
Kiryanov, Yu. I.—169
Kiselyov, A.—445
Klibanov, A. I.—71
Kliment, Bishop of Vinnitsa—180

Kliment, Metropolitan—43
Klyuchevsky, V. O.—57
Kogan, Yu. Ya.—109
Kolchak, A. V.—272-74
Kolokolnikov, Ye. A.—205, 207
Konoplyov, Dmitriy—74
Konstantin, Grand Duke—156
Konstantin Vsevolodovich, Prince—44
Kopanev, A. I.—64
Korenevsky, N.—98
Korf, Baroness—253
Korniliy, Hegumen of the Pskov-Pechery Monastery—69
Kornilov, L. G.—263
Kotlyarevsky, S. A.—262
Kozhevnikov, V.—213
Krasnitsky, V.—285, 298, 301, 304
Krasnov, P. N.—272
Krasotin, P.—304
Krusche, Werner—401
Kryukov, Nikita—131
Kudryavtsev, V. D.—370, 372
Kuritsyn, Fyodor—72-74
Kuroyedov, V. A.—429

## L

Lapin, P.—78, 82
Leikina-Svirskaya, V. R.—169
Lenin, V. I.—134, 135, 152, 155, 175-77, 187, 188, 196, 197, 267-69, 271, 279, 366, 445
Leon, Bishop—43
Leon, Metropolitan—24
Leontiy, Bishop of Rostov—33, 46
Leontiy, Metropolitan—28
Leontyev, Pyotr—182
Likhud, Joannikius—103
Likhud, Sophronius—103
Login, Archpriest of Murom—89
Lomonosov, M. V.—95, 129, 130
Loris-Melikov, M. T.—158
Lossky, V.—382
Lavmieński, G.—27
Luka Chryzoverg—39
Lukyanov, V.—445
Lurye, Ya. S.—71, 72
Lvov, A. M.—89
Lvov, V. N.—258
Lyubimov, D. N.—180

Lyubimov, N.—260
Lyubinetsky, N. A.—169

## M

Macarius, Patriarch of Antioch—98
Makarios III, Archbishop of Nova Justiniana and All Cyprus—16
Makariy, Metropolitan—65, 82, 95, 340
Makariy, Metropolitan of Moscow and All Russia—66, 69, 76
Makariy, Metropolitan of Moscow (formerly Bishop of Tomsk)—179, 190, 224, 256, 258
Maksim, Metropolitan of Kiev—50
Maksim, Patriarch of Bulgaria—15
Maksim the Greek—68
Maksimov, Ivan—74
Mankov, A. G.—84, 86
Mansvetov, I. D.—91, 92
Manuil, Bishop of Smolensk—43
Manukhina, T.—171
Markell, Bishop—174
Martemyanov, Shestak—92
Marx, Karl—70, 87, 100, 132, 164, 327
Massa, Isaac—79
Matvey, editor—92
Maykova, T.—117
Medvedev, Silvestr—103
Meletiy, Hierodeacon—153
Melgunov, S. P.—150, 151
Menander—72
Mengu-Timur—48
Michurin, I. V.—366
Mikhail, Bishop of Grodno—256
Mikhail, Bishop of Samara—260
Mikhail Fyodorovich—84
Mikhail, Metropolitan—24
Mikhail (Mudyugin), Archbishop—420
Mikhail Olelkovich (Aleksandrovich)—71
Mikhail (Semyonov), Archimandrite—222
Milovidov, V. F.—109, 144, 161
Milyukov, P. N.—266, 267

Mitrofan, Bishop—214
Mityai, priest—51
Mogila, Pyotr—90
Morozov, B. I.—89
Moses Maimonides—72
Muravyov, Mikhail—154
Musatov, A. A.—222
Musin-Pushkin, I. A.—105, 111

## N

Napoleon—140
Nechayev, S. D.—146
Nechkina, M. V.—142
Nelyubov, A.—394
Neofit, Metropolitan of Chernigov—28
Neronov, Ivan—89, 94, 96, 97, 100
Nesmelov, V. I.—213, 324, 370, 372
Nicholas I—135, 137, 142, 143, 145, 147, 162
Nicholas II—174, 180, 192, 194, 199, 275, 282, 438
Nicolas IV, Pope and Patriarch of Alexandria and All Africa—9
Nicolas, St., Bishop of Myra in Lycia—47
Nifont Archbishop of Novgorod—40, 43
Nickanor, Archbishop of Kherson—172
Nikanor, Metropolitan of Warsaw—146
Nikodim (Rotov), Metropolitan—341, 343, 347, 350, 354, 357, 358, 378, 382, 392, 407, 410, 414
Nikolai, Archbishop—217
Nikolai, Archbishop of Finland—180
Nikolai (Kasatkin), Archbishop—20
Nikolai, Metropolitan—378
Nikolai Nikolaevich, Grand Duke—205
Nikolai (Yarushevich), Metropolitan—384
Nikolayevsky, P. F.—92
Nikolsky, N. M.—88, 93, 117, 120, 125, 142

Nikon, Bishop of Serpukhov—190, 217
Nikon, Patriarch of Moscow—81, 84, 87-102, 450
Nikonovich, F. I.—214, 218
Nil of the Sora—67
Noulens, Joseph—275
Novikov, N. I.—130

## O

Obolensky, A. D.—192, 194, 209, 218
Obolensky, I. V.—58
Odoyevsky, N. I.—97, 99
Oleg, Prince—44
Olga, Grand Duchess—24
Osipova, Ye. S.—257-59, 261, 262
Ostrogorsky, G.—25
Otto II—25
Ovchinnikova, Ye. S.—90
Ozerov, Ivan—92

## P

Paisius, Patriarch of Alexandria—98
Paisius, Patriarch of Constantinople—96
Panin, P. I.—128
Panin, V. N.—149, 150
Panwitz—433
Pariysky, L.—363
Pashuto, V. T.—43, 51
Paul, Apostle—383
Pavel, Bishop of Kolomna—95
Pavel (Paul), Archbishop of Karelia and All Finland—19
Pavel (Paul), Emperor—135, 139
Pavel, St., of Obnora—277
Pelgusiy-Filipp—51, 52
Peresvetov, I. S.—74
Perun—24
Pestel, P. I.—142
Peter I—12, 103, 105-107, 109-19, 133, 395, 450
Peter II—119
Peter III—121
Peter, a nephew of Khan Batu—52
Petrishchev, A. B.—200
Petrov, Anton (Sidorov, A. P.)—152

Petrov, G. I.—172-74
Petrov, G. S.—205, 207
Photius, Metropolitan—60, 66, 70
Photius, Patriarch of Constantinople—23
Pimen, Archbishop of Novgorod—69
Pimen (Izvekov), Patriarch—321, 323, 344, 346-48, 356, 358, 384, 385, 390, 394, 396, 417, 424, 425
Pistolkors, F.—253
Pitirim (Nechaev), Metropolitan (formerly Bishop and Archbishop—323, 329, 356, 371, 379
Pitirim (Oknov), Exarch of Georgia—256, 258
Pitirim, Patriarch of Moscow—81
Pitirim, St., of Tambov—277
Platon, Bishop of Chigirin—204
Platon, Exarch of Georgia—260
Platon (Levshin), Metropolitan of Moscow—136, 144
Platonov, N. F.—179
Pobedonostsev, K. P.—158-61, 163, 172-74, 185, 187-89, 192, 209, 212, 218, 219
Pokrovsky, I. M.—92
Polyansky, I. V.—193
Pomerantsev, Pavel—131
Pope, Alexander—130
Popov, A. A.—215
Poppe, A.—25, 27, 31
Potapyev, Kh.—366
Potashinskaya, N. N. 193
Potter, Philip—410, 411
Potyomkin, Spiridon (Simeon)—89, 101
Pozoysky, S. I.—172
Preobrazhensky, I. V.—157
Prokhorov, G. M.—55
Prokopovich, Feofan—114, 115, 119, 120
Protasov, N. A.—143, 145, 146, 158
Prozorovsky, A. A.—103
Prugavin, A.—143
Pugachov, Yemelyan—104, 125-28, 451
Putsek-Grigorovich, Veniamin—126

Putyata—26
Pyotr (Alekseyev), Archpriest—130
Pyotr (Polyansky), Metropolitan—303, 309, 310

R

Radishchev, Alexander—130
Ramsey, Arthur Michael—395
Rapov, O. M.—26
Rar, G. A.—440
Rasputin, G.—254-56, 258
Rayev, N. I.—255, 256
Razin, Stepan—272
Regelson—413
Rodzyanko, M. V.—262
Rogov, A. I.—90, 103
Rogov, Mikhail—92
Rogovich, A. P.—218
Romanovs, the—220
Rosen, A. E.—142
Rozanov, N. P.—162
Rozhdestvensky, A.—260
Rtishchev, F. M.—89, 90, 103
Rumyanov, A. V.—207
Rumyantseva, V. S.—90, 99-101, 103
Runcie, Robert—395
Rybakov, B. A.—44
Ryleyev, K. F.—142
Rzhevsky, Timofey—123

S

Sabler, V. K.—174, 217-19, 253, 254
Saburova, Solomonia—68
Samarin, A. D.—254, 255, 262
Samuil, Bishop of Krutitsy—128
Sarychev, V. D.—322
Savva, Bishop of Lutsk—62
Savva, St., of Storozhi—277
Savvatiy, editor—92
Schwartz, Ye. G.—253
Scott, Edward—410
Seraphim, Archbishop of Athens and All Hellas—16
Serafim (Chichagov), Bishop of Oryol—200, 220
Serafim (Gladolevsky), Metropolitan of St. Petersburg—141-43, 146, 147